Delirium and Resistance

Delirium and Resistance

Activist Art and the Crisis of Capitalism

Gregory Sholette

Edited by Kim Charnley

Foreword by Lucy R. Lippard

First published 2017 by Pluto Press
345 Archway Road, London N6 5AA

www.plutobooks.com

British Library Cataloguing in Publication Data
A catalogue record for this book is available from the British Library

ISBN   978 0 7453 3688 6   Hardback
ISBN   978 0 7453 3684 8   Paperback
ISBN   978 1 7868 0059 6   PDF eBook
ISBN   978 1 7868 0061 9   Kindle eBook
ISBN   978 1 7868 0060 2   EPUB eBook

Typeset by Stanford DTP Services, Northampton, England

For Olga

Contents

List of Figures

Abbreviations

AAND	Artists Against Nuclear Destruction
AMCC	Artists Meeting for Cultural Change
AWC	Art Workers' Coalition
CAE	Critical Art Ensemble
CETA	Comprehensive Employment and Training Act
CK	Conflict Kitchen
CLT	Community Land Trust
CMU	Carnegie Mellon University
COLAB	Collaborative Projects
DDoS	Distributed denial-of-service
DIY	Do It Yourself
DSLR	Department of Space and Land Reclamation
EK	Enemy Kitchen
EU	European Union
FIRE	Finance, Insurance and Real Estate
GULF	Global Ultra Luxury Faction
GAAG	Guerrilla Art Action Group
IA	Imaginary Archive
IDNS	Illinois Department of Nuclear Safety
LAPD	Los Angeles Poverty Department
LARP	Live action fantasy role-play
MAVAN	Marxism and Visual Art Now
MBA	Masters of Business Administration
MFA	Masters in Fine Art
MoMA	Museum of Modern Art
NYLPI	New York Lawyers for the Public Interest
NYPD	New York Police Department
OWS	Occupy Wall Street
PAD/D	Political Art Documentation/Distribution
SPARC	Social and Public Art Resource Center
UL	Universal Lab
WAGE	Working Artists and the Greater Economy

Acknowledgments

This book would simply not have been possible without Kim Charnley. I am beholden to him not only for his smart and meticulously researched introduction to this volume, but also for the generous labor, encouragement and insightful assistance he provided throughout the process of its development as it grew from a vague idea to a completed work. Likewise, I recognize the luminous contribution of my friend and fellow cultural activist Lucy R. Lippard, whose concise, superb preface opens *Delirium and Resistance* with precisely the right mixture of verve, history and critical analysis. It is equally not possible to overstate the importance of Professor of Modern and Contemporary Art Christa-Maria Lerm Hayes, whose continuous insights and discerning analysis, together with the valued critical appraisal of Professor Jeroen Boomgaard, shaped these essays into a dissertation submitted to the Amsterdam School of Heritage, Memory and Material Culture at the University of Amsterdam (UvA). I am indebted to both the UvA and to the Andrew W. Mellon Seminar on Public Engagement and Collaborative Research at the Center for the Humanities at the Graduate Center, CUNY, for financial aid during the development of this project, as well as to Helen Carey and Liz Burns of the Fire Station residency in Dublin, Ireland for endowing me with time to think and work on this project. I wish to extend my great appreciation to David Castle, Sophie Richmond and the entire editorial and design team at Pluto Press, as well as to Imogen Charnley, Larne Abse Gogarty, Eric James Triantafillou, Noah Fischer, Aaron Vanek, Jennifer Avril and Ottie Theires for their assistance and input on the manuscript, and also to Chloe Bass and Jeff Kasper who kept the Social Practice Queens MFA project moving forwards while I concentrated on these writings. And finally, though listed last, my devoted and extraordinary wife, Olga Kopenkina is thanked for keeping me from succumbing to delirium without resistance, before this book was completed.

Record of Publication

A number of the essays in this book were previously published either in their present form or in a comparable version and they are presented here with the acknowledgment of these sources: "Fidelity, Betrayal, Autonomy: Within and Beyond the Post-Cold War Art Museum," *Beyond the Box: Diverging Curatorial Practices*, edited by Melanie A. Townsend for Banff Centre Press (Canada, 2003); "Let's Do It Again Comrades, Let's Occupy the Museum!" *Texte Zur Kunst*, a special issue entitled "Art History Revisited" (Berlin, March 2012); "Nature as an Icon of Urban Resistance: Artists, Gentrification and New York City's Lower East Side, 1979–1984," *Afterimage: The Journal of Media Arts and Cultural Criticism* (Rochester, NY, Sept./Oct. 1997); "Mysteries of the Creative Class or I Have Seen the Enemy and They Is Us," *MUTE* magazine (London, 2004); "Occupology, Swarmology, Whateverology: The City of Disorder versus the People's Archive," for the *College Art Association Art Journal, Internet Edition* (NYC, Winter 2011/2012; and this essay has also appeared in the *Critical Digital Studies Reader* edited by Marilouise Kroker and Arthur Kroker, University of Toronto Press, Canada, 2013); "Counting on Your Collective Silence: Notes on Activist Art as Collaborative Practice," also from *Afterimage* (NY, November/December 1999); "Dark Matter: Activist Art and the Counter-public Sphere," *As Radical as Reality Itself: Essays on Marxism and Art for the 21st Century*, edited by Matthew Beaumont, Andrew Hemingway, Leslie Esther and John Roberts for Peter Lang Publishers (Oxford, UK, 2007); "On the Maidan Uprising and Imaginary Archive, Kiev," *Hyperallergic* (NYC, July 2014); and "Delirium and Resistance after the Social Turn," *FIELD: an Online Journal of Socially Engaged Art Criticism*, issue number one (San Diego, 2015).

Gone is the first mad delirium ... The show is over ... Into the disillusioned atmosphere of pale daylight there rings a different chorus; the hoarse croak of the hawks and hyenas of the battlefield.

Rosa Luxemburg*

*   *The Junius Pamphlet: The Crisis of German Social Democracy* (Feb.–April 1915), reprinted in *The Rosa Luxemburg Reader*, edited by Peter Hudis and Kevin B. Anderson (New York, Monthly Review Press, 2004), pp. 312–313.

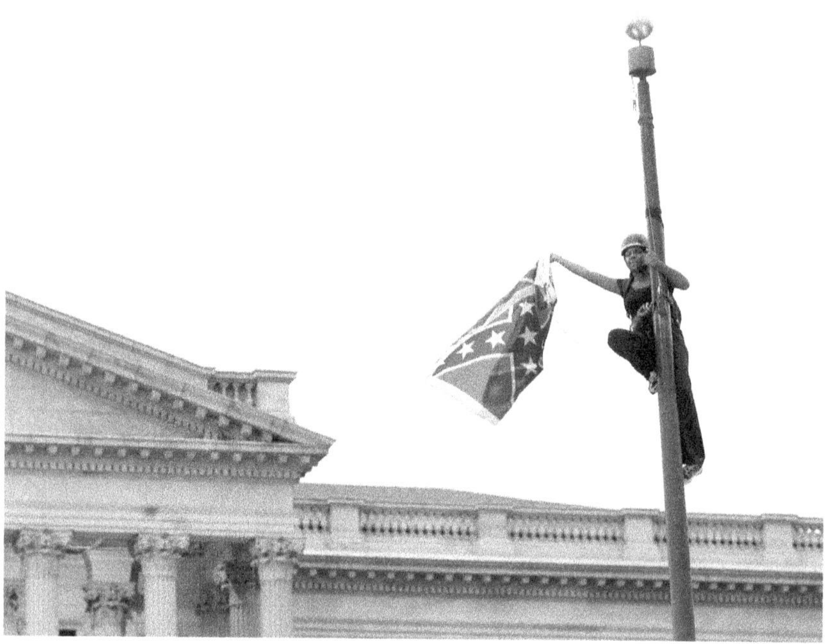

Figure 1 Activist and media artist Bree Newsome removing the Confederate flag from outside the South Carolina State House, June 27, 2015. Newsome was arrested immediately after descending the pole

(Photograph Adam Anderson, Reuters Pictures)

Foreword:
Is Another Art World Possible?

Lucy R. Lippard

Amnesia attacks and ongoing reinventions of the wheel are two things that have plagued social activist art and the left for as long as I can remember (and I cut my activist teeth with the Art Workers' Coalition in the anti-Vietnam war era). For the two decades represented in *Delirium and Resistance*, Greg Sholette has been educating us about the threads connecting past and present trajectories of activist/ community/ political/ socially engaged art. His brilliant essays are based in active participation, lived experience and unrelenting critical examination of art from the early 1980s to the present, with all its complex global twigs and branches, visible and invisible successes and failures. He consistently questions and undermines conventional ideologies, as he did when I first worked with him in Political Documentation/Distribution (PAD/D) in 1980. Since then he has continued to catalyze with passion while theorizing with subtlety. No-one else does precisely what he does, or does it as well.

That said, this book inevitably raises more questions than solutions. Or the solutions described are open ended. Times change and we don't always change fast enough with them. Tactics and strategies for artists trying to be effective allies of social movements vary in different times and places. In the 1970s, activist (and feminist) artworks with any impact were often condescendingly labeled simplistic, heavy-handed, didactic and naïve—"just social work," too low to make it into the high art pantheons, even when (or especially when) such works were sparking consciousness and playing a new role by underplaying aesthetics and objecthood. In the 1960s the counter-culture was inventing image wars, and in the 1980s we were responding to a mainstream overdose of irony and obscurantism often posing as "political."

In the 1990s, intervention—soon to be epitomized by The Yes Men—was the activist's response to mere spectacular provocation, as parsed by the Situationists. Sholette's writings on "the interventionists" are particularly acute (even as he wryly concedes that the road to hell "is paved with good interventions"). All of us hoping to see and facilitate social change are best served when the models and lessons are at once complex and accessible. Sholette writes from the front lines, from PAD/D and REPOhistory to Occupy Wall Street, Gulf Labor and beyond. He writes as an artist, not as an academic onlooker, not as a politico dismissing art as peripheral to serious action. His theorizing illuminates rather than obfuscates. His essays also offer a path for readers to grow in critical acumen with the author over time, expanding the impetus to critical thinking that is, or should be, the goal of all art education.

The "move beyond representation" traced here began long before "social practice" was baptized. Conceptual artists in the 1960s rejected the commodification of art, while focusing on information and daily life, critiquing art institutions tied to the aesthetic and political status quo. Today's hacktivists can be traced back to the public access TV movement in the 1970s and a now-ripened eco art also emerged in those days. These "escape attempts" from the art world became subversive elements within the mainstream, which, despite today's apparent adoption of beyond-the-gallery, socially engaged art, still doesn't quite know what to do with them. In the interim, we've all been through several cycles of art and activism, several moments when it looked as though artists were finally partners in political change, only to watch as even the best efforts proved unsustainable, while simultaneously sowing seeds for future initiatives. Some of us remain convinced that nothing matches face-to-face discussions and collaborations, and that social media, for all its potential, tends to flatten both affects and effects. (Reading *Delirium and Resistance* is a recommended antidote.)

*   *   *

Sholette inhabits an urban art world where gentrification, police brutality and governmental neglect of those struggling to survive are long-standing issues that surround the often complicitous art institutions. He has always worked collaboratively and collectively, with "politically engaged and [mostly] non-hierarchical" structures, aspiring to provide them with "their own analytical approaches."[1] Over the years his contacts and activities have extended across the world. He lectures and curates globally, bringing back to his national base the issues, concerns and lessons learned from encounters beyond the comfort zone. His reports and analyses of a vast number of small independent groups of art activists around the world are invaluable for those of us who stay home, exponentially increasing our models for further action and offering an influential model for students of studio, art

xviii

history and theory, who should be grappling together with pressing issues in integrated programs.

Years ago it became clear that there was fertile ground in social energies not yet recognized as art, and the term "social practice" (a bit clinical) has come to occupy that space where, as Sholette puts it, art "treats the social itself as a medium and material of expression." (The Beuysian term "social sculpture," often used as a synonym, regresses toward the object.) Despite what he calls the "paradoxical ascent of social practice art in a socially bankrupt world," and "an inversion of artistic taste" from the periphery to the center of the art world, small audiences, inadequate funding, and lack of long-term thinking remain obstacles to true florescence. He writes that contemporary art is simultaneously capital's "avant garde and its social realism."

Sholette's solid grasp of economics (at the heart of his last book, *Dark Matter*) is rare among art writers. As artists begin to understand the corporate world, they are also in danger of being consumed by it, just as activist artists have always worried about being co-opted when (and if) finally courted by mainstream institutions. Similarly, grant-making bureaucracies have become a business model but can stifle creativity. Crowdsourcing is the tactic most compatible with social practices. In a fearful, eroding democracy, it remains to be seen whether art continues to be free to act in the public sphere or is driven underground once more. Too many solutions involve continuing sacrifice by artists bucking the system, who are rarely rewarded for their hard work. Sholette himself has been a target.

There is a tipping point at which art topples over into the real world and loses its power to surprise and instigate. It is a very subtle point at which the always precarious balance between art and life, art world and "real world" threatens to collapse. But like even the best of the community arts, successful social practice is public service light, usually intended as a catalyst rather than a plan. That of course is the role art should play—a jolt from unexpected and previously unconsidered angles. It seems significant that Bree Newsome, who scaled a flagpole in South Carolina's capitol to remove the Confederate flag, identifies herself as an artist.

Is another art world possible? Will political organizations ever really respect, encourage, collaborate, instead of censoring or ignoring artists' contributions and innovations? It's hard to be optimistic after the 2016 elections. But it is crucial to be hopeful. Sholette shows us how to imagine art's future in a social context without losing our minds or our integrity.

Art on the Brink: *Bare Art* and the Crisis of Liberal Democracy

Kim Charnley

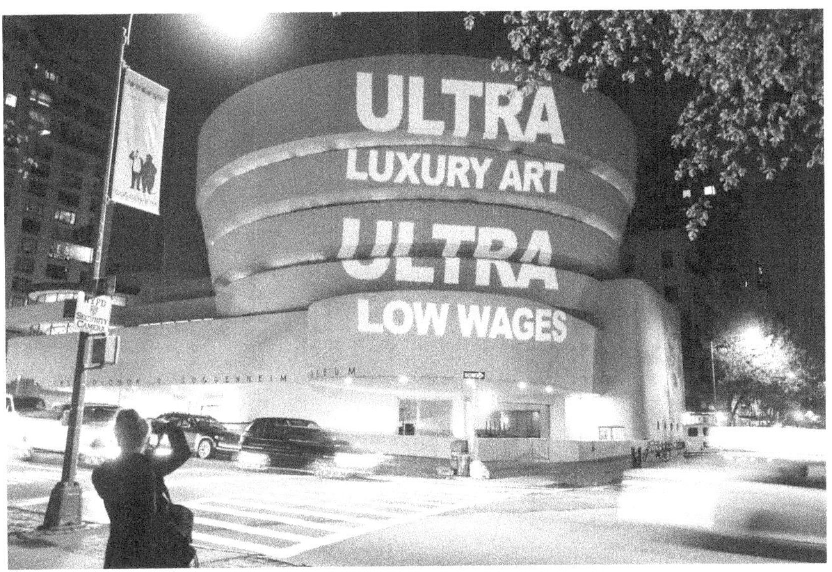

Figure 2 The Illuminator/GULF, April 18, 2016. Gulf Labor Coalition, Global Ultra Luxury Faction (GULF), Occupy Museums and The Illuminator respond with a night-time guerrilla projection onto the Guggenheim Museum, New York, April 27, 2016 following the museum's refusal to discuss with these activist art groups the improvement of wages and working conditions for migrant laborers in Abu Dhabi, where a new Guggenheim museum has been in the works

(Image courtesy GULF/The Illuminator)

Over the past two decades, artist, critic and curator Gregory Sholette has produced an important body of theoretical work exploring the shifting relationship between contemporary art and politics. Sholette uses the concept "dark matter," explored in his 2011 book of the same name, to describe the art world "from below": taking the part of the imaginative and creative energies that are excluded from visibility because the art system requires a surplus of "failed" artists in order to function.[1] Although this art system allows a gestural politics into contemporary art, it also regulates dark matter by excluding the most politically committed work. Dark matter, is therefore a "missing mass" or "surplus archive," metaphors that are kept in play to allow Sholette's analysis to range across critical frames of reference. Indeed, the instability of the imagery that Sholette finds in dark matter seems to be required by the bizarre logic that permeates neoliberal culture, where record numbers of museums are built, where art markets boom as financial markets crash, and where gentrification spirals out of control.

Activist art, for Sholette, is part of the dark matter of the art world: representing the labor of artists at the base of the art pyramid, far from the market and its penumbra of artistic celebrity. His essays, published in *Afterimage, Third Text, e-flux, Text zur Kunst* and *Mute*, have contributed to the many debates around the "social turn" in art since the 1990s, playing a key role in the resurgence of interest in art activism, artists' collectives, and artistic labor. In this volume, the texts have been organized into three sections—Part I "Art World," Part II "Cities without Souls" and Part III "Resistance"—each focusing on one aspect of the complex relationship between activist art and neoliberal capitalism. In each part, the essays are arranged in chronological order, culminating in reports upon the present, so that fault lines can be traced from the triumph of neoliberalism in the 1980s through to the Great Crash of 2008 and its aftershocks, which continue to reverberate through social and political institutions almost a decade later.

Rather than consider each text separately, this introduction will explore one line of thought from among the many suggestive possibilities presented by Sholette's work. The central focus here will be *bare art*, the term that Sholette uses to examine the now banal obviousness of art's subservience to the interests of capitalism. Sholette's analysis is attuned to the crisis conditions that have emerged in a period when the revolution in communications technology makes possible new forms of resistance but also reveals the disfigured social relations of capitalism. As with dark matter, though with a different emphasis, *bare art* is art on the brink of tipping over into politics, forming a space in which to assemble resistance against the neoliberal capitalist order.

Throughout the neoliberal period, emergency conditions have existed on the margins of global capitalism, often deliberately created to allow rapacious exploitation of the commons. Now, however, after the crash of 2008, the austerity policies that sought to revive the ailing capitalist system are the proximate cause of the rise of the far right in Europe, the Tea Party in America, Brexit and of course the anarchic populism of the successful presidential campaign waged by Donald Trump. Spending cuts have stripped back welfare provision, punishing the most vulnerable. Even where they are not directly affected, fear of downward mobility has taken hold in the middle class to the extent that unstable political energies have been unleashed. Crisis conditions now affect the institutions of liberal democracy in the wealthiest capitalist states. Political elites long to return to the politics of consensus, the listless indifference that was always the most important precondition for neoliberal reform. It seems unlikely that any such return will take place, but even in its weakened condition liberal democracy loathes and fears the left—Sanders, Corbyn, Podemos— far more than it does the xenophobic far right. This political conjuncture threatens to move in a frightening direction. Such is the terrain in which the political implications of *bare art* must be evaluated.

Activist Art and Neoliberal Culture

The emergence of neoliberal capitalism is usually dated to the mid 1970s, linked to the collapse of the Bretton Woods agreement in 1973, the market reforms and suppression of left-wing organizations that took place after the coup against Salvador Allende in Chile, and comparable economic restructuring that took place in New York, after the city became bankrupt in 1975.[2] It was not until the electoral success of Ronald Reagan and Margaret Thatcher, however, that neoliberal economic policy was placed at the heart of a new hegemonic political project. It was also during the 1980s that the expansion of the art world gathered pace, which is why changes in art since this time, driven by speculative capital investment, are often cited as having been symptomatic of neoliberal capitalism. Under the influence of neo-liberalism, contemporary art has become a global phenomenon, but it has also become incoherent, over-abundant, a proliferation of styles that are corrosive to any stylistic category. This art world assimilates critiques of the prevailing system that never quite amount to a qualitative transformation of it, but instead add material to the relentless expansion. Sholette's polemical engagement with the art world that was created by an influx of financial capital has been coruscating, and it is worth quoting him at length:

Contemporary art appears indiscriminate in appetite; a maw perpetually opened in uninterrupted consumption as vats of chemicals, butchered animals, dirty mattresses, mass-produced commodities, disposable packing tape, cast-off pieces of cardboard, even acts of coitus enter the art world through its specialized showrooms in New York, Los Angeles, London, Berlin, Paris (and, minus the sex, also now in Beijing, Shanghai, Dubai, and Abu Dhabi). Animal, vegetable, mineral: like a steady flock of coarse penitents, the more profane in outer appearance, the greater the artistic yield. For there seems to be one constant leveling everything entering this global cultural matrix: faith in the institutional art world's ability to drag some aesthetic meaning out like a confession from any object, person, or situation.[3]

How is this transformation of the art system related to the characteristics of neoliberal capitalism? This depends on the definition of neoliberalism that is employed. For a long period, art theorists have tended to assume that neoliberalism is a self-reinvention of capitalism, characterized by intensified exploitation and the "restoration of class power," in the terms first used by Gérard Duménil and Dominique Lévy and developed by David Harvey.[4] Others have disputed this account because it seems to concede the ruling class an unprecedented mastery over the contradictions that grind away within the capitalist system. For the Marxist economist Andrew Kliman, for example, the term "neoliberalism" is misleading when it is used to suggest a new period of capitalist development, free from the contradictions that Marx first identified in the nineteenth century.[5] Certainly, the era of neoliberalism, from the 1970s onward, can be understood equally well as one in which ruling elites have tried and failed to address crisis tendencies that first emerged in the 1970s, leading to successive financial and economic crises culminating in the Great Crash of 2008.

Sholette's essays make use of the concept of "neoliberalism," or the closely related ideas of "post-Fordism" or "enterprise culture," because they seem indispensable to the discussion of the transformation of art since the 1980s. The concept *bare art* strategically repurposes Giorgio Agamben's formulation "bare life" to speak of a moment in which the art system has revealed, in all its banality, the extent of its subservience to the interests of global power elites. The final text in this collection, "Delirium and Resistance after the Social Turn" (chapter 11), examines the most recent effects of the transformation of art under neoliberalism. Sholette observes that the art market has, up to now at least, entirely avoided the effects of the crash of 2008. In fact, it has prospered: there is a boom in museum building and auction sales for contemporary art continue to rise. Even a few years ago, art dealers were reported to avoid revealing the commercial dimension of their practice for fear of undermining the value of their wares.[6] Now they openly refer to art as an asset class, a "hedge" or an alternative currency: the financialization of art is apparently complete.[7] The art system, bloated by finance capital, has become delirious and cynically disenchanted. Art has been insulated against the crisis tendencies of neoliberal capitalism but also restructured to serve the interests of finance capital. After 2008, the art market showed itself to be immune to financial collapse, not least because it became a useful place to hedge investments, using the money pumped into the system by "quantative easing."

In some respects, art activism has prospered within this situation. "Social practice," a term used to describe the various legacies of activist art, is increasingly accepted by the status quo, as Sholette notes in two of the essays in this book, "Art after Gentrification" and "Delirium and Resistance after the Social Turn" (chapters 7 and 11). At the same time as prestigious art world prizes have been awarded to groups and individuals whose work might be described as social practice—for example the collective Assemble and the artist Theaster Gates, who were both honored in 2015—signs of class struggle have emerged within art, discussed in "Art after Gentrification" (chapter 7), an essay written for this volume.[8] Artists' groups such as WAGE (Working Artists and the Greater Economy) are working to address the low wages and poor working conditions that are endemic within the sector, while also linking this political action to struggles beyond art. Gulf Labor and GULF (Gulf Ultra Luxury Faction), operating in the same spirit, have undertaken a successful series of actions to highlight the exploitation of laborers working on the Guggenheim Museum's new outpost in Abu Dhabi.

Crisis conditions are making themselves felt within art, even within artworks, but it is difficult to understand the kinds of changes that they may presage. Activist art is increasingly acknowledged as an important presence within politics, especially since the global insurrections of 2010/11. The "Movement of the Squares"—in Spain, Greece and then the international Occupy movement—was inspired by the "Arab Spring," but also drew upon imaginative organizational methods and media interventions that are part of the art activist tradition.[9] The discussion of *bare art* addresses this complex situation: an art world where the interweaving of art and capitalism is self-evident, at the same time as critical categories are distorted by the social upheaval that emerges behind their backs. Sholette has developed a compelling examination of the way that neoliberal crisis has permeated art by examining the contradictions that drive this instability. His aim is to clarify the political stakes of art, in the hope that art, now that it is laid bare, might uncover new forms of solidarity.

Histories of Art Activism

Based in subversion on the one hand, and empowerment on the other, activist art operates both within and beyond the beleaguered fortress that is high culture.

Lucy Lippard[10]

The emergence of the term "art activism" is closely linked to Lucy Lippard's critical advocacy in the 1980s, though the category has since grown to accommodate new waves of radical practice, including tactical media and interventionist art.[11] Taken from "Trojan Horses: Activist Art and Power," an essay published in 1984, the definition cited above is remarkable for its concise report of the stakes involved in activist art: to subvert existing cultural forms while simultaneously working to permeate culture with radical democratic principles. The Black Power movement, the anti-Vietnam counterculture and later radical feminism all had an important influence on collectives like the Art Workers' Coalition, Women Artists in Revolution, the Black Emergency Cultural Coalition and the Artists Meeting for Cultural Change. Subsequent New York-based art activists were also influenced by politicized post-conceptual art, exemplified by figures like Margaret Harrison and Conrad Atkinson, which emerged in Britain in the 1970s. Experimental art in Latin America was also important, having been politicized in the 1960s by struggles against reactionary dictatorship, most famously in the work *Tucumán Arde* (Tucumán is Burning), created by the Rosario group in 1968.

All of these forms of activist practice continue to have an influence on the present, as Sholette observes in the essay "Let's Do it Again Comrades, Let's Occupy the Museum" (chapter 2 in this volume). Activist art combines the ideals of participatory democracy, the community art tradition, as well as avant-garde experimentation in art and theater. For this reason, the label disrupts conventional art historical markers of style and periodization: art activism does not designate a movement located in a particular time and place, but instead connects struggles ever more widely, on the boundary between art and politics. It would be misleading to look for an origin of activist art in any one time or place, therefore. There can be no *history* of art activism, only *histories* of art activism, where art in its broadest anthropological sense is linked to political struggle.[12] For this reason, "art activism" has been regularly reinvented to describe the new forms of aesthetic protest that have accompanied the alter-globalization movement from the 1990s up to the present.[13] In short, art activism resists any linear model of cultural transmission, though strategies do return, often after long periods during which they are seemingly forgotten.

These historical peculiarities are captured in Sholette's work, which aims to amplify the challenge of art activism by inverting the "figure and ground" of art historical narrative.[14] Some of the groups that Sholette writes about—Group Material, Political Art Documentation/Distribution (PAD/D), Red-Herring and Artists Meeting for Cultural Change—are now increasingly incorporated into art historical revisions of the development of contemporary art. However, it is characteristic of Sholette's essays that they open out onto a strange cosmos of other names, some of them extremely obscure: Carnival Knowledge, Madame Binh Graphics Collective, the Royal Chicano Airforce, Syracuse Cultural Workers, La Raza Graphics workshop, Kearney Street workshop.[15] These historical references resonate with the many groups who work in the present on the margins of artistic visibility, whose local struggles become stronger by being interconnected, even across time.

Having said all this, it is also true that for Sholette the early 1980s are a recurring point of reference, and it will form a starting point of sorts for the narrative explored here. This was the period in which he was a founding member of PAD/D, the collective that is discussed in a number of the early essays in this book. PAD/D was closely linked with Lippard's integral contributions to the flourishing of political art in New York, founded in response to a meeting advertised on the reverse of an invitation for an exhibition that she curated at Artist's Space in 1980. In retrospect, the vibrant activist scene that emerged around PAD/D, but also across the United States and the UK, as well as in Australia, appears to have been a late flowering of the radical legacy of the New Left, doomed to be overtaken by the rise of neoliberalism. At the time, however, it was to all appearances to be a "massing of energies," harnessing the discontent that had grown among the capitalist crises of the 1970s, and focusing it against the unpopular early Reagan and Thatcher administrations.[16] The neoliberal onslaught against unions, resistant subcultures and state funding for the arts was yet to reach its full intensity; the legacy of the "left shift" among artists of the 1970s was still potent.[17]

PAD/D features in a number of the essays in this book, approached from different perspectives in the essays "Nature as an Icon of Urban Resistance ..." and "Counting on Your Collective Silence" (chapters 4 and 8) for example. For Sholette, the group exemplifies tensions that affect art activism, the precarious relationship to history and to the rise of gentrification that has been a key effect of the transformation of culture under neoliberalism. Although the archive of political art collected by the PAD/D has been held by the Museum of Modern Art since the collective disbanded in 1988, outside of Sholette's and Lippard's writings, the activities of PAD/D were largely overlooked in histories of 1980s art. This fate, to be buried in the heart of the institution and seemingly forgotten there, has certainly influenced Sholette's account of the subversive potential of dark matter as "an antagonistic force simultaneously inside and outside, like a void within an archive that is itself a kind of void."[18] There are echoes in this enigmatic statement of Lippard's definition of art activism as a "Trojan horse," "within and beyond" high culture. However, Sholette's work responds to the complexity of a period in which capitalism has become increasingly subversive, and an art world in which the relation between inside and outside has in turn become more elusive.

From Dark Matter to Bare Art

Theorization of activist art practices not only has to avoid codification inside and outside the conventional canon, it also has to develop new concept clusters in the course of its emergence and undertake to connect contexts not previously noticed in the respective disciplines.

Gerald Raunig[19]

Bare art, like dark matter, is a "concept cluster" of the kind described by Gerald Raunig, one that allows the political stakes of the interpenetration of art and neoliberal capitalism to be examined. By approaching the art world "from below," Sholette develops a distinctive perspective on the task of criticism and its response to crisis. The early signs of a "crisis in criticism" were already evident in the early 1980s, as the influence of neoliberal policies began to be felt in the cultural sphere. Hal Foster's famous essay "Against Pluralism" was among the first to diagnose the early effects of speculative capitalism upon the art market. Since that time art has become increasingly protean, shot through with the capillary action of financialization, while at its boundaries myriad art projects blend into daily life. Pluralism, for Foster, described a position in which "no style or even mode of art is dominant … for in a pluralist state art and criticism tend to be dispersed and rendered impotent."[20] There were two causes of this malaise, he suggested at the time: "an art market confident of contemporary art as an investment" and "the profusion of art schools—schools so numerous and isolate as to be unaware they constitute a new academy."[21]

In his book *Anywhere or Not at All*, the philosopher Peter Osborne cites "Against Pluralism" as an early identification of the "constantly renewed, self-declared crisis" of criticism.[22] For Osborne, the way out of this trap is to develop a more philosophically robust account of judgment in contemporary art, via a clarification of the complex temporal stakes involved in the description "contemporary" and an exploration of the way that the "transcategorical" forms of post-conceptual art might be made legible within criticism.[23] Osborne's ultimate aim is to restore the philosophical cogency of art criticism, as a means of examining, through dialogue with artworks, the stakes involved in our present. Undoubtedly, this is a philosophically powerful project, but there are other implications that might be drawn from Foster's remarks, which are prescient because they understand change within art to be driven by the interplay of demographic and institutional factors—resulting in increased numbers of artists—as well as by the altered demands of financial capitalism.

In *Dark Matter*, Sholette identifies the political significance of the "glut" of artists, which has steadily increased since Foster spoke of the proliferation of art schools in the early 1980s. The 2005 US census shows that over 2 million American citizens claimed "artist" as their primary occupation, and 300,000 as their secondary occupation. The 2010 census puts the figure at 2.1 million. As Sholette observes: "This makes the 'job' of being an 'artist' one of the largest single professions in America, just slightly smaller than those employed in the active-duty military."[24] He cites figures that show the number of employees in the European Union cultural sector to be 5.8 million, more than the combined working population of Greece and Ireland. Of course, statistical categories can be deceptive, especially because the growth of service and cultural industries has created professions that are difficult to classify. In the US census results, the terms "artists" and "fine artists" are used to describe both designers and animators. Nonetheless, Sholette makes a powerful polemical point, which focuses attention on the changing role of cultural production under neoliberalism.

In the words of art historian Carol Duncan, whose work is a key influence on Sholette, art organizes "vast amounts of artistic labor" to "spill most of it down the drain in order to get a little of it to show in a few places for the benefit of a few people."[25] The violence of this system has the potential to politicize artists, just as it shows the deep connections between art and the capitalist system. Sholette's interpretation of this argument is anchored in a simple sociological observation: "failed" artists form the most important audience for museums and galleries, fill administrative roles within the art world and purchase art supplies. At the same time, the "failed" artist represents all those who judge their success in terms different from those dictated by the mainstream art world: the art activists who turn art to political ends. Finally, and most importantly, the reserve of dark matter contains the suppressed fantasy and creativity of the working class, those who are both economically exploited and excluded from acquiring protocols of elite taste, as discussed in "Dark Matter: Activist Art and the Counter-public Sphere" (chapter 9 in this volume).

Sholette's examination of *bare art* begins from the same problematic as Osborne and Foster, but refuses the idea that problems manifested in the art world can be addressed from within art criticism, however thoroughly it may be reformed. The transformation of art is too fundamental to be resolved in this way, because art can no longer be held apart from the forces that seek to integrate it into neoliberal capitalism. This does not spell the end of art's critical potential: rather, that critical potential now derives from the contradictions within capitalism that have been exposed by the rapid expansion of the art system. Sholette's criticism, rather than responding to discrete works, identifies, through the precarious working conditions of artists under post-Fordist capitalism, the lineaments of a political subject that might come to resist it, alongside new forms of class struggle. Art plays an important part in these debates because it has become the model for flexible, high-reward labor under neoliberalism, where a small number of creative workers experience enlightened working conditions.[26] For the majority, however, the esteem in which artists are sometimes held becomes compensation for a precarious existence.

The complicity between art and neoliberal capitalism becomes the pivot of Sholette's analysis: "Is it possible that this enterprise culture has so de-radicalized art that something approaching an historic compromise or *détente* is taking shape whereby artists gain improved social legitimacy within the neoliberal economy while capital gains a profitable cultural paradigm within which to promote a new work ethic of creativity and personal risk-taking?"[27] Artists tend to be inured to uncertain cycles of income, and high levels of self-exploitation, spurred on by the gratification of creative autonomy and the possibility, though never the promise, of reward. The dissembling and ruthless competition that is encouraged by art's hierarchical structures has been identified and criticized by politicized artists since at least the 1970s.[28] For ideologists of neoliberalism, art's highly motivated, individualistic and unregulated labor offers a compelling model for new forms of work in the service sector. The cultural theorist Andrew

Ross suggests that the role of the artist has been exalted by new forms of labor under neoliberalism primarily because it has a glamour which masks the "the infiltration of models of non-standard employment from low-wage service sectors."[29] The reality of creative labor is not self-fulfillment but endless self-development, in pursuit of a reward that never arrives.

Sholette captures these conditions through shifts of perspective that are made possible by the flexibility of the metaphor "dark matter," which establishes a concept cluster with many theoretical points of references, including the art criticism of Lucy Lippard, the institutional critique of Martha Rosler and Hans Haacke, the analysis of the public sphere developed by Alexander Kluge and Oscar Negt, and the autonomist Marxism of Antonio Negri.[30] The ramifications of art's incorporation into neoliberal forms of the exploitation of labor are tracked across many of the essays included in this volume, where art is found on the brink of becoming politics in response to changes in the socioeconomic field. Rather than address the disorganization of critical judgment in contemporary art, as Osborne does, Sholette identifies in crisis the potential for new forms of political agency, as he puts it in *Dark Matter* "a new sustainable political culture of the Left."[31] Whether it will be possible for art to revitalize politics in this way, it is difficult to say. However, it is clear that under current conditions it would be unwise to rule out any possible reconfiguration of the political and the cultural. We are in a situation where it is impossible to predict definitively what will happen.

Crisis

Something has ended, or should have ended; everyone can feel it. It is a sort of interregnum. A miserable lull, backlit everywhere by the sense of declension and fires flaring across the planetary terrain of struggle. The songs on the radio are the same—awful, astonishing. They promise that nothing has changed, but they never do keep their promises, do they?

Joshua Clover[32]

"Something has ended" as Joshua Clover puts it, but it is not yet clear what may have begun. Certainly, since the emergence of neoliberalism, it has been clear that the relationship between art and politics has been in play. The discussion of pluralism in the previous section is illuminating because it shows that competing interpretations of democracy are woven into the ideological shifts that have taken place within art throughout the neoliberal period. Art cannot be free of what Joshua Clover describes as the "snares of the political."[33] For Foster, pluralism in art is a false *e pluribus unum*:

the co-option of criticism by the market creates pseudo-diversity, which he described in the 1980s as a "postmodernism of reaction."[34] In this respect, Foster's diagnosis was undoubtedly correct: art under neoliberalism feeds the culture of "spectacle." However, art activism must be recognized as a critical pluralist practice that also emerged from the crucible of the 1980s, one that was grounded in collective models of artistic labor and intent upon infiltrating a radical image of diversity into the domain of culture. For Sholette, this legacy feeds into *bare art*: sometimes as resistance, sometimes as complicity.

Marx argued in *Das Kapital* that capitalism is defined by its internally conflicted and predatory drive to accumulate surplus value. Large capital, which must grow still larger or risk dissolution, preys upon smaller capital, which is ill-prepared to withstand the shocks generated by the chaotic process of development. Meanwhile, the working class is forced into penury and intermittent employment, at the mercy of cycles of growth and decline and of the changing technical demands of capitalist industry. Competition between capitalists drives technological development that creates greater productivity and a decline in the numbers of workers relative to the scale of production. The result is polarization between, on one side, a small number of capitalists controlling vast social wealth and, on the other, a mass of immiserated workers. This, in a severely compressed form, is Marx's account of the internal contradictions that lead to capitalist crises, which create "overproduction, speculation crises and surplus capital alongside surplus population."[35]

Since the crash of 2008, a Marxian theory of capitalist crisis has been rehabilitated. Many analyses now seek to situate the present moment through fresh readings of crisis theory.[36] Although the Great Crash seemed to have been stabilized until the political upheaval of 2016, the combination of austerity measures and quantitative easing which created what the collective Endnotes has described as "social stasis": "maintained only by means of massive ongoing state interventions, which have ensured that the crisis remains that of some people, in some countries, instead of becoming generalized across the world. How long can this holding pattern be maintained?"[37]

It is clear that the holding pattern is now breaking. Advanced capitalist democracies are all committed to the idea of social mobility, but they are less and less able to achieve it, because there is insufficient surplus available after the ruling class takes their accustomed share. These crisis conditions, though they have intensified since 2008, may date back all the way to the beginning of neoliberalism. As discussed in Part II of this book, "Cities without Souls," advanced capitalist countries have conspired in the spoliation of their own working-class communities since the 1970s, in a way that has destabilized the democratic polity. During the same time period, the artist has been a holding pattern of sorts for the contradictions evident in a system that bases its legitimacy on the idea that social mobility is possible for all: a promise that can no longer be fulfilled. The artist is highly educated, required to take out enormous loans, in America and the United Kingdom at least, in order to pay the price of entry to the art system, as Sholette identifies in "*Bare Art*, Debt, Oversupply, Panic! (On the Contradictions of a Twenty-first-century Art Education" (chapter 3). Artists are able to claim access to the symbolic resources of elite culture while existing hand to mouth in precarious working conditions that suggest a return to the labor practices of the nineteenth century. Sholette's writings on dark matter and *bare art* situate the history of art activism within these contradictions. At the same time, they explore the ramifications of the new kinds of visibility that are afforded by the communication revolution that is another precondition of neoliberalism. Mass participation in social media has opened up the public sphere to reveal its distortions, its concealed wounds.

In *Revolutionary Time and the Avant-garde*, the theorist John Roberts writes in sympathy with Sholette's argument about dark matter, identifying a "second economy of art" that has been created amid the increasingly precarious forms of labor that exist within the service and creative economies: "the exponential increase in under-employed and unemployed artistic activity exists in the gap between the relative decline of industrial labor and the rise of new global proletariat comprising all those excluded or partially excluded from wage-labor."[38] For Roberts, the "second economy" of art, supported by new forms of distribution provided by the internet, is the basis for a "suspensive avant-garde" that exists beyond the art market. In Sholette's analysis, however, the technological revolution plays a slightly different role: the internet makes the redundant populations of capitalism more visible, where "dark matter is getting brighter."[39] Network culture has made art activism more prominent and more effective, but it has also revealed the distortions of imagination and desire which are latent within capitalist sociality. Invoking Nietzsche's famous analysis of the emergence of slave morality from the *Genealogy of Morals*, Sholette suggests that social media makes possible "networked *ressentiment*."[40] The indiscriminate connective power of the web feeds anti-capitalist movements, but also the far right, including US anti-immigration groups like the Minutemen and the openly fascist Stormfront Media Portal and the alt-right news site Breitbart News, among many others.

In this way, Sholette situates continuing global struggle against neo-liberalism within a wider technological transformation that has released subversive energies:

> One thing is clear, whether merely bitter or revolutionary, undeveloped or reactive, this survival project inevitably makes use of whatever resources it finds at hand, including the misappropriation of the "master's" own voice, the principal means of expressing political will today ... non-market dark matter ... is shot through with just such stealthy, frequently ambiguous expressions of resentment and rebellion. It is replete with acts of theft, rich with *double entendre* and knowing acts of indirection.[41]

Sholette's argument draws upon Oskar Negt and Alexander Kluge's rich theoretical work on the public sphere, which points to the distortion of working-class fantasy by the systems of oppression, as discussed in the essay "Dark Matter: Activist Art and the Counter-public Sphere" (chapter 9 in this volume). Since *Dark Matter* was first published in 2010, the resurgence of the populist right which has manifested all over Europe, and Britain's "Leave" campaign, have reinforced the significance of this analysis. During Trump's ascendancy, the incipient fascism in recent political debates has become full blown and the most prescient cultural critics have rightly identified this change as an issue that politicized artists must now address.[42] The systematic pillage of the state by neoliberal reforms has released unstable political energies that state intervention in social welfare was adopted to contain in the first place. This is a moment of political awakening, and the activism of the right is more vigorous within it than is that of the left.

The early signs of this political change were identified by theorists of art activism in the 1980s. Brian Wallis, for example, in an important essay published in the *Democracy* project created by the artist collective Group Material in 1991, suggested that the distinctive contribution of art activism is that it "takes democracy at its word," instigating "a crisis brought about by too much participation, too much democracy."[43] However, the flip side of this struggle was the prevalence of right-wing activism in the hegemonic politics of neoliberalism. If the 1960s saw the emergence of the combination of media activism and grassroots organizing on the left, laying the ground for activist art, the 1980s saw these techniques adopted by anti-abortion campaigners, and conservative campaigns against the "liberal" media.[44] The mass rallies of the Tea Party in the US, Marine Le Pen in France, the rise of UKIP (the UK Independence Party) and the cynical populism of the Brexit campaign in the UK in 2016 see this legacy bringing about what seems, without any trace of exaggeration, to be a new mutation of fascism.

Most chilling of all these developments has been the success of Donald Trump's presidential campaign. In one sense, Trump is an appropriate figurehead to oversee the decline of liberal democracy, which has been underwritten by neoliberalism. Although he inherited great wealth, his fortune was magnified by the real estate boom in New York that accompanied the emergence of neoliberal capitalism in the 1980s. His crass personal style recalls the era too, but most significant of all is the fact that a shambolic, crisis-ridden campaign was able to take him to the White House. Under neoliberalism, economic rationale supervened over political debate. Trump's success represents on one level the resurgence of overt racism, but his supporters, whatever else they may hope from his presidency, also repay the system in its own nihilistic coin. They know that Trump is inconsistent, but all politicians have been. Some may even know that Trump is unstable, but, after decades of neoliberal managed decline, it becomes difficult to imagine that instability can be any worse than stability.

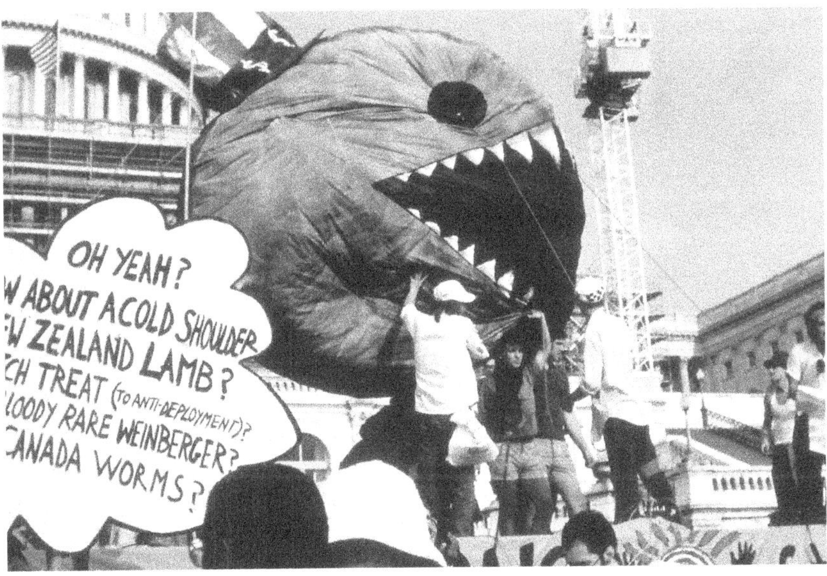

Figure 3   Uncle Sam Pac Man demonstration inflatable artwork by PAD/D, circa 1984 (Image Herb Perr)

Art activism presents, in this context, a complex symptom of liberal democracy's combined and uneven decline, in which the conception of art itself has come under immense pressure. It may be that democratic failure has prepared the ground for systemic upheaval. The economist Wolfgang Streeck has argued that the decline of capitalism has been precipitated by its success in disrupting and fragmenting internal opposition. Internal dissent in capitalist states, the more or less "loyal opposition" of unions and left-wing parliamentary parties, helped to moderate the excesses of the system in the 30 years after the Second World War. Neoliberalism, as a political project, has broken the regulative power of this internal dissent, often by tapping right-wing populist energies, and has irrevocably damaged the integrity of liberal democracy, the political form within which capitalism seemed to flourish. Streeck's predictions for the trajectory of capitalism, written in 2014, bear repeating after the upheaval of 2016:

> What is most likely to happen as time passes is a continuous accumulation of small and not-so-small dysfunctions; none necessarily deadly as such, but most beyond repair, all the more so as they become too many for individual address. In the process, the parts of the whole will fit together less and less; frictions of all kinds will multiply; unanticipated consequences will spread, along ever more obscure lines of causation. Uncertainty will proliferate; crises of every sort—of legitimacy, productivity or both—will follow each other in quick succession while predictability and govern-ability will decline further (as they have for decades now). Eventually, the myriad provisional fixes devised for short-term crisis management will collapse under the weight of the daily disasters produced by a social order in profound, anomic disarray.[45]

This may not be the track upon which capitalism is set, but it is a plausible reading of recent events. In the writings presented in this book, and in *Dark Matter*, Sholette offers a way to think about art's politics that acknowledges the disorder inherent in this situation, which derives not from the spectacular power of capitalism, but from its profound internal contradictions. There is no consolation in perceiving weakness rather than strength at the heart of capitalism, because it creates the conditions for barbarism—for fascism—more easily than it does for a redemptive politics. However, it is the power of capitalism's decrepitude against which a progressive politics must be measured, even as democratic systems are further driven into convulsions of kaleidoscopic fragmentation and refor-mulation. Under these conditions the prefigurative politics of art activism must surely be part of the effort to resist ruling-class attempts to reimpose their hegemony. When we are on the brink, after all, it is the promise of a beyond that becomes increasingly important to our political struggles. Although art has been transformed by neoliberalism it has been able to suggest this promise, even in the throes of delirium.

Part I

Art World

Introduction I:
Welcome to Our Art World

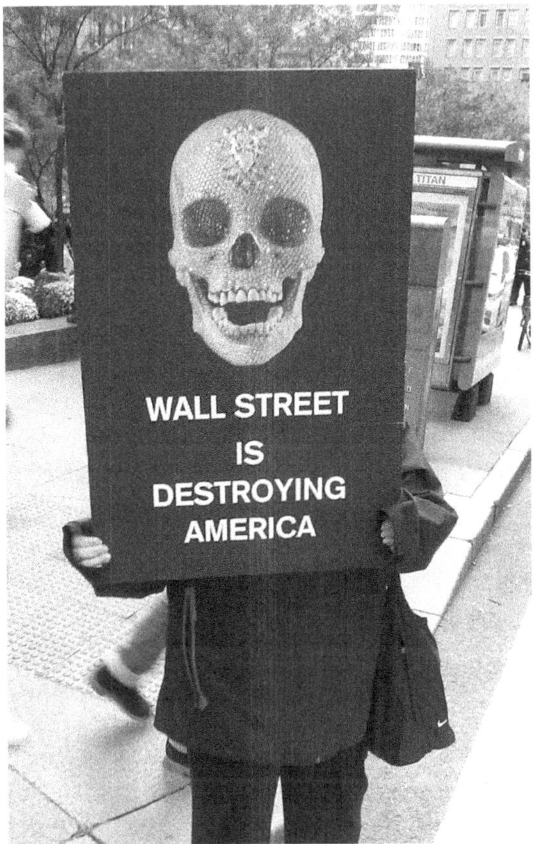

Figure 4   Protester with Damien Hirst sign during the first week of Occupy Wall Street, September, 2011

(Image Chris Kasper, 2011)

Having died twice, the artist is neither modern nor postmodern, yet caught in the order of time conditioned by her relation to the symptom, her relation to the art world.

Marc James Léger[1]

How does the growing embrace of socially engaged art practice by mainstream culture relate to unprecedented fiscal indebtedness among students and artists? And what do we make of provocative claims that Occupy Wall Street was in fact a contemporary art project? Part I examines these entwined issues through the common denominator of our art world, a term difficult to define, yet ubiquitous in use. For people directly involved in it, the art world is a familiar space (or system, or economy) that stands apart from the so-called real world and yet is also increasingly entangled with the real world (which curiously appears less and less real itself of late). This introduction argues that the art world must be analyzed as a "totality" whose features are simultaneously more exposed and less exceptional thanks to the broader crisis of deregulated capitalism and erosion of liberal democracy at the start of the twenty-first century.

City of God

One phrase, the art world, appears throughout this book with great frequency and for two reasons above all. First, it designates a field of cultural practice and, second, it delimits my chosen area of critical enquiry. Most often the expression is used in commonsensical way, appearing with adjectives such as "contemporary," "mainstream," "institutional," or "elite" preceding it. It was not until after my early essays were completed that I further qualified what *the art world* actually means analytically. In 2007 I wrote: "By the term art world I mean the integrated, trans-national economy of auction houses, dealers, collectors, international biennials, and trade publications that, together with curators, artists and critics, reproduce the market, as well as the discourse that influences the appreciation and demand for highly valuable artworks."[2]

Two features of this definition color my subsequent research into contemporary art. First, is the implied lack of impartiality evident from the definition's focus on the art world as a set of business relations within a capitalist marketplace. No doubt this bias has its roots in my own development as an artist, writer and activist lending all my writings a partisan, anti-capitalist tendency. Likewise, most of my writings engage with the absence/presence of a countervailing sphere of invisible or overlooked art production and its history, a missing mass that makes the art world possible in the first place. Thus, my point of view has primarily been one of constantly looking up, from down below, or looking in perhaps from a marginalized but parallel dimension of artistic dark matter. The second contention made here is that the art world *is* an integrated system of production, and *not*, as some postmodernist critics contend, merely a bundle of overlapping practices, discourses or subcultures with varying degrees of autonomy, connectivity and interdependence. For even though the art world may appear piecemeal, it is, as is capitalism, a totality that is typically visible only as localized phenomena or in a fragment, which is, in Adorno's terms, "that part of the totality of the work that opposes totality."[3] Or, to place a bit of spin on a maxim by György Lukács, despite its fragmented semblance our art world is an objective totality of *delirious* social relations.[4]

To clarify this point, it is helpful to consider a famous definition of the art world, made by the philosopher Arthur Danto in a celebrated meditation on Warhol's *Brillo Boxes*. As Danto put it, "the art world stands to the real world as the City of God stands to the Earthly city." In order to gain admission, Warhol's *Brillo Boxes* required an indiscernible difference to mark them out from other mass-produced commodities (although Warhol's boxes were, in fact, built from wood and silk-screened, an issue that Danto overlooked). Danto's solution is devastatingly simple: "To see something as art requires something the eye cannot descry—an atmosphere of artistic theory, a knowledge of the history of art: an art world."[5]

This definition of the art world is very well known, but its full implications are rarely discussed. In the opening stages of his thought experiment, Danto introduces "Testadura," the "philistine" who cannot see the artwork, just another object. It is helpful sometimes to remember that very few people are born speaking art theory, or reeling off the lineage of contemporary art. That is to say, we are all "philistines" at some point. It is art education that shows artists the City of God, though it doesn't let them through the gates. Instead, perhaps, it reveals the art that seems now to be everywhere: in the underwhelming objects, in gatherings, even perhaps in an Occupy Wall Street (OWS) protest. Stranger still, this art has been stripped bare, first via a long process of artists questioning the power relations that inhabit the theories that they inherit and, second, by the myth-melting processes of capital. To understand these contradictions, it is necessary to view the art world with Testadura's bluntness as I do, from "below." The key axis of Part I, therefore, is between the art school, where everything is learned, and the museum, where initiates forget they ever had to learn anything as they perform the rituals of art.[6]

Danto's Artworld thesis appeared in 1964, and since then these cultural rituals have been integrated into those of capitalism. As architectural historian David Joselit recently suggested, a new wave of museum construction seems to "function as the art world's central banks." Designed for cities "around the world by star architects like Frank Gehry, Renzo Piano, Jacques Herzog, and Pierre de Meuron": "in a time of economic instability, precipitated by worldwide financial failures since 2008, people now see art as an international currency. Art is a fungible hedge [that] must cross borders as easily as the dollar, the euro, the yen, and the renminbi."[7]

Perhaps it was Haacke's real estate mappings, real-time projects and critical provenance tracings of Monet and Seurat paintings in the early 1970s that first indicated all that what was once so solid, including works of art, were beginning to melt into thin air. "There is nothing so edifying," writes W.J.T. Mitchell, "as the moral shock of capitalist cultural institutions when they look at their own faces in the mirror."[8] And along with notions of cultural privilege the idea of artistic autonomy was also dissolving. Since then, these moments of breakdown and demystification have only accelerated. To this assault was added museum interventions by Art Workers' Coalition and the Black Emergency Cultural Coalition, artistic deconstructions by Daniel Buren and Michael Asher, the cultural utilitarianism of Artists Placement Group, theories of institutional critique from Art & Language, museum maintenance performances by Mierle Laderman Ukeles, and the dematerialization of art world privilege via Lucy R. Lippard's copious writings. A bit later on came the critical practices of Martha Rosler, Carol Condé and Karl Beveridge, Mary Kelly, Alan Sekula, Fred Lonidier, Conrad Atkinson, Artists Meeting for Cultural Change (AMCC), Art Against Apartheid, the militant art journals *Red-Herring* and *The Fox*, and still further on Political Art Documentation/Distribution (PAD/D), Black Audio Film Collective (UK), Group Material, followed by John Malpede's LAPD (Los Angeles Poverty Department), Bullet Space, Artists Meeting Against US Intervention in Central America, Guerrilla Girls, and Gran Fury, so that by the end of the Cold War a process was unfolding whereby the previously unseen (I do not mean unseen as in unseeable, but instead intentionally unseen) conditions of cultural labor began to be foregrounded. All of this was paralleled by the rise of a social history of art in the US and the UK starting in the 1970s with figures such as T.J. Clark, Carol Duncan, Linda Nochlin, Frances K. Pohl, Andrew Hemingway, Alan Wallach, Fred Orton and Griselda Pollock.

Rather than "new," as the "avant-garde" is often defined, this self-critical artistic work represented a disenchanted revelation of the power that sustains the art world. At the same time, these moments of resistance were spurred along by changes in the working conditions of art as capital subsumed artistic practices into its own forces of production. On the one hand, art has been stripped bare by critical artists who have labored to reveal the workings of power within it. On the other, the speculative incursions of oligarchs who want to put the "City of God" to work as a kind of eternalized asset class have turned autonomous art into an unregulated investment market. And here we arrive at this book's central observation. Culture's internal aesthetic character is now manifest as so many flagrant, unconcealed and utterly ordinary attributes, so many data points, so that the desire by 1960s artists to transform their elite social position into that of a "cultural worker" has finally been fulfilled. Today artists are simply another worker, no more or less. We might best describe this new *mise en scène* as simply *bare art*.

Ironically, the activities of critical artists have been assisted by capital's own hegemonic reach, in which it "mobilizes to its advantage all the attitudes characterizing our species, putting to work life as such," explains Paolo Virno, or as Jameson explains following Marx, capital is "the first transparent society, that is to say, the first social formation in which the 'secret of production' is revealed."[9] The "secret" of artistic production is also revealed to be social production, a disclosure that has occurred as the pursuit of surplus value comes to dominate all fields of human activity. Like a hallowed covenant we reluctantly pledge ourselves to follow, there is little time or need now for older, ideological facades and cover stories. Claustrophobic, tautological, our *bare art* world is our *bare art* world is our *bare art* world. It emerges in successive and accelerating states of shadowless economic exposure following capital's ever-quickening swerves from crisis to crisis—the oil crisis and stagflated 1970s, the Savings & Loan meltdown 1980s/1990s, the dotcom bust 2000s, Argentinian default at about the same time, and of course the "Great Recession" starting late in 2007 with 8.7 million lost jobs between 2008 and 2010. But this does not mean all artists like it. As Caroline Woolard of BFAMFAPhD asked with added incredulity, "what is a work of art in the age of $120,000 art degrees?"[10]

Clearly a growing number of previously invisible cultural producers have begun to see themselves as a category in and for themselves as the social nature of art is unavoidably made visible. Like some weird redundant agency, this no-longer dark matter is commonplace—the art fabricators, handlers, installers whose own art practice always takes a back seat—and simultaneously bristling with a profound potential for positive change as well as an unpredictable and deep-seated sense of resentment. Tuition-indebted artist and co-founder of Occupy Museums Noah Fischer sums up the situation with frustration: "The contemporary art market is one of the largest deregulated transaction platforms in the world—a space where Russian oligarchs launder money, real estate tycoons decorate private museums for tax benefits, and celebrities of fashion, screen, and music trade cash for credibility."[11]

Pushing Back

Capitalist communication networks serve to quicken and thicken these resistant formations so that groups such as WAGE (Working Artists and the Greater Economy), Occupy Museums, Gulf Labor, Debtfair, Arts & Labor, MTL (Nitasha Dhillon and Amin Husain), Decolonize This Place and BFAMFAPhD, among others, openly acknowledged that they are indeed an art labor force whose work should not simply benefit the 1% of the art world's global superstars and mega-galleries. Speaking as artist and organizer of WAGE, Lise Soskolne bluntly lays out the view of a *bare art world* from below:

> Even though it is made up of a for-profit and a non-profit sector, the world of art is an industry just like any other. All of its supporting institutions, including philanthropy, contribute to its perpetuation and growth as such, and all those who contribute to its economy by facilitating the production and distribution of art products, including and especially artists, are wholly unexceptional in their support for and exploitation by it. The role of art and artists within this multibillion-dollar industry is to serve capital—just like everyone else.[12]

While some artists organize for better "working conditions," others parody enterprise culture, cunningly montaging the leftovers of a broken society into "mock institutions": DIY organizations that sometimes work as well as or better than the bankrupt institutions their founders initially sought to mimic. Debtfair derides the concept of the Art Fair by offering an open invitation to all artists in Houston, Texas, to submit work while also relaying their level of student debt: "Total debts amongst the artists are tabulated in a running tally while identifying the institutions in which these debts are rooted, [thus] while many feel isolated by their economic reality, Debtfair works to build solidarity and community around our shared economic conditions."[13]

At this point, we must pause to consider how these forces of resistance actually exist within an art world that is so intimately tied to the interests of the 1%. And consequently, does the past, present and anticipated future defeat of artistic opposition just return us to the age-old complaint of co-option, where every vestige of resistance is pre-deceased, because it will only find itself serving the interests of capital in the end? This was the issue that I took up in "Fidelity, Betrayal, Autonomy: Within and Beyond the Post-Cold War Art Museum" (chapter 1 in this volume). As I put it at the time: "no matter how imperfectly actually existing museums fulfill their social obligations, the symbolic position of the museum remains inseparable from notions of public space, democratic culture, and citizenship itself."[14] The essay also suggests a reason for this attraction to the art world, even by critical, politically driven artists because: "if institutional power persists in attracting even its opponents, perhaps it is because we love it, or at least the unselfish image it projects, more than it could ever love itself. That is the scandal my essay seeks to comprehend."[15]

The key issue, to reframe these concerns, is how the totality formed by the art world is understood. Crucially, it must be grasped as a dynamic system, one that adapts but also one that breaks down, if only momentarily, to expose underlying contradictions. Thus, the key observation I put forward in 2003 (chapter 1 in this volume) was the recognition that museums, universities and corporations are rife with administrative malfunctions, redundancies, and even occasional destabilizing contradictions. Perhaps it is not too much of a stretch to say that the prevalence of *bare art* is itself evidence of this kind of destabilizing conflict, pulled this way and that by the different forces that constitute the art world. Undeniably, just as everywhere else, this is not an equal struggle: the resources are almost all in the hands of the patrons, their hedge fund managers and the administrators who do as they are told. However, the point is still pertinent: the art world absorbs resistance and seeks to neutralize it, but its processes do not always succeed.

OWS was a moment of resistance and the overcoming of inertia that also stood in close relation to the New York art world (though the global Occupy camps were all quite different in character). "Let's Do It Again Comrades, Let's Occupy the Museum!" (chapter 2 in this volume) addresses the presence of an off-stage archive that ripples through the actions of Occupy Museums as a kind of repetition that is also strangely novel: the rediscovery of the art activist tactics of the 1970s and 1980s by a new generation of interventionists. The essay focuses on Occupy Museums, one of many post-Occupy groups that has gone on to develop, gradually, a new set of values with which to oppose capitalism, including the aforementioned Debtfair project. These groups have emerged from the fundamental contradiction within the art world, and the wider neoliberal economy: there is not enough room or resources for everyone (or so we are constantly reminded). A few experience the exalted version of an artistic career, but most will find themselves barely existing as precarious cultural laborers. For along with revealing the obscene top-heaviness of neoliberal institutions, OWS has also underscored the utter redundancy of most workers in the present economy, including artists.

OWS and the contemporaneous rebellions in other parts of the world also represented for me and other social commentators a critical denouement about contemporary art. Examples include theorist Stevphen Shukaitis who interprets the 2011–2012 wave of public square risings as heralding the formation of a New Left constituency that drew upon such Situationist tactics as psychogeography, *détournement* and *dérive* to create "the time and space for the emergence of new forms of collective subjects, rather than a politics formed around already given demands."[16] Curator Nato Thompson argues that the significant presence of contemporary artists in OWS, the Arab Spring, and other twenty-first-century uprisings is proof that culture's role in oppositional movements must be taken seriously, linking this amalgam of art and politics to the late twentieth-century anti-globalization movement. For Thompson, what these uprisings share in common is a preference for leaderless leadership, non-hierarchical organizing, and the "creative and productive unity of art and activism."[17] Thompson also defends Occupy's frequently criticized lack of political demands by explaining that, "one cannot understand this radical refusal until one appreciates just how intensely OWS sought to avoid its language being used against the movement in the court of public spectacle."[18] Here I am reminded of Michel de Certeau's description of the everyday tactical resistance that keeps no territory or winnings, and "has no image of itself."[19] Likewise, the humble OWS tactician neither wants nor owns anything and is instead engaged in what Stephen Wright terms "usership," an activity comparable to a bee colony whose pollinating labor collectively generates a far larger economy than the colony requires to sustain and reproduce itself.[20]

Occupying the Totality

While Shukaitis and Thompson acknowledge the central role of artistic vanguards, or a certain interpretation of these practices, in twenty-first-century left politics, historian Yates McKee goes one step further in his book *Strike Art!* by proposing that OWS might be read as a work of contemporary art in itself. Acknowledging his own divided position as both critic and activist, McKee describes the surrealist atmosphere of the OWS encampment as follows: "for those steeped in contemporary art theory, walking into Zuccotti Park was an uncanny experience."[21] But in order to firmly set up the role played by contemporary art and avant-garde aesthetics in Occupy he turns to the concept of prefigurative politics as this is defined by one of the movement's primary architects, the anarchist and anthropologist David Graeber. For Graeber, as for McKee and many other commentators on Occupy, the concept of prefigurative politics involves first visualizing a non-alienated society as a means of realizing its future actualization: "Surely there must be a link between the actual experience of first imagining things and then bringing them into being, individually or collectively, and the ability to envision social alternatives."[22]

Graeber proposes a link here between aesthetic imagination and political prefiguration. McKee threads the needle: "Graeber's text is an essential point of reference in tracking the political and artistic ethos that would inform Occupy, an ethos that, as we have seen, developed in relative autonomy from the art world itself even while drawing nonacademically on the discourses of avant-garde art such as Dada, surrealism, and the Situationists."[23]

Strike Art!'s emphasis on the aesthetic dimension of prefigurative politics is reinforced throughout McKee's book, including a reference to the late 1960s street theater of the San Francisco Diggers, and also when he cites the ingenious media-oriented creativity of ACT UP in which artists were essential "not merely as decorators or designers, but rather as organizers and tacticians in their own right."[24] Finally, with cards almost revealed, he writes: "Occupy as a totality—rather than just this or that phenomena within it—can itself arguably be considered an artistic project in its own right, assuming we reimagine our sense of what art is or can be."[25]

This project, McKee asserts, also represented the end of socially engaged art, at least in so far as the latter seeks to be a vanguard practice "defined by its very flirtation with dissolving the category of art altogether into an expanded field of "social engagement."[26] Remarkably, McKee's prediction has come to pass, and has also simultaneously been flipped over on its head. For, on the one hand, the direct interventions of Global Ultra Luxury Faction (GULF) and Liberate Tate, among other activist art groups, reflect the dissolution of art into social activism while, on the other, social practice art is now being taken up, selectively, by mainstream art institutions, including the Guggenheim Museum, which is the very target of GULF's direct art activism.[27] Therefore, regardless of whether OWS did or did not serve as the furnace fusing the categories of art and politics into a new amalgam, the resulting state of affairs might best be characterized as a delirious state of resistance and subsumption at one and the same time.

Perhaps this is another permutation in the trajectory that has been followed by *bare art* since the 1970s. Imagining such a history for socially engaged and activist art inevitably raises the question of our art world, and the role it plays in normalizing such practices, which is why I insist on grasping the art world as "a world," or, if you prefer, as a unified, but internally conflicted, political economy grounded in its own endless reproduction and expansion. To reject this notion of the art world as a totality set within the larger totality of capitalism inevitably generates interpretive limitations that not only constrict cultural criticism but also political analysis. McKee's otherwise excellent *Strike Art!* runs afoul of this shortcoming when he writes that he will use "the phrase 'art system' as a way to displace the deeply engrained figure of the 'art world.'" McKee continues: "The latter term connotes a unitary, self-enclosed cultural universe of likeminded cognoscenti making, viewing, judging, and sometimes buying and selling works of art. Even when used disparagingly, as in the phrase 'art world elites,' the phrase homogenizes and neutralizes what is in fact a highly complex and uneven landscape."[28]

I certainly would not argue with the metaphor of the uneven cultural landscape, but would add that it is still very much a landscape with definable properties and topographies, regardless of how it might appear from any particular angle at any given time. Because, like capital, the art world, manifests itself *as* a fragmented and highly localized phenomenon, though in one significant way the situation is quite the reverse. For what the art world's exhaustive power relations aim to reproduce is its own restricted economy: a system of structured immobility, competitive hierarchies and false scarcities. And rather than call it a *system* and leave it at that, the art world is better grasped as a *system of reproduction*, one that, no matter how granular in appearance, generates real-world effects on the way artists live and work. In other words, the art world is both a real, material economy *and* a comprehensive symbolic whole, not a monumental whole, but an oblique and roundabout narrative that we typically glimpse only in moments of crisis and breakdown, such as the current period following upon the 2008 financial collapse.

Rejecting the concept of an integrated art world has other consequences. For one thing, there can be no such thing as activist art, political art, interventionist art or socially engaged art without the adversarial presence of our art world. This does not mean activists or social movements do not produce cultural artifacts or aesthetic concepts that could be described as art were we to, as McKee suggests, "reimagine our sense of what art is or can be."[29] On the contrary, just like what is produced by hobbyists and amateur artists, Live Action Role Play (LARP) enthusiasts, Crop Circle makers, zinesters, or the ultra-left and largely self-taught Madame Binh Graphics Collective, whose silkscreen posters show fugitive Black Panther Assata

Shakur breaking free of white chains (Figure 5), such works will never be displayed as "art" without first passing through a mandatory filter of disinterested detachment. This is, after all, how artists such as Sharon Hayes or Jeremy Deller are able to display politically charged artifacts within the art world context, as much as it is the logic behind the presence of the PAD/D Archive of socially engaged art that is located within MoMA, although in PAD/D's case the detachment is literal since its archive is off-site and out of view to regular museum-goers).

In order to move these practices out of a state of sheer "usership," to cite Stephen Wright's terminology, and into the ontological category known as art, their specific social provenance must be bracketed out and replaced

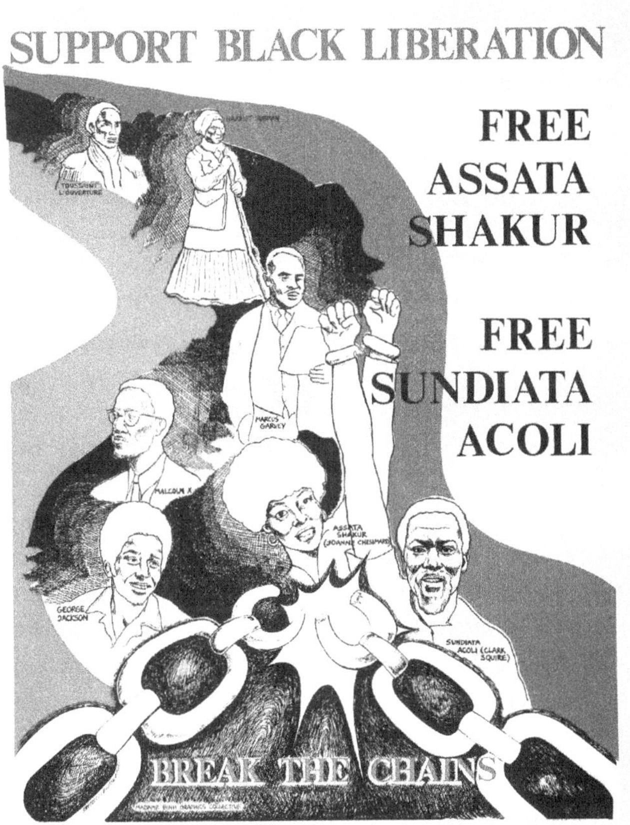

Figure 5 *Support Black Liberation/Free Assata Shakur/Free Sundiata Acoli*, Madame Binh Graphics Collective, Mary Patten, lead designer, NYC, circa 1978–1979

(Image M. Patten)

with a new frame of neutralized or ironic reference. The typically fraught outcome of this procedure is apparent whenever an earnest, socially conscious curator attempts to display the "authentic" life settings of activist artworks within the solitude of the white cube by using documentary photographs, newsreels, artifacts and so forth. Most often the exercise results in a visual menagerie with the ultimate example found in the 2012 Berlin Biennale where curators Artur Żmijewsk and Joanna Warsza invited Occupy Museums and other art activists from Zuccotti Park to establish an encampment on the ground floor of the Kunstwerk for the duration of the exhibition. This "administered occupation," as Olga Kopenkina describes it, was also labeled a "human zoo" even by its participants.[30] Nato Thompson's exhibition *The Interventionists* and Martha Rosler's *If You Lived Here* exhibitions, as well as installations by Group Material fared better by confronting the art world framing as part of the critique. The question remains, however, how are we to understand this new aesthetic frame if OWS really is to attain the status of an artwork? How are the terms of the struggle over culture to be reconstituted?

At moments like this we see the art world firmly set within that larger whole that is capital. This is not an entirely new situation. Writers such as Chin-Tao Wu and Julian Stallabrass argued this reality for years, as did artists such as Hans Haacke and Martha Rosler. But there is one caveat today, and that involves scale, even if it is not always clearly visibile as such. Because while Jameson reminds us capitalism is never visible as a totality and can only ever be perceived as a set of symptoms that manages crisis through "mutation onto larger and larger scales," so too has the art world scaled up to the point that it has become a literal surrogate for capital.[31] A new generation of cultural critics has arrived at a similar reading of the art world's imbrication within capitalist production including John Roberts, Melanie Gilligan, Kerstin Stakemeier, and Marina Vishmidt, Kim Charnley and Hito Steyerl. Some of their views are discussed in "*Bare Art*, Debt, Oversupply, Panic! (On the Contradictions of a Twenty-first-century Art Education)" (chapter 3 in this volume). As Steyerl has recently observed "art's organizing role in the value-process—long overlooked, downplayed, worshipped, or fucked—is at last becoming clear enough to approach, if not rationally, than perhaps realistically."[32] Which is perhaps why, when I look at a monumental work produced by Jeff Koons's studio, or a diamond-dotted platinum skull by Damien Hirst, what I see is a very real ailment puffed up to the size of our too-big-to-fail twenty-first-century reality. And what strikes me, as it does so many other people, is not the presence of a powerful idea or a remarkable manifestation of artistic expressivity, but the raw accumulated resources of money and wage labor necessary to bring this work into being. I also remember one other thing. On September 17, 2011, just before the actual occupation of Zuccotti Park began, the first thing I saw when visiting OWS was a lone protester carrying a placard with an image of Hirst's skull on it that read, "Wall Street is Destroying America." To many, the art world is the primary symptom of the 1% economy.

This is also why the delirium and crisis of capitalism is also the delirium and crisis of the art world. Two realities demonstrate this turmoil above all others. One is the art world's need for an ever-increasing pool of unremunerated creative workers indebted to the art world system of reproduction, which is why art education plays an important role in the final chapter of Part I "*Bare Art*, Debt, Oversupply, Panic!" Art education is one of the key points of entry into this surplus labor pool and riven with its own contradictions as a result. Like the rest of university education, the price for being shown the City of God is a lifetime of debt that will force you to labor, paradoxically, to keep it out of reach. The super-profits from the loan system no doubt feed into the unremitting art world expansion visible today in the supercharged art market, certainly, but also in the wave of global museum construction, including in nations propped up by extremes of inequality and repressive political regimes such as the United Arab Emirates. What is remarkable, however, is the way so many art world pundits, institutions and policy makers continue to use the language of social justice and democratic ideals while remaining faithful to capitalist principals of maximum growth, unremunerated cultural labor, and deregulated supply and demand thus blatantly contradicting the ideal image of art as an exceptional mode of human activity.

Bare Art

If the latest iteration of system failure has left art naked, with no clear way of restarting the old narrative about art as an autonomous sphere of ideas and creativity no matter how entangled its system is with the marketplace, then this rupture also reveals a significant negation at work for all to see. What I term the art world's dark matter, and what John Roberts more narrowly describes as art's "second economy," generates resources necessary for survival within, across, as well as beyond the art world, operating through networks of gift giving and the exchange of services and knowledge, rather than through a self-limiting market of buyers and sellers.[33] Much like Georges Bataille's notion of a "general economy," as opposed to a "restricted" economy, this other support system involves expenditure without precise limits and broadly distributed, rather than concentrated, forms of compensation and expectation.[34] And no doubt it was this beehive colony effect that occupiers in Tahrir Square, Puerta del Sol and Zuccotti Park, among other encampment sites, were testing out, fine-tuning and trying to make self-sustainable.

The undeniable aesthetic dimension of this experiment in horizontal generosity, its prefigurative vibrancy, is ultimately what I suspect many art world oriented observers of OWS and other uprisings in the 2010–2012 time frame have interpreted as contemporary art's gift to the movement, as McKee suggests. "Occupy took the avant-garde dialectic of 'art and life' to a new level of intensity," he writes, though one could also cite similar statements by Thompson, Shukaitis, Holmes, Gokey, Raunig and Grindon among many others, including even CNN in, predictably, a more conventional manner, "How art propels Occupy Wall Street."[35] Nonetheless, in truth, neither contemporary artists, nor creative class workers have any special monopoly on these informally networked, non-market methods of survival. These are the weapons of the weak.[36] Which is why the most important lessons of *bare art* cannot help but point to new forms of potential solidarity within, but also beyond our art world.

1

Fidelity, Betrayal, Autonomy: Within and Beyond the Post-Cold War Art Museum[*]

Certainty, fidelity
On the stroke of midnight pass
Like vibrations of a bell
W.H. Auden (*Lullaby*, 1937)

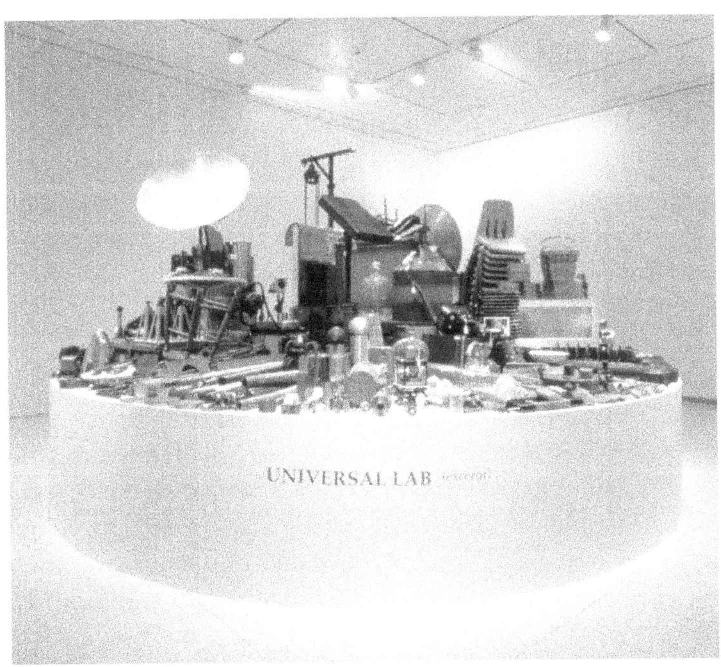

Figure 6   Dan Peterman, Universal Lab, Smart Museum of Art, University of Chicago, 2006
(Courtesy of the artist)

---

* This chapter was first published in 2003.

Today, the socially committed artist, writer, curator or administrator must face one very unpalatable fact—large, basically conservative institutions, including museums and universities, eventually charm even their most defiant critics and radical apostates. If the end of the Cold War (and of Modernism) has brought a new level of inclusiveness to these cultural institutions, what has become of the once defiant notion of a counterculture? Writing as a heretic, I believe that while institutional power is certainly no phantom, the "institutional function" (to rework a term borrowed from Michel Foucault's essay "What Is an Author?") is seldom precisely directed. Rather, museums, universities, even corporations are rife with redundancy and internal conflict.[1] Their greatest effectiveness is often more the result of a magnitude of scale than organizational efficiency. Naturally, administrators and curators will, in the last instance, always side with the institutional function, but at any point prior to that critical juncture, there arise intrigues, affairs and infidelities of great potential to political activists. And if institutional power persists in attracting even its opponents, perhaps it is because we love it, or at least the unselfish image it projects, more than it could ever love itself. That is the scandal this chapter seeks to comprehend.

I want to begin by describing my own troubled history. I have worked inside art institutions as well as outside and against them. I want to address this space of ambivalence, but I also want to confess a still deeper, long-standing disloyalty—toward the practice known as contemporary art, and toward the increasingly global market that supports it. As a practicing artist and curator who teaches in an arts administration program, this confession is nearly seditious. Yet, like all complex relationships, it also betrays my co-dependency on institutional authority as a means of achieving what are in effect contrary, democratic goals.

I can trace my declining faith in the institutions of art back to 1979, the year I graduated from The Cooper Union School of Art. No longer a student, I began to attend meetings where other artists spoke not about their art but about their opposition to racism and apartheid, sexism and militarism. Rather than visiting studios or planning exhibitions, we focused on supporting Third World liberation movements, labor unions, the ecology movement and public housing. Art was at best a vehicle for accomplishing these ends. Besides, there was serious work to be done that had nothing to do with career building. Among those active at these gatherings was the critic Lucy R. Lippard, the writers Clive Philpot, Irving Wexler and Barbara Moor, and the artists Ed Eisenberg, Tim Rollins, Jerry Kearns, Richard Myer, Julie Ault, Janet Koenig, Doug Ashford, Mike Glier, Mimi Smith, Herb Perr and Rudolph Baranik. Many were veterans of other organizations, including Artists Meeting for Cultural Change (AMCC) and the feminist group Heresies. Before long, an organizational mission was being formulated that would transform these informal meetings held in Lower Manhattan into a coherent association with its own offices and bank account. In principle, the new group was to focus its activities on archiving and circulating the many boxes of materials about political and activist art that Lippard had been collecting for several years. At the moment of institutionalization, Philpot, then the director of the MoMA library, proposed the appellation Political Art Documentation, or PAD. When several members raised concerns about the service-oriented connotation of this name, it was modified to become Political Art Documentation and Distribution, or PAD/D.[2]

The PAD/D archive was intended to be an instrument for expanding left-wing activism among artists. By accumulating and distributing models for politically engaged practices, the archive would serve as a sort of tactical toolbox. The greater expectation was that this informal network would grow into an entirely autonomous system for distributing and exhibiting activist culture. This countercircuit would be woven out of a combination of new and existing sites not strongly tied to the dominant art world. It would include university art galleries, community centers, labor union halls and various public venues. Work would also be made for demonstrations and picket lines. Note, however, that most alternative art spaces were not part of this network because these artist-run institutions were perceived as outposts and stepping stones for the very cultural hegemony that PAD/D opposed. To underscore this desire for critical autonomy, consider the group's mission statement from 1981, in which PAD/D proclaimed that it "cannot serve as a means of advancement within the art world structure of museums and galleries. Rather, we have to develop new forms of distribution economy as well as art."[3]

Today, even the most formal art claims social relevancy. As Bruce Ferguson noted in his opening address for the 2000 Banff Curatorial Summit, it has become almost *de rigueur* to make explicit reference to issues of politics, cultural diversity, gender, and sexual identity (although, I must add, seldom to class or economic inequality). Indeed, such routines can be lamentable for political as well as artistic reasons. Yet, from the perspective of a politically engaged activist artist or organizer this kind of intra-institutional, liberal ambition can indeed be useful, if frustrating. Useful, because a certain amount of actual political work can be "leveraged" through it. At the same time, this tendency to display one's politics on one's sleeve (or via an interpretive wall text) is frustrating because curators, artists, museum administrators and academics easily confuse the kind of symbolic transgression that takes place inside the museum with the political activism that occurs at the judicial, penal, even global levels of society.

The reflex to make art socially relevant is itself a recent phenomenon (as well as a return to a much older one). It appears to have accelerated following the demise of the Soviet Union and the end of the Cold War. Perhaps this is because US artists no longer needed to display to the world an uncompromising individuality exemplified by abstract expressionism. At the same time, however, new grounds for justifying culture were needed. Social purposefulness and community-based art fit that need. By contrast, in the late 1970s and early 1980s, art with overt social subject matter was dismissed as utilitarian or as protest art. As difficult as it is to imagine today, in 1975 resistance to any sullying of high culture with politics actually helped topple the short-lived editorial team of John Coplans and Max Kozloff at *Artforum.* Coplans and Kozloff brought to the influential trade magazine a raft of radical art historians, artists and essayists, including Carol Duncan, Allan Sekula, Lawrence Alloway, Alan Wallach, Eva Cockcroft, Ian Burn and Patricia Hills. These writers dared to suggest that art was not an autonomous expression of transcendental truth, but an integral part of the social world. Hilton Kramer, then the principal art critic for the *New York Times,* as well as an ardent cold warrior, openly called for art dealers to boycott the magazine. In what might be considered a virtual coup d'état, both Coplans and Kozloff were soon dislodged from their positions.[4]

Meanwhile, by the late 1970s, politically engaged artists were becoming increasingly sophisticated in their mixing of the symbolic realm of art with the practical needs of political activism. Unlike an earlier generation, exemplified by Donald Judd or Carl Andre, who both strongly opposed the Vietnam War yet remained devout minimalists, many post-formalist artists collaborated with one another as well as with environmentalists, anti-nuclear and housing activists, and community workers, producing a heterogeneous range of artistic forms and styles that directly addressed social causes. Even PAD/D soon veered away from its stated archival and networking mission to make performances and agit-art for public rallies and demonstrations, including the 1981 action in Lower Manhattan titled *No More Witch Hunts.* The Reagan administration had recently passed anti-terrorist laws giving the government expanded powers of surveillance over US citizens. Many understood these so-called anti-terrorist laws as a thinly disguised legal justification for spying on domestic supporters of the FMLN (the Farabundo Marti National Liberation), a Salvadorian-based insurrectionary organization opposed to the US-backed regime of José

Napoleón Duarte. *No More Witch Hunts* brought together religious activists, a local progressive union, legal activists and artists. Meanwhile, Group Material, another New York City-based artists' collective founded about the same time as PAD/D, performed a mocking, military-influenced disco dance outfitted in hybrid "uniforms" that grafted together standard GI camouflage with the bright red colors of the FMLN. Such reflexive and playful use of visual signifiers marked the increasing experimentation and confidence of a new "political art" that was consciously distancing itself from the banners and murals of the past.

Along with PAD/D and Group Material, a partial list of organizations that operated in the New York area between 1979 and 1982 included the anti-nuclear organizations Artists for Survival and Artists for Nuclear Disarmament; the community-based Asian American group Basement Workshop; media activists including Deep Dish and Paper Tiger Television; and the feminist art collectives No More Nice Girls, Heresies, and Carnival Knowledge. And this list could be sorted differently by highlighting specific projects, including *The Women's Pentagon Action* and *The Anti-WW III Show*; *The Real Estate Show*, an anti-gentrification exhibition, organized by a splinter group from COLAB (Collaborative Projects), that was staged in a squat space on the Lower East Side; *Bazaar Conceptions*, a pro-choice "street fair" organized by Carnival Knowledge; and an art auction to help fund a women's center in Zimbabwe organized by the ultra-left Madame Binh Graphics Collective, some of whose members later served time at Rikers Island in connection with the infamous Brinks robbery in upstate New York.[5]

Therefore, when one speaks about political activism taking place *inside* the museum, as a prominent Chicago curator of contemporary art Mary Jane Jacobs once asserted, it is important to contrast the sort of critical and material engagement I've described above with attempts to "subvert the institutional frame" or to "transgress" conventions of representation or modes of display. Needless to say, and for reasons too detailed to go into here, by the later part of the 1980s, the category "political art" had become widely accepted, even as PAD/D dissolved. Meanwhile, the PAD/D archive is now housed in the mother of all establishment art institutions, MoMA in New York City. And while activist cultural work continued to evolve within organizations such as ACT UP, Gran Fury and the Guerrilla Girls, by the time MoMA organized its 1988 "political art" survey, *Committed to Print*, the very possibility of an alternative or counter-network of affiliated activist artists and autonomous exhibition spaces such as PAD/D proposed could no longer be sustained, either in practice or in theory. Perhaps even more disconcerting is that today, some 20 years later, much of the art documented in the PAD/D archives remains invisible, in spite of the apparently required observance of political correctness within the contemporary art world.

The degree to which collectives such as PAD/D or Group Material or the Woman's Building on the West Coast participated in this normalization of politically and socially engaged art has yet to be studied. Nevertheless, when the terms "political art" or "multiculturalism" or, more notably, "activist art" are invoked today, they raise for me specific historical as well as theoretical questions regarding definitions and context. They also remind me that history is premised on such lost opportunities, just as activism is a process of recovering what the past has betrayed.

To briefly summarize then, from the perspective of a politically engaged art practice, whatever the motive is for the post-Cold War art world's alliance with social content, it must be read as a potential site for rendezvous. To think otherwise, to remain opposed to all institutional intercourse, is to assume the most ideologically accommodating position possible. It leaves the institution in the hands of those administrators and intellectuals who dismiss the impulse for economic and political justice as impractical, turning instead to a melancholy exploration of personal meaning or an unreflective indulgence in popular culture. Therefore the current fashion for political correctness (to use a term I despise but one that makes perfect sense in this context) is useful if for no other reason than that it provides leverage for a certain measure of engaged, political work.[6]

Perhaps the clearest way to frame this dilemma then is in the form of a question. How can artists learn to siphon off a portion of institutional power while maintaining a safe distance and margin of autonomy from the institution? At the same time, we need to ask what ethical questions this raises—not only for artists but also for sympathetic curators and arts administrators working on the "inside." In other words, what is the nature of the contradiction such potentially dangerous liaisons can produce? One answer can be found in the work of several contemporary artists, including Dan Peterman, his associates on the South Side of Chicago, and the collective REPOhistory.

Peterman's project, *Excerpts from the Universal Lab: Plan B*, was on display in the summer of 2000 at the David and Alfred Smart Museum of Art at the University of Chicago's urban campus. The Smart Museum is located not far from Peterman's multipurpose studio that, prior to a suspicious fire in 2001, included a neighborhood organic garden and housed a bicycle recycling and woodworking business as well as the offices of *The Baffler*, an iconoclastic left-wing journal featuring articles about global media culture and the so-called "new economy."[7] On one level, the artist's project for the Smart Museum resembles an unassuming display of outdated scientific equipment painstakingly arranged on a cylindrical platform or dais. The initial effect is of a display meant for a science fair that was mistakenly delivered to the wrong institution. But the "excerpts" that Peterman has used in the installation were in fact drawn from the collection of a former University of Chicago research associate named John Erwood (the man's actual name, but Peterman chose not to identify him in his project). By using the history of this collection, the artist is able to launch his subtle process of leveraging institutional power.

For several decades, Erwood had been diverting scientific materials from the university into a warehouse north of the campus. Initially, Erwood's accumulations formed the basis of an unregulated science laboratory under the utopian-sounding name Universal Lab or UL. This "laboratory" was intended to be a free space in which science projects that were not sanctioned by the university could be explored by almost anyone wearing a lab coat. (At least one viable scientific project involving solar-voltaic technology did result from the work done at UL.)[8]

The Universal Lab was therefore something of an institutional parasite. It recycled outmoded equipment and materials while remaining invisible to any oversight by its host, the university. However, Erwood's free space eventually became so choked with discarded apparatus and hazardous chemicals that it was no longer anything but a storage depot. By 1999, the Universal Lab devolved into piles of Geiger counters, autoclaves, lab ovens, oscillators, computers, radio equipment, plastic buckets of mercury, and hundreds of chemicals in brown glass bottles, all of which were stacked from floor to ceiling inside a cavernous former factory on Chicago's South Side. If the University of Chicago was not concerned with this pilfering, it may have been because Erwood was "disappearing" obsolete, even dangerous holdings that would have been expensive to dispose of in the proper manner.

UL might have remained invisible indefinitely if the building's ownership had not changed hands around 2000. In the meantime, Erwood had become destitute. With nowhere to turn, and no cost-effective way to dispose of the mountains of archaic technology, the new owner called on the assistance of the Resource Center, a Chicago-based non-profit recycling organization. Closely associated with Peterman's own recycling projects, the Resource Center allowed the artist to selectively catalogue some of the anonymous equipment and display it at the Smart Museum as part of an exhibition titled Ecologies: Mark Dion, Peter Fend, Dan Peterman, which was organized by curator Stephanie Smith.[9] By physically relocating some of the University of Chicago's lost "assets" back to its campus, Peterman was able to provoke a series of political and aesthetic challenges that extend beyond the immediate art context. As Smith notes, through this collaborative project, these objects, many of which were scavenged from the university's loading docks and trash bins, spiraled back in a new context. They did not complete a circle/cycle but instead accrued new layers of use, value and meaning as they were temporarily incorporated into the systems and physical spaces of the University of Chicago's art museum.[10]

If the apparatus Peterman transported to the museum is viewed simply as art, it neatly falls into the now familiar and relatively safe category of found object. However, if *Excerpts from the Universal Lab: Plan B* is looked upon as materials momentarily freeze-framed, yet still in a process of circulation and recovery, Peterman's project raises a far broader spectrum of issues. Perhaps the most provocative are legal questions about the University of Chicago's responsibility toward environmental safety in the largely African American community surrounding its South Side campus. The project also brings up questions of a more theoretical nature, including how UL, an extremely unconventional model for scientific experimentation, could exist, even briefly, in the shadow of an enormous institution such as the University of Chicago. Again, in terms of practice, what would it take to ensure the stability of a "free space" like UL? Equally compelling is the way that the moment Universal Lab was made visible within the legitimating authority of the museum, it was transformed into both a cultural asset (as "art") and a danger to the institution. One year after the exhibition closed, *Excerpts from the Universal Lab: Plan B* continued to haunt the university. In 2002 the University of Chicago Department of Radiation Safety, under the supervision of the Illinois Department of Nuclear Safety (IDNS), entered the UL site and identified and removed four potentially dangerous radioactive items. Following this the university again absolved themselves of any responsibility for the cleanup, Peterman noted, and Erwood's former laboratory was quarantined. Erwood was essentially evicted from Ulab and locked out while landlords puzzled over how to get rid of the Ulab inventory. Eventually the private owners of the space took on the cost of decontaminating the Ulab site.

The threat Peterman's artwork delivered to the Environmental Protection Agency (EPA) and other regulatory agencies prevented the landlords from recklessly disposing of the hazardous contents of the lab. But the importance of these crossovers between art and local politics depends on how Peterman's work is contextualized. With little more than a shift in discourse, the work veers between an engaged artistic practice that uses the museum for its own extra-artistic purposes and the now familiar mode of institutional critique, a point I will return to.

Yet if artists can leverage the institution's tendency to confuse symbolic and actual political action, this same ambivalence can also serve the interests of the institution. For instance, the semblance of self-criticism and a move toward cultural inclusivity can have direct economic benefits for the museum. This has become especially true in a funding climate where guidelines for (what is left of) public money in the United States explicitly call for "outreach" to "underserved" communities. Notably, within the hierarchy of the museum, this outreach usually falls to the education department, even if the education department and its staff seldom recuperate the financial rewards for such virtuous work. Needless to say, power and status in the museum come down to how much of the budget you receive (regardless of what you earn) and how much programming space you are permitted to command. This is one reason why every possible move an artist or curator makes inside the museum is always already a political one.

Much of the practice of the artist's collective REPOhistory also remains largely invisible within the institutional discourse of the art industry. One possible reason for this is that REPOhistory, an informal group of artists and activists established in 1989 by myself as well as several dozen other individuals, produced work that is unapologetically didactic and that appears to subjugate visual imagery to strategies of communication. By repossessing lost histories, the group simply, and in some ways naively, assumed that an intelligent, concerned citizen actually exists and would take the time to read the often bounteous information REPOhistory posted in public spaces. More than that, the group held out a genuine belief that some portion of the political and social critique REPOhistory was raising about the representation of history and the use of public space would be communicated, even acted upon. The New York-based group operated from 1989 to 2000, and, while no empirical proof has been collected regarding this model of what Jürgen Habermas would call communicative action, the substantial amount of mass media (as opposed to art) press it attracted, as well as the negative response by city officials to several REPOhistory projects, suggests that the group's operating assumptions were not entirely baseless. Perhaps the project that best illustrates this is the 1998 public installation *Civil Disturbances: Battles for Justice in New York City*.

Civil Disturbances developed out of a unique collaboration between the REPOhistory collective and a non-profit law office, New York Lawyers for the Public Interest. The latter provides legal assistance to poor and under-represented people and communities in the New York City area. Working with a team of socially concerned lawyers, REPOhistory established 20 topics and sites that designated pivotal battles in defense of the legal rights of the politically and economically disenfranchised. Using the same approach the group had developed for past projects, in which artist-designed street signs were mounted on city lampposts (temporarily permitted through the Department of Transportation), *Civil Disturbances* aimed to mark publicly subjects such as the mistreatment of citizens by members of the NYPD (New York Police Department), the legal fight to save various public hospitals, a class-action suit brought against the Giuliani administration in defense of abused children, and the passing of laws to protect women from domestic abuse and to provide low-income public housing. Yet, despite the group's record of obtaining two temporary installation permits for its public work from the city in 1992 and 1994, REPOhistory was first stonewalled and then refused permission by the Giuliani administration to proceed with the installation of *Civil Disturbances*. It required the intervention of a major law firm, Debevoise & Plimpton, to force the city to relent. However, the victory over City Hall in August, 1998 did not end the battle over *Civil Disturbances*. Once the project was installed, following many months of delays taken up with legal tactics, several individual artists' signs "disappeared" from city streets. Among these were Janet Koenig's work documenting the Empire State Building's prolonged non-compliance with the Americans with Disabilities Act, Marina Gutierrez's piece critiquing housing discrimination by the city against Puerto Rican families in her Brooklyn neighborhood, and a sign by William Menking that "landmarked" the site of an illegal "midnight" demolition of low-income housing on the lot where a luxury hotel now graces the "new" Times Square. As it turned out, in each case the art was being removed by building managers or local politicians.[11] This underscores a principle about so-called public space: it is never "empty" and simply waiting to be filled. Instead, it is always already occupied by political and economic power that claims entitlement to that space regardless of its designation as "public."

Nevertheless, these harsh lessons in *RealARTpolitik* that REPOhistory, PAD/D and Peterman endured have a counterpart within the hallowed heart of the museum. For many cultural laborers of my generation (artists, critics and scholars educated during the late 1970s and early 1980s), the inner workings of museums and other art-related institutions were rendered visible through the artistic practice known as institutional critique.

Exemplified by Hans Haacke and Daniel Buren in the 1970s, and continuing today with Andrea Fraser and Fred Wilson, among others, institutional critique is characterized by work that is less concerned with the formal aspects of art than with the unseen economic and social structures that buttress art's institutional setting. These unseen forces include the boards of directors, corporate underwriters, wealthy benefactors and affiliated dealers and collectors for museums, foundations and similar cultural entities. What has been revealed by the institutional critique is one persistent and disturbing fact: many cultural institutions are led by the private interests and personal tastes of an invisible elite, rather than by their stated philanthropic and educational mission. Yet while institutional critique has directly focused significant attention on this cultural contradiction for the past 30 years, it now appears to provide a degree of closure by reinforcing the notion that the museum offers an uncompromising democratic zone for engaging in civic dialogue. Even the preservationist obligations of the traditional museum are being redeemed in the work of Mark Dion, whose installations have increasingly become less an exposition of institutional limits than a rediscovery of the primary conservationist role of the museum. Once again, it is Dan Peterman's work that proves the more nuanced. Indeed, if there is the possibility of leveraging the all too conspicuous benevolence of the art museum, and of proceeding where

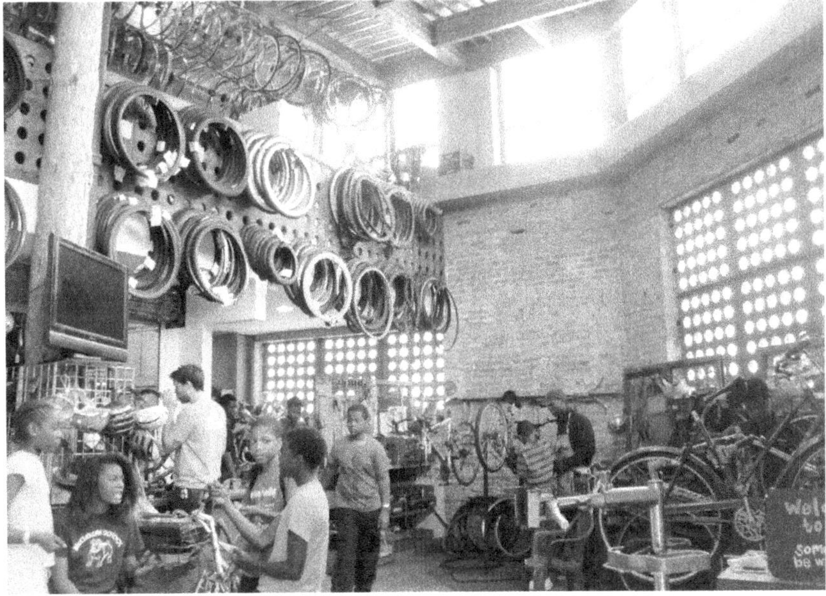

Figure 7 Blackstone Bicycle Works at Experimental Station, the South Side of Chicago, 2016

(Image Dan Peterman Studio)

institutional critique has left off, it is through work that extends off-site politics into the museum, then propels it back out into the public arena. Yet this raises still another question. Just who and what is outside the museum and how do these off-site, institutionally resistant spaces and practices perceive their relationship to the authority of the institution?

Speaking from my own experience, those artists working out of abandoned warehouses and in basement workshops, cooperative centers and urban squats believe that large institutional structures operate with a military-like precision to strategically defuse grassroots and resistant practices. In response, any viable counter-practice is compelled to constantly re-establish itself at the ever-greater perimeter of the institution's expanding hegemonic zone. Within this scenario, globalization clearly poses an unprecedented challenge to any possible counter-hegemonic cultural practice. Yet even within this outermost post, at a safe distance from the discourse and economy of the museum, there is a form of unspoken fidelity to the museum's institutional marrow. There is even a vague recognition that the passion that drives and sustains opposition is motivated just as much by an affinity for the failed ideals of such institutions as by any overt hostility to institutional power.

What does it mean, therefore, to suggest that even a critical discourse that refuses to serve the institution can remain faithful to it? Simply this: that informal antagonistic formations such as Peterman's *Excerpts from the Universal Lab*, REPOhistory or PAD/D actually share a pivotal semblance to what they, by their very constitution, must necessarily reject. However, in the case of these small, anomalous organizations, this similarity is based on an allegiance to what many museums and universities have already abandoned in practice, if not also in theory: the passionate commitment to explore the social, political and aesthetic dimension of art, coupled with the desire to transform the material world into an egalitarian and de-alienated living environment.

There is yet another level at which the institution and its antagonists converge. Even the most fleeting and decentralized collective, art group or political collaboration requires some form of operating structure, some kind of institutional arrangement, however ad hoc or informal.[12] To think otherwise is to naturalize and mystify what is a specific type of contractual relationship among individuals with common concerns (among them is often the actual or perceived threat of being crushed by institutional hegemony)! At some level, both the museum and its *other*—those resistant, residual and informal cultural organizations recognize that the centralized institution *proper* does not exist. Instead, it is constructed within a field of ideas as well as economic variables that are jointly, if unequally, shared by the center and the margins. This means that activists must develop the cunning to see the museum, as well as the university or corporation, as virtually predicated upon the collective productivity of those whom it regulates. In the case of the museum, this naturally includes artists, but also the museum staff and the public that patronizes it. To paraphrase the philosopher Gilles Deleuze, the institution is an apparatus of capture. But what does it seize? The answer is the enthusiasm of artists such as Peterman or REPOhistory or PAD/D. And, at least for a brief moment, it manages to entrap this dynamism. (Yet, one must also ask, what dangerous, even treasonous ideas now spread within the institution as a result of this abduction that is also an infection?)

Finally, in order to describe oneself as both artist and political being, or what Pier Paolo Pasolini termed a "citizen poet," one indeed must remain ill at ease with the neoliberalism of post-Cold War institutions, especially those that seem all too willing to embrace a prudent form of political dissent, including the unstated demand that curators be culturally inclusive and socially progressive. Despite this uncertainty, and regardless of one's divided loyalties, we might now seriously consider re-approaching the idea of critical autonomy that PAD/D, as well as the Universal Lab, attempted to establish more than 20 years ago. I'm not referring here to the modernist notion of autonomy, in which the art object is celebrated as something solely in and for itself, transcending everyday life. Rather, I want to propose reintroducing the concept of a self-validating mode of cultural production and distribution that is situated at least partially outside the confines of the contemporary art matrix as well as global markets. In other words, a self-conscious autonomous activism in which artists produce and distribute an independent political culture that uses institutional structures as resources rather than points of termination. As the theoreticians Michael Hardt and Antonio Negri argue in *Empire*, capitalism may be evolving into a circulating phantom in the global arena but: "around it move radically autonomous processes of self-valorization that not only constitute an alternative basis of potential development but also actually represent a new constituent foundation."[13]

Naturally, such critical autonomy could not exist in close proximity to voracious institutions like art museums, Kunsthalles or international biennials for very long. That lesson was learned from the 1980s all too well, when a select group of artists were chosen to represent "political art" within the mainstream culture industry.[14] No, what is required is a program of theft and long-term sedition aimed at rupturing and reappropriating institutional power for specifically political purposes. Once more, the work of autonomous collaborations, including Peterman and PAD/D, as well as groups such as REPOhistory, RTMark, Les Sans Papiers, Temporary Services, UltraRed, or Ne Pas Plier, Colectivo Cambalache to mention a few now active in the United States and Europe, can serve as provisional models.

But what of us? Us faithless intellectuals, artists, curators and administrators—myself included? We need to *actively* forget the convoluted nature of our predicament. We need to break with the guarded routines of fidelity and betrayal that circulate both inside and outside the museum and move toward recognition of the radical potential already present in collective action. As Pasolini mused:

Corporeal collective presence:
you feel the lack of any true
religion: not life but survival[15]

2

Let's Do it Again Comrades,
Let's Occupy the Museum![*]

If exchange is the criterion of generality, theft and gift are those of repetition. There is, therefore, an economic difference between the two.

Gilles Deleuze[1]

There is an art world haunting the specter of the Occupy movement. It's January 14, 2012. Gathered on the second floor of a café near MoMA is a cohort of conspirators known as Occupy Museums. They are stitching together a public art intervention plotted in a few simple directions: split

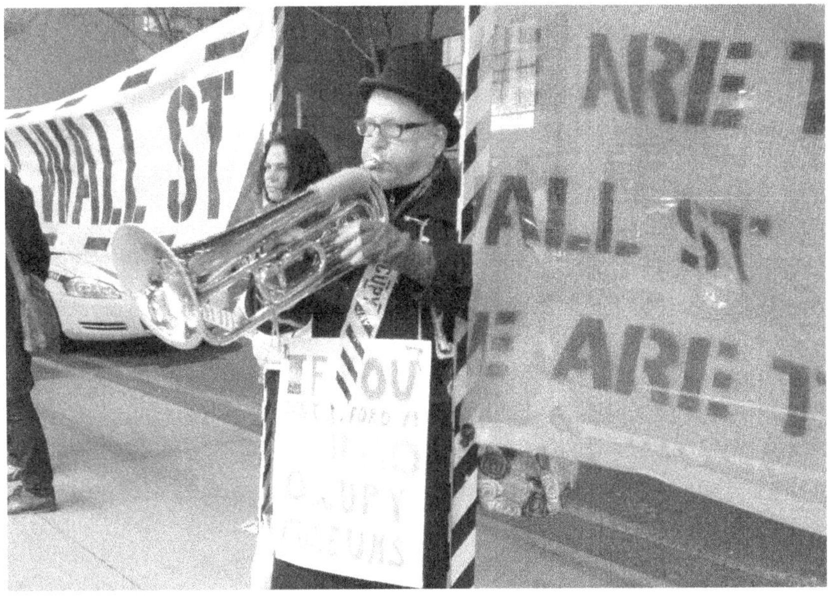

Figure 8 Aaron Burr Society's Jim Costanzo and Occupy Museums protesters outside the Museum of Modern Art, New York during the Diego Rivera Murals exhibition, January 17, 2012

(Photo courtesy of Sak Costanzo)

* This chapter was first published in 2012.

47

up and enter MoMA individually … reconvene on the second floor within the Diego Rivera exhibition … point out to those present that the radical Mexican artist would have been opposed to his work being on display in such a bulwark of capitalism … initiate a General Assembly and discussion about who the museum serves … drop a banner into the atrium at 7:00 p.m. that reads:

MoMA: When Art is Just a Luxury/Art is a Lie
Sotheby's: Hang Art Not Workers/End Your Lockout

Outside the museum Jim Costanzo of the Aaron Burr Society dons a top hat and bellows out a tune from the *Rise and Fall of the City of Mahagonny* on his baritone bugle. Passersby are handed informational flyers as museum guards watch on warily. But the artists entering the museum that night, myself among them, did not dress in paint-spattered blue-jeans as their 1969 counterparts had when they demanded that MoMA establish a wing for women, Black, and Puerto Rican artists, and open its doors to the public for a free evening and weekends for working New Yorkers. (Technically MoMA is a privately owned museum, yet since it functions as both a tax haven and public relations mechanism for wealthy individuals and corporations one could argue that it is at least partially by default a publicly owned institution.)

By contrast, the 2012 invasion was carried out by post-studio *creatives*, that surfeit of young men and women with Master's and Bachelor's degrees in fine art who are beginning to recognize a sobering fact: their seemingly privileged place in the economy is not substantially different from that of the millions of other professional workers who have lost employment since the economic meltdown. In short, they are just more surplus labor gathered like dross within the "jobless recovery." It is their rapid politicization that has generated interest. In this they follow a pattern set by previous artists. And yet somehow, what is happening is also simultaneously new. By way of repetition something is undone, "repeated, the same line is no longer exactly the same, the ring no longer has exactly the same center, *the origin has played*."[2] And undoubtedly, the center is *in play* today, again.

American artist Tim Rollins once scornfully quipped that the term "political art" conjured up charcoal sketches of Lenin, and muscular workers with clenched fists. It was the 1980s, but his reference was to the radical proletarian art of the 1920s and 1930s often associated with the John Reed Clubs, publications like *The New Masses*, and the Communist Party USA. Fifty years later Rollins, together with Julie Ault and a dozen other people, co-founded Group Material, a youthful collective of 1980s art school graduates hoping to resurrect the withered spirit of the avant-garde then languishing between the exhausted vocabulary of post-minimalism on one hand, and regressive neo-expressionist painting on the other. Group Material had no doubt about the connection between art and politics; both were cut from the same cloth of social dissent. Rather, it was social realism, and political propaganda that they dismissed with righteous contempt. The objective of Group Material was to forge links between art and politics and popular culture in a complex, aesthetically engaging way. Nor was Group Material alone in this pursuit. Paper Tiger television, Artists Meeting for Cultural Change (AMCC), Political Art Documentation/Distribution (PAD/D), Artists Against Nuclear Destruction (AAND), and the feminist art collective Carnival Knowledge, were more or less contemporaries with Group Material in New York City during the late 1970s and early 1980s, with the Guerrilla Girls, and the anti-AIDS activists Gran Fury emerging mid decade. Meanwhile, on the West Coast groups such as SPARC (Social and Public Art Resource Center), the San Francisco Poster Brigade, Urban Rats, and Border Arts Workshop represented a similar wave of collaborative, socially engaged cultural intervention.

Nevertheless, most of these short-lived collectives and their actions have largely vanished from the art historical narrative, just as much of the work they generated has little or no representation in museum collections (though admittedly, now and then, one or another example of this artistic dark matter is trotted out like an official dissident whose presence proves that the art world is not the homogeneous monolith it appears to be). Group Material, probably the best known of these communal art experiments, is typically treated as the singular representative of 1980s art activism. Rollins's contempt for the cliché-bound "political art" of past generations notwithstanding, the actual history of this engaged art activism has generally fared only somewhat better than social realism. Alternatively, one could view this missing artistic matter as part of a phantom archive filled with practices and practitioners either too political, or simply too anomalous for mainstream cultural institutions to acknowledge in any complex way. But then came the Occupy movement, charging that "the 99%" were being systematically excluded from visibility, including within the art world. The phantom archive spills open (yet again). Its dark content threatens to contaminate the sterility of white cube ideology. And refusing to acknowledge this danger is not really an option. Therefore, just as in the past, the art world haunts these occupiers and dissidents. Haunts them and hunts them, as if waiting to obtain specimens of this energetic phenomenon for its treasured vaults and repositories. Not missing a beat, the Whitney Museum featured one or more artists associated with OWS in its upcoming 2012 biennial, reinforcing the process of institutional capture. To paraphrase the philosopher Gilles Deleuze, the institution is an inexorable apparatus of capture. It was no different in the late 1980s as "political art" became briefly popular in the art world and several New York museums staged "radical" exhibitions. This, after all, is the logical way to manage dissent. Still, one must also ask, what, if any, dangerous ideas might be spread as a result of this abduction. Was not the communist modernist Diego Rivera's waltz with MoMA and the Rockefellers also a long-range plan of infection? (At the same time, aren't museums experts at managing fever?)

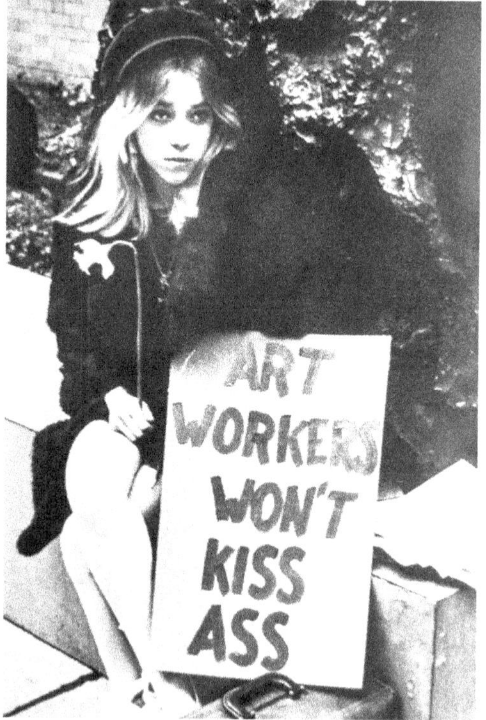

Figure 9   Art Workers' Coalition, circa 1971
(Photo Mehdi Khonsari)

Some 40 years ago another wave of informal collectives—Art Workers' Coalition (AWC), Guerrilla Art Action Group (GAAG), Angry Arts—demanded that the mainstream art world be held accountable not merely for the wellbeing of living artists, but that museums and other cultural institutions take part in a broader critique of capitalism and imperialism, including opposition to US intervention into Southeast Asia. One of the few concrete gains made by AWC was the establishment of free admission one night of the week at MoMA in New York.

Today, MoMA calls this public gift Target Friday, prominently displaying the big-box store's Kenneth Nolan-looking logo inside its lobby. Occupy Museums pointed to this irony, although they only became aware of it recently during their January 14, 2012 intervention at the museum:

> As it turns out, this free day was initiated not by the mega-retailer, but rather by pressure from a group of artists/activists called the Art Workers Coalition in the 1970s. Their struggle then, and our shared struggle today is to put culture into the hands of the 99%—the artists, art lovers and workers who are largely invisible to the museum.[3]

Asserting an adversarial dualism such as "we are the 99%" can be viewed as factual distortion, or simplistic sloganeering, or it might be viewed as a discursive weapon tactically wielded by the politically disempowered. Nonetheless, it is important that the movement begin to precisely define this occluded population since clearly it is not merely the negation of a ruling, 1% elite, any more than the sizable percentage of artists invisible to the mainstream would refuse success in the art world on sheer principle. However, there is another way to look at the recent "discovery" of asymmetrical power by the Occupy movement, one that requires wheeling out that rusted Marxian apparatus of base and superstructure, even if only as a kind of demonstration device. Rather than view this gadgetry as offering a literal explanation of the current crisis, that is, the strict determination of cultural labor by the capitalist market system, we could visualize it in a state of spectacular malfunction as the sphere of economic activity below erupts into the realm of ideological production above. For along with revealing the obscene top-heaviness of neoliberal institutions, OWS has also underscored the utter redundancy of most workers in the present economy. This includes artists, many of whom are forced to find work fabricating, framing, transporting, or installing the work of other, more successful colleagues just to keep on making their own art. It is this sense of failure and superfluousness that may also help explain why OWS has, as a movement, identified itself with the homeless by garrisoning its General Assembly in public spaces that resembled the shantytowns of unemployed workers in the 1930s.

Exemplifying these perverse divisions of artistic labor and tacit class privilege was the 10-month long lockout of Sotheby's unionized art handlers that ended in June, 2012. This same period of time happened to be a banner year for the auction house, with its CEO's salary jumping from $3 million to $6 million. By contrast, the corporation offered its workforce a seriously compromised contract leading the art handlers to go on strike, after which Sotheby's set about hiring replacement workers.[4] On January 14, 2012, Occupy Museums staged a public action that was linked to the lockout at MoMA, because the museum uses Sotheby's for some of its transactions, but also because a labor strike during an exhibition of Rivera's work underscored the indifference of the museum to these contradictions. Nevertheless, much more difficult to convey is the way the art world depends upon the majority of its participants to remain both unseen and undeveloped, even as this same invisible multitude continues dutifully to reproduce the economic and symbolic structures that systematically exclude them.

Occupy Museums, along with the Arts & Culture and Arts & Labor working groups, have openly embraced the surplus imagination of the phantom archive, transforming its dark matter into a bright carnival of protest. This is a significant start. But, as Adorno cautioned in somewhat different words, it's a privilege to critique privilege.[5] The real occupation of culture will not begin until a different set of values is developed, both between artists, and between artists and their audience. And this more ineffable challenge to invisibility will require more than slogans and banner drops. Yes, unquestionably, let's occupy the art world, or better yet, let's do it again comrades. And then? And then?

3

Bare Art, Debt, Oversupply, Panic! (On the Contradictions of a Twenty-First-Century Art Education)

To play at life one must win over the economy.
Randy Martin[1]

Debt, Oversupply, Panic

Much has been written regarding the seemingly irrepressible rise of student financial debt, especially in the United States where by June, 2016 a record $1.3 trillion in higher educational loans has accumulated.[2] Alarm bells ring louder still when the students in question are studying fine art, and for good reasons. Two years of tuition at a top ten US MFA (Master of Fine Art) program leaves behind a debt burden of some $76,000. This sum does not factor in such essentials as the cost of living and art supplies, which in

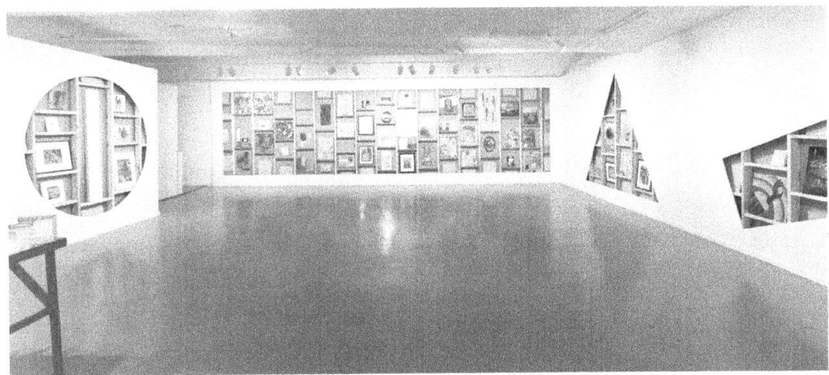

Figure 10   Debtfair installation at the Art League, Houston, Texas, 2015. Debtfair is an ongoing artistic campaign seeking to expose the relationship between economic inequality in the art market and artists' growing debt burdens, exploring the idea that the most active layer of artistic practice is not what we see on the wall, but the "economic reality" which lies below the surface. Debtfair is a project of Occupy Museums
(Photo courtesy ALH)

New York, Los Angeles or Chicago, the cities where most of these programs are located, is far from a minor expense.[3] Critics point out, correctly, that the average art graduate is less likely to find regular, well-paid employment when compared to other, similarly educated professionals, thus diminishing the likelihood loans will be repaid or economic solvency attained.[4] "Nearly one-third of borrowers in repayment were in default," writes Andrew Ross about total US student debt, with overleveraged artists undoubtedly making up a large proportion of this group.[5] This explains why most artists operate in a constant state of financial deficit: the ability to borrow capital requires a steady income and maintaining a good credit score, a challenge not just in the US or UK, as a Warsaw-based study found artists "Do not have borrowing capacity enabling them to purchase property or credit, which puts them in a worse situation than the average Polish employee."[6] And yet the number of individuals choosing art as a career path has been growing steadily, sometimes rapidly, starting in the late 1980s, and may only now be leveling off in the past couple of years.[7] With artistic labor apparently at an all-time record high, a chorus of anxious voices contends that these numbers are simply unsustainable. That may be so, but my argument takes a step back to insist most artists have *never* been sustained by the actual art world economy. This chapter therefore examines the veracity of these claims about the oversupply of artists, proposing an alternative reading that argues there are exactly as many artists as the system requires for reproducing itself, just as there always are in a market-driven artistic economy. What has changed is the capacity to conceal this fact as the privileged status of art, its autonomy, and the exception it represents to capitalist markets is subsumed by post-Fordist enterprise culture. What remains might best be described as a *bare art* world.

Panic

Figures from the US National Center for Education Statistics in 2012 indicate that Master's degrees granted in the visual and performing arts have "been rising every year in the last decade," and the Center for an Urban Future reported in 2015 that "while traditional economic drivers like finance and legal services have stagnated in recent years, several creative industries have been among the fastest growing segments of the city's [New York's] economy," with 24% of this growth attributed to visual artists.[8] Similar statistics show a simultaneous expansion of the artistic labor force in other developed nations such as Australia, where one-fifth of the nation's entire population is engaged in the arts and the number of visual artists rose by a third between 1987 and 2011 before leveling off.[9] A 2011 Canadian study indicates there has been "higher growth in artists than the overall labor force," twice the farm worker population, two and a half times larger than real estate employment with visual artists, artisans and craftspeople making up some 22% of the 136,600 artists surveyed.[10] Nicholas Mirzoeff states that a German "opinion poll found that 24 percent of young people expressed the desire to become an artist."[11] And British artist Derek Harris flatly states that there are "more fine art courses per capita in UK than anywhere else in the world." (Perhaps this is an exaggeration but the statement also parallels American anxieties about an oversupply of artistic labor.)[12] Europe's already large population of artists has grown as well, but less rapidly between 2011 and 2014.[13] What to make of these facts? It would seem that one of the world's most precarious professions, poet and philosopher aside, suddenly became alluring, even irresistible, to a generation growing up as their economic prospects and presumable class mobility rapidly declined.

This ever-expanding, always precarious glut of creative labor also destabilizes the urban environment, as discussed in Part II of this book, on gentrification, inadvertently leading to rising rents, small business closures and the expulsion of long-term, low-income residents. As sociologist Sharon Zukin explained in her classic study *Loft Living: Culture and Capital in Urban Change*, "cities with the highest percentage of artists in the labor force also have the highest rates of downtown gentrification and condominium conversion."[14] Placing the blame on speculators first and cultural workers second, artist Martha Rosler insists that real estate speculators are eager to offer concessions to "artists and small nonprofits in the hopes of improving the attractiveness of 'up-and-coming' neighborhoods and bringing them back onto the high-end rent rolls."[15]

Whatever the exact mechanism and whoever is really to blame, the belief that artists cause or significantly accelerate the process of gentrification has become a truism. The greater the number of artists emerging out of MFA and other certificated education programs, the more this axiom solidifies and becomes part of a knot of panic that extends beyond issues of housing and displacement to encompass changing perceptions about the stability of the cultural economy in general. One result has been for commentators to apply macroeconomic paradigms such as "supply and demand" to the problem, a terminology once anathema in proper fine art circles. Even the noted artist and commentator Coco Fusco exclaimed that the situation is simply "unsustainable" at a public discussion on the topic of gentrification: "[its cause is the] expansion of MFA programs that produces an impossibly large demographic of artists, there are many many more artists than there ever have been … the pool [of artists] has expanded to an absolutely untenable degree and without means of controlling access it would be impossible for the market to contend with the numbers."[16]

Among responses to this issue, we find an unexpected convergence as bewildered policy wonks, conservative and liberal art critics, including some on the left, confront with alarm a deluge of newly minted art professionals poised to inundate a field where there are already too many players and too few resources. One outcome of this state of approaching terror is a surprising degree of soul-searching and honesty regarding the political economy of art. It turns out that many now see the cultural economy as nothing special. Art is just another commodity, and the iron law of supply and demand rules over the art world just as it does over everything else. A small but influential group of commentators either raise the issue or actually advocate curbing the apparent oversupply of artistic labor:

> At a time of flattening demand there is increasing supply, as noted above, in terms of both the sheer number of organizations and the supply of product. Neither the audience nor the public or philanthropic sector can support this level of oversupply.[17]

> The Australian arts sector is grossly "oversupplied." In the first decade of the century, Australian participation in creative arts work increased dramatically—in some arts activities it more than doubled or tripled! At the same time, artists' relative incomes have declined … Australia's cultural policies predominantly work on stimulating supply, and so are likely to have made matters worse.[18]

> Neither the audiences nor the public or philanthropic sector can support this level of oversupply [in cultural products].[19]

> Demand is not going to increase, so it is time to think about decreasing supply.[20]

> We have an overstocked arts pond.[21]

Stripped of all romance or peculiarity, a demystified art world emerges into view, one in which pragmatic notions of supply-and-demand economics seem suddenly applicable. Today, art's allegedly exceptional economy has been permeated by the grammar of finance, forcing its integration with the new normal of ultra-deregulated enterprise culture about which Randy Martin observed, "if money was, even in the recent past, what people were thought to be more defensive about than any other subject, the veil has, in many ways, been lifted."[22] It is as if everyone suddenly woke up to discover they had been speaking capitalist prose all along. In other words, we have arrived at the condition of *bare art*, whose peculiarities I will explore in this chapter.

The Contradictions of Enterprise Culture

Not so long ago, the art world was largely the province of the wealthy upper classes. Their guardianship of art might be chalked up to nostalgia for aristocratic values, or simply a practical means of sheltering rentier incomes from taxes, not to ignore the cultural prestige that an association with art provides for elites. Regardless, the stewardship of art remained within the purview of high society and a small circle of trained connoisseurs drawn from elite universities. Though serving the public interest may have been their officially stated mission, any real effort at democratizing art collections, opening museum doors to the masses or funding academic scholarships probably had more to do with limited government support than acts of *noblesse oblige*. Art was not a populist project and certainly not a consumer-oriented affair; rather it needed to be protected from the multitude. Challenges came in response to the Great Depression, and then with the GI Bill after World War II, which was itself a kind of concession to the socialist critique of capitalism. Even then, a tendency toward custodianship of high culture was prevalent in post-war art theory, most obviously in the writings of Clement Greenberg and Michael Fried, the two pillars of formalist art criticism. Nevertheless, things were already shifting thanks in part to the growth of artistic graduate degrees during the period of the Cold War.

Howard Singerman observes that some 320 candidates received diplomas from 32 institutions between 1950 and 1951, five times as many as a decade earlier.[23] From the perspective of the post-war state, broadening access to high culture harmonized with the West's ideological campaign against the Soviet Union, even if that meant funding dissident works of art and granting working-class people limited access to high culture's inner sanctum. The number of MFAs has only grown since. But once the Cold War ended a new paradigm for cultural funding was required. Art was reborn as a creative instrument for sparking broader economic development, just as a generation raised on popular art unseated some of the established privileges associated with high culture, its form and its content. Art under neoliberal ideology was enterprising and creative. As a 2010 United Nations sponsored report summarizes, along with technology and business, culture helps to "circulate intellectual capital" thus providing part of a powerful engine "driving economic growth and promoting development in a globalizing world."[24]

According to Chin-Tao Wu, key indicators of this paradigm shift can already be glimpsed in certain high-level museum appointments right before the onset of neoliberalism, such as that of Thomas Hoving who served as director of the Metropolitan Museum of Art, New York, between 1966 and 1977. With his big business background and training in medieval art, Hoving, Wu observes, "deliberately ventured into costly undertakings—new wings, blockbuster exhibitions and expensive acquisitions—thus forcing the museum into a desperate search for new sources of income."[25] Decades later we see this tendency playing out with massive real estate ventures by such institutions as the School of the Art Institute of Chicago, and the The Cooper Union, forcing the latter to impose tuition for the first time in its 150-year history, and leading to protests by faculty and occupations by students. But if Hoving embodied the emerging spirit of enterprise culture, then former Guggenheim director Thomas Krens, who held the position from 1988 to 2008, represents its fully developed archetype, signaling once and for all that capital had unapologetically come to dominate the art world. Wu cites a *New York Times* profile of the Guggenheim director written shortly after his appointment in which Michael Kimmelman notes that, despite the discomfort brought about by the "Globe Straddler of the Art World" within certain elite art circles (including, despite Hoving, the less overtly entrepreneurial Metropolitan Museum), Krens is "pursuing the American cultural system to its inevitable conclusion."[26]

Substitute "capitalist" for "American" and a great deal falls into place. Because it's not just the art fairs and auction houses or the fact that the majority of museum trustees now come from the corporate sector, what we see is the hegemonic effect of capital across the board, even if we focus solely on the non-commercial, not-for-profit art sector. Consider the overtly entrepreneurial approach of both the National Endowment for the Arts (NEA) and British Arts Council's creative economy models that intentionally dovetail with the broader economic emphasis on flexible, knowledge-based work and the development of private–public culture industries. Take note of the unabashed application of finance management tools useful for meeting consumer demand as proposed by a prominent not-for-profit arts foundation, "if society demands and deserves more relevant, accessible, and dynamic art, we emphasize capitalization as the means to that end."[27] Often the language of these programs and policy forums borrows directly from the world of technology start-ups. What we find is the promotion of incubator spaces, pop-up shows, experimental labs and clusters, and yet the underlying gambit aims to extend state-supported cultural endeavors globally by financing collaborative projects in developing countries such as Vietnam, Nigeria, Kenya, Brazil and Egypt. Parallels with corporate models of globalization are impossible to avoid. By now, all this creative economy and corporate-culture-speak may be rather obvious to many close observers of the art world; however, what is necessary to underscore here is that not-for-profit administrators and policy makers are now *obliged* to join with their art market counterparts in asserting, often indirectly, a constant-growth economic model, identical with that of capital. This is so, even as commentators call for moderating the supply of artists to better match the "demand" that exists in the form of art careers.

Regulation

However well-meaning it may be, the call to limit the supply of artists—even if this were somehow possible—is at the same time a coded call for a return to a position of superintendence with regard to culture, one that raises uncomfortable questions about who is to decide which aspiring artists, or art schools, will make the cut. In other words, art's alleged "oversupply crisis" looks very different depending on which end of the art economy you inhabit, or whether or not your art school degree is more vocational or liberal arts oriented. For artists positioned somewhere along the narrow central peak of visibility, the pressure in the system may seem like a threat; for others—most artists—extreme competition to gain some measure of visibility is already part and parcel of a place at or near the bottom of the art world pyramid. Here, among the artistic dark matter, what will additional artists really do to fundamentally alter that situation?

It may be, however, that it is not possible, or really desirable from a pro-market perspective, to stem the tide of artists. When it comes to the arts, "disequilibrium seems to be a sort of permanent critical situation," affirms French sociologist Pierre-Michel Menger.[28] Art's economic dementia reaches back at least to the seventeenth-century Dutch painting market, which allegedly produced "between five and ten million works of art" of which "perhaps less than 1%, have survived."[29] However, Menger's disequilibrium condition really kicks in with the formal subsumption of artistic production under nineteenth-century capitalism in France. It was then that the exhausted academic art system fell into disarray, opening up space the free market came to dominate. What came next was a wave of innovative artists and movements operating on a:

more flexible and also much riskier basis of open competition involving dealers, critics, painters, and buyers. Supply was no more to be regulated, so that oversupply was known to become a permanent feature of that market … periodic panics about the glut and the high rate of unemployment didn't deter students from entering art schools in growing numbers.[30]

Art education is integral to this chaotic system, where established producers may begin to feel "trapped in a disintegrating market while new aspirants continue to flood in," as Menger cautions, adding, "the training system may play an unintended role in the self-congesting spiral of oversupply."[31] Elaborating on the role higher education plays in producing an art supply glut, Fusco also maintains that the "proliferation of degrees does not translate into more jobs for graduates; it is just another way to lure more people into assuming debt."[32] This is, of course, true, but it is not only art that experiences this problem. Across the humanities and social sciences, there are more highly qualified postgraduates than can possibly find long-term academic employment. Without doubt, in the US, the marketing and monetization of higher education programs is a pernicious trend, where falling government education spending forces schools and universities to scramble for every tuition dollar increasingly generated by private lenders. Still, the argument that the development of more art programs, sexier programs, more cleverly advertised programs, is the primary reason for the oversupply of artists is not entirely convincing, or at least it is only a part of the story. The sheer intensity and pace of change within the art system makes monocausal diagnoses of the problem of an "oversupply" of artists implausible. Ideology is to blame insists Hans Abbing, a Dutch artist who is also a trained economist. In the minds of the majority, he claims, art remains a near-spiritual endeavor, not a commodity-oriented business as in other types of work. In his view, it is state funding that encourages the glut of artists, feeding their delusions by allowing them to just about scrape a living, resulting in the ascetic mindset of artists whose unremunerated devotion to their field "looks a lot like a ritual sacrifice."[33]

Abbing lays out his solution to this problem in his book *Why Are Artists Poor?*:

If governments were to interfere less in the arts and offer fewer subsidies, the economy of the arts would become less exceptional and, as a result, artists would not be nearly as poor. Nevertheless, for the time being this remains an unlikely scenario because governments are just as locked into the present mythology of the arts as the other participants are.[34]

Whether or not government subsidy really is to blame for the delusions of artists, it has become increasingly difficult to argue, outside of a few European countries, that art is clearly separated from the rest of the economy any longer. Record-breaking sales for individual artworks (including works by younger, living artists), the increasing capitalization of the art world by financial speculators, as well as the explosion of museum building seem to show an art system that is integrated into the expansionist tendencies of capitalism. Influential Professor of Creative Industries Ruth Towse tells us that it is "risk taking behavior" in which "artists overestimate their (average) chances of success prior to entering the labor market."[35] For Towse, like Abbing, the solution to oversupply is more and more being viewed as a matter of regulating production. This takes such forms as allowing "market forces to bring the supply of artistic labor down," as Dave Beech skeptically summarizes Towse's advice to the British Arts Council, or, in more socialized European economies, the answer proposed is to "reduce overall [cultural] subsidization."[36]

It is curious that for both Abbing and Towse the real culprit behind the hazardous behavior of artists is state intervention and support for culture, rather than the prevalence of neoliberal ideology, which openly advocates for a universal embrace of risk throughout the entire population (knowing of course, that some are more exposed to failure than others). For many wannabe artists there is an irrefutable attraction to a highly unregulated market whose overall value in 2013 was estimated at $35 billion, which is about half the size of Microsoft Corporation's sales revenues two years earlier.[37] Most likely it is this same barely supervised economy that attracts hedge fund operators, though the stakes and consequences of failure are strikingly different. Still, in a capitalist society, where one's very livelihood is contingent on taking risks, placing an $80,000 wager on an MFA degree, or on a painting by a 20-something artist, may not be as irrational as it first seems.[38] The student gains entry into what appears to be a growing economic sector that some claim outpaces the stock market, while the capitalist gambler might be the first to discover a "flippable" new art star at a discount price.[39]

As Randy Martin put it, as if he was anticipating the presidential campaign of Donald Trump, today one must firmly believe that the system can effectively be gamed.[40] In truth, neither the so-called economic exceptionalism of art, nor the neoliberal economy in general, operates consistently through rational decision making (though watching such incoherent behavioral phenomena enter the very seat of presidential authority within a nuclear superpower such as the United States is an alarming and unforeseeable turn of circumstances, even for an era rife with capitalist delirium).

Art, Class Conflict and Capitalism 4.0[41]

As with all things in our ultra-high-risk society, individual rates of financial solvency and professional success are skewed toward those with pre-existing access to capital, or toward those who have a good working knowledge of money management, two elements that often converge in one and the same privileged person. Recent studies have shown that the overall student loan default is actually less for those attending expensive, Ivy League-type schools when compared to that for low-income and low-earning students who are attending far less costly state community colleges.[42] One likely reason for this is that elite institutions provide their students with significant stockpiles of accumulated social capital with which to successfully launch oneself into a well-paying job, including a successful art career, upon graduation.[43] By contrast, even a modest tuition hike represents an onerous expense for those from less affluent backgrounds, as those of us who teach in the public school system know so well. Add to this the fact that peer networks at less prestigious schools are likely to offer lower social capital value. While certainly, the job market for artists is weak or non-existent, regardless of your class background, those with more resources remain a few, often crucial steps ahead of others.

Graduating students with prosperous upbringings also come pre-bundled with financial resources and social skills, as well as pre-existing family networks, all of which help them make up for the job deficit, while low-income students scramble to learn what others take for granted in a kind of DIY fashion. While the art world's class differentiation seems to start here, stratification was already in development during art school. Not only does higher education do little to prepare students for the economic realities of the art world but, as art historian Katy Siegal points out, the "real class divide in the art world [is] between the art workers and the art thinkers," because "places like Ohio State versus, say, the Whitney program still teach manual labor skills ... as opposed to ... conceptual problem solving and networking."[44] One need hardly guess which art school graduate will be fabricating the other one's projects in due time. At the same time, the lending of public capital for education in the post-war, post-Sputnik era helped to open up the field of arts and humanities to a broader composition of participants in terms of class and race, ironically priming the pump, at least in theory, for potential resistance or rebellion, a point to which I will return shortly. With the shrinking of government support for academia and increased private debt-lending, together with rising tuition fees, that diversity is in jeopardy.

Class, then, is not really so difficult to see at work in the art world. One need only follow the money and, for many, that begins with the extreme indebtedness of so many art students. Which is why the absence of debt as a topic related to class in Ben Davis's influential essay "9.5 Theses on Art and Class" seems like such a remarkable oversight.[45] In some 90 concisely worded segments, Davis explains that being middle class means "having an individual, self-directed relationship to production," as opposed to being working class and possessing but one thing with which to leverage the system: labor power that one sells as a commodity in the marketplace. All of which feels solid enough if we are speaking of economic conditions in the nineteenth or early twentieth century, or perhaps in underdeveloped nations today. However, in a fully developed neoliberal economy, Davis's schema is upended by two seemingly obvious factors. First, except for the most precarious and homeless segment of the population (who would not classically be considered part of the proletariat), most modern workers have more resources at their disposal than only their commodified labor power. In fact, it is precisely the aggregate consumer capacity of the working classes that capitalism has transformed into a means of bolstering its flagging rate of profit in recent decades. And, second, the composition of this consumer power is increasingly derived not from salaries or wages, but from financial lending institutions as leveraged credit.[46]

And therein lies the rub.

Rather than only focus on student debt, consider home ownership. In the US and UK this hovers around 65%, with a good portion of this segment undoubtedly consisting of "blue-collar," unionized workers. If we overlay onto these numbers the 80% average debt of GDP (gross domestic product) carried by US and UK households (87.4% in the UK, 78.4% for the US in 2016)[47] that is in excess of income, and we factor in the 4.4 million US home foreclosures since 2008, then Davis's very concept of the "middle class" begins to take on water.[48] In reality, the so-called middle class consists of working people who aspire to be in control of their own means of production, who want to become property owners, even perhaps stockholders, and yet who frequently fail, or have been failed, by the system, never quite reaching escape velocity other than in name or in their own imagination (or apparently in the mind of some art critics). This is not to suggest those who self-identify as painters, sculptors, performers or other types of artist are workers in the way nurses, dishwashers, truckdrivers or even programmers are when they are engaged in the type of labor that pays their wages (or that pays off their credit card debt). But many of these same artists, most of them, will be doing some other kind of labor, often several other types of work, in order to support themselves.[49] So while Davis asserts

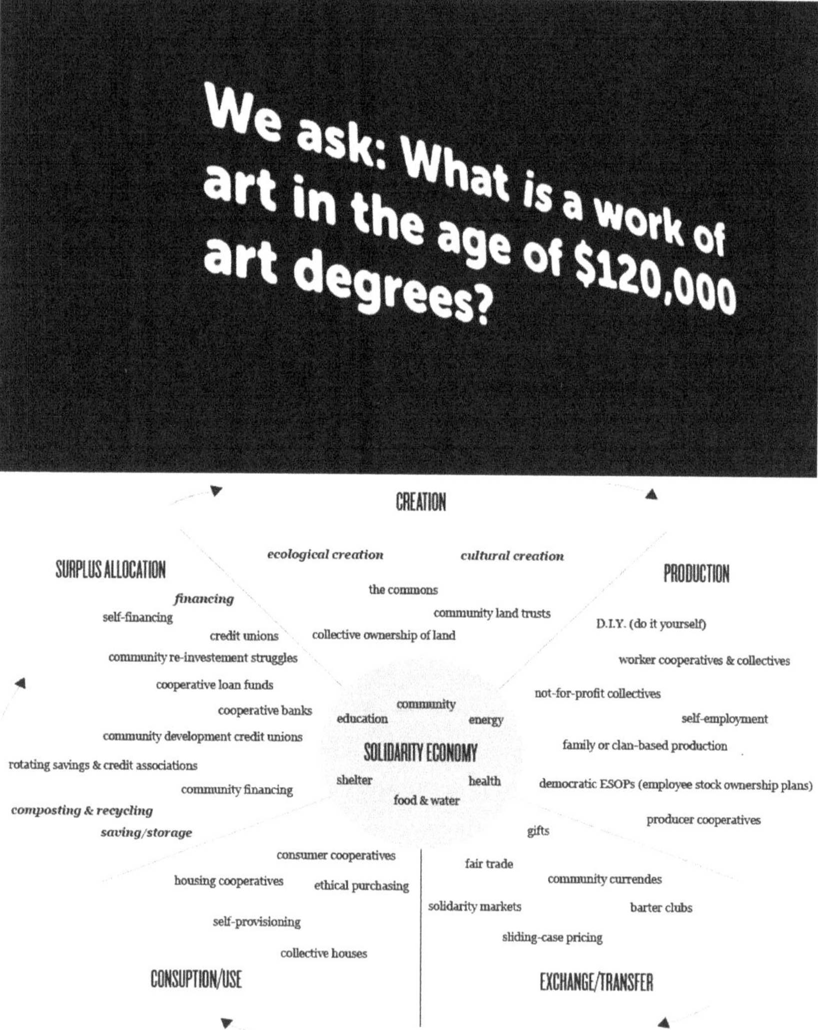

Figures 11 and 12   Top graphic by BFAMFAPhD; bottom by Andrew Persoff/Caroline Woolard, illustration for SolidarityNYC, updating Ethan Miller/JED collective diagram from 2008, new vector graphic, 2010

(Used with permission of C. Woolard)

that, "the sphere of the visual arts has weak relations with the working class," it requires only the slightest nick at its surface to expose the class differentials manifest within it. Such disparities produce divergent effects, both before and after graduation, not unlike an unspoken caste system, where, for example, the state-school MFA graduate builds the art star's projects for the next biennal or art fair.

The real question therefore is not whether artists are or are not middle class—an inquiry made especially ambiguous given the extensive redrawing of social rank, including the economic immiseration of the working class and lower middle classes within the population as a whole—but why the majority of professionally trained artists continue to reproduce the system and its hierarchies when the actual distribution of aggregate benefits is skewed towards the top tier of the art world. This is a question Davis cannot address and not only because of his oversimplified concept of class composition. Ultimately, the critic's outlook is underpinned by an unreflective conservative viewpoint that, as Kim Charnley notes, presumes that "it is the job of the artist to make art, of the audience to look at it, and of the critic to let the audience know whether it is good."[50] Even though Davis embraces a self-described Marxist analysis of class, his definition of culture recalls the privileged custodianship of art that was last seen at the height of Modernism. Since the beginning of the twentieth century, avant-garde artists and other cultural workers have labored to blur or even upend this hierarchical and categorically segregated arrangement. That is not to say this destabilization of categories has been consistently successful or even always sincere, however, this internal critical process—as well as the contradictions it generates—should not be overlooked by art critics who are concerned with the politics of culture, as is Ben Davis, genuinely I believe.

Looking back over the period since the end of World War II, and especially since the 1960s, the transfer of power from an older patrician class to that of enterprise culture has undeniably improved entry into the art world for a more diverse population of participants and audiences. The neoliberal spirit of entrepreneurship has lowered barriers of entry into high art, perhaps just enough to allow museums and other elite cultural institutions to claim, not always incorrectly, that they are unique havens for an otherwise missing democratic public sphere. The most obvious illustration of this accessibility is the growing embrace of social practice art, a topic discussed in this book's final chapters. And yet, for many, including women and people of color, the art world, especially at its highest levels of institutional governance, remains still a privileged territory for wealthy, male, white gentry, even if the formerly aristocratic make-up of this or that board of directors, for instance, is now infiltrated by financiers, real estate moguls and media barons. Recent struggles by marginalized artists over issues of cultural representation, sometimes referred to as "decolonization," also continue to erode these barriers. However, it is important to acknowledge that under enterprise culture the world of high art has come to be dominated by something else, something lacking either taste or social consciousness, and that is capital itself, capital as a thing-agency.

Alongside capital's intensive domination of the art world via neoliberal entrepreneurialism, a different sort of patrician class arises, with arguably less attachment to bourgeois values of tradition and stability, but whose ethos is grounded instead in the "financialization" of life. This makes for some rather obvious paradoxes. On one hand, a condition of *bare art* emerges in which art's mystique and romance has boiled away, where laws of supply and demand can be invoked without irony. The conditions of *bare art* also blatantly transform culture into a new, secure investment category. A senior manager of the global financial consulting firm Deloitte goes so far as to insist the complete monetization of art will actually serve the public interest because its: "financial activities will have ripple effects on other sectors of the economy. This evolution should create a new era for the art markets and for the benefit of the society as a whole by fostering culture, knowledge and creativity."[51]

Welcome to the obligatory platitudes of the new art patron class; though unwilling to give up art's mystique, they cynically work at minimizing the difference between art and capital. Once fully accomplished, today's art flippers will be tomorrow's oligarchs, managing talent like stocks and bonds. Perhaps as a result we find an attempt to wrap art's nakedness with a new critical task, derived from notions of autonomy and economic exceptionalism. Theoretically, a demystified *bare art* may set the stage for a return of artistic autonomy as critique. Jeroen Boomgaard has suggested that "the artist's symbolic act can consequently propagate the idea of freedom even more strongly than it could in the days when autonomy was still the hallmark of art—if only because that autonomy no longer has an ideological background."[52] Is art somehow still exceptional within the capitalist economy even as it is being colonized by it?

Reorganizing the Exceptional Economy of Art?

Artist and theorist Dave Beech rejects both Hans Abbing's mythologizing explanation for the apparently exceptional economy of artistic production, as well as Ruth Towse's rationalistic approach, each of which ultimately leads, he argues, to the normalizing of artistic production through mechanisms of market correction, including managing supply and demand. Beech instead reaches back to Marx's *Capital* and to classical economics in general in order to assert that an artist's practice is *essentially* anti-market regardless of what anyone thinks art is about, whether it is or is not mystified, or how a painting or sculpture is priced or circulated later on after it leaves the artist's studio. This makes artistic labor fundamentally alien to capital's means of production, as Marx proposed when he wrote that "Milton produced *Paradise Lost* in the way a silkworm produces silk, as the expression of his own nature."[53] Although John Milton's book ultimately became a commodity, distributed through a capitalist market, it did so only after the author completed his epic poem, doing so to his own standards.

Perhaps, had Milton been in desperate financial need, he might have been forced to sell his talent directly to capital as artistic labor, thus tethering his freedom to its system of production. As it is, however, both silkworm and Milton produce things naturally, and would presumably continue to do so regardless of whether their creations were useful or interesting to anyone, including to capital, always in search of profit. In this sense, both artist and silkworm are "unproductive workers," to use Marx's terms, because only living labor harnessed as labor power can add value to the capitalist's initial monetary investment, producing more capital than was there to begin with. This type of labor, Beech argues, is not that of the artist.

Once purchased from the labor market, (non-artistic) living human labor is fully enclosed within capital's apparatus of production, where it is put to work alongside objectified dead labor (machinery) in order to generate "a commodity greater in value than the sum of the values used to produce it."[54] Thus, the mystery of capital is theft, the taking away of a worker's time and labor in either mental and/or physical form without full compensation when compared with the return on the sale of a commodity. Extrapolating from this premise, Beech argues that "no capitalist makes a profit merely from the existence of potential wage laborers, but only, as Marx says, by putting them to work."[55]

Unproductive work, like art, is *not* incorporated, or not fully incorporated, into that system of exploitation, and cannot be because, first, unlike exploited wage workers, artists take the necessary time to generate a final product and, second, just as with the *Bombyx mori* caterpillar's automatic silk-spinning, the artist freely deploys his or her mental and physical energy autonomously, just as they please, regardless of pressure from capitalist regimentation. Personal time and labor are at the artist's command, which is why Beech understands the politics of art to be located here, at the very basic level of cultural production, and not necessarily in any specific content or activist engagement. Beech's concept of artistic production also shares qualities with Walter Benjamin's interest in childhood play. As Ester Leslie interprets, "in play, and in learning, children animate objects [bringing] to life past energies now slumbering in objects. The reification of commodities is to be dissipated in the process."[56] Thus art is doubly anti-capitalist, first because of how it is made and, second, because of the way it appears to release ossified social labor out of inanimate things and materials.

It is beyond the scope of this chapter to delve into all of the argumentation Beech brings to his engaging thesis, but a couple of tentative challenges to his proposition may shed light on issues related to the current oversupply panic, as well as artistic resistance more broadly. The first question has to do with history, because it is necessary to ask, along with Sven Lütticken, at what "dialectical tipping point does an exception become the norm?"[57] In other words, art's exceptionality from the market may need to be rethought at a time of sustained capitalist crisis and falling profits, and not because Marx did not see it coming, but because he did.

Plausibly, capitalism has continuously evolved, reacting to its own economic contradictions as well as to those of labor's resistance, by replacing more and more living workers with machinery in response to intra-capitalist competition, but also to working-class opposition. This has generated an increasing surplus of workers who are not employed, or who are only barely employed. Just as Marx predicted, these developments have also brought about rising productivity, along with falling rates of profit, and also a spreading immiseration or precariousness for much of the population. Such conditions now appear to be a chronic feature of modern capitalism. With no viable socialist or other alternative, this incongruity takes on an almost farcical quality, as capital scrambles to "normalize" its contradictions. Responding to its own shrinking surpluses, capital tests out financialization schemes, negative interest rates, credit default swaps, technology bubbles and other alleged fixes that, sooner or later, always fail, sending catastrophic ripples across the global economy.

Inventing new ways of managing the tremendous surpluses of labor is another attribute of twenty-first-century capital. Low-wage jobs in the service sector only soak up a portion of this excess, and do so inadequately. A recent study shows that $153 billion in annual US government welfare payments is being spent to subsidize employees of corporations with multi-billion dollar assets such as Walmart and McDonald's.[58] Demands for better pay gave rise to the "Fight for $15" movement that eventually forced pay hikes by some fast-food chains. At the same time, the increasing *precarity* of the workforce has led to previously unthinkable calls for socializing the economy as shown by the popularity of presidential candidate Bernie Sanders' left-leaning anti-Wall Street message. In the UK, former Prime Minister David Cameron was essentially forced to commit to a rise in the minimum wage (though many insist it is not a "living wage"), and arising across Europe is a growing call for a Basic Income Guarantee or Guaranteed Minimum Income, another response to the chronic nature of capitalist crisis. In other industries, flexibilizing the means of production into post-Fordist systems of fragmented just-in-time manufacturing helps capital decentralize labor, thus making unionization and other forms of organized resistance much more difficult to bring about. But by becoming dependent on distributed forms of outsourced labor capitalists risk exposure to politically repressive regimes and unstable "failed" states, where resistance can break out in outright rebellion as we have seen in Syria.

The refugees fleeing conflict in Syria and coming to Europe, as well as other parts of the Middle East, are a highly visible symptom of the instability that has been caused by neoliberal capitalism, which in turn feeds xenophobic far-right narratives in Europe and the US, despite the staggering 5,000 deaths among asylum seekers in 2015, with predictions of double that figure for 2016. While capital thrives on such instabilities at the margins, their "spillover" into the economic center is—Angela Merkel's shortlived policy exception in Germany aside—entirely unwelcome. One reason so many refugees aim to live in London, to take the example of just one "global city," is the same reason some polls show one in six people worldwide wish to move there: it harbors a creative economy with multicultural diversity, precisely as the city promotes itself via the global mediascape. The stability at the center draws the effects of disorder toward it. The very same communication technology that allows cities to compete with one another and for capital to disseminate production over greater distances, compressing space and time, as Harvey and Virilio contend, also generates an informal capacity for resistance. Spreading post-Fordist global networks aid or actually give birth to collective practices such as tactical media, Occupy Wall Street, Black Lives Matter and other forms of activist culture. As John Roberts and I have claimed, this broadening of access to technologies, resources and distributed labor effectively provides tools for building a parallel cultural sphere where, as Roberts writes, "energies and strategies pulled in from a range of skills, competences and interests, across the divisions of professional and non-professional, artist and non-artist, artistic practices and non-art practices" that operate without recourse to the hierarchies of the official art world allow, as I have put it, a "formerly invisible sphere of imaginative productivity [to come] spilling out of the archive," brimming over with all manner of past and present resistance from below.[59]

For Beech, on the other hand, modern production technologies and collective networking assets remain outside art's true sphere of activity, not necessarily always in practical terms perhaps, but at the deepest level of artistic production: "Insofar as the economics of artistic production have not changed significantly since the Renaissance in some respects and since the eighteenth century in others, post-Fordism appears to coincide with the pre-industrial."[60] Beech rejects assumptions about the convergence of capital with artistic production, arguing that art's potential anti-market resistance does not pivot on collective forms, conceptual strategies and activist practices, but instead arises from the nature of its essentially unaltered production model. Activist art is of incidental political value in this regard.

That said, his claim for art's inherent anti-capitalist attributes is based more on ontological than on tactical grounds: art as non-productive labor remains a kernel of opposition, regardless of how deeply buried under capitalist offal it becomes. This is Beech's aesthetic of resistance, one that inevitably raises the danger of romanticizing art's revolutionary promise, but is an assertion that is not without merit. Still, his understandable desire to repossess art's singularity in this manner runs the risk of wistful futility. As Kerstin Stakemeier cautions: "The modernist figure of a somewhat prior autonomy of the arts fulfills a solemnly affirmative function within catastrophic financialized capitalism. It reiterates a nostalgic figure that can linger on only at the price of its social remoteness and conservative discursive function."[61]

While Stakemeier doubtless underestimates the potential value something like *tactical nostalgia* might play in countering the psychological damages prevalent in our high-risk society, the gambit Beech proposes would nevertheless be available only to those privileged enough to be able to withdraw into autonomous productivity in the first place. Given the state of the art world, the window of opportunity for artists to construct for themselves a time and space for critical, autonomous or non-commercialized cultural labor, while also accruing or paying-down enormous debts, is very brief. This is not in itself an invalidation of Beech's thesis, but it is a reason to hit the pause button when it comes to art's oppositional potential. Beech himself does not entirely avoid addressing this problem, though after first dismissing the potential critical effect of recognizing a counterproductive sphere of non-professional dark matter creativity on the established art world, he concludes by admitting that only when culture becomes common property, and general "philistine" creativity (perhaps akin to general intellect?) is manifest in the fullest sense, will art fulfill its capacity for universal liberation "both through the extension of collective decision making about the consumption of art and collective participation in artistic production."[62]

It is difficult to see how art defined as a truly autonomous practice, and not merely a tactic of resistance, could accomplish this goal, or how it can even survive modern-day circumstances. As neoliberalism, in its desperation to salvage falling profits, seeks out ever more intrusive means of monetizing the totality of life, it seems to increasingly generate what Mario Tronti called a "social factory": a world in which capitalist markets enclose social relations previously located outside the factory or workplace proper.[63] Does this mean that art has become wholly subsumed within capital as well? And if so, does that spell the end of its oppositional power? With art education, cultural institutions, foundations and urban centers simultaneously more diverse than in the past, but also more like a financial marketplace than ever before, the wellspring of resistance originating from within artistic labor production per se seems less and less tenable, not without radical change.

However, reification and the blockage of desire have differing outcomes depending on the level of one's political awareness. "Objectification is an unavoidable aspect of all signifying systems, all abstract thought, and all art forms," writes Andrew Hemingway with regard to György Lukács' classic 1923 study *History and Class Consciousness*, adding, "the point is that reification comes in beneficial and harmful forms."[64] Being subjected to the illusion that capitalism is an ahistorical inevitability is a negative deformation caused by reification, for example, but confronting head on the condition that I call *bare art sans illusions* would be a potentially positive utilization of objectification. Let me sketch out an alternative scenario to art's adversarial ontology, one that is not entirely at variance with what Beech proposes.

The Growth/Oversupply Paradox

What if the essential uniqueness of artistic labor is not its anti-market form, but its ability to mimic productive modes of work without being "productive"? As artists, Beech and I both know that making art is both pleasurable and a task, except that our taskmaster is internalized. More than that however, artists commonly describe what they do as work. And though people with nine to five jobs may find this description infuriating, such working at *not-working* is both real and dissimulating at once. It could even be described as art's subsumption of capitalist modes of production: capturing, reflecting and ultimately mocking the absurdity of being forced to generate surplus value for private appropriation, a sort of reverse theft in other words. As philosopher Jacques Rancière has written with regard to Plato's ban on imitative artists, the shoemaker, carpenter, baker, blacksmith all must remain tied to their stations in life due to the fact that: "artisans cannot be put in charge of the shared or common elements of the community because they do not have the time to devote themselves to anything other than their work. They cannot be somewhere else because work will not wait."[65]

However, the "office" of the artist, is ambiguous with regard to time, space, communal duties and so forth. Art is like a phantom profession, one that permits the artist to simultaneously work and not work, to have a "real" job and to have a fictional job. And nothing is more subversive than showing other workers the pleasure of not engaging in productive labor. Furthermore, artists have always been able to slide between social barriers; sometimes even "passing" for members of another class. More to the point, the offices of contemporary art are now filled with imitative projects that are not replicas of objects, but of the administrative institutions and affective economics of neoliberal enterprise culture.[66] One need only think of the many institutes, centers, bureaus, offices and schools whose reality has been forged by contemporary artists. Sometimes these mock institutions even overtake and substitute the actual institution they imitate. Therefore, unlike the silkworm, which by the way has been genetically modified in recent years to increase its output, artistic work exists as a natural counterfeit, or conversely, a counterfeit nature. And once art's mimetic non-productivity is subsumed within capital its real threat appears once a *bare art* world arrives: art becomes the single most conspicuous demonstration of capital's delirious con game.

Still, it's what the art world needs from this counterfeit, unproductive artistic labor that leads to the multiplication of MFAs and the so-called oversupply of credentialed artists. Before addressing that let us consider one other part of the system, how the growth maxim is communicated to art world participants. In truth, the signaling mechanisms are as ubiquitous as they are easily overlooked. They are aimed at cultural administrators, municipal policy makers, but also individual artists, adding up to a pervasive, though implicit law driving the art economy toward a constant state of expansion. To illustrate this, I have selected three of many excerpted statements drawn here from (1) the *Creative New York* report, (2) the British

Arts Council and (3) a program director of the Andy Warhol Foundation respectively:

> The economic impact of all this innovation and growth is enormous. As creative workers multiply and experiment and their companies grow, they spend more on support services and suppliers. This benefits thousands of ancillary businesses across the city, including lumber, equipment and catering companies, as well as manufacturers producing everything from clothing to furniture … They're building institutions. They're building an incubator for themselves, and they're working across mediums.[67]

> If investment in the arts is to positively impact upon the growth and competitiveness of the creative economy, which in turn will re-invest in and exchange other types of value with the arts, then "innovation and growth" are the investment imperatives for the Arts Council and its co-investors.[68]

> Our general principle is that if a project moved an artist's practice forward, allowed him or her or a group to experiment, try something more ambitious, less familiar, in collaboration or conversation with someone or something new, then it is a success.[69]

Taking these expansionist directives at face value their aim is clear enough: generate more and bigger cultural projects, creative placemaking programs, ever-larger organizations, budgets, staff and, of course, art careers. Compounded growth is, in other words, institutionalized within the art world. It is present through investment in the administrative apparatuses of art, including not only a continual proliferation of arts organizations, but also, significantly, through indirect systems of re-granting, educational programing, student lending and other capital services to the arts community that appear to be taking place robotically, regardless of any corresponding rise or fall in the demand for artistic labor or its products. But now we are faced with an obvious inconsistency, if not a contradiction. How to square the imperative for growth with the kind of statements found at the start of this chapter whereby another group of panicked policy makers advocate tightening the alleged oversupply of artists, art institutions, staffing and so forth. What drives this blatant growth/oversupply paradox?

One answer is the exceptional nature of the art economy, its very strangeness generating inevitable contradictions. We might add to this the possibility that, given its exceptional nature, art generates an allure, drawing individuals to it precisely because it is not completely subsumed within capitalist markets. This attraction operates regardless of the limited chance of success. For Abbing this allure leads to the growth/oversupply paradox, it stems from art's historically venerated social position; we always want more culture, but until we bring culture into better alignment with capitalism most artists will remain poor. For Beech, following Marx, the inherent autonomy of artistic practice means there will likely always be more artists than there are available resources to support them in a market-based economy. Why? Because at bottom, there is no economic discipline regulating the making of an artwork, the market only becomes important after production is complete. If art making were to be rationalized the negative outcome would be critical and fundamental because such radically heteronomous art could no longer be art, at least not in the form celebrated by the contemporary art world, its institutions or its market. We can add to these problems Fusco's criticism regarding the unethical overselling of art education to young people. All of these may indeed be involved in the growth/oversupply paradox; however there is another, arguably more dominant mechanism generating this paradox, bringing us back to the reality of *bare art* in a post-Fordist economy.

In the book *Dark Matter*, I address the fascination the arts hold for neoliberal enterprise culture, arguing that this attraction is not entirely based on the "imaginative out-of-the-box thinking or restless flexibility" of cultural workers, but involves: "the way the art world as an aggregate economy successfully manages its own excessively surplus labor force, extracting value from a redundant majority of 'failed' artists who in turn apparently acquiesce to this disciplinary arrangement. There could be no better formula imaginable for capitalism 2.0 as it moves into the new century."[70]

If we seem to have too many artists today, that is because what was once exceptional to artistic economies in relation to capitalist markets has, under conditions of post-Fordism and *bare art*, become increasingly less extraordinary. The extraction of value from a large surplus population is what drew neoliberalism towards artistic production in the first place, at least according to Boltanksi and Chiapello's "artistic critique" argument, in which capital appears to assimilate aspects of its own Bohemian-inspired refutation.[71] The integration of art and capitalism also explains the necessity for a constant expansion of creative labor, a process analogous to the unfettered compound growth inherent in all capitalist forms of economic organization. Capital, David Harvey writes, requires an ever-expanding output of social labor, "a zero-growth capitalist economy is a logical and exclusionary contradiction. It simply cannot exist. This is why zero growth defines a condition of crisis for capital."[72] What we are witnessing under conditions of *bare art*, just as with capitalist crises more broadly, is this aggregating compulsion in overdrive. It has become an accelerating demand machine, seeking to extract ever more marginal and dispersed gains from an expanding pool of widely distributed participants—including indebted art students, underpaid cultural workers, unpaid artists and interns, as well as the innumerable networked contributors, with or without credentials, who assist in reproducing an increasingly *bare art* world.

And it is here that we glimpse the danger that an imagined oversupply of artistic labor generates. It is twofold. If the aggregating process continues to speed up, thus contributing to the demystification of the art world economy, it may lead to the solution sought by panicked oversupply advocates: the decreasing numbers of artists entering the system. Some studies, as well as the highly publicized walkout of students from MFA programs in the US, suggest this possibility.[73] Assuming my thesis is correct and that art in an age of enterprise culture requires a prodigious excess of unremunerated participants, the contemporary art world as we know it will simply cease to be under these circumstances. But there is another set of reasons that may

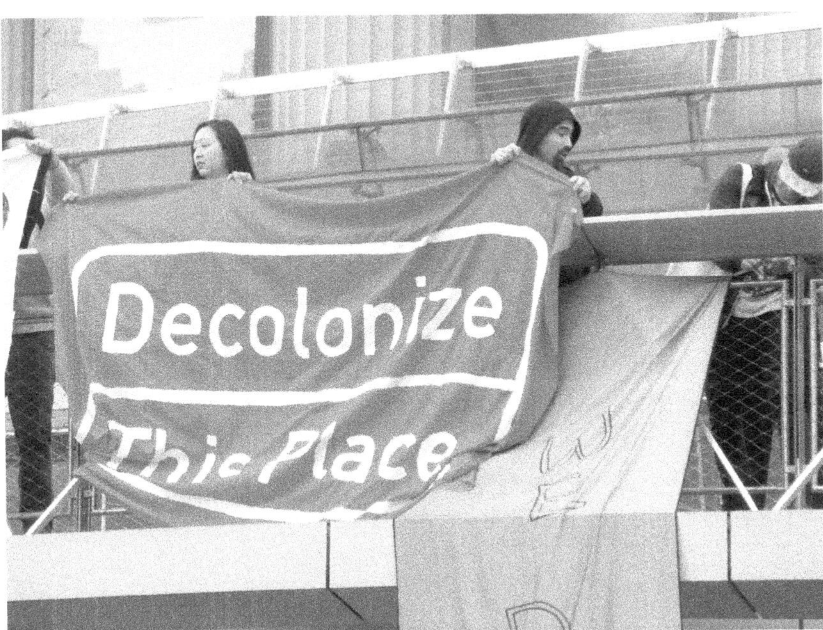

Figure 13   Decolonize This Place action at the Brooklyn Museum of Art protesting neighborhood gentrification and marking Native peoples' and Palestinian rights, May 7, 2016

(Image G. Sholette)

underlie this oversupply anxiety. What if this surfeit of invisible producers demanded economic justice? This appears to be the tactic of Working Artists and the Greater Economy (WAGE) and others seeking exhibition fees for artists. Or, contrarily, what if the majority of artists simply decided not to participate in the art world, perhaps following Stephen Wright's sardonic suggestion that contemporary art is seeking to break away from itself, a process that even generates a new area of study he calls escapology.[74]

Who would be left in that case to teach art, fabricate projects, subsidize museums and conferences and industry journals? Where would the art world's hierarchies and value production be in that situation? Even more terrifying, to echo a question raised by Carol Duncan some three decades ago, what if the majority of those whose creative potential has never even been tapped by the system were to suddenly be illuminated within it as a *bare art* world sweeps into view that vast surplus army of dark matter creativity? What was previously (and perhaps in some cases as we shall see, thankfully) hidden from sight now becomes painfully manifest in the *bare art* world.

Bare Art *World: Conclusions*

Rather than approach the crisis of artistic "overproduction" as if we were dealing with an inelastic, Malthusian closed system of supply and demand, we can now see that there are today, just as there were in the past, exactly as many artists as the system requires to reproduce itself.[75] Too many artists is a steady and central feature of the art world's means of valorization and propagation, and the mechanism of exclusion does not operate outside of, but rather from within the very center of the system.[76] This makes gaining an MFA more like a subscription to an online service that one signs up for, and only later realizes the charges never stop piling up, plus interest. Why is this current state of oversupply, perhaps better described as plentiful *pre-supply*, different and potentially calamitous for the status quo (including myself as a disloyal opposition figure)? The answer is again found in the emergence of a *bare art* world where freedom is just another word for nothing left to buy (leaving only subscription plans purchased on credit). Thus the one difference between oversupply panic today and in the past is that in a *bare art* world the situation is impossible to ignore.

If the extraordinary accumulated debt incurred by an ever-expanding population of individuals prepared to gamble away a great deal of their resources in order to join the art world is not an actual constraint on the growth of total artistic production, if it is instead a kind of delirious stimulus, then, as argued here, it is time to look elsewhere for the culprit behind this crisis of so-called oversupply. And that would almost certainly be the total aggregate demand for cultural consumables, a category that art now finds itself in, along with such bizarre commodities as financial derivatives, risk management instruments and highly leveraged mega-real estate developments, thanks to the dubious celebration of "innovative" creative and cognitive labor power as a highly distributed, abstract economic force. It is a strange situation in so far as this reality has perhaps never been more apparent, while at the same time capital, as we will see in Part II, "Cities without Souls," is developing new ways to attach artistic prestige to its endeavors. This means any attempt at developing non-capitalist models of sustainability must begin with an analysis of this new cultural algorithm and its "set of bureaucratic and linguistic instructions and their effects," as theorist Marco Baravalle points out with regard to "Creative Europe."[77]

What then actually makes this historical oversupply of artists different from those of the past? Two things stand out. First, the intense matter-of-factness of this precarious majority, who now perceive one another through the eyes of a *bare art* world: so many interchangeable elements making up an overarching art system. This *RealARTpolitik* is as conspicuous as it is delirious, merging what the brilliant and sadly missed theorist Mark Fisher called "Capitalist Realism" with the vertiginous feeling of having no viable alternative.[78] For as much as the condition of *bare art* yields predatory behavior and panic, so too does it give birth to bad deeds in the form of boycotts, strikes, occupations and demands for equality. And here, in a nutshell, sits point number two concerning the delirious irrationality of the typical oversupply crisis argument. Any attempt at "normalizing" the situation, especially through austerity-style economic constraints or neoliberal cultural policies, will also almost certainly destabilize everything that the status quo wishes to preserve about *its* art world.

Part II

Cities without Souls

Introduction II:
Naturalizing the Revanchist City

The rebuilding of public spaces since the 1980s shows signs of the same homogenizing forces of redevelopment … smooth[ing] the uneven layers of grit and glamour, swe[eping] away traces of contentious history … This is another way the city loses its soul.

Sharon Zukin[1]

Aggressive mimicry often involves the predator employing signals which draw its potential prey towards it, a strategy which allows predators to simply sit and wait for prey to come to them.

Wikipedia[2]

Romulus broke down and wept at Remus' funeral.

Arthur Cotterell[3]

The emergence of a distinct art activist scene in New York City in the 1980s was closely related to a gradual recognition of, or perhaps refusal to accept, artists' involvement in processes of gentrification. The relationship between art and gentrification is now widely acknowledged, and it is a feature of all global cities. However, New York has become the most cited example of the volatile combination of utopianism and artistic careerism that fuels gentrification, and accompanied a wave of young, white and primarily middle-class newcomers as they took up residence in the economically impoverished and ethnically diverse neighborhoods of Manhattan island in the early 1980s. The artists' communities in SoHo, and then the East Village, seem to have made way for the "regeneration" of inner-city neighborhoods, which, in the process, displaced existing communities. This pattern has since been reproduced in other boroughs of New York, and in major cities of the world, as artists are increasingly considered integral to urban regeneration. At the same time, artists and other creative laborers have proven a willingness to critique, protest, boycott and occupy neoliberal institutions and policies. The essays collected in Part II situate my work in this particular place and time, as a member of the art "gentry" and one of its critics, while noting the shift in urban mythology from a feral, post-industrial city, to the present-day creative city where nature and the remnants of an industrial past are symbolically reconciled, as attractions for tourists, investors and an expanding urban gentry, sometimes giving rise to moments of upheaval and resistance.

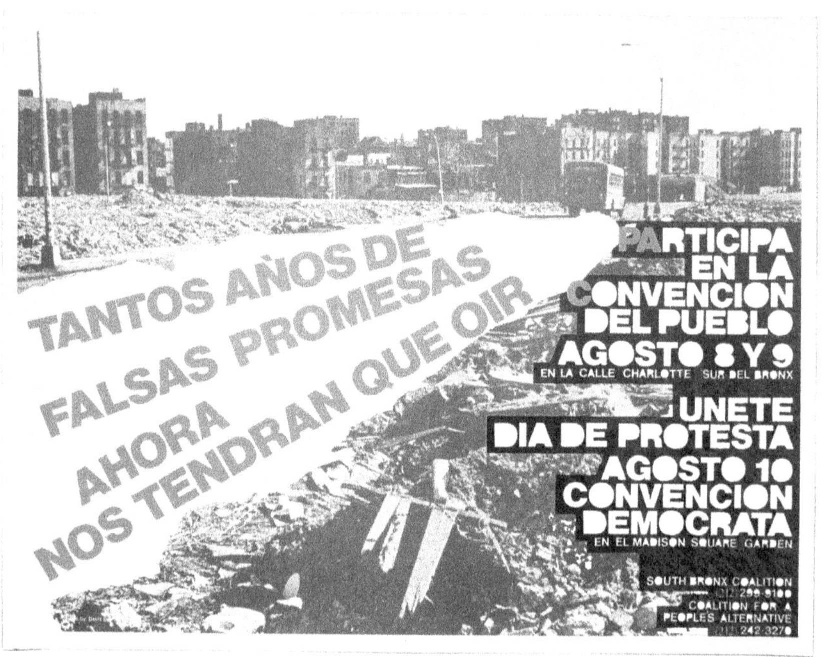

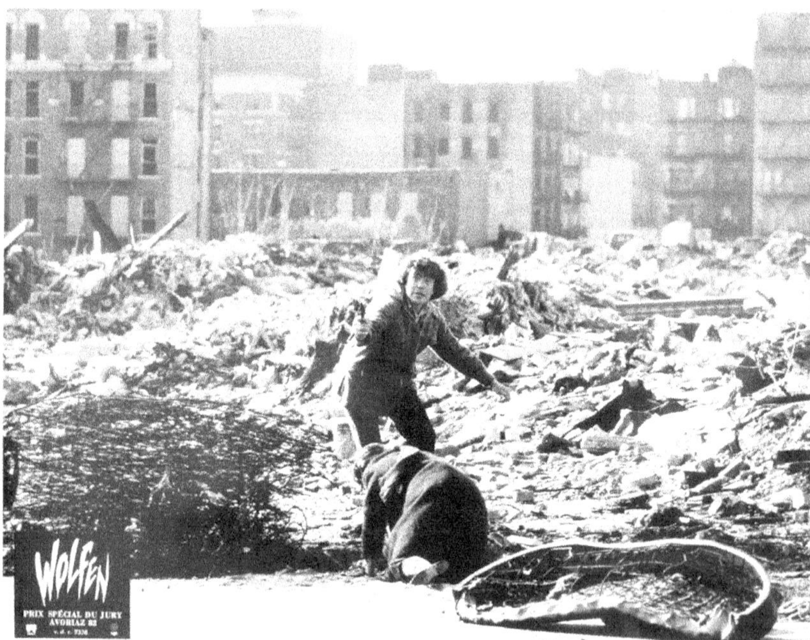

Figure 14   *Every Crack is a Symbol,* a mixed-media video installation by Emanuel Almborg incorporating footage from the 1981 film *Wolfen* (2015)

(Video still E. Almborg)

Unnatural City

For three eight-hour days in May, 1974 German artist Joseph Beuys confined himself with a living coyote to a secure enclosure inside the René Block Gallery in Southern Manhattan. Beuys was engaged in fieldwork, writes Christa-Maria Lerm Hayes, transforming art into "applied or active/activist anthropology."[4] In one photograph, shot towards the end of the piece we see man and canid lying side-by-side and looking out the window like a couple of warm, mammalian siblings.[5] This was the point in the project where the beast is said to have grown docile after hours spent in Beuys's shaman-like presence. (Still, just as the artist is seen wearing his signature felt hat, so too is his heavy wooden shepherd's staff visible close at hand.) But other than this one view out the window, Beuys allegedly saw very little of New York. As per his instructions, the artist was hustled from the airport by ambulance, wrapped entirely in felt, and taken directly to the gallery's inner compound. He later returned for his flight back to Germany in exactly the same fashion. What he did not see therefore was a city on the brink of bankruptcy, its infrastructure in ruins and increasingly abandoned by race-panicked White European-Americans.

A little over one year after Beuys's *I Like America and America Likes Me* performance piece, President Gerald Ford publicly rejected bailing out the largest municipality in the country, leading the tabloid *Daily News* to declare "Ford To City: Drop Dead." Once a deal was struck, however, it required austerity measures that included freezing the salaries of city employees, closing hospitals, libraries and fire stations, and raising public transportation fares to make way for the new masters of the city, the Finance, Insurance and Real Estate industries, or simply FIRE. These same policies would later be expanded and applied to the entire US and UK economies under President Ronald Reagan and British Prime Minister Margaret Thatcher, this has now been recognized as a watershed moment of neoliberal economic policy. In other words, the founding of the *new* New York City came at the expense of trade unions, the working poor and the public sector. But unlike the she-wolf's foster child Remus, no public officials wept as they vanished from the city, cleansed to make way for high net worth individuals, as the FIRE economy fundamentally changed the class composition of the city.

The first chapter of Part II, on gentrification, entitled "Nature as an Icon of Urban Resistance on NYC's Lower East Side, 1979–1984" (chapter 4) was written in 1997 for the journal *Afterimage*. It addresses the hopes and paradoxes of activist art in the pre-gentrified and ethnically diverse 1980s Manhattan neighborhood where I lived when I first came to New York.

Without lionizing the various but too-few efforts at resistance against gentrification and displacement by artists, the chapter attempts to map out the way several specific projects engage with images of the natural world in order to make sense of the city, or to critique the failing world of urban capitalism. One of the projects discussed took place in the early hours of 1980 when a group of artists from the COLAB (Collaborative Projects) collective broke into a city-warehoused building on the Lower East Side and installed an impromptu exhibition called the Real Estate Show. Before the day was over, the NYPD had shut down the illegal squat gallery.[6] As it happened, Joseph Beuys was back in New York for his Guggenheim Museum retrospective. After the German celebrity took part in a press conference in support of the shuttered exhibition an embarrassed Mayor Ed Koch relented, eventually giving the COLAB artists another nearby location to reinstall their project. The Real Estate Show reopened a few weeks later with Rebecca Howland's street drawing of a monstrous white octopus crushing tenement buildings pasted on the façade, an image exemplifying the participating artists' hostility to both municipal policies of urban abandonment and commercial strategies of property speculation.

Political Art Documentation/Distribution (PAD/D) soon picked up where the Real Estate Show left off, mounting the Not For Sale street art project in 1984 that not only protested gentrification but explicitly linked the phenomenon to the rise of the entrepreneurial East Village art scene on New York's Lower East Side (which was, we insisted, "not for sale"). "Nature as an Icon of Urban Resistance" (chapter 4) tries to catch sight of a future city that is as different as can be from the present revanchist, neoliberal model. Resistance, it seems to propose, will come in the form of an inner-city zone of autonomy, informally organized by a scruffy cadre of long-term residents, housing activists, progressive artists and an intransigent detachment of persistent vegetation and animals that, despite all odds, continue to thrive at the margins. For some eight years PAD/D generated art for political demonstrations, published a newsletter, hosted monthly public forums and did all of this with virtually no public funding relying instead primarily on the volunteer labor of its activist art membership.

PAD/D's activities wound down in 1988, just as the Cold War was coming to an end and NYC's gentrification stepped up apace with an event that even the *New York Times* described as a "police riot," as dozens of NYPD assaulted squatters and homeless people living in Tompkins Square Park.[7] One could easily describe the horror of that day as a wolfpack in blue uniforms turned loose upon their prey, precisely the words written on an anti-police brutality protest sign only one year after Richard Luke, a 25-year-old black man, was killed by white officers in Queens, New York. The wolfpack "in blue" description was itself a cutting reference to the media's portrayal of five young men of color falsely accused of beating and raping a white jogger one month earlier on April 19, 1989. The media condemned the Central Park Five, describing their activity as "wilding." It was not until DNA tests proved their innocence 13 years later that forced confessions by police were targeted as endemic facets of racial profiling by the NYPD.[8] Thus, in more ways than one, a baleful bestiality seemed to lurk within the New York City of the 1970s, 1980s and early 1990s.

Feral City

The image of a coyote gazing out at skyscrapers evoked the loss of connection to the natural environment: the wound that Beuys's activist-ethnography was intended to locate, perhaps to heal. Ironically, as the city continues to gentrify, the rats, pigeons, roaches and other scavenging species of the financially deteriorated 1970s and 1980s have been forced to make room for animals better known in rural settings, including deer, raccoons, skunk, opossum, the occasional black bear and, of course, coyotes. On Staten Island, white-tailed deer populations have risen over 3000% in six years, and the Gotham Coyote Project now tracks a couple of dozen animals that first moved to the Bronx around 2006 and have now fanned out into other boroughs. In 2015 one coyote even wandered about the Chelsea art district in Manhattan, an unknowing tribute to the nameless creature who performed alongside of Beuys almost four decades earlier.[9] Coyote populations have also been established in Chicago and Pittsburgh, two cities discussed in Part II.

This resurgence of urban-based wildlife—which may be due to increasing maintenance of city parks—has given rise to nature tourism in the form of guided walking tours and family kayaking trips. Vanished from the 2016 New York City is the image of a wild malevolent jungle with its obvious racialized undertones. Gone too are the Wild West "trail blazers" who "tamed, domesticated and polished" various rundown neighborhoods, as one full-page 1983 real estate advertisement in the *New York Times* proclaimed (by now these "settlers" have probably fled escalating rents and the city's colorless docility). What remains is itself like a sci-fi movie, a parallel urban universe completely removed from any future that might have been extrapolated from the devastated 1970s or 1980s. Unreal nature in a real 1980s city has today become real nature in an unreal city.

One symbol of this urbanized nature stands out above all other contenders: New York City's High Line Park.[10] Covered in wildflowers, ailanthus trees and carpets of weeds, an abandoned mid-nineteenth-century elevated railway in Lower Manhattan served—like so many forsaken parts of the city once did—as the illicit destination for graffiti artists, photographers, informal urban explorers, as well as homeless people, drug users, runaways and prostitutes. In 2009, it was repurposed into a city park by a team of architects, designers and engineers using funds drawn from both public and private sources. Less than a decade later the High Line has become a prime global tourist attraction as well as the anchor for a burst of nearby real estate developments, including luxury condominiums, upscale hotels and restaurants, blue-chip art galleries and the new Renzo Piano designed Whitney Museum art building. Not surprisingly, the High Line's elevation of a cultivated wild space set above urban commotion, as well as its seemingly magical powers of spillover regeneration, has spawned copies elsewhere. London's proposed Garden Bridge follows the NYC prototype by pooling sizable sums of public money with privately raised capital in a project that will regularly shut down for private events. Similar endeavors are planned in Philadelphia, Chicago, Sydney and Rotterdam.

The return of nature to the neoliberal city has an obvious ideological message: urban space has erased the past and achieved an uncanny urban pastoral, or neoliberal eudaimonia. The violence of the city has been tamed, at least on an aesthetic level. Of course, the obverse of this tranquility is the experience of the working-class, marginalized populations who were once subjected to racialized imagery of the urban "jungle" or the "frontier," and have been replaced by another "nature," one that has been cleansed of all antagonism, as if performing a semiotic inversion of Rosalyne Deutsche's critical observation from the early 1980s that the city was *socially* cleansing public spaces of unwanted humans, including of course the homeless.[11]

Within a few decades of the urban devastation that I witnessed in the early 1980s a new metropolis emerged that did not completely erase the past, but rather encapsulated this malignant history as a souvenir for memory-wiped gentry. The third essay in Part II, from 2004, acknowledged that the battle to realize a non-gentrified *city from below* had, for the moment, already failed. "Mysteries of the Creative Class, or, I Have Seen the Enemy and They Is Us" (chapter 5) is almost unique amongst my writings in so far as its sardonic, first-person voice addresses my own return to NYC after several years of teaching in Chicago. In it I am confronted with the reality of what Neil Smith called the revanchist city whose elite retaliate toward those they are displacing by seemingly crying out: "Who lost the city? And on whom is revenge to be exacted?"[12]

"Mysteries of the Creative Class" addresses the predicament of being a socially engaged artist in a city metamorphosing into an enormous gated community for the ultra-wealthy. I write with alarm that I encountered the visage of a city that I once knew which is now "being transmuted from lead to gold," a process of alchemical conversion affecting both its physical and mnemonic traces of the past.[13] Such profound disenchantment is not mine alone. Richard D. Lloyd's neo-bohemia is a soulless theme park; Martha Rosler's reclaimed city is saturated with "naturalized creativity and hipster-friendly memes"; while Sharon Zukin's *Naked City* has simply lost its soul.[14]

Nonetheless, "Mysteries of the Creative Class" does at least manage to wind up with a positive thought experiment—one that seems to anticipate events in Zuccotti Park some eight years later. At the conclusion of the essay I imagine the recently built Millennium Hotel suddenly occupied by its own service workers acting in cahoots with luxury establishment's creative class clientele:

> The bartenders and the brass polishers and cooks, the laundresses and bell hops throw down their aprons and spatulas to join in mutinous celebration with artists, web designers and musicians. Raiding the wine cellar, they open up all 33 executive-style conference rooms, set up a free health clinic in the lobby, transform the hotel into an autonomous broadcasting tower and party in a universe of creative dark matter.[15]

The insurrection finally came in the Fall of 2011; a rebel festival swiftly spreading across the US and into other countries (but also preceded by uprisings in public squares from Cairo and Madrid to Athens and Tunisia) as the contradictions within different sectors of unemployed people following the 2008 financial crisis turned into a wave of protests targeting economic austerity and neoliberal policies more generally. Particularly visible in Occupy Walls Street (OWS) was the so-called Creative Class. The penultimate essay of Part II, "Occupology, Swarmology, Whateverology" (chapter 6), returns to the theme of the surplus archive explored in *Dark Matter* (see chapter 9) by proposing that a type of *archival agency* was at work within OWS. This archival activation generated speculative expectations simply by constituting a massive assemblage of once-shadowy productivity and resistance now brought into light in the present. Ultimately I suggest that Zuccotti Park's cardboard encampment with its inventory of *no* political demands and its free OWS library existed in a state of creative lawlessness temporarily at odds with neoliberal capital and its revanchist urban policies, but with a definite desire, if unknown trajectory, towards the future. Those on Wall Street took singular advantage of the massive *Charging Bull* sculpture located close to the New York Stock Exchange; intended to be an icon of capitalist perseverance following the 1987 Black Friday market collapse, it is primarily a favorite with selfie-snapping tourists (though it is assigned a 24/7 NYPD guard detachment). Some credit the occupation of Zuccotti Park as inspired by a poster of a woman striking a ballet pose atop the masculinist beast's back. The poster was created by the Canadian culture-jamming group Adbusters and, as Yates McKee writes, it graphically flipped the bronze bovine's power "against itself in what would become the foundational meme of Occupy Wall Street."[16] In any case, the pro-capitalist metallic creature remains standing as if it were also an uncanny, burnished totemic counterpart to the actual return of abundant animal life in the new New York City.[17]

Repurposing the Wolfen

Creatively reusing the past is a paradigm well suited to an era where no specific vision of the future sits on the collective horizon: this is the secret of our own time, of course. In order to understand the banal utopia of the neoliberal city historically, I will return to 1980, the year the filmmaker Michael Wadleigh began shooting a film adaptation of horror novelist Witney Streiber's story *The Wolfen* on East 172nd Street in the South Bronx, an area of the borough so damaged from neglect that, a few years prior to this, a German film crew used it as the set for a movie about the firebombing of Dresden in 1945.[18] In retrospect one can see how this odd urban thriller, retitled simply *Wolfen*, captured the vertiginous transition of a crumbling working-class city that would later be reborn as an ultra-gentrified metropolis, a neo-Bohemian enclave celebrating creative workers and delirious development schemes benefitting the global elites. As a historical document the film shows the sheer scale of destruction that had been wreaked on the city by de-industrialization and calculated neglect.

Wolfen's plot parallels such post-war cinematic terror films as Jacques Tourneur's neo-gothic *Night of the Demon*, Don Siegel's paranoiac *Invasion of the Body Snatchers* and Nigel Kneal's sci-fi *Quatermass* series in so far as scientifically minded skeptical protagonists gradually acknowledge the presence of a menacing, unnatural force capable of disturbing the normal course of everyday things. But while 1950s popular culture often addressed anxieties over communist infiltration or homosexual contamination, *Wolfen* appeared at a time when the left, both old and new, was in decline and as identity politics rather than international class struggle was on the rise. By the early 1980s, not only had Keynesian policies of social spending failed to stabilize the economy, but also much of the leftist organizational energy stemming from 1968 was either being consumed by factionalism or disintegrating in the face of a well-funded right-wing backlash. To many, this political and cultural entropy found expression in crumbling post-industrial cities whose metonym was the South Bronx. Whatever *Wolfen's* menace was, it did not come from without, but from within a space of a decomposing unreality, one that is nevertheless fully enclosed within the logic of capitalist crisis.[19]

The movie's narrative is set in motion by the execution-like slayings of a wealthy, Donald Trump-like developer, his trophy wife, and bodyguard, all gruesomely beheaded with near-surgical precision. Police begin to suspect a terrorist conspiracy. My memory is that this scene symbolically played out the racial and class resentment many New Yorkers felt at the time towards the white establishment elite. And, while the organized New Left was in disarray and decline, 1981 was far from lacking in militant left politics, though of a highly factional nature. For example, that year saw the bombing of a bathroom at JFK airport by the Puerto Rican Resistance Army, the kidnapping of a US Army general in Italy by Red Brigades, and the armed robbery of an armored van just north of New York by a black splinter group of the Weather Underground known as the May 19th Communist Party that included three fatalities among bank guards and police. *Wolfen's* terror, however, turns on a different threat. In a pivotal scene, the lead police investigator (Albert Finney) enters a smoke-filled bar frequented by Native Americans. Physically enervated by false leads, more killings and a close encounter with the killer whose identity has left him stunned, he is warned by an older man (Apache actor Dehl Berti) that what he is after is in fact an ancient race of wolf-like predators who once lived alongside indigenous humans, hunting with them. It was only later, after Europeans arrived, that the smartest went underground to feed on the homeless or the addicted among urban decay in "the new wilderness: your cities … the great slum areas, the graveyards of your fucking species … in their eyes, you are the savage."[20]

In their canny collaborative essay, "Werewolf Hunger (New York, 1970s)," cultural theorists Alberto Toscano and Jeff Kinkle persuasively argue that *Wolfen* represents a "critical moment in the collapse of radical politics and the emergence of a feral neoliberalism against a backdrop of urban dereliction and real estate speculation."[21] I am going to spend a bit of time building on their interpretation, not only because the film's anti-capitalist imagery stayed with me for decades after first seeing it during the year of its release, but also because, like Toscano and Kinkle, when looking at issues of gentrification some 35 years on—a timeframe that runs almost parallel with the introduction of economic austerity measures, deregulation and privatization in NYC and elsewhere—*Wolfen* appears as an ever more prophetic statement.[22]

The film certainly captures themes present in the four chapters that make up Part II of this book, including the place of naturalized (and unnatural) white anxiety about what is lurking in the failed post-industrial city, as well as the figure of the artist, who appears sometimes as gentrifier or capitalist regenerator, and at other times as an activist and an angry spirit of marginalized resistance just biding his/her time for the day of revenge. In Toscano and Kinkle's reading, the Wolfen are an ambivalent resistant subject that rises up against capital. *Wolfen*'s political unconscious—to apply Jameson's hermeneutic—portrays a world teetering on the point of implosion from every possible angle. Pointing to the physically fatigued white police detective, Toscano and Kinkle observe that every character in the movie appears worn out, including the city, which is surrounded by an "exhausted working-class and radical left."[23] In fact, almost all of the characters in *Wolfen* will be dead or might as well be before the film ends. As another Native American played by Edward James Olmos says ominously to protagonist Finney, "you don't have the eyes of the hunter, you have the eyes of the dead," but he could also be talking about capitalism in 1981. Toscano and Kinkle, however, interpret the Wolfen as akin to gentrifying artists who move into run-down inner cities in search of low-cost housing, only to become "unwitting collaborators with capital." Artists exploit the weak and clear away debris, thus preparing neighborhoods for development, before they themselves are displaced later on. Therefore, what Finney saw, Toscano and Kinkle suggest, was "not the shock troops of gentrification, but its janitorial squadron."

And yet, as an artist living in NYC during *Wolfen*'s summertime premiere, my reading is somewhat different. It's not so much that Toscano and Kinkle get it all "wrong," they just don't allow the movie's political unconscious to fully play itself out. I recall not a sense of shock while viewing *Wolfen*'s docu-depiction of the South Bronx, but of familiarity. That devastated neighborhood closely resembled my own on the Lower East Side, a partially ruined zone where the carcasses of overturned, tireless cars accompanied collapsed buildings filled with refuse that nonetheless served as impromptu homeless shelters and shooting galleries for heroin addicts, later to become crack-smoking dens in a year or two. While artists undoubtedly played their part in regenerating these spaces, helping sweep in the no-collar creative class and FIRE economy, they almost always found themselves in turn the victims of its machine-like processes of displacement and expulsion. In addition, some artists, though certainly too few, attempted to fight back against these circumstances.

On several occasions Toscano and Kinkle seek to answer a central question, "The South Bronx and Wall Street, what's the connection?"[24] In Wadleigh's film, the speculator breaking ground for the construction of a luxury high-rise located inside the Wolfen's South Bronx hunting grounds instigates their ruthless retaliation. This is the ostensible reason he is hunted down and exterminated. However, intentionally or not, the filmmaker also establishes a conspicuous symmetry, linking two unproductive surplus populations: the class of wealthy speculators, financiers, rentier-capitalists and pseudo-aristocratic social freeloaders who skim value off the top of society while adding little or nothing back to it, and the sick and dispossessed whose failed lives bear the brunt of capitalism's failure. Thus the ruined South Bronx of 1981 and Wall Street connect at the level of cultural signification.

Toscano and Kinkle are right, therefore, when they identify the movie as an oblique treatise on the arrival of what we now call neoliberalism, with its privatization schemes, gated communities and aggressive enclosing of the commons, but, rather than the beasts signifying merely the feral counterparts of self-serving artists and *creatives*, Wadleigh's depiction of the Wolfen is far more ambivalent. It is important to note that the Wolfen kill without prejudice or remorse, much as Nietzsche's amoral beasts in *Beyond Good and Evil* devour weaker prey. They appear to be a force of nature that transcends humanity, like the Big Other of Jacques Lacan's symbolic order, a sort of impersonal superego "that relieves us of responsibility for what we desire" theorist Marc James Léger remarks, with reference to certain forms of community art practice.[25] In this repurposed scheme, as Toscano and Kinkle propose, the Wolfen are artists foraging at the edges of a ruined capitalist city, but these monsters also mark the otherness of capital as nature, red in tooth and claw; its thing-like drive that is inherently alien to life. In this sense the artist-Wolfen play Renfield to Dracula, promised eternal life in a delirious space where Wall Street and the South Bronx, the center and periphery, are impossibly conjoined on East 172nd Street, in an uncanny spatial collision where capital's normally hidden contradictions become visible in vertiginous free-fall.

Wadleigh goes to some lengths to show us the beasts at home within this breach. Thanks to infrared heat-sensitive film we "see" with the predator's preternatural vision as they stalk us from a hallucinatory *near-beyond* just adjacent to our own world. Before the movie ends, we witness a zoologist, the chief of police and the city coroner meet the same end as the fated tycoon van der Veer. Tellingly, Finney's character survives the massacre, first by casting rationality aside, and then, with head almost bowed, by accepting not only the fact that the Wolfen exist, but that they, and not the police, or intelligentsia or financial elites, are the city's truly uncontested top predators. Toscano and Kinkle conclude their allegorical reading by stating that: "what lies in tatters beneath the rubble is the precarious social-democratic compact of postwar New York City. What rises in its wake is a city where the memories have largely been wiped and the ruins elided, the unrestrained voraciousness of capital now but an everyday appetite."[26]

The placid wanderers of the High Line need to be read through, or understood as, the ciphers of the Wolfen's predatory subjectivity. Werewolf hunger has become an "everyday appetite," in the sense that it is equally banal and aestheticized, though it continues to tear capitalist sociality apart from the inside and brings us to another moment of disintegration. It is not only artists, but a pervasive class consciousness that is marked by this contradiction: a simultaneous avid competition with and contemplation of nature.

Regenerating Cities without Souls

A principal concern of the final text of Part II is to look at how the displacement from art into life, or perhaps more accurately art into capitalism, has led to disputes and encounters with labor unions, financial administrators, the law, police, and other social agencies typically located outside the literal and historical boundaries of a work of art. "Art after Gentrification" concludes Part II by focusing on three recent socially engaged art projects in which a contemporary art aesthetic breathes new life into existing, frequently failed urban structures mixed with creative industry business enterprises. But it also reflects on the prominence and challenges faced by social practice artists who are now selectively being recognized by the art world mainstream, even as states and municipalities appear increasingly incapable of either governing or reasonably managing the social sphere, as accelerating urban gentrification makes apparent.

The first case study examines Assemble, a London-based designer-collective and their collaborative regeneration project in a devastated neighborhood in Liverpool, England. Following the analysis of Assemble, I present an evaluation of Theaster Gates and his work, including Dorchester Projects, the South Side Chicago art enterprise that is poised for replication in economically challenged cities around the globe. The chapter concludes with an appraisal of Conflict Kitchen in Pittsburgh, Pennsylvania, an art project that has morphed into a successful fast-food business in a city rated by the Movoto real estate brokerage firm as one of America's top ten most creative cities.[27] The link between creative industries, gentrification and upper-class indignation is not a simple one, and it has taken years to come into focus. Still, as early as 1984, Rosalyn Deutsch and Cara Gendel Ryan formulated an answer to a question not yet asked. The primary target of the affluent urban gentry is "directed against those who will never serve the interests of 'postindustrial' society, as either workers or consumers." It is a retribution that carries with it "the

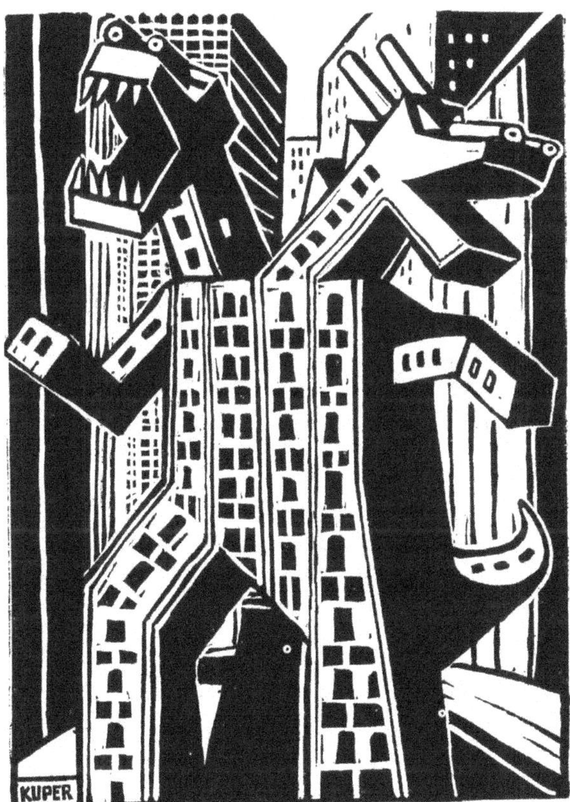

Figure 15 Gentrification, drawing on paper, © Peter Kuper, 1984
(Image P. Kuper)

full vengeance of two hundred years of capitalism," in which, as Deutsch and Ryan pointed out decades ago: "people, dwelling in the lower strata of what Marx identified as capital's surplus population, are [viewed as] victims 'chiefly' of their own 'incapacity for adaptation,' an incapacity which results from the division of labor."[28]

Or, as then NYC Mayor Ed Koch is alleged to have put it, "If you can't afford to live here, mo-o-ove!"[29] Meanwhile, the fetishization of the wild and untamed within the ultra-gentrified metropolis, like a saccharine reworking of the city's *Wolfen* past, is served up in a pastoral, family-friendly Disney movie manner for the tourists, city-boosters, FIRE denizens, and the elite glitterati. Its version of urban nature is grafted seamlessly onto the fossilized remnants of a now-distant, troubled past to emerge as a resplendent, made-to-order enclave for the twenty-first-century ruling classes and their administrators. The dark side, as Saskia Sassen and Neil Smith have noted, is that the neoliberal city's gentrifying policies are vengeful, predatory expulsions, not merely "displacements," to adopt the less brutal sounding and preferred terminology of the creative economy. Because once victims are "displaced," the truth is they can no longer return.[30] And so perhaps Beuys was right (or was it Romulus?), to think beyond present contradictions—of capitalist cities and failed nations, of class divisions and socially engaged collective art—is to lead us back into a world of feral signifiers and rough beasts, slouching and scavenging about the margins of the new normal crisis economy, a repurposed predatory art species ideally suited to this time and this place.

Soulless City Limits

On October 29, 2012, the largest hurricane of its type on record struck the New York region, killing 233 people and causing some $75 billion in property damage. "Superstorm Sandy" shifted the discourse around sustainability and the city's collective future. That we now face amplified natural forces made catastrophic through anthropocenic human intervention is without doubt. And yet, if Sandy was this decade's "Big Other," made all the more monstrous by surplus carbon emissions and negligent governmental politics, its uncontrollable terror was prophesied by other, man-made creations run-amok, including the legendary Golem, and Shelley's tragically reanimated experiment in *Frankenstein*. While the storm, like the Wolfen, dealt its fury evenly to both wealthy and poor neighborhoods of the city, those with fewer resources suffered longer, more severe periods of post-disaster rehabilitation. In response, post-Occupy Wall Street activists, including many artists, mobilized to voluntarily fulfil civic obligations in low-income storm-damaged neighborhoods that the city, state and federal governments were, unlike Rome's mythic she-wolf, simply incapable or unwilling to care for. 95

4
Nature as an Icon of Urban Resistance on NYC's Lower East Side, 1979–1984[*]

The state of this Lower East Side of New York City provides pictures for painters, operas for actors and poets from urban shambles of a slum where monstrous inequity is met with savagery, a nearly perfect specimen of malignant city life ... yet this neighborhood has also functioned as a cultural insulator. Within it bosom minority cultures have remained intact, and new ideas have incubated.

Alan Moore[1]

Urban cycles of decline, decay, and abandonment followed by rebirth through rehabilitation, renovation, and reconstruction may appear to be natural processes. In fact however, the fall and rise of cities are consequences not only of financial and productive cycles and state fiscal crises but also of deliberate social policy.

Martha Rosler[2]

Loisaida's wounds are bandaged with posters, stencils, and graffiti that bear witness to the internal struggles and triumphs of its diverse populace.

Lucy R. Lippard[3]

Metaphors of urban decay and trauma, but also of rebirth and incubation suggest natural processes above all. Likewise in pulp fiction, detective novels and *film noir* cinema the city often appears as a malevolent creature whose effect on humans is typically corrupting. And yet, as Martha Rosler points out, urban cycles of expansion and contraction, construction and demolition, are anything but natural phenomena. Why then does the naturalization of culture, and in particular the representation of the inner city as natural forms or processes, so often appear in the work of artists? In this chapter I look at the figurative use of "nature" in the work of several visual artists and artists' groups active on the Lower East Side of Manhattan from

* This chapter was first published in 1997.

Figure 16 Becky Howland's photocopied flyer for The Real Estate Show, 1980
(Image B. Howland)

the late 1970s to the mid 1980s. What makes these artists' works cohere is that each uses natural iconography—nature as image or as idea—to critically respond to the entwined processes of real estate speculation and class displacement known as gentrification, while effectively treating the neighborhood itself as a thing brimming with "malignant city life."[4]

By and large the work examined below was initially seen in outdoor locations, often on abandoned buildings. These "street" settings presented their own artificial ecology, where competing species of images inhabited an environment of licit and illicit visual noise that included: wheatpasted hand bills, commercial advertising, signage from retail businesses, fluorescent graffiti, as well as stencils and posters, some of which also presented anti-gentrification messages to the public. One response to urban speculation involves satirizing the naturalizing language of the real estate industry itself. Through advertisements and press releases, land developers, speculators and even the city administrators described low-income neighborhoods like Hell's Kitchen or the Lower East Side as "untamed territories" where upwardly mobile white renters were called on to serve as "trail blazers" or "urban pioneers."[5] The other way artists "naturalized" or challenged the myths surrounding gentrification on the Lower East Side is less straightfor-ward. It involves what Craig Owens described as a search "for lost difference [that] has become the primary activity of the contemporary avant-garde." Owens's critical remarks were aimed at the shallowness of the East Village art scene in the early 1980s which: "seeks out and develops more and more resistant areas of social life for mass-cultural consumption."[6]

Owens's acerbic analysis frames in historical terms what he called the "shifting alliances" between artists and other social groups, by comparing the fascination of the 1980s avant-garde with the "racial and ethnic, deviant and delinquent subcultures" of the Lower East Side to the infatuation of a previous avant-garde with the "ragpickers, streetwalk-ers and street entertainers" of mid-nineteenth-century Paris. Yet, despite Owens's important insights, he misses some of the irony generated by the artist's role in gentrification. For example, Owens applies arguments made by Thomas Crow in his essay "Modernism and Mass Culture" to the phenomena of the East Village art scene. Crow understands what he terms "resistant subcultures" to be the source material for high-art avant-garde recycling. But like Crow, Owens also bestows upon these marginalized groups an "original force and integrity" that is later appropriated by high art and turned into a commodity, thus tacitly investing subcultures and marginalized communities with an exploitable, organic richness manifested as "difference."[7]

Against the "puerilism" of the East Village art scene, Owens champions the anti-gentrification imagery produced by members of Political Art Documentation/Distribution (PAD/D), a project that I helped organize in 1983–1984, and which I detail below. Yet in describing PAD/D's work as "mobilize[ing] resistance against the political and economic interests which East Village art serves,"[8] Owens fails to notice the way the same search for "lost difference" also operated within progressive cultural formations, including the work of PAD/D, even if this longing occasioned more reflexive practices, as I hope to reveal. In various and often unexpected ways, therefore, the work under consideration naturalizes urban culture, extending this process to all parts of the Lower East Side, including the streets, the political economy, the history and even the heterogeneous population of the neighborhood. Within the work of these artists, "Loisaida" (as the local Latino population called the region, based on a 1974 poem by Nuyorican writer "Bimbo" Rivas) is represented variously as an endangered species or as one that is biologically out of control; a tableau in which predators and prey are locked in a primeval struggle; a cyclical organic process revealed to be man-made; or a corrupted ecological utopia in need of liberation. It is this last instance that I will turn to in my conclusion, when examining some of the art from the late 1990s that reworks the ecological themes of the last decade but so far remains primarily wedded to art world display.

Malignant City

Like myself, many of the artists immigrating to the Lower East Side in the mid to late 1970s were voluntary refugees from the managed communities of New Jersey, Long Island or towns in the Mid-West or California, places where life's rough edges and natural disorder had been displaced in favor of the regularity of landscaped yards, shopping malls and parking lots. To these children, whose parents had themselves fled the cities, the mix of Afro-Caribbean, European and Asian cultures proved enduringly vital, despite the crumbling tenement buildings and empty lots. In many places the Lower East Side circa 1979 indeed looked like a B-movie version of life amid the ruins of a nuclear or ecological catastrophe. Overturned cars, resembling animal carcasses, with their chassis' stripped of parts, were strewn along the sides of streets, especially on the alphabet avenues B, C and most of all D. Burnt-out or demolished properties cut spaces between tenement buildings. These openings became filled with rubble, trashed appliances, syringes, condoms, as well as pigeons, and rats. Often they appeared to be returning to a state of wilderness as weeds and fast-growing locust trees began to sprout from the piles of fallen bricks and mortar. Along some stretches of avenues B, C and D there were more square feet of this antediluvian-looking scenery than there was extant architecture.[9]

Still, residents in this predominantly Hispanic community could be seen organizing gardens amid the rubble and hurrying in and out of tenements to work (always elsewhere), fetch food or to go to social clubs. In the summer, older Ukrainian men played checkers in Tompkins Square, while the women would sit together on the opposite side of the park conversing near kids dressed in black leather with Mohawk haircuts, the remnants of an already fading punk scene. Both groups shared their space with street vendors, graffito writers and children chilling in opened fire hydrants. Always a conga drum sounded, meting out a near 24-hour pulse. Even the neighborhood's ethnic and cultural vitality could be read as a dense forest of signs where typographical tracings, some in Spanish or English but others in Hebrew, Chinese or Slavic characters, overlapped on brick or stucco walls and in shop windows. Along with this melange of texts was the visual chaos of newsstands, billboards, wheatpasted handbills, graffiti, political slogans and murals that depicted angry looking brown or yellow workers raising their fists. The total effect was that of a mongrel thing: part living, part mineralized ruin, part text, but always more authentically "natural" than the genteel communities of either SoHo or Nassau County. Before discussing the art in detail, let me present a highly abbreviated history of the neighborhood and the arrival of a new wave of artists beginning in the late 1970s.

The Anti-suburb

Celebrated by many who were raised on the Lower East Side, this working-class neighborhood formed the first home to generations of Americans entering the United States beginning in the 1850s. Along with consecutive waves of Irish, Germans, Italians, and later eastern European Jews, Chinese, Puerto Ricans, it was also a place where the artistic avant-garde—from the publishers of the radical paper *The Masses* to the first cooperative galleries to the Beat poets—flourished alongside one another. Like an American Left Bank, it was here that aspiring actors and artists drank coffee, ate ethnic foods and encountered the urban poor, the chemically dependent and the slumlord.

By the late 1960s the Lower East Side was still a place for political activists, small businesses, hippies, Yippies and junkies, and a vibrant Hispanic culture (mostly Puerto Rican but also Dominican) of social clubs, sidewalk domino games, botanicas and bodegas. At this point the falling property values sped on by bank red-lining and municipal neglect, made much of the intact rental property a target for arson, as some landlords who preferred insurance money over some unlikely rise in property values contracted for the destruction of their own miserable investments.

Then, in the latter half of the 1970s, came a new wave of young immigrants. Many of these young people who moved to the streets west of the Bowery, south of 14th street, and north of Delancey were artists—a class of individuals traditionally willing to forgo bourgeois comforts, even risk their safety, in the pursuit of two goals. One of these was to be discovered in the traditional manner by a patron, a ticket out of the East Village for the lucky few. The other hope was to come into contact with something authentic, such as the imagined organic quality of other peoples (ethnic) communities. However, the national and regional economy of the 1970s was in a virtual depression and the low-income areas of the city were the worst hit. This malaise was reflected in the *fin-de-siècle* spirit of the art and club scene in the Lower East Side. Downward mobility caused by high unemployment and a tight money supply literally cut off any route leading out of low-rent neighborhoods and back into the middle class (at least until the boom years of the mid 1980s, and then at the price of 70-hour work-weeks).

Yet in spite of this sense of "zero" options, combined with such ominous signs as the energy "crisis," when people shot each other at gas stations, or the unprecedented global nuclear build-up of the 1970s, the punk years were filled with a sense of macabre festivity. As one observer put it:

> The first generation to grow up under the specter of nuclear annihilation angrily came of age in an era of diminishing expectations. It was in this atmosphere that a rock club CBGB opened in New York's East Village [in 1975] … CBGB launched the punk movement, and it's no coincidence that many of the early punks looked like survivors from a nuclear holocaust.[10]

Ronald Reagan became the Republican presidential contender in 1979, offering steep tax cuts for the wealthy, and promising a demolition of the liberal welfare state established after the Great Depression of the 1930s. Dubbed "Supply Side Economics," Reagan's policies were interpreted by the working classes and poor as little more than trickle-down leftovers, and unending attacks on the social safety net. Today we refer to this ultra-free-market outlook as neoliberalism, in which the deregulation of markets, and the privatization of public assets go hand in hand to move capital up the class ladder. But in 1980 the former Hollywood actor was elected president and immediately began implementing his "Voodoo Economics" (as his own staff referred to these policies in private), as well as making occasional bizarre remarks in public about a coming biblical showdown. All of this left some thinking that President Reagan was proof enough that the world had all but ended, and that the only option that remained was to party (or to imitate a party at any rate). The tone was set for the 1980s as one of extremes: excessive consumption on one hand; homelessness and poverty on the other.

Nevertheless, throughout the 1970s some Lower East Side artists inevitably folded into this anarcho-apocalyptic moment did pull back somewhat. They attempted to develop a specifically political and resistant agenda to the forces of gentrification and displacement. Still, these art-activists understood that they were themselves central to these processes as typically white, well-educated young people whose very presence enhanced the desirability of a given neighborhood for more mainstream middle- and upper-income residents. Some also began to grasp that later on they were themselves going to be displaced by the same processes artists helped set in motion. Finally, when a second wave of artists began arriving in the late 1970s and early 1980s, these political possibilities became exceptionally sharpened, if only temporarily, before the juggernaut of gentrification overwhelmed all resistance.

Copping an Octopus

The smoke of burning buildings fills the street… Rats and dogs are coming out to eat … the rich have been buried in the basements of their buildings … throw away your clothes you no longer need them.[11]

In the last weeks of 1979, a splinter from the four-year-old artists group Collaborative Projects (COLAB) entered a city-owned building on Delancey Street that had been sitting empty in Loisaida for years. Aiming to liberate and occupy the site as a means of exposing "the system of waste and disuse that characterizes the profit system in real estate,"[12] the Committee for the Real Estate Show opened their "squat-gallery" to friends and the public on January 1, 1980. The show was filled with coarsely made artworks that decried rent-gouging landlords, city-run development agencies and what would become a favorite target of the new scene: the "suburbs," as a series of suburban real estate photographs with sardonic captions like "3 BR, no rats, no unemployment" demonstrated.[13]

Outside the building, in a move that prefigured the pop-piracy of East Village art, Rebecca Howland copped the image of a monstrous octopus—the consummate left-caricature of big business—and painted it onto the bland facade of the Real Estate Show. In the creature's tightly coiled arms were two tenement buildings, a bundle of cash, a gem (signifying the speculator's perception of the building), and a dagger. But one of the beast's arms had been violently severed. The artist positioned this liberated limb just above the entrance to the building forming an arrow that directed the eyes of the neighborhood toward both the exhibition and to the example set by the artist's collective action. Within the context of the Lower East Side, with its graffiti-covered brickwork, handmade store signage, street graphics and didactic murals, the Real Estate Show's polymorphic sea creature appeared inevitable, natural, like a denizen attracted to the region's visible ecological fatigue. Howland also put her octopus icon on the Real Estate Show's fliers and posters, some of which were printed over actual page-spreads from the *New York Times* real estate section, thus turning the creature into a veritable logo for the squat-action.

Howland would in fact continue to use the mollusk-image in her work for years, her most ambitious version a large three-dimensional sculpt-metal piece from 1983 titled *Real Estate Octopus with Dead Horse* that she made for the walkway of the Williamsburg Bridge. *Real Estate Octopus …* presented Howland's now emblematic invertebrate writhing beneath the towers of the World Trade Center as if it were the radioactive spawn of a secret Port Authority experiment. One likely source for Howland's initial octopus effigy may have been the mural "Chi Lai—Arriba—Rise Up!" by Alan Okada on a building just five blocks to the south of the Real Estate Show. Within Okada's four-story-high painting a squirming cephalopod, draped in a US flag, clings like a parasite to the figure of a money-grubbing landlord. Another source for Howland's image is undoubtedly the 1901 novel *Octopus* by radical socialist author Frank Norris, where the railroad is represented as a many-armed monster. This connection is all the more interesting in that Norris's beastie symbolizes the expansion of capital into the western frontier. In the following passage Norris's protagonist Presley first encounters the rail-road monster: "Presley saw again, in his imagination, the galloping monster, the terror of steel and steam, with its single eye, Cyclopean, red, shooting from horizon to horizon … with tentacles of steel clutching into the soil, the soulless Force, the iron-hearted Power, the monster, the Colossus, the Octopus."[14]

It is difficult to miss Howland's version of real estate speculators with their "tentacles … clutching the soil" of the Lower East Side. But the real estate "insurrection" was itself a mixture of anarchistic bravado and analytical naïveté. The artists mimicked the direct action strategies of 1968 and in doing so they imagined that the community would be inspired to take similar action and stop the irrational warehousing of useful property. There was, however, nothing irrational about the city's plan for the neighborhood. It was part of a long-standing grand design to weaken investment and living conditions in certain low-income areas so that re-development could later be carried out that would attract real estate developers and upper-income residents.[15] Neither did neighborhood people necessarily get the point of the exhibit. According to artist Joe Lewis, a fellow COLAB member, "a lot of people saw the show, the community people, they thought it was just a group of artists protesting that they could not show their work anywhere."[16]

The day after the opening of the Real Estate Show, the city padlocked the building. Then, after receiving some bad press helped along by the appearance of artist Joseph Beuys, the city reversed itself and offered the artists a smaller space a few doors away to resume the exhibition. Soon after the Real Estate Show debacle, the city offered artists still another storefront, a few blocks north on Rivington Street to use as an ongoing gallery. The new space was named ABC No Rio after a garbled nearby sign reading ABOGADO NOTORIO. Since 1980 the space has occasioned changing exhibitions, musical events, happenings and an occasional educational art project with neighborhood kids. (And most recently the No Rio building was discovered to be structurally unsound: it will be replaced by a state-of-the-art green building designed by Paul Castrucci.)[17] The Real Estate Octopus was just one specimen in an ersatz natural history of the Lower East Side targeting landlord abuse and neighborhood degradation. While Howland's tentacled speculator cast the real estate wars in terms of natural predation and defense, artists such as Christy Rupp and Michael Anderson presented images of animals as signs and victims of an urban environment gone wrong.

Rats, Kingfishers and Voodoo Economics

In works like *Rubble Rats* and *Rat Patrol*, artist Christy Rupp approaches the Lower East Side as if it were the locus of an ecological disaster. In 1979 Rupp pasted some 4,000 offset images of running rats throughout the city. The action, titled *Rat Patrol,* was intended to make "visible during the day what went on at night."[18] Rupp also played on traditional images of plagues or miasma, where corruption spreads like an infection throughout the urban body. What was the source of this contagion? In an interview with the *New York Post* in 1980 the artist stated "Rats are not terrorists … I see them as part of the history of ecology, in the whole chain of things. It's simply that they're out of control in the cities."[19] Elsewhere the artist has commented that "Rats are a symptom," insisting that garbage and "the environment and economics" are the cause, presumably of natural imbalance in cities.[20]

The success of *Rat Patrol* was followed by a series of rodent-sized sculptures such as *Rubble Rat.* In 1980 Rupp made the work by casting a rat with cement directly onto a pile of bricks she found in the debris and weed covered backyard at ABC No Rio. In keeping with the camouflaging common to the animal kingdom, Rupp's small concrete sculpture is at first indistinguishable from other chunks of broken building that littered the area. Partly embedded in the debris it is only when the rat figure is at last discerned that are we tipped off to the artifice of the work. A somewhat different reading of the work places it in the category of the post-traumatic souvenir, along with other petrified curiosities such as the melted watches in Hiroshima or the mummified inhabitants of ancient Pompeii. The piece first appeared in No Rio's inaugural exhibition, put on by the anti-nuclear coalition Artists for Survival in May, 1980. In contrast to Rupp's more recent, skillfully crafted and assertively beautiful animal sculptures, these scabrous rodents retain a strong ambivalence about art as commodity production. The abject look of Rupp's sculptural vermin hints at another ambivalence by reflecting at once the rawness of "malignant city life" on the Lower East Side as well as an uneasiness over the absence of bourgeois standards. Once again my speculation is that, for Rupp as well as other East Village artists, the inner-city landscape appeared as pathological, as "malignant city life." And whether her representations of rodents were intended to make visible a nocturnal urban ecology or to amplify the already abundant evidence of New York's social and environmental crisis, these works are symptomatic of art that used the poor ecological hygiene of the city to agitate for social improvement.

In 1984 the activist art group PAD/D launched the second of two anti-gentrification projects on New York's Lower East Side, and artist Michael Anderson added another specimen to Loisaida's expanding zoological garden. Anderson's silk-screened poster "In Memorium" featured the unusual pairing of an endangered animal, a bird known as a kingfisher, together with an altogether different endangered species, the neighborhood "mom and pop" store, in this case the Orchidia, which was a popular Lower East Side restaurant serving a unique combination of Ukrainian and Italian cuisine. The Orchidia had recently been forced to close down because of unregulated commercial rent increases brought about by the "upturn" in the neighborhood's property values. But it was also one of the focal points for neighborhood anti-gentrification activists such as the Lower East Side Joint Planning Council, who used the Orchidia situation to expand community participation and garner media attention. Anderson was an exhibition preparator for the American Museum of Natural History at the time, and was also actively involved in anti-gentrification work in Brooklyn and on the Lower East Side. The poster, which was made for a neighborhood-wide art project called *Out of Place: Art for the Evicted*, has a bold headline that is dedicated: "To those felled by environmental/economic pollution." On the left side of the 24×30-inch piece is the image of a dead bird. Beneath it in small type is a label-like caption reading: "BELTED KINGFISHER (*Ceryle Alcyon*) Found in New York City alive but with legs paralyzed. Died August 25th 1983 of suspected poisoning by environmental pollutants." To the right of the kingfisher memorial Anderson has printed an image of the neighborhood eatery along with another testimonial that reads: "ORCHIDIA RESTAURANT After almost 37 years at 2nd Avenue at 9th street, landlord Sydney Wiener, in defiance of community opposition raised rent from $950/month to $5,000/month. The Orchidia, despite protest, closed April 11, 1984." Surrounding both images is an irregular color smudge—one blue, one red, like the color of the dyes used to stain microscopic specimens—and within these blots are images of roses and hovering cherubs.[21]

Along with Anderson's memorial to economic and environmental pollution was another lament for a lost neighborhood business that was part of the *Out of Place* project. The Garden Cafeteria had been a Jewish cafeteria-style restaurant located on East Broadway, which had recently been bought out by a Chinese restaurant (more likely a symptom of the changing demographics of the Lower East Side than real estate gouging). The artist Marianne Nowak paid tribute to the establishment's passing in the form of color Xeroxed images of actual gardens interspersed with Cafeteria diners. Arranged in the form of a single horizontal panorama on the delapidated building that would temporarily be known as the Guggenheim Downtown, the work linked urban life and personal memory with natural cycles of growth and dissolution. But where Anderson's graphic lament "In Memorium" worked as a visual and conceptual pun, mixing document with lamentation and patently confusing the categories of nature and culture, "Garden Cafeteria" resolves this opposition by using nature to invoke the rapture of dwelling on what has recently been lost.

In general, the reconfiguring of the economic sphere—labor and capital—into a metaphor of natural processes is not unlike the ideological sleight of hand that Marx and Engels charged the young Hegelian philosopher Ludwig Feuerbach with perpetrating when they insisted he: "does not see how the sensuous world around him is, not a thing given direct from all eternity, remaining ever the same but the product of industry and of the state of society."[22]

The authors further demystify Feuerbach's idealization of the German landscape using the history of a species of tree arguing: "the cherry-tree, like almost all fruit-trees, was, as is well known, only a few centuries ago transplanted by commerce into our zone, and therefore only by this action of a definite society in a definite age it has become 'sensuous certainty' for Feuerbach."[23]

Sensuous certainty may have been on the minds of Ronald Reagan's publicity handlers when they "spun" their offensive against working-class interests in terms of bucolic national resources. The Republicans' vision of the American landscape was not unlike that of Feuerbach's Germany over 130 years before, only here just as melting snowcaps on mountain peaks wondrously find their way to your kitchen's faucet, so too Reagan claimed would an unprecedented federal tax cut for the wealthy mysteriously and assuredly "trickle down" to those in the economic lowlands. This is the background from which artist Ed Eisenberg's street poster titled *Reaganomic Galleries* is derived as a silvery waterfall surrounded by informational graphic boxes. Upon close inspection these parenthetical captions carry out two operations. First they attempt to trace the history of the economic assault on the neighborhood in terms of the trickle-down metaphor and, second, they relate this deregulatory spirit to the emergence of the East Village Art Scene of the 1980s.

Eisenberg's waterfall street artwork starts with the 1981 tax bill cutting taxes to corporations and the upper class, splashes its way down to the revitalization of the luxury art market before passing through the gush of the East Village Art Scene, and finally lands in a pool where the caption reads: "some young art stars profit handsomely; communities poor residents continue to dehydrate." Other works generated by the PAD/D Not For Sale group were similarly "exhibited" in the streets and invoked concepts of natural history in a more ethnographic mode, including the ironic poster by Nancy Sullivan that depicted an iconic cowboy on horseback with a bold caption that read "Area Natives make your Reservations Now." Behind the lasso-wielding horseman is an image of a desert in the Southwest. Both images appear on a sheet of graph paper, suggesting the rationalizing of natural landscape in the wake of invading capital. This Euro-expansionist sentiment carried over to Hokeayevi Edgar Heap of Birds' poster with the word Natural spelled backwards:

ЈАЯUTAИ
WE DON'T WANT INDIANS
JUST THEIR NAMES
MASCOTS
MACHINES
CITIES
PRODUCTS
BUILDINGS

LIVING PEOPLE

Like artist John Fekner, whose spray-painted slogans "Growth/Decay," and "Broken Promises," were stenciled onto the exterior of crumbling buildings and torched car bodies both downtown on the Lower East Side and uptown in the South Bronx, Hachivi Heap of Birds' (aka Hock E Aye Vi) and Sullivan's posters functioned as ironic warnings about the effects of what might be termed ecological urban colonialism. Although, as artist Janet Koenig and member of the PAD/D *Not For Sale/Out of Place* project cautioned, the contradictions involved in making art against gentrification were not going to be resolved within the cultural sphere:

> In many Manhattan communities the leading edge of gentrification has been artists ... What relationship then, do politically conscious artists have to this situation? For artists, mere awareness of their roles in gentrification is not sufficient. On the one hand, this project attempts to raise consciousness about the issue, on the other hand, it can be seen as another "Off Off West Broadway" encroachment on the Lower East Side community.[24]

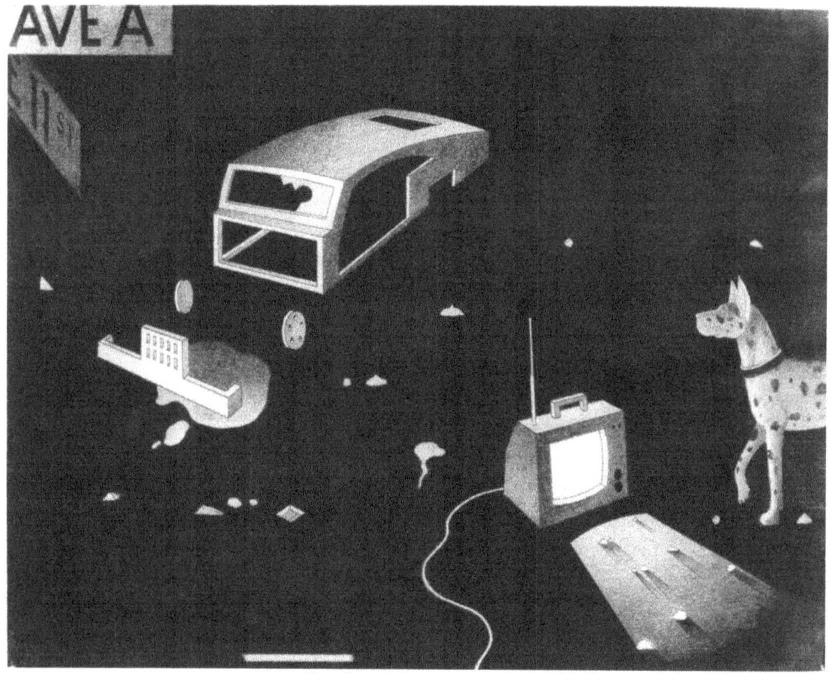

Figure 17   Anton Van Dalen, *Abandoned Car with Dog and TV*, pencil drawing, 1977 (Image Anton Van Dalen)

Ecotopia on the Lower East Side?

Within these varied reconfigurations of city as nature and nature as city, another tendency is visible. This includes artists who presented designs, often of a fantastic nature, for a new ecological-urban utopia. In fact the Lower East Side already had a tradition of both pragmatic and fantastical ecological undertakings that combined the recycling of natural resources with the existing architecture and community. Though beyond the scope of this chapter, a short list of these attempted projects would include: La Plaza Cultural and garden on East 9th Street, Adam Purple's Garden of Eden, buildings with solar panels and windmills located on East 5th and East 11th Streets, the Quondo urban agricultural collective on Houston Street and even a purported fish farm in the basement of an abandoned tenement building. At one time even Buckminster Fuller had been involved in demonstrating to members of CHARAS (a Nuyorican community center run by artists and poets) and former members of the Puerto Rican Young Lords Party how to construct geodesic living structures for the neighborhood. The list could also include the home of Anton Van Dalen, a senior member of the East Village art scene. Born in Holland during the Second World War, Van Dalen moved to the Lower East Side in the mid 1960s. On the roof of his building were pigeon coops and in the first floor an indoor "farm" of rabbits and chickens. Van Dalen's surrealist-inspired art enlarged upon this improbable urban agrarianism by offering a three-dimensional wooden pigeon-coop car and the Auto Botanica: a Ford made of leaves, as well as emblematic street stencils of a woman's shoe with a dove nestled inside, a flying bus launching missiles, and an x-rayed arm with a vine sprouting from its lace-like arteries suggesting a dual reference to drug-shooting galleries that proliferated in the neighborhood's partially demolished buildings, and the ever-present potential for a grassroots revival of Loisaida's "mean streets."

In a more theoretical hybrid of ecology and activist ideals, artist and architect Peter Fend, who was active with the Real Estate Show, presented his plan for a project he called OECD or Ocean Earth Construction Development. Fend's idea was to set up a "community corporation" that would design environmental engineering projects and then channel the profits from these into neighborhood improvements. This green-stock would be held exclusively by residents of the Lower East Side, who would in turn democratically vote on how profits would be used. Under the slogan of "Delancey Street Goes to the Sea" Fend aimed to secure autonomy for the neighborhood by establishing "an independent energy and wastes-conversion cycle, possibly in Jamaica Bay or the shoals off Staten Island, and to build structures which—being elevated above existing structures or lots—are virtually exempt from taxes or rents." Exactly where the "profit" would come in Fend's project is unclear. Together with fantastic

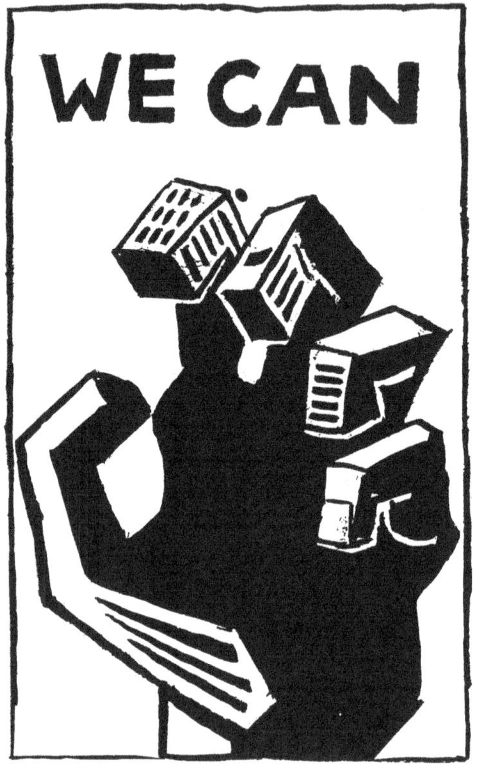

Figure 18   Seth Tobocman, *WE CAN*, linocut on paper, 1988
(Image S. Tobocman)

reworkings of topographical maps so that nations might be organized around shared resources and drainage basins, Fend was a sort of East Village version of the conceptual art team of Helen and Newton Harrison. But Fend's libertarian-like schemes fitted the entrepreneurial style of the 1980s more than the anti-commercialism of early 1970s conceptual art.

The theme of proposing to fix the environmental and social-economic problems of the inner city through conceptual projects reappeared in the work of 1990s artists like Mark Dion and Nils Norman. Dion's project for the exhibition, Culture in Action in Chicago in 1992/1993, combined a high school science project with a field trip to a South American rainforest, and resulted in temporarily recycling an abandoned building in Chicago into what Dion described as an "eco drop-in center and clubhouse." According to the curator of the project, Mary Jane Jacob, the participating young Chicagoans learned "to frame nature in art context and to frame art in relation to the natural world. It initiated in the students a way of thinking about nature."[25]

Closer to issues related directly to the Lower East Side as a site of social and political contestation are the conceptual schemes and prototypes made by British born artist Nils Norman. In an exhibition at American Fine Arts in 1997, Norman presented detailed scale models and blueprints for a number of utopian architectural and/or garden projects including the Sky Village for Tompkins Square Park (designed for both habitation and defense against city marshals and police), a communally owned solar-powered news kiosk for senior citizens, and a proposed agricultural workers collective to be known as the Underground Agrarians. This micro-utopia would be constructed at Norfolk and Delancey Streets on the Lower East Side (recall that the Real Estate Show was held on Delancey in 1979). With each of the precise plexiglas-covered miniatures in the exhibition is a Site Analysis. The model-site is broken down in the document into various life-sustaining functions including: "Food Coop, Specialized info/book shop (gardening, tenant rights, autonomous energy use), Prosthetic Gardening Limbs Shop, Self-composting toilet, and Sustainable model permaculture roof garden." The Organizational Structure is composed of work detachments and democratically elected commanders who supervise "composting, watering, weeding, sowing." Norman even proposed re-naming Delancey Street Wobblies Street, after the radical turn-of-the-century workers' organization known as the Industrial Workers of the World or Wobblies. Norman's models, even more than Dion's largely symbolic investigations, borrow from the little-known history of left politics and ecological utopianism, including the kind of iconographic and polemical uses of nature that I have touched on in this chapter. Nevertheless, in light of the present anti-progressive and the self-satisfied insularity of the 1990s art industry, it is this often less-than-ideal history of actual political work by artists in places like the Lower East Side that is in danger of being forgotten, or romanticized like an exotic, organic thing.

There is a seductive pleasure in the new ecological art, not least derived from the conceptual linkage, especially strong in Norman's projects, to the history of collective practices and militant political resistance. And while New York City's Lower East Side continues to serve as the "natural" site for locating these alternate histories, what cannot be stressed enough is the need to move beyond idealized exhibition settings into long-range commitments where conceptually refined concepts are put to use in the malignant cityscape that gives birth to such urban art activism.

5

Mysteries of the Creative Class, or, I Have Seen the Enemy and They Is Us[*]

The full-page advertisement in the Sunday edition of the *New York Times* depicts a trio of smartly clad, sophisticated young white people conversing over a glass of wine. Intentionally rendered in a retro-1930s Art Deco style, the illustration is captioned "An Oasis In Times Square." The ad goes on to explain that the illustrated place is where the traveler who is weary from business can discover tranquility and a "new level of self-indulgence," right in the midst of busy Manhattan. This was 1999 when, with bank-rolled panache, the Hong Leong Group launched the Millennium Premier hotel. It was the global real-estate group's first New York project, and immediately I sensed the arrival of something different at work, some shift in tactics within the decade-old project of "upclassing" the city. I also knew something troubling about the hotel's recent past that made my hunch even more compelling, and deliriously logical.

A veteran of anti-gentrification activism on the city's Lower East Side some 20 years earlier, I still recall the clumsy call for "pioneers" to brave the city's harsh urban frontiers. But by the late 1990s this type of gambit had largely played itself out, at least in Manhattan. Already most of the island was well on its way to full-blown gentrification and what was left of the poor and working class largely scattered by force or rising rents in the wake of reverse white flight that began in the 1980s.

However, this late 1990s wave of gentry wanted nothing to do with leaking pipes or chasing away crack-heads from street corners, and under no circumstances would they wear overalls. Yet the hotel's curiously retro illustration also avoided references to the fevered, techno giddiness of those blissful, pre-crash 1990s. Instead, the unknown artist lovingly invoked the modernist conceit of the machine age some 60 years prior. Nor was it camp, for the irony was too far adrift from any rhetorical moorings to signal "spoof." Instead, like an arcane plot out of a Philip K. Dick novel, the very visage of the city I knew was being transmuted from lead to gold. The more I

[*]   This chapter was first published in 2004.

112

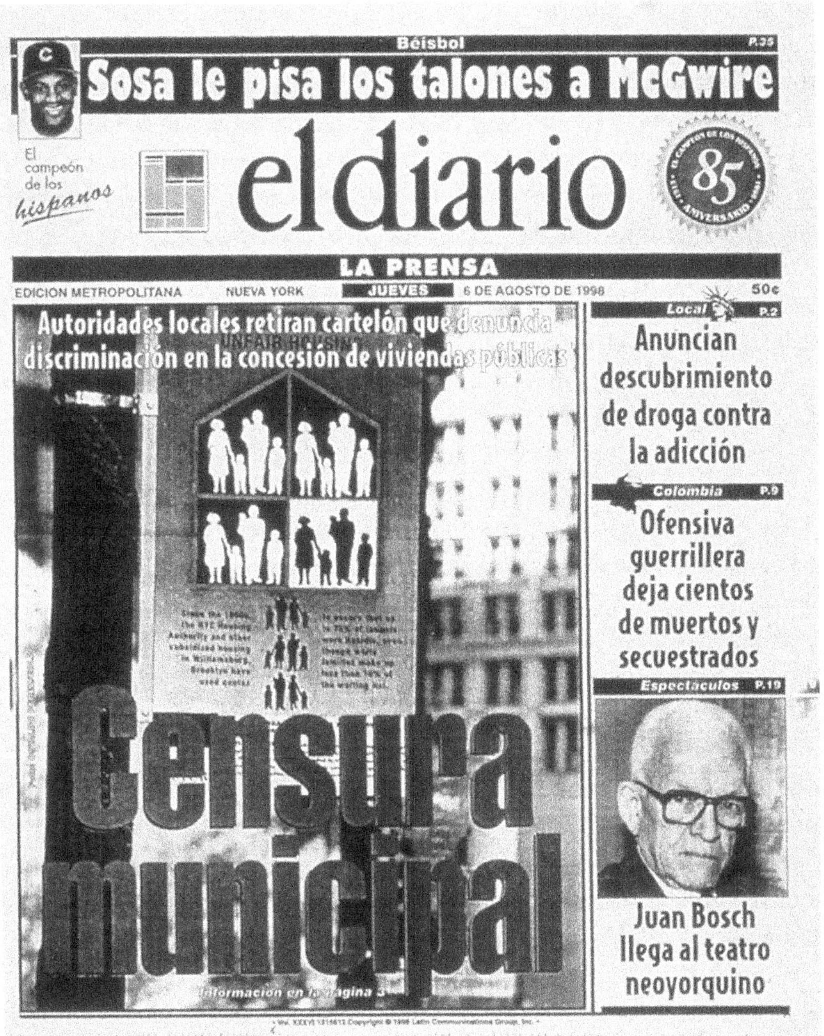

Figure 19 Cover of *El Diario* newspaper showing Marina Gutierrez's controversial REPOhistory street sign, which focused on a quota-system regulating public housing by race that favored white residents and was illegally removed from public display by local politicians, 1998

(Photo G. Sholette Archive)

looked, the more I saw. Quaint cafés replaced actual coffee shops. Futuristic bars and art galleries took over food processing and light industrial shops. An ersatz cosmopolitanism was everywhere and the millennium was a part of this larger whole that involved wiping clean not merely the physical traces of the past, but its memories. What filled up the ensuing breach were artful surrogates and clever replicas of a city that no one had ever lived in but that nevertheless looked strangely familiar. Certainly it is easier to see this in retrospect, but the Millennium campaign signaled the start of an entirely new era in the administration of free market urban renewal. More abstract, more inspired, more creative. The question I wanted to answer most, then and now, is whose minds the hotel chain's marketers hoped to, well, gentrify, and what ghosts they sought to keep at bay?

It was the artists collective known as REPOhistory that provided the key to unlocking this mystery, but its startling solution, like Poe's purloined letter, turns out to have been right in front of me all along.

Located on West 44th Street, the Millennium Premier Hotel stands in a once largely Irish and working-class neighborhood, formerly known as Hell's Kitchen but re-christened with the sanitary-sounding moniker "Clinton" by real estate speculators in the 1980s. This new Times Square is no longer the porn playground of the fiscal crisis 1970s. It has been rehabilitated: safe for families, safe for business, efficiently emptied of homeless people and sundry other uninvited sorts. In May, 1998, however, a metal street sign appears outside the Millennium. The sign is flagged off of a lamppost, meters away from the hotel's tastefully subdued, black marble façade. Mounted low enough for passersby to read, its text begins portentously: "What is now the Millennium Broadway Hotel used to be the site of 4 buildings including an SRO [single room occupancy] hotel that provided badly needed housing for poor New Yorkers …"

Artist and architect William Menking designed the plaque to look like a busy montage of newspaper clippings. The story of the hotel's less than tranquil past continues in bold type:

In 1984, New York City passed a moratorium on the alteration of hotels for the poor. Hours before the moratorium was to go into effect, developer Harry Macklowe had the 4 buildings demolished without obtaining demolition permits, and without turning off water and gas lines into the buildings. NYC officials declared, "It is only a matter of sheer luck that there was no gas explosion." Attempts to bring criminal charges against Macklowe for these actions were not successful. Macklowe built a luxury hotel on the site, then lost it to the current owners. The demolition of hotels for the poor during the 1970s and 1980s added to the city's growing homeless population. While streets of the "new" Times Square seem paved with gold—for many they have literally become a home.

Like the materialization of an army of Dickensian apparitions, the Millennium/Macklowe sign was one of 20 temporary historical markers specifically sited around New York that made up the public art project *Civil Disturbances: Battles for Justice in New York City*. Sponsored by New York Lawyers for the Public Interest (NYLPI) and produced by the art and activist group REPOhistory, its aim was to publicly landmark legal cases in which civil rights were extended to disenfranchised peoples. The content of the signs ranged from the famous *Brown vs. the Board of Education* desegregation case to the first woman firefighter sworn into service in New York City. Others, however, pointed to occasions when the law had failed to protect as promised and Menking's sign was in this category. Initially, for a time the city tried to stop REPOhistory from installing *Civil Disturbances*. After weeks of legal maneuvers however, the signs went up from spring 1998 to late winter 1999. Nevertheless, right from the start several signs vanished after installation. Menking's was among them.

Responding to an inquiry, the Millennium freely admitted having its staff confiscate the legally permitted artwork. They even returned it to the group. However, along with the returned sign came a letter threatening legal action if any attempt was made to reinstall it. The grounds? REPOhistory was damaging hotel business. It seems the return of an inopportune past can prove a powerful trigger, revealing hidden ideological tendencies in what appears otherwise to be a purely market-driven process of privatization and gentrification. After considerable debate that internally split REPOhistory roughly along lines of activists versus artists, Menking's sign was reinstalled, but now at a greater distance from the hotel. And, despite further threats, the sign stayed in place, the project's permit ran its course, and neither side took legal action. It is five years on. Aside from this text and other scattered citations, Macklowe's "midnight demolition" is forgotten along with those he cruelly displaced. At the tranquil oasis in old Hell's Kitchen stylish guests still sip wine, discuss art and continue to manufacture content for the information economy.

All of this is familiar now: the 1990s affection for the 1920s and pre-crash 1930s, its weird merger of avant-garde aesthetics, high fashion and post-Fordist management theory all dolled-up in a neo-modernist longing for limitless progress. So what if the occasional act of terror was, and remains, indispensable to make it all seem real? Why dwell on conflict? If the creative class has supplanted the traditional laboring class in many places it has done so by greeting capital as potential equal, not as adversary. Winners are admired. Losers, on the other hand, are truly abject, lacking the aptitude to become exploiters themselves. Asserting a collective disarray, an enduring ahistoricity and a belief they have transcended labor/management antagonisms, creative workers think they can even avoid being exploited in the long run because their big, table-turning breakthrough is always just around the corner, always about to make that longed-for reservation at the swanky Millennium tower a reality.

Anyway, it's 2004, and billionaires abound. According to Forbes' recent survey they number a record 587.[1] Still, it's difficult not to notice a connection between this fact and the new economy, with its deregulated markets, rampant privatization, decaying worker protection and widening gap between rich and poor. Nor are the super-rich all petroleum refiners and armament producers. Many belong to the so-called creative class. Among those joining the ten-figure income bracket include the rags-to-riches writer of Harry Potter stories, J.K. Rowling; Google creators Sergey Brin and Larry Page; and Gap clothing designer Michael Ying. So why am I still surprised when I walk down formerly forbidding streets to see such upscale consumption? Designer outlets, smart eateries, bars radiant with youthful crowds, and taxis shuttling celebrants to and fro. Block after block the scene resembles a single, unending cocktail party strung like carnival lights up and down nearby 7th and 8th avenues. Between these cheerful stations other men and women, mostly in their forties and fifties, haunt the shadows, gathering glass and metal recyclables from public waste bins. Certainly losers can't harm you. But what about ghosts?

I enter bar "X": its ambience probably not much different from bars in the Millennium New York, or Millennium Shanghai, or Millennium London. I shout for a dry, gin Martini over the mechanically generated industrial music. (A cartoon thought-bubble appears, "Am I the only person in here with a beard?")[2] My mind returns to REPOhistory and its altruistic necromancy some six years earlier. "If the enemy wins, not even the dead will be safe," Walter Benjamin once declared.[3] Not safe from whom? Perhaps it was the noise and the alcohol, but a surprising correlation asserts itself. REPOhistory was part of the creative class. While its objectives were different, REPOhistory, like RTmark, The Yes Men and similar artistic agitators made use of available technologies and rhetorical forms to reach the same erudite consumer-citizens this swanky bar hoped to attract. The Millennium had been correct all along: we were the competition. With a little toning down of its righteous antagonism REPOhistory could have even taken its place among the web designers, dressmakers, MTV producers and other content providers of the new, immaterial economy. And come to think of it, right before the group folded it was increasingly being asked to travel outside to this or that city or town and install public markers about the quaint olden times; the local barber shop, the saloon, the red-light district and parade grounds. I had indeed found the enemy: it was me.

Like forgotten letters in some dimly lit archive, those not immediately part of the radical shift in the means of production remain out of sight, out of mind, fleeing from demolitions, downsizings and sometimes rummaging for cans. Not that this zone of dark matter was not always present and surrounding the upwardly mobile types such as the Millennium crowd. What is new, however, is the way this far larger realm of unrealized potential can gain access to most of the means of expression deployed by the burgeoning consciousness industry—that ubiquitous spectacle essential to the maintenance of global capitalism. By the same token, the so-called "insiders" might, if circumstances permit, decide to cast their collective lot in with the losers and the ghosts. REPOhistory et al. prove it can happen. Because even the new creative class, with its 80-hour work-week and multiple jobs has a fantasy, one half-remembered perhaps and a bit mad, yet still evident in times of stress and economic uncertainty. It goes like this: the bartenders and the brass polishers and cooks, the laundresses and bell hops throw down their aprons and spatulas to join in mutinous celebration with artists, web designers and musicians. Raiding the wine cellar, they open up all 33 executive-style conference rooms, set up a free health clinic in the lobby, transform the hotel into an autonomous broadcasting tower and party in a universe of creative dark matter.

I finish my drink and return home to wrap up the essay I promised the fine, creative folks at *Mute* magazine.

6

Occupology, Swarmology, Whateverology: The City of (Dis)Order Versus the People's Archive[*]

Figure 20 The People's Library, Occupy Wall Street (OWS), Zuccotti Park, NYC, October 1, 2011
(Photo G. Sholette)

I

The archive, with its icy temperature and motionless repose, may seem like an unlikely place to begin thinking about Occupy Wall Street (OWS), a dynamic and still-unfolding phenomenon (in November, 2011) whose precise nature appears impossible to determine, let alone file away like a

[*] This chapter was first published in 2012.

stack of dog-eared documents. Unlikely, if we approach the idea of the archive as a physical collection located in a specific time and place, or as a set of historical documents that uphold this or that interpretive school. But what if we invoke something like an archival agency, something that now and then animates the *longue durée* of resistance "from below." After all, things have changed since we witnessed the power-scrubbing of Zuccotti Park's People's Library and the mulching of the encampment's 100-page opus of dissent written on corrugated scraps of cardboard and inverted pizza boxes, some torn, trimmed, or simply folded down into manageable dimensions for extended protest.[1] We witnessed the demolition as an echo of the Baghdad library's destruction eight years earlier in 2003, when US and UK troops stood by as that archive was reduced to ashy pulp. It is this we must grapple with and theorize, this residue that authorities determined to be expendable, or even threatening, even if such engagement takes us places we would, under other circumstances, prefer to avoid. (For, after all, doesn't the act of conquest demand the erasure, in whole or part, of an enemy's communal identity, just as resistance centers on defending or recreating the archive?)

OWS has an odor. Its lustful, repetitious and messy imagination is articulated not only through fat felt markers on tent flaps and recycled materials, but also on naked bodies, and on moving and dancing bodies, as well as the multicellular superorganism known as the General Assembly. Still, to describe this as an archive—or *swarmchive*—is to suggest that OWS is more than an accumulation of conceptual, biological and material textures. It is also something being written, call it a promissory note, an obligation to a future reader from a place already dislocated in time (though admittedly aided by time-bending cybertechnologies like YouTube and Twitter). Not what does, but what will, the archive mean, Derrida once asked, to which he then replied: "We will only know tomorrow. Perhaps."[2] Tomorrow began at 1:00 a.m. on November 15, 2011 for OWS, the hour of Zuccotti Park's brutal erasure on orders given police by Mayor Michael Bloomberg. The NYPD raid seemed to express something else. Call it a repulsion toward damp, cardboardy smells and commingled sweat, or a fear of the breathy exhalations emanating from the People's Microphone, with its mandatory intervals of listening and hearing, and its uncanny pantomime of mechanical apparatus as if some inert thing were being jolted back to life. But perhaps most unsettling of all was the way OWS established a link with the dispossessed and discarded homeless at the very center of private real estate and finance capital, a tactic Mike Davis perceptively contrasted recently to the university sit-ins of his generation in the 1960s that, while certainly confrontational, nevertheless remained bound up within less contested academic spaces.[3] It seems that when today's *creatives* rebel, they take no hostages; they make no demands.

So there it was, occupied Zuccotti Park, filling up, hour after hour, with multiple signs of urban dispossession and homelessness, from sleeping bags to makeshift shelters, virtually everything that the "quality-of-life" city detested about the vanquished liberal welfare city, and everything it wanted to forget, including the drifters and hustlers, addicts and graffiti taggers who are nevertheless continually generated by its deregulatory policies.[4] There was no bold objective, such as forcing ROTC (Reserve Officer Training Corps) off campus, or establishing a Black studies program. Instead, facing inward, the OWS General Assembly painstakingly constructed systems of communication, grew antennae, spawned internal laws and methods of governance, all the while appearing from the outside to be so much dead capital, a homeless hive of unemployed kids with too much time on their (jazz) hands, growing, festering, like a blot or a bruise, directly on the belly of the global finance leviathan. Is it any wonder city patriarchs sent police to punish Richard Florida's children turned warrior class?

II

"Leave us alone!" asserts the towheaded cadre of mind-melded children in the 1960 British science-fiction film *Village of the Damned.*[5] Mysteriously born all at once to the unimpregnated women of a rural English hamlet, the children possess collective powers of telepathy and worse. They also have an enormous appetite for knowledge. A professor played by George Sanders, the one human they tolerate and who serves as their teacher, eventually destroys them in a suicide attack. But even as the final credits roll, we never fully understand who, or what, they were. We never learn what they were after.

III

Police, not protesters, were visible on day one of Occupy Wall Street, September 17, 2011. They massed in all directions, ringing Wall Street, shielding storefronts, securing Citibank, Chase, Wells Fargo, and Morgan. And then there were those two, slightly chagrined officers standing watch over *Charging Bull,* the bellicose bronze sculpture that dominates the northern edge of Bowling Green Park. An irony likely lost on most who passed by is that artist Arturo DiModica's giant bovine was an unannounced "gift" that he dropped in December, 1989 to lift Wall Street's downcast spirits after the crash of 1987. Initially seized by police as illegal street art, the statue was soon born again as a 7,000 lb (3.5 tons) photo-op relished by tourists, filmmakers, city boosters and anti-capitalist protesters.

One intrepid demonstrator stood out on the first day. She carried, sandwich-board style, a photographic reproduction of Damien Hirst's *For the Love of God*, the diamond-spattered platinum skull allegedly valued at over £50 million. No other statement or slogan was present, as if the no-longer "Y" British artist's profligate *memento mori* was the indisputable portrait of our epoch. But only a few days into the occupation at nearby Zuccotti Park—the privately owned public space that demonstrators ultimately settled into after failing to take possession of Wall Street proper—a functioning commonwealth had germinated. It was complete with daily meetings aimed at self-governance; food and trash services; recycled gray-water treatment systems; a generator-powered digital media station; and an expanding collection of books and publications dubbed the "People's Library," nestled in rows of boxes with handwritten labels like International Relations, Music, Religion, Fiction, Non-fiction, Feminism, and Racial Justice. According to movement librarians, an estimated 5,000 volumes were located at Zuccotti Park prior to the NYPD raid of November 15.[6] The encampment also gave life to dozens of smaller subdivisions, including Jail Support, Medics, Direct Action Painters and, one of the largest, Arts and Culture, with its own subdivisions, including Arts and Labor, Alternative Economies, and Occupy Museums. Among other immediate necessities is restoring knowledge of past attempts at organizing cultural workers such as Art Workers' Coalition, Artists Meeting for Cultural Change, Political Art Documentation/Distribution (PAD/D) and Group Material. Much of this history has been shorn from the record to form a missing mass or cultural dark matter.[7] The articulation of this shadow history is now taking place through teach-ins, email exchanges and archival websites, all of which are, so far, beyond the reach of police.

IV

"What do they want?" demands the mainstream media. OWS has no response. No policies, no demands, and only a stated desire to be left alone. "The 1% is just beginning to understand that the reason Occupy Wall Street makes no demands is because we aren't talking to them. The 99% are speaking and listening to each other."[8] Zuccotti Park: *Das Unheimliche.*

V

Scrawled dollar signs, credit cards, monstrous octopuses, mutated American flags: like pages torn from a faded copy of *The New Masses* (rather than *Adbusters*), Zuccotti Park's artistic iconography was replete with anti-capitalist slogans, clenched fists and top-hatted millionaires. But this time the slogans were a great deal cheekier than those printed in the radical leftist magazine of the 1920s and 1930s, and the fists were attached to people wearing Guy Fawkes *V for Vendetta* masks rather than muscular "workers." Meanwhile, the millionaire—pulled down from his pedestal, bearded and broke—did not refer to the sketchbooks of communist artists William Gropper or Hugo Gellert, but was appropriated straight from Parker Brother's Monopoly board game. One sign simply implored "Occupy through Art." Yet, despite the twenty-first-century self-consciousness, OWS released a repertoire of protest tropes that, like a grammar of dissent waiting in the wings, came to the fore as the encampment participants discovered they were legally bound by New York City ordinances to pre-electronic forms of protest. Thus there were citations, statements, manifestos and entire letters directed to the public. "Did you lose your home? Wall Street stole from you." One text with blue-on-red writing proclaimed tragic loss as a leftover handhold from what was once a cardboard box floated off to the side like an errant exclamation mark. Along with the ubiquitous beige of cardboard signage there were silk-screened T-shirts, a few oil paintings, and profession-ally designed typographic posters by *Adbusters*, the Vancouver-based culture-jamming magazine that first called for a Wall Street occupation which officially began on September 17, 2011. Shepard Fairey, of *Andre the Giant* stencil-art fame, morphed his own controversial Barack Obama election poster "Hope" into an explicit reference to Anonymous, the online hacktivist entity strongly associated with new forms of digital civil disobedience. But the President wearing a Guy Fawkes mask with the tagline "We Are the Hope" simply did not go over well with some OWS organizers. Fearing that Fairey's graphic promoted links to the Democratic Party, the former street artist was taken to task and asked to revise his design in what amounted to a series of online studio critique-sessions: long-distance learning, OWS-style. "While it definitely looks cool, whether intended or not, this sends a clear message that Obama is co-opting OWS."[9] The movement may not have demands, but it is exceedingly conscious of its image, as befits a twenty-first-century rebellion.

VI

*I'm not a smooth writer and am barely managing to focus now on something
i need to finish* [writes the Egyptian artist Maha Maamoun in an email]
*but in general, positions, attitudes and temperaments are changing here
with every headline. its a constant tug and pull. a constant recalibration of
expectations. many players rising that were not known before, and many
known ones falling. its interesting to see this "organic" process play out. its
not easy. every detail is a battle … it's definitely taking a huge amount of
time away from work. most of our time is spent following the news in every
form. resulting eventually in loss of concentration and burnout. personally,
i feel that previous drives in my work have been halted or changed. there is
some kind of rupture but its not clear where exactly and what it will lead
to. result is a need to be quiet and research and find one's (new) center
of gravity … i think activists and artists, and those who are both, are all
putting in time and effort when and how they can. and since this is a
prolonged situation, it is understandable that participants come in and out
of action depending on their ability and time. burnout is experienced by all,
and thus the need to take time out in order to be able to come back in. that
is to say, divisions of roles are not so clear.*[10]

If a real-world crisis politicizes artists and cultural workers, sometimes to
the point that they abandon their studios and galleries to engage in agitation,
organizing, the production of ephemeral street art or direct action, then is
this to be understood as an aesthetic lacuna similar to a mason throwing
cobblestones at soldiers, or a seamstress smuggling food to demonstrators in the hem of her skirt? Or is art's occasional venture into radicalism
something else altogether, perhaps an inescapable phase of aesthetic
investigation that ironically must jettison aesthetic investigation itself (or
temporarily seem to discard it)? Must it be the case that, when artists take
their turn on the barricades, along with the partisans and oppressed, the
dispossessed and the evicted, they are there because, aside from playing *for*
the enemy, they simply have nowhere else to go? Or are they, along with
the practice of aesthetics itself, a kind of blockage or lesion found within
society's disciplinary structures, only functioning fully as a grammar of
dissent in times of crisis?

VII

I visited the encampment again on October 1. Immediately following the
evening's General Assembly, OWS protesters streamed out of Zuccotti Park

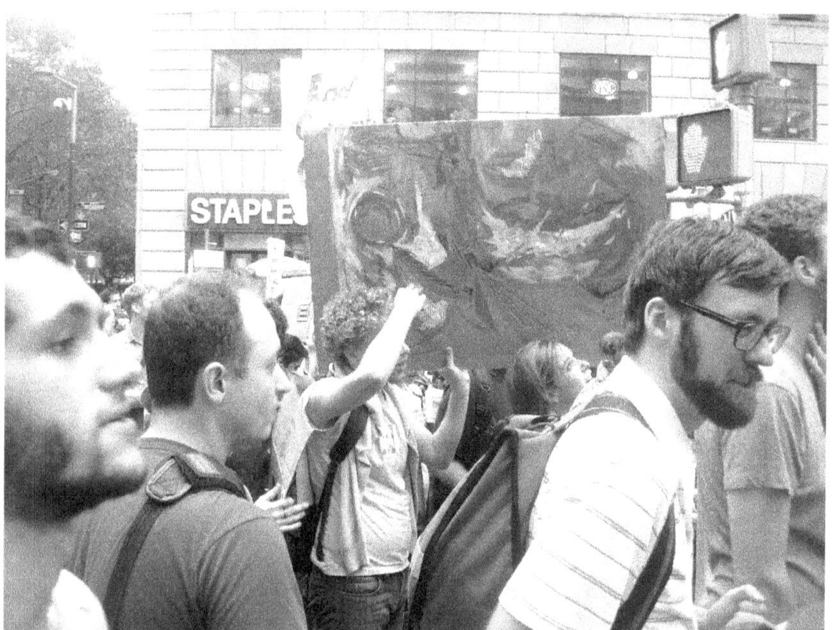

Figure 21   A painting on cardboard carried aloft up Broadway by OWS Zuccotti Park demonstrators, October 1, 2011

(Photo G. Sholette)

and swarmed up Broadway. Within the torrent of handmade protest placards—"Workers Rights are Human Rights," "Jail Bankers, Not Protesters," "Occupy Everything"—I spotted a trio of art students (they must have been art students), who lofted what looked like an abstract painting over their heads. Watery, colored shapes have soaked into a rectangle of beige cardboard. In truth, it was an elegantly odd picket sign that looked a bit like a DIY Arshile Gorky, and was oddly fragile, bobbing up and down in the crowd. A short time later OWS flocked onto the Brooklyn Bridge, where 700 demonstrators were arrested. God only knows what became of the corrugated Gorky.

VIII

Take another look at the infamous University of California, Davis, pepper-spraying video on YouTube. Watch it to the end to see the power reversal that follows the abusive violence. Students surround police. After the crowd uses the People's Microphone, one student begins to chant, "You can go." Others gradually follow in unison, "You can go." "You can go." "You can go." Like a colony of insects guided by pheromones, the police turn and march away. Applause.

IX

Capitalism, like nature, has no "history," hisses the ghost of Milton Friedman from the great beyond. Perhaps this explains why the *city of disorder*—Alex S. Vitale's sarcastic moniker for post-Giuliani New York— loathes the archive. It's too ungainly for a town that is always investing in its present, a city that worships the erotics of gentrification and delights in the joyful liquidation of memory. In truth, this state of affairs may have been perfectly acceptable for a generation of precarious workers, artists among them. Until recently, the creative "cognitariat" demanded neither a past nor a future, but only an opportunity to be productive all the time, 24/7, as a mode of life. That was tolerable, until capital placed its boot on the big hand of time. Suddenly both history and hope lurched into view, and memory, an archaic vestige, was foisted onto them like a millstone. Liberating the future becomes the logic of the archive, and perhaps this is why the political scientist Jason Adams argued that OWS is "increasingly complicating static images of space: it is, in short, occupying time."[11] If encampments at Zuccotti Park and other squares and public spaces around the globe marked nothing else, they marked the lawlessness of the law, or what passes for law. The real crisis is less about finance than about the social ruins that are no longer allegorical memories archaically dotting a forward-looking, modernist landscape, such as Walter Benjamin held dear. Nor are they merely ungovernable disaster zones or self-contained spaces of decay within stateless states and collapsed cities. In short, ruins have become our destiny. Do you remember Occupied Berkeley and its revolt of anointed intellectual heirs decrying their education as a necrosocial graveyard "of liberal good intentions, of meritocracy, opportunity, equality, democracy?"[12] Despite batons, pepper spray, rubber bullets, buckshot, tear gas, polycarbonate shields, orange dragnets and military sound amplifiers, what has been occupied is the long duration of resistance: Trenton's Army of Unoccupation, the Flint Michigan sit-down strike, the Woolworth cafeteria sit-in strike, Berkeley's "plant-in" at People's Park, an attempted occupation at New Hampshire's Seabrook Nuclear Power Plant, the Seneca Women's Peace Encampment, Tompkins Square "Guilianiville" in New York, as well as Seattle, Genoa, Iran, Tunisia, Egypt, Greece, Spain, Wisconsin, Wall Street—all impure, repetitive, and often self-mythologizing, occasionally sentimental, sometimes resentful, even reactionary. It is the murmur of the *other* archive, with its excesses, and magic gift-economies, its aesthetics of attraction, and its reanimation of dead time. Now there is only *after OWS*, no longer is there a *prior to*.

X

Immediately after the police raided Occupy Oakland, a protester spoke to a radio reporter and assured her that OWS had been dispersed for now, but would soon collect again in other locations, "like water." Spores, buds, mushrooms, swarms, rhizomes, air, water; the swarmchive has emerged as a thing that seems to ask: What Am I? The answer is very simple: You Are the Swarmchive. You Are the Social.

7
Art After Gentrification

Young creative professionals who operate in these collective spaces are blurring the lines between commercial and non-commercial work, shifting from one to the other, depending upon the project.[1]

The ability of art to "accumulate" all social phenomena as instances of itself comes to resemble what capital does, in its self-expanding movement as the automatic subject.[2]

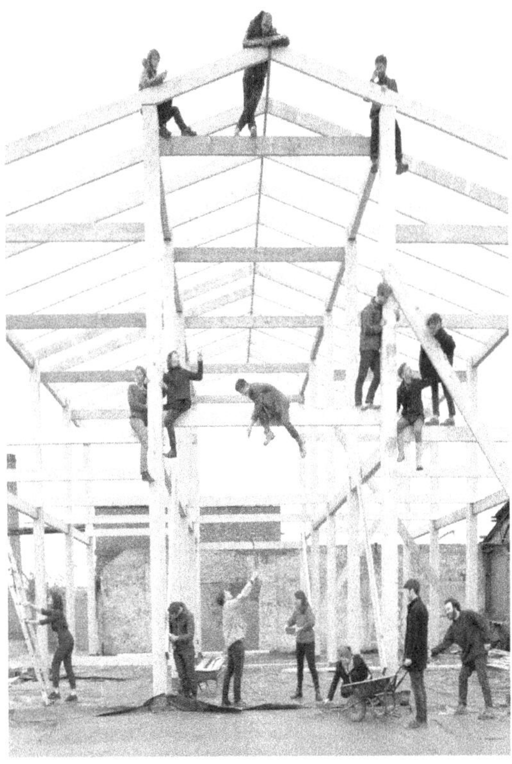

Figure 22 Assemble collective's Yardhouse studios for London creatives under construction, 2015
(Courtesy Assemble)

The practice of repurposing resources that already exist—versus innovating or engineering new ones—is an area of significant overlap between contemporary art and twenty-first-century capitalism. Low-risk and relatively low-cost, the process of creative reuse generates fantastic value-adding possibilities. Or so it seems. Where a defunded inner-city neighborhood previously lay in tatters, a rising spirit of self-repair and hope now emerges, and where once the overlooked working class was forced to devise survival tactics along the edges of formal capitalist markets, they are now part of the urban "placemaking" paradigm, if not in the flesh, then at least evoked in post-industrial, upcycled decor. At the same time, "change agents" orchestrate redundant populations (viewed from capital's perspective) and discarded assets (unrealized profits) into art projects that symbolically resolve decades of racial and class-based maltreatment by police and abandonment by city planners in post-industrial regions such as Toxteth, Pittsburgh and Chicago. Just as real estate speculators and city planners discovered the value of culture for upgrading urban infrastructures, so too have a growing number of contemporary artists learned to mimic and perhaps intentionally mistranslate neoliberal enterprise culture into a repertoire of ex-onomic tools and "art+realty" hybrids that game the system against itself. Complex mutual strategies of imitation and mimicry between art and neoliberalism rediscover, in strange new forms, the contradictions that underlie this phase of capitalist development. As social regenerative art projects mobilize underutilized workers, for example, labor conflicts that were once identified with the economic sphere emerge within art. Real workers, even when their labor results in art, have a tendency to resist and push back in search of their own interests and security, sometimes even seeking recognition for their own creativity, as we shall see. One aim of this chapter, therefore, is to explore the place of gentrification in a *bare art world*. The mainstream embrace of socially regenerative art practices may, sometimes, turn the system against itself, but it is by no means immune from discord; especially because the logic of economic crisis permeates everywhere, even the boundary between art and life.

Assemble

Sixteen cosmopolitan hipsters lean against, squat atop or straddle across the skeletal wood frame of a three-story building in early construction stage. Wearing subdued street garb rather than sensible work clothing, one passes a square point shovel to another who dangles overhead, three engage in conversation, still another is steadying a ladder though no one seems to be on it, and high above on a roof joist sits a lone figure gazing into her mobile. None engage in actual work (why is a tool used for shoveling gravel and soil handed up?), instead they mimic acts of physical labor. The measured spacing between each of the 16 also implies a mode of loose collectivism particular to our time, as if those present were a flash mob responding to a text message: 'meet at such and such location, pick up a tool and/or find a place to sit, pose and wait for the photographer to arrive.'[3] Note the remnants of a damaged brick wall visible in the distance? This is definitely not a community barn-raising in some wind-swept prairie, but a redevelopment project located in a neglected inner city. Though it could be set in numerous inner-city regions or forgotten neighborhoods abandoned to ultra-free-market neglect the photo was taken in a former industrial area in London known as Sugar Hill Lane, now undergoing "regeneration." And the image is popular. As of this writing some 5,000 websites host digital copies of the image, which makes it "viral" by art world standards.[4] Its popularity is simple. We are looking at the London-based collective Assemble, a self-described cadre of designers, builders, artists and organizers who in December, 2015 were awarded Tate's prestigious Turner Prize for contemporary art.[5] For some, including members of Assemble, this art world recognition came as a surprise. For others, including those who wish to fortify a link between urban regeneration and social practice art, it was all but inevitable.

Assemble's Turner award primarily honored another inner-city regeneration project involving residents of Granby Four Streets, an ethnically mixed area of Toxteth, Liverpool. For decades, inhabitants organized themselves into DIY work committees and guerrilla gardening teams to repair damage left over from a racially charged, anti-police rebellion some 30 years earlier.[6] "After the riots an invisible red line was drawn around the area," explained a resident of Granby of 40 years, before describing an "unspoken policy of no maintenance and no investment."[7] Successive neoliberal governments, nominally right- and left-wing, continued the policy and refused to address Granby's plight, actively disinvesting in the neighborhood for decades. As the recently released papers of a former Thatcherite minister admitted with regard to the government's official practice of inner-city abandonment, Toxteth represented a "tactical retreat, a combination of economic erosion and encouraged evacuation."[8] Locals fought back with the weapons of the weak, blocking bulldozers and planting vegetables in the rubble, though not always entirely successfully. Some residents gave up and left, but a resistant core remained to establish a Community Land Trust (CLT) in 2011, giving Granby greater control over municipal funds and guidelines. Two years later, social investment company Steinbeck Studio Limited commissioned Assemble to develop a social regeneration project with the Granby Four Streets CLT, restoring to date a ten-unit section of building stock with plans for a winter garden and local artisanal cooperatives in the development stage.

Comparable stories can be identified across Europe and North America, where disinvestment in former working-class areas has been a key consequence of neoliberal reforms. Deserted by policy makers, the residents of marginalized zones develop their own micro-political agency pivoting on a DIY skillset of salvaging, recycling, grassroots entrepreneurship and forms of direct resistance that sometimes target both conservative and liberal policies (especially given that for many years neoliberal agendas have dominated both the UK Labour Party and the US Democratic Party, although battles within these parties, involving Corbyn and Sanders respectively, represent challenges to this alleged *fait accompli*). Granby Four Streets is one of many examples that include neighborhood improvement projects, homespun cultural programs, and cooperative food/urban gardening projects, as well as tactics for evading eviction. Though each of them is defined by its particular context, comparable examples can be identified across the world, including the Detroit Black Community Food Security Network; the Focus E15 Mums in Newham, East London; Radical Housing Network in Tower Hamlets, London; Experimental Station and Reuse Center on Chicago's South Side; the Brooklyn Anti-gentrification Network; Baltimore Development Cooperative; or the Kaptaruny Art Village where sculptor Artur Klinau is transforming an abandoned town in rural Belarus into a literal "Straw Village" for himself and his artist friends.

While some of this activity involves artists or finds support from internationally based non-governmental organizations and even occasionally from enlightened municipal governments, in large part these grassroots rejuvenation and resistance projects are carried out through the pooled labor of local residents. It comes as no surprise, therefore, that one obvious solution to governmental neglect is found at the heart of the very same regions that capitalism withdrew from as it sought to stabilize itself following the economic collapse and racial and class-based rebellions of the 1970s and early 1980s. This socioeconomic self-repair prototype appears to be voluntary, but it is in fact virtually obligatory, forming the coercive rationale for twenty-first-century, top-down forms of "creative" urban redevelopment such as "Placemaking," a quasi-privatized initiative popular with cultural foundations and municipal agencies, as well as real estate developers.[9] The social practice art template fits here perfectly, and seems to be a win-win for all concerned. City managers leverage low-cost cultural and community assets to solve seemingly intractable infrastructure problems; blighted neighborhoods are made livable again; and artists get an opportunity to apply their talents to real-world problems outside the solitude of their studios. Typical of the enthusiasm for "arts-initiated revitalization," a 2010 National Endowment for the Arts (NEA) White Paper described job creation and the reuse of "vacant and underutilized land, buildings, and infrastructure."[10] And while it raises the issue of gentrification and displacement of long-term residents, the solution offered aimed to retain affordable spaces for members of the creative class, without a single proposal for shielding minority and low-income residents from permanent expulsion.

Like the US, the UK Arts Council has promoted the Creative Industries approach since the end of the Cold War in the 1990s but, as Josephine B. Slater and Anthony Iles also point out in their critique of regeneration art projects, "state-led regeneration proper developed in the wake of the inner city riots which erupted across Britain's cities in 1981, in London (Brixton), Liverpool (Toxteth), Birmingham (Handsworth) and Leeds (Chapeltown)."[11] The regeneration efforts that were made, of course, need to be understood in the context of a widespread post-industrial decline, especially in the north of England, which is widely credited as a key factor in the outcome of the Brexit vote to leave the European Union. Whether state-led regeneration, or creative placemaking, has ever been anything more than a token gesture is a moot point. Similar observations could be made about the South Bronx, Detroit, Baltimore and parts of Los Angeles where creative placemaking is being tested out or is already under-way in communities dominated by people of color. Irrespective of the effectiveness of these interventions when set against the structural tendencies that exist within capitalism, however, the 2015 Turner Prize Jury should be understood as a tribute to the Granby citizens themselves, including their bottom-up form of self-governance, which managed to salvage a story of hope from the maelstrom of neglect and disinvestment. This story is easily lost in the arguments about the extent to which Assemble's work is art: the decision to award the prize to Assemble certainly highlighted differences of opinion among artists, and shows that the contemporary art world's so-called social turn—as Claire Bishop pronounced it a decade ago—has arrived on the doorstep of the mainstream art establishment.[12]

Social practice art confronts us with a disarming sincerity that is refreshingly at odds with the typically contrived affect of the contemporary art world. As Turner Prize jury member Alistair Hudson explains his decision to award the prize to Assemble, the collective is "not in the hierarchical structure of the art world [and] not about making art forms but about changing the way the world works, making the world a better place, making life more artful."[13] The power of this William Morris-like aesthetic affirmation radiates back into the collective. In a profound moment of de-alienation, one member of Assemble states about her experience in Toxteth that, "the sense of community is much stronger than anywhere I've ever experienced in my whole life."[14] This same unassuming euphoria can also be seen in Assemble's group portrait in which their neatly choreographed bodies feign blue-collar toil while playfully making allusion to nineteenth-century forms of communal work. This curious, even jocular, detachment from "labor," underscores the group's blithe relationship to the complex political stakes involved in what they do. After all, theirs is not an image mocking work itself, but neither is it a classic depiction of nineteenth- or early twentieth-century emancipated socialist labor either. The group's ironic workerism is more likely a form of collectivism after modernism, as Blake Stimson and I termed this phenomenon, which is to say, it is communalism grounded in plasticity, unity founded on difference.[15] One might even describe it as "whatever" collectivism in so far as social solidarity is staged via a networked aesthetic, more than it is through physical togetherness or the immediate relationship to work.

Still, there is no satisfactory escape from the contradictions bound up with contemporary high culture, especially under present conditions of *bare art*, as discussed in Part I of this volume. This is a post-avant-garde situation robbed of deep historical resources, and devoid of future utopias, with only the cunning technology of reuse available. Not surprisingly, one of its primary competencies is superimposing a certain spontaneous naïveté onto clever cosmopolitanism, precisely what we see manifest in Assemble's mass-selfie. Whatever real gains it may achieve, social regeneration art is tailor-made for a non-revolutionary now-time, covering up the effects of crisis with the infinite return of the same.

Theaster Gates

Perhaps no artist embodies this curious blend of urban sophistication and uninhibited enthusiasm better than the virtuosic Theaster Gates. Like Assemble, Gates ducks the label "artist" (or at least he does some of the time), and yet like Assemble he is the recipient of a distinguished art world prize, the Artes Mundi. Known for leveraging sizable sums of public and private capital, Gates purchases and renovates vacant real estate on

Chicago's fiscally depressed and primarily Black South Side. Gates casually and somewhat credulously sets aside the label artist in order to describe his work as "practising things—practising life, practising creation."[16] His reputation is embellished with a delirious combination of real and fictional monikers such as designer, architect, social worker, archivist, and urban planner, with the last of these listed on his actual curriculum vitae along with ceramicist.[17] An African American originally from the Near West Side of Chicago, Gates has rehabilitated some 32 abandoned South Side homes in what he calls the Dorchester Project. Most of this work is carried out under the auspices of his non-profit umbrella organization the Rebuild Foundation. With 2014 assets of about half a million dollars, Rebuild is the quintessential embodiment of a sustainable, artist-driven regeneration enterprise. Its mission statement promises to reactivate "underutilized properties," invest in "creative entrepreneurs" and empower "neighborhood transformation" through artist-driven "Intentional Aesthetics," the latter term a possible tweak on the expression "intentional community."[18] Yet, while this represents Gates's community advocacy, it is a different side of his practice that most distinguishes him from Assemble.

Gates departs from his British counterparts in two fundamental ways. First, his connection to the University of Chicago, where he was appointed Director of the Arts+Public Life initiative in 2011, and, second, via his skillful capitalization of art world prestige and his own ethnic identification, resources mobilized not only for the South Side rejuvenation projects, but also for his individual art practice. By actively repurposing building and industrial materials such as lumber, wooden doors, tar, tires, roofing tiles, furniture, and even decommissioned fire hoses into works of art, Gates is able to sell these mixed-media assemblages for considerable sums of money at the top tier of the global art market while concurrently making reference to African American culture. While Assemble also retails what they call "upcycled" furniture made from urban detritus, so far these pieces have not rocketed to blue chip status; perhaps because not even the Turner Prize can overpower an art collector's preference to possess an individually authored art object. Notwithstanding the recent embrace of socially engaged art, when it comes to commercial investments by wealthy patrons, the art world remains a fundamentally conservative economic system, one that can, however, be repurposed. To whatever degree gambling with art as a financial investment strategy has always been present, playing itself out behind the closed doors of the art world, today there is no concealment needed: intervening within the system is an unabashed hallmark of *bare art*, just as financial scheming is of capitalism in general.

Figure 23   Theaster Gates, *Bank Bond*, limited edition artwork, 2013, marble, 6 1/8 × 8 5/8 × 13/16 in. (15.5 × 21.9 × 2.1 cm) © Theaster Gates. Photo © White Cube (Photo: Ben Westoby)

In 2012 Gates purchased the abandoned Stony Island Savings & Loan bank building from the city of Chicago for $1, repurposing a portion of its marble interior, including material from the water closet, into a limited edition of 100 "Bank Bonds," or more accurately, "Art Bonds." Acid-etched into each sardonic collectable is the motto "In Art We Trust." (Some of the marble came from the bank's urinals, thus reinscribing the Duchampian readymade not only with acid but also a dose of Nietzschean *ressentiment*?)[19] The following year at the Basel Art Fair in Switzerland Gates's White Cube gallery offered the satirical securities for $5,000 a piece: "I found myself with a failed bank, and here I was being invited to Basel, the land where banking never failed. So what did I do? I asked bankers to help me save my bank. That felt poetic."[20]

Gates exhibits a witty, even facetious, disposition towards money, including the question of how it is acquired and what it can do. The capacity to toggle back and forth between a market-based art practice and not-for-profit social entrepreneurship provides Gates with several advantages, including managing multiple taxable income streams and expenses such as his studio of assistants. This same financial *RealARTpolitik* carries over into virtually all of the artist's practices, sometimes appearing in a mischievous form as in the Duchampian "Art Bond" gambit, but at other times taking on a more indignant expression, almost as though one finally catches a glimpse behind the Gates phenomenon of a vexed class and racial frustration at work: "It's unreasonable to think that only collectors should have the luxury to be conscious of that [investment value of the art object], and that if an artist ever became conscious of the economics associated with the art world then they would no longer be pure. That's bullshit."[21]

Much of the power and moral authority of Gates's work derives from its engagement with race: "For as long as I can remember the everyday things of black people have had deep resonance for me ... It's from this place of thankfulness and reverence that I start a more critical examination of how the world sees blackness and, by extension, how the world sees me."[22] The relationship between appearance and identity, especially in the visual art world, is too complex to tackle meaningfully in this chapter except to say that perhaps more than any other frequently cited socially engaged artist Gates's "unapologetically black" (his phrase) practice has singularly rebooted the color spectrum emitted by art as social intervention, permanently altering what African Canadian artist Deanna Bowen calls "optical politics."

What is curious here is that Gates is not the first artist of color to work in the medium of direct social engagement; that distinction typically goes to African American artist Rick Lowe's *Project Row Houses* (1993) that transform abandoned real-estate into art installation, and which is clearly a strong influence on Gates, but also Asian American Mel Chin's *Operation Paydirt* (2006–ongoing), if we stick with the social practice genealogies developed by Tom Finkelpearl, Shannon Jackson, Nato Thompson and Grant Kester, among others, and if we hold to Claire Bishop's 2006 historical bracket for the start of the "social turn."[23] Other precedents also exist in this regard, including Tania Bruguera's *Behavior Art School* (*Cátedra Arte de Conducta*, Havana, Cuba: 2002–2009); Coco Fusco's anti-Guantanamo Prison performance *Bare Life Study* (2005); William Pope.L's interactive cross-state vehicle *Black Factory* (2004); Daniel J. Martinez and VinZula Kara's West Side Chicago protest parade *Consequences of a Gesture* (1993); and also perhaps David Hammons infamous snowball vending action *Bliz-aard Ball Sale* (1983), or Adrian Piper's *Funk Lessons* (1983–1985, though Kester considers the latter more pedagogical than socially partic-ipatory). However, none of these social medium works by artists of color have made "blackness" a topic of discussion for social practice artists to the same degree, and in just a few short years, even before the #BlackLivesMat-ter hashtag went viral in 2013. Perhaps this is because, in a social practice field primarily populated by non-commercial careers, Gates has not shied away from an individual studio practice or from the market, thus bringing him into more eyeball-to-eyeball contact with the dominantly white art world pecking order. Or maybe it is because he has consistently asserted his *otherness* within this supposedly neutral, color-blind framework, as he did in a statement from a 2013 live-blog interview, "I don't have to perform blacker, but that I become blacker in the presence of all you white people."[24] And with regard to the artworks he produces for a largely white art world, "Black art is art that can triple code."[25]

Further complicating the riddle of Gates's meteoric career is that he was almost certainly introduced to the possibilities of material salvaging and creative reuse by fellow South Side (white) artist Dan Peterman. A long-time proponent of recycling who is better known in Europe than in the US, Peterman is also the co-founder of Experimental Station (ES), a mixed-use cultural center or "border institution," as Peterman describes it, where Gates has shared a small studio for the past decade along with a bicycle refurbishing shop, a local farmer's market, a vegan delicatessen and a documentary production studio known as Invisible Institute that was instrumental in forcing the city to release the sequestered dash-cam video of the 2014 police murder of black teenager Laquan McDonald.[26] Peterman owes his own association with the art of recycling to Chicagoan Ken Dunn, a waste reuse maestro who founded the Chicago Resource Center in 1973. Dunn began experimenting with urban sustainability by employing jobless South Side residents picking up discarded cans and bottles. First of its kind in the city, the Center now has over two dozen employees and hosts the Creative Reuse Warehouse where artists, among other reusers, pay modest fees to locate and release the possibilities latent within what Chicago has simply forsaken.[27] Peterman likens the idea of reuse to "a medieval economy or someplace where everything is still in the loop, where everything is being reworked, everything has the potential to be viewed with a new perspective."[28] However, the notion of keeping it small and keeping it local is simply not part of the *bare art* equation, or of an art world intent on unbounded expansion. By contrast, Peterman's recycling loop almost resembles an autonomous gray zone economy: "We can actually seriously build an economy for the city of Chicago based on what are conventionally conceived of as liabilities: all the vacant lots and vacant land, the food waste and yard waste can be turned into valuable compost and turned into farms that can provide materials."[29]

While Peterman and Dunn emphasize sustainable community-oriented economies that attempt to gain some degree of political autonomy, their approach to material reuse differs from Gates in so far as the latter extends his recycling strategies not only into the mainstream art market, using a more or less Duchampian strategy to attract the surplus value of art collectors, but also expands the paradigm into such highly ambitious regeneration undertakings as Dorchester Projects or the Stony Island Savings & Loan library.

Peterman's "recoverable liabilities" include for Gates not only housing stock, but also undervalued and underutilized human capital, thus his direct artistic intervention into the social as a material in its own right. In addition, with some 60 people now in his employ, and the prominent rejuvenation projects as proof, the artist has delivered a significant, though still largely symbolic retort to capital's problem of waste and surplus, material and labor. And, by gaming the autonomy of high art (real or not, artistic autonomy still has cachet in the market), Gates gradually expands his practice beyond its initial locality. While he cut his teeth on Chicago's South Side, the artist now insists his real challenge is "the same as it is in Liverpool, or wherever, it is: what do working people do now the industry has gone?"[30] As a lecturer and policy adviser in the ravaged Mid-West cities of Detroit and Gary, but also the austerity-choked nation of Greece and the racially and class divided city of Bristol, UK, Gates will likely be disseminating his Dorchester Project model far beyond Chicago.

In this broader context, the significance of the 2008 real estate bubble implosion for Gates's practice is impossible to overlook. The artist's first property was purchased with a sub-prime mortgage loan, and when the housing collapse hit Chicago he leveraged additional properties.[31] Simultaneously, post-crash quantitative easing by the US Federal Reserve helped to boost the upper tier of the art market, as historically low interest rates pushed capital towards stocks, but also art, whose notoriously opaque and unregulated market was flooded with cash. This was certainly a key reason why the art market did not collapse along with other high-income investment instruments, and one of the reasons why Gates's individual art practice could operate so effectively: there was stimulus money, guaranteed by the state, surging into the art market.[32] And if all of this peels back a layer or two to Gates's renown it is also important to note that hidden genealogies and economic stimuli are common to the under-theorized, and under-historicized, field of socially engaged art. Neither should this diminish the artist's effort to establish through his own creative reuse activities a Black art consciousness, though it does situate this ambition within a long history of such practices on Chicago's troubled South Side. Because, along with alternative economic experimentation and regeneration projects, this regeneration paradigm also collides with a decades-old, complex history of racial tension between the University of Chicago and the surrounding African-American community: the former consisting of a traditionally white and privileged enclave that for years virtually blockaded its campus from residents of the surrounding low-income African American South Side community. However, as sociologist Julia Rothenberg writes, with the hiring of Gates the university now suddenly appears as "a magnificently generous benefactor and font of support for Black cultural life in the community." Such is *RealARTpolitik* in the creative city.[33] And it is also possible that Gates, as well as other social practice artists such as Conflict Kitchen that I now turn to, really did began their projects by slyly mocking the creative city model itself, only to discover over time that they had become essentially indistinguishable from it.

Conflict Kitchen

An art project that poses as a successful fast-food restaurant in a post-industrial American city may seem like an odd inclusion in this chapter on regenerative social practices, but the creative city must be fed, figuratively, as well as literally, and the consumption of food is, after all, our primary embodied relationship to the abstract forces of social production (Gates has also recently opened up a coffee shop on Chicago's South Side he calls the Currency Exchange Café). Contemporary artists have approached commodification in their work for decades, primarily focusing on issues of fetishization in relation to the work of art itself. Approaching group consumption itself as a site of potential intervention is less typical, though precedents reach back to Rirkrit Tiravanija's gallery-framed curry dinners, or further to the artist-run FOOD restaurant in New York's SoHo art district between 1971 and 1974,[34] but neither Tiravaniga nor FOOD was organized as an entrepreneurial social art project, especially one that could effectively be franchised to other regenerative city settings. In 2010 artists Jon Rubin and Dawn Weleski opened Conflict Kitchen (CK) in Pittsburgh, Pennsylvania, "a take-out eatery that only serves food from countries with which the United States is in conflict."[35] Sometimes described as a "Trojan horse" by founder Rubin, CK specializes in a rotating menu of cuisine from Iran, Venezuela, Cuba, Afghanistan, North Korea, Palestine and, as of this writing, the indigenous nation's alliance of the Haudenosaunee Confederacy: all countries that are in political and/or military conflict with the United States.[36]

According to the project's website, CK operates seven days a week using "the social relations of food and economic exchange to engage the general public in discussions about countries, cultures, and people that they might know little about outside of the polarizing rhetoric of governmental politics and the narrow lens of media headlines." Fulfilling such a solemn mission involves cooking authentically prepared ethnic dishes and serving them in graphically designed informational wrappers that focus on the culture, people and politics of a given adversarial nation. Though CK offers diners a flavorful and inexpensive meal, it also compels patrons into an intimate encounter with their alleged enemies. In other words, there is a mischievous, even ironic dimension to the project's stated ambitions that reminds us that CK is also a work of contemporary art. Location also matters. Twice selected for an All American City Award (by contrast, New York City has never won), Pittsburgh is a small northeastern service-oriented city that nevertheless represents itself as a beer drinking, blue-collar sports town.[37] Pittsburgh is moderate in size and politically liberal in outlook, and CK has naturally attracted a great deal of local media attention. When CK began serving Iranian food in 2010, not only did they discover Pittsburgh's previously cloistered Persian community, which began to flock to their restaurant, but their project's regional media focus went national and then international.

With bright blue and gold colors alluding to ancient Persia, the "Kubideh" Kitchen wrapper included short paragraphs about such topics as the 1979 revolution, conflict with Israel, the US perception of Iran, and nuclear power, as well as such less charged subjects as tea, bread, film and fashion. But when, in the Fall of 2014, the kitchen staff began turning out traditional Palestinian meals, including Shawarma roasted chicken, falafel and baba ganoush, things got ugly. The new menu was wrapped up in a packaging design citing a range of topics raised by Palestinians living in Pittsburgh, but also from interviews conducted during a ten-day visit to Palestine in May, 2014 by CK director Rubin, and co-directors Weleski and chef Robert Sayer. One wrapper reads in part, "Israeli soldiers shot our friend Bassim [with a tear gas canister] it made a big hole in his chest and killed him. The canister was made in Western Pennsylvania." Still other short texts focus on marriage, dating and olive trees, and all of this was printed on CK food wrappers.[38]

Almost immediately after CK began to serve Palestinian food, the project received a death threat, forcing Rubin and Weleski to shut down operations for several days as authorities investigated. Previous to the threat, pressure from conservative Jewish organizations forced one of the project's sponsors, the University of Pittsburgh's Honors College, to withdraw their funding. CK later reopened under police protection but with heightened media attention from global news agencies including the *Washington Post*, *Al Jazeera*, the

BBC and *El Mundo*. Media attention has grown steadily over the years with even *Tonight Show* humorist Jay Leno once referring to the art project in one of his stand-up routines. But this comedic connection is less baffling when one learns the importance of humor to Rubin's aesthetic tactics:

> Humor is the thing the visual arts have that gets you in the gut … I'm doing a project with my friend who lives in Iran to have a sitcom in Los Angeles and Tehran. The family will be stuck in two realities at the same time. The kid knows what's happening and the others don't. Conflict and miscommunication is the core of comedy.[39]

Rubin concludes by rhetorically asking if it is possible to "create an innocuous environment to bring up political issues without censorship?" The "Trojan horse" recipe he and Weleski operate from is clear. Smuggle politics in through the back door of a familiar setting, in this case a fast-food restaurant. This artistic subterfuge built upon CK's previous iteration as the Waffle Shop, a late night Pittsburgh eatery where customers could order vegan waffles and take part in a live television broadcast involving "the storytelling vernacular of a talk show."[40]

The Waffle Shop developed out of an undergraduate art seminar Rubin taught at Carnegie Mellon University (CMU) between 2009 and 2012. Before long it evolved from a social art experiment into a full-fledged enterprise in which a series of rotating hosts conversed with patrons in the type of empty patter typical of televised talk show programming. Supported in part by the Center for the Arts in Society at CMU, though mostly funded by its own sales, the Waffle Shop was located in the East Liberty section of the city. According to a 2009 article in the *Pittsburgh Post-Gazette* the once economically blighted neighborhood was "on a rocket's trajectory," with upscale food stores, hotels, a Home Depot and more than a dozen developers actively transforming its bankrupt infrastructure into an attractive target for capital investment.[41] As in so many similar rejuvenation scenarios, East Liberty's mostly black, low-income residents were systematically edged out of the neighborhood in order to make way for middle- and upper-income residents, who are also predominantly white.[42] Much of this renewal was taking place via public–private partnerships. In this regard, the Waffle Shop was both similar and different. Rubin managed to get a reduced rent from the landlord and that cost was picked up by CMU. At the same time the Waffle Shop soon managed to generate its own revenue from sales, reportedly employing some 450 students over the course of its business life.[43] Rubin's student-run art project operated between the hours of 10 p.m. and 3 a.m.; giving it the air of a nightclub for insomniacs. The Waffle Shop's curious mix of food enterprise plus a side of reality TV seemed made-to-measure for the so-called creative class: knowledge-based professionals whose flexible, adrenaline-charged work schedules favored a place with cheap coffee and sugary confections for knocking out that website design, concert deal or press release on a tight, redeye deadline.

In practice, however, most regular waffle eaters came from the Shadow Lounge, a late-night hip-hop music club located next door. That did not prevent Pittsburgh policy shapers from seeing the Waffle Shop as a creative cities type venture, useful for anchoring broader urban changes. Assistant city planning director for development and design cited the project when she stated "art can stimulate development. For example, the Waffle Shop became an East Liberty destination that contributed to the neighborhood's development buzz, officials said."[44]

Whether or not grabbing a midnight snack plus a side of *realitytainment* led to the kind of buzz that transformed the East Liberty neighborhood into one of the city's hottest rental locations is unclear but, as cuisine, the Waffle Shop ranked fair to good on Yelp.com.[45]

As television, it was no less trite than most broadcast fare. But as art, the Waffle Shop, just like Conflict Kitchen, put forth an imposing organizational model that Rubin insists, "hybridized many social identities as it simultaneously functioned as a restaurant, talk show, business venture, public artwork, and classroom."[46] What presumably keeps it ontologically grounded as contemporary art is CK's dialogically aesthetic ambition. For art historian Grant Kester, dialogical art draws indirectly on the ideas of Russian Formalist Viktor Shklovsky and German playwright Bertolt Brecht. At the start of the Russian Revolution in 1917, Shklovsky's technique of *ostranenie* (остранение) or defamiliarization sought to make what is familiar strange, thus freeing it from cultural ossification. Notably, his estrangement process contrasts with the aesthetic approach of artists Vladimir Tatlin, Lyubov Popova and Aleksander Rodchenko, whose concept of Constructivism sought to replace existing cultural forms with a completely new society merging art and life. It was Brecht who blended aspects of both avant-garde tendencies in his own estrangement effect, by instructing actors to alienate their performance from traditional bourgeois theater's illusionary *mise-en-scène*. Ideally, once the fourth wall separating audience from stage was lifted, a real time-space remained behind in which candid and improvised reflections on art and politics and revolutionary change could unfold.

Sensing that the late twentieth-century neo-avant-garde had stripped these practices of their social and political context, Kester takes issue with the resulting tendency to serve up cultural alienation for its own sake, without the secondary process of critique, reflection and reassessment provided for in earlier avant-garde theories. Pointing to the paradox of "liberating" a subjugated population by cruelly negating the comfort of representational conventions and clichés, Kester proposes that the next step after shocking the viewer is engaging in participatory conversation about the shortcomings of existing social conditions. The resulting dialogical aesthetic aims to reimagine art and society as a more democratic collaborative project.[47] Curiously, CK splices Kester's dialogical aesthetic directly into the context of a carefully staged world of deception in which patrons' expectations are reprocessed through an intimate encounter with their alleged geopolitical enemies. That there is humor in this confrontational platform there is no doubt. Whether or not diners leave the kitchen more enlightened is difficult to assess, though perhaps Rubin and Weleski will make outcome evaluation part of their project going forward. Still, it is probably more accurate to suggest that both the Waffle Shop and CK's version of audience estrangement is not an attempt to resurrect pre-war avant-garde techniques, but instead derives from secondary or even tertiary pop-cultural sources, including *The Daily Show* and *Saturday Night Live*, whose reality television parodies and mock-news broadcasts borrow indirectly from early twentieth-century art innovators, including Brecht.[48]

Notably, Conflict Kitchen's name and mission closely resemble another food-related art project entitled Enemy Kitchen (EK) developed six years earlier by Iraqi-American artist Michael Rakowitz. While neither Rubin nor Weleski have officially commented on the similarities of the two projects, Rakowitz amiably grants that, "there is room in the world for both projects to exist." EK's origins are also in the classroom where, beginning in 2003, concurrent with the US invasion of Iraq, the artist taught middle-school students how to make his Iraqi-Jewish mother's chewy Kubba dumpling dish. The classroom became a space for "dispersing cooking technique and a space for conversation making as an act of resistance." EK later evolved into a Chicago food truck that employed US veterans of the Iraq War as sous-chefs/servers taking orders from Iraqi refugee chefs. The ensuing conversation between truck operators and residents is the heart of Rakowitz's project that he believes inverts power relations between military personnel and refugees so that "friction and discomfort is made visible."[49] Rakowitz, trained as a sculptor, explains that "instead of the kind of didactic approach Conflict Kitchen take with their wrappers, I am interested in having people in relation to the object": the paper plates on which EK's food is served are replicas of Saddam Hussein's hospitality dinnerware, and

EK's kitchen knife was forged for Rakowitz by Hussein's personal sword maker. And while Rubin and Weleski have not sought to expand the range of what constitutes actual "conflict" to include their own city, one could easily imagine a curated African American cuisine phase, complete with wrappers exploring issues of displacement in a gentrifying creative city like Pittsburgh.[50]

Bare Art/*Real Estate*

Up to a point, Assemble, Gates's Dorchester Projects, the Waffle Shop and Conflict Kitchen all pivot on a similarly anomalous logic, in which participants' reality frame is undermined and sustained at one and the same time. On one hand this brings the laws of capital, as well as state and municipal regulators, directly into art's ontological frame. Whether post-Fordist capitalism now resembles art or vice versa, virtually everything we thought we knew about "serious" culture has been peeled away with astonishing force, leaving behind a raw, and in some ways vulnerable thing: a *bare art* world, fully congruent with the political and economic emergency that marks our contemporaneous present. On the other hand, in a society dominated by entrepreneurship and risk, such "real-world" practices as regenerative social art inevitably serve to map the tactics of a certain artistic vanguard directly onto the raw and unmediated capitalist reality of the twenty-first century.[51] Without contesting the dialogical value of these practices at a local level, as Marina Vishmidt warns, the transfer of art from the sphere of culture into the realm of real estate, contract law and business, permits:

> art to stop *being art*, or to stop being *only* art, and allows it to start playing a much more direct role as a channel of empowerment, governance, and even accumulation—if only of "social capital"—for specific communities and in specific contexts … we thus seem to be living through a moment of semantically frictionless yet socially devastating fusion between the social and capital.[52]

I would go a step further, but also one step back, by suggesting this slippery transition from art to life is more real than a mere semantic integration, one that is therefore free of neither class conflict nor racial and gender discord. Since contemporary art no longer has any meaningful contextual or formal limits, it is also no longer possible for any art practice to radically exceed or subvert the field's existing boundaries or discursive framing. This *bare art* condition is a state of cultural overexposure in which the horizon of art's future possibilities is also its infinite conventionality made visible as an exhausted canonical finitude, and it is not always clear that empowerment can be the result. *Bare art* has merged with life, while life is permeated by capital. What was once capital's crisis is now also that of art, institutionally as well as epistemologically and ontologically. What is overlooked by Vishmidt's understandable pessimism, therefore, is that this change of status forces art into an encounter with social frictions operating within capitalist forces of production. This is especially evident when socio-economic art practitioners mobilize the undervalued labor power of other artists for their own projects. Probably, almost certainly, it always was this way, though now, under the stark conditions of *bare art*, there is no reliable means of concealing this fact. The truth will out, leading to conflicts of a decidedly real-world nature once perceived as largely external to art.

In a 2009 University of Chicago public forum, Theaster Gates confessed to listeners that his temporary staff wanted "healthcare benefits … they want their family members to fly free to Documenta … they made me rich …what do I do?"[53] Musing on this situation, but also on divisions of labor within the contemporary art world in general, John Preus, a former Gates studio manager and fabricator, rhetorically asks:

> how is it that the image of labor is still so compelling? From the early yearnings to turn lead into gold, to the fountain of youth, we have returned to the blue collar transformations of hands and material as a sort of spiritual placeholder, reifying the Laborer as the inarticulate alchemist, the one whose knowledge of the material world is true and pure … Is this simply another instance of the poet falling in love with the shipbuilder, ostensibly amplifying the plight of the common man against the supposed frivolity of the upper classes and academics? Could we call this phenomenon Bluewashing? And how far can such populism stretch, as the celebrity of the artist increases?[54]

These days Gates produces his studio based art by himself, while assistants are deployed to fabricate projects related to the Rebuild Foundation side of the artist's career. Nevertheless, whenever "intentional aesthetic" practices tap into actual legal, economic and social production frameworks labor-related conflict inevitably arises. In August, 2015, staff members of Conflict Kitchen decided to form a union: "Inspired by food service workers across the country fighting for fifteen dollars an hour, we the workers of Conflict Kitchen have decided to come together to organize for living wages, fair benefits, and recognition of the key role we play in the [art] project."[55] The project's business success has required a staff including a full-time chef, a couple of management personnel and project researchers, as well as over a dozen kitchen employees, who voted to join Local 23 of the United Food and Commercial Workers Union in an effort to improve working conditions at CK. As one employee explains: "I've had eight jobs in Pittsburgh since I moved here ten months ago. Like Conflict Kitchen, not getting paid enough is the baseline for all of these jobs."[56] Another staff member, however, focuses on the aesthetic dimension of the job, reporting that, along with better wages:

> about half the staff wanted to be more involved in researching and programming. All of us are interested in harnessing our skills and interest and applying them to a project in a small way, and making more money and having the benefits we deserve will give us the power and confidence to make small changes and programing ideas that might change the direction of Conflict Kitchen.[57]

CK's employees have come to realize that they are not merely artistic representations of food preparation workers who perform their tasks as if on display in some historical village re-enactment, but are instead actual food service employees on the payroll of a socially engaged art project known as Conflict Kitchen. No doubt Brecht would be amused by this double estrangement procedure in which an allegedly non-alienated artistic labor force undertakes its own self-alienation in order to generate a more "real" mode of collective solidarity that demands recognition for the value it adds to a work of contemporary art, which also happens to be a profitable commodity. It is important to add that the CK labor conflict is directed less at Rubin and Weleski, or at the art project, than it is towards CMU which contracts the kitchen's workers. Nevertheless, it is clear that a socially engaged artwork such as CK that is virtually inter-changeable with reality also inevitably thrusts all of its participants into a day-to-day struggle with the legal, inter-social, and economic minutiae of contemporary life operating beyond the sphere of autonomous art's safety zone. That same up-scaling of an art work to fully synchronize with life, in fact to become interchangeable with the everyday world, would once upon a time been celebrated as a triumph for the avant-garde but, under current circumstances, this shift reflects conditions particular to the crisis of capitalism, as well as art's own response to the impoverished status of the *bare art* world.

Social Practice/Social Labor

The ethos of socially engaged art makes managing worker-oriented concerns an especially knotty affair. Which is to say, in a *bare art* world, contemporary artists, especially social practice "regenerative" artists, find many of the conflicts and dilemmas inherent to autonomous bourgeois art not only remain in effect, but have now been raised up to a higher level of concreteness. While Rubin and Weleski allowed the CK unionization to take place, and Gates has publicly struggled with such issues, there is a broader transformation under way as contemporary art and labor disputes spread.

Since the 2008 economic crisis we find art fabricators, cultural interns, studio managers and so forth collectively growing more assertive about their right to better working conditions and higher pay. In early summer of 2016, art world megastar Jeff Koons is alleged to have abruptly "laid off" 14 of his painting staff in response to an attempt at unionization. Whether or not this proves accurate is perhaps less important that the fact it seems perfectly plausible because enterprise culture has made such day-to-day conflicts just another facet of the *bare art* world phenomenon. To these

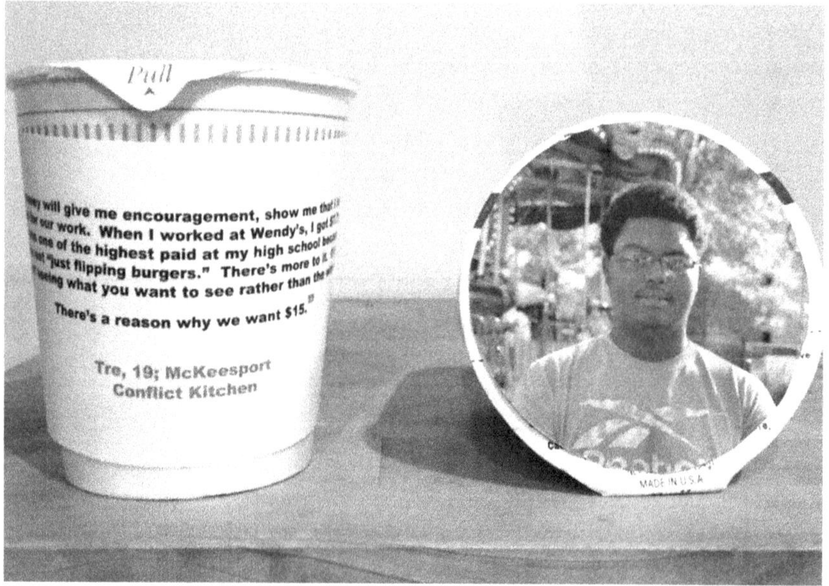

Figure 24   Fight for 15 (dollars per hour wages) take-away cup o' noodles with statements and portraits of pro-union Conflict Kitchen workers on each lid (pictured is former CK employee Mr. Trevor Jenkins). A project by Madalyn Hochendoner and Clara Gamalzki, 2016

(Courtesy the artists)

labor-related tensions we can add the activism of WAGE (Working Artists and the Greater Economy), Arts & Labor, Gulf Labor, GULF (Global Ultra Luxury Faction), Debtfair, and BFAMFAPhD.org discussed in the Introduction to Part I, "Welcome to Our Art World," but also the recently formed Artists' Union England, the art as social factory research of the Free/Slow University of Warsaw, the investigation of divisions of artistic labor by the European think-tank Former West and, even as I write this, the Guerrilla Girls are organizing a joint action with the Precarious Workers Brigade in London focusing on unpaid art world internships, and WAGE is preparing to roll-out a new coalition program called *WAGENCY* that seeks to go beyond issues of fair pay to tap into the developing political potential of artistic labor in general, while in the Basque region of Spain the educational staff of the Guggenheim Bilbao are protesting in the streets to denounce the "McDonaldization" of major museums by arguing, "We live a moment without precedents in museum history, which has lost respect for the cultural worker, turned into staff throwaway."[58]

This is not a comprehensive list. What it evinces, however, is the fact that we are experiencing a phase of long-overdue reflection, advocacy and action focused on the working conditions of artists and cultural workers. This reaction is spurred on by the chronically unmanageable repercussions of the financial collapse. But if cultural labor's response is to rise above the important, though limited, need to improve the distribution of art world benefits by addressing deeper structural and political concerns, it may depend on our ability to link present conditions of *bare art* to the crisis and delirium of capital. As capitalism's long-term contradictions deepen, in the form of an ever-weirder symptomatology of bizarre negative interest rates, persistent underemployment and excess populations, an oversupply of artists and an ever-accelerating series of Ponzi-like schemes involving bubble-and-burst debt and investment cycles, fundamental questions arise about the role of art. Art now speaks the grammar of finance, doing so with such aptitude that no accent is evident (though one is frequently affected), but labor disputes and signs of class struggle arise within it. At the same time, the sincere and sprightly good will of socially committed artists and urban rejuvenators stretches out far beyond the province of high culture in a desperate search for a solution to the failures of neoliberal capitalism, and mainstream art prizes are awarded to them. Even though the art world is insulated from the economic effects of crisis, it becomes disorganized by it. One newly advertised project in NYC pretty much sums up the situation with uncanny precision (and note the reference to "Intentional Community"): "Art Condo is a professional real estate project and an

'Intentional Community' based in the social sculpture ideas of Joseph Beuys [and] a community-drive real estate enterprise that helps creative individuals purchase and develop buildings, collectively, in partnership with neighborhood residents."[59]

Expect more, not less, of these hybridized art and business enterprises as the crisis drags on. More Beuys-inspired condos, pop-up cultural ventures, university-funded art eateries and public–private creative placemaking initiatives. However, if cultural entrepreneurship and creative reuse represent art's gift to capital, the gift is not free of a contaminating animus, or even a degree of venom. On the one hand, we find low-income residents and communities of color raising charges of "art-washing" and heightened gentrification when such projects are brought into discussion. On the other hand, social regeneration art illustrates a means of temporarily reappropriating and distorting mainstream market enclosures, adding local value to people and spaces abandoned by capital. In the crisis management portfolio, social regenerative practices are one tool among others, and probably the preferred mechanism for taming, or at least seeming to tame, a system spinning out of control: small in scale but high in visibility, such projects keep at arm's length difficult ideological questions about the role that state and municipal agencies might play in moderating the deleterious effects of capitalism.

In order to save itself, capital goes to extraordinary lengths, absorbing alien modes of production into its repertoire of perseverance, including experimental modalities of avant-garde art, even if these are assimilated only superficially, at a formal level. And yet the more capital subsumes what was once "other" to it, including labor as Negri and others pointed out decades ago, or the reproductive systems of biopower as Silvia Federici and other feminists have insisted, or dark matter creativity for that matter, the more capital returns to itself the destructured society it has created, sometimes with a vengeance.

Part III

Resistance

Introduction III:
Critical Praxis/Partisan Art

What do we do now? Since the Revolution Egyptian artists have been running about like headless chickens. Their concerns have taken an almost existential dimension. What do we do now? Do we keep doing what we used to do? Where do "we" end and our art begin?

Cos Aly[1]

Without a critical understanding of how, when and why oppositional movements repeatedly rise and fall, each time as if anew, no sustainable activist art or partisan praxis is possible. But history is more than just another trope among others. The dark and overflowing archive of many past failures and a few temporary successes does make possible this or that genealogical narrative, but it also is a concrete agency in its own right offering up a type of resistance all its own. Part III brings together six essays about art activism written at different historical moments in which "habitual" art practices confronted real-world events taking place "beyond" the comfort zone of the studio, gallery or museum including: the rise of the counter-globalization movement (Counting on your Collective Silence, *1999*), *an attempt at formulating a broader thesis about art as resistance via what I somewhat roguishly call the dark matter of the art world* (Dark Matter, *2003*), *the cultural and political complexities of the Maidan uprising in Kiev Ukraine* (On the Maidan Uprising, *2014*), *and finally a reflection on a decade in which social practice art became accepted within contemporary art* (Delirium and Resistance, *2015*). *Over the span of time represented in Part III, several significant changes take place with regards to activist art, including what I consider a fundamental paradigm shift in how such engaged practices conceive of their own political and cultural resistance in theory and practice. Nonetheless, one underlying question remains throughout: how might a truly oppositional art emerge within the overwhelming political and economic reality of an omnipresent consumer culture and an ever adapting capitalist hegemony. One answer attempted here is to insist that while resistance is never futile, it does come with its own demands and paradoxes often involving the way history is ignored or invoked, used or abused by those who invoke the materiality of its archive. My appeal to explore the past as a means of grasping*

BOYCOTT THIS SHOW!

The De Young Museum of San Francisco and John D. Rockefeller III have collaborated on selecting from his private collection: 'American Art'. (Sic) In our initial protest against this particular exhibition and the policies that make this kind of exhibition possible in general, Artists Meeting for Cultural Change enumerated the crimes of cultural institutions like the Whitney Museum of American Art in accepting and promoting 'American Art' as if it were simply what it says it is.

Among the outrages charged are:

■ A staff of experts constructing a 'history' of American art from the viewpoint of the ruling class; a 'history' that systematically ignores not only 'the last decade of cultural and social reassessment' but worse: the entire history of people struggling and organizing for social/cultural transformation.

■ This show attempts to pass off as representative a private, discriminatory collection of art. 'American Art' only succeeds in representing the values of John D. Rockefeller III and his class. This is accomplished with the complicity of cultural institutions with a legal obligation to remain politically neutral and to consciously reflect the social realities of all of the people.

■ This exhibition has in it the work of only one woman and no blacks. This is particularly offensive in light of the past Whitney administration promises to the Black Emergency Cultural Coalition to at least make use of professional black curatorial staff in curatorial or even sub-curatorial ranks and the hard-won advances of women in all sections of society. To these promises the present Whitney administration obviously feels no obligation.

Why protest? Because our social section has an obligation with respect to the general problems of these 'point of production' struggles. This reflects the terrain of contradiction which must be dealt with respect to social responsibility.

Rockefeller, the De Young and Whitney Museums, etc. appropriate people's work in their attempts to perpetuate both a specific and a general concept of Official Culture. They promote art as a set of commodities. They conceal and confuse the class character of art and art practice.

——AMCC——

Figure 25   A page from *An Anti-Catalog* produced by Artists Meeting for Cultural Change in 1976 as a counter-history of the visual arts in the USA

(Image G. Sholette Archive)

the present and future is probably no different. Still, the general orientation of my writing was and remains concerned with how shifting social, economic and historical realities directly impact the way I, and other politically engaged artists, produce our work, as well as what forms of oppositional praxis are opened up, or closed down by the changing conditions of artistic production over time.

A Post-Cold War Activist Aesthetic?

Even before the end of the Cold War and the dissipation of what remained of the New Left's oppositional energy, the dominant neo-conservative politics had already led many cultural producers to turn inward in the 1980s. They moved away from a class analysis and a conception of capitalism as a whole, towards an exploration of personal identity as a form of resistance. In the art world, postmodernism celebrated a new aesthetic of depthlessness, or what cultural critic Fredric Jameson summarized as "surrealism without the unconscious," and the dismantling of the Keynesian welfare state by neoliberalism heralded the formation of an entrepreneurial cognitariat or knowledge worker stratum, who occupied, often precariously, what sociologist Saskia Sassen described as the luxury zones of new global metropoles, Richard D. Lloyd defined as Neo-Bohemia, and the late Neil Smith denounced as the revanchist city.[2] Then, in the 1990s, a fresh wave of activist art and cultural collectivism emerged to immediately challenge many key assumptions held by an earlier generation of politically engaged artists still linked to the rebellions of May, 1968. Dovetailing with the rise of the counter, or "*alt*" globalization movement, this new cultural activism was less concerned with demystifying ideology than "creatively disrupting it." Unlike most of the critical art practices of the 1970s and 1980s, in which dominant representational forms were systematically analyzed through a variety of methods ranging from Semiotics to Marxism, Feminism and Psychoanalysis, the new approach plowed directly, some would say gleefully, into what Guy Debord described as the *Society of the Spectacle*. Groups such as RTmark, The Yes Men, Yomango, Electronic Disturbance Theater, Nettime, and Critical Art Ensemble, among other artists' collectives, took full advantage of increasingly widespread and affordable digital communication networks in order to practice what was often referred to as "tactical media," a concept inspired as much by the Zapatista rebellion as it was by the Situationist International. According to key theorists of tactical media David Garcia and Geert Lovink, the practice involved appropriation of cheap, available technologies for the purpose of engendering political resistance amongst socially disenfranchised populations.[3]

What is unique to these 1990s antagonistic practices is that these technology-based artists took advantage of post-Fordist capital's distributed communicative networks in order to generate acts of disruption within their very structure. Tactical media did this by mobilizing its own secondary economy of informal dark matter productivity by organizing in cellular fashion, much like a social club or rock band, or by establishing ersatz institutions, or mockstitutions, with intentionally unstable public identities. In so doing they diverged even further from the more hierarchically structured art activism of the 1960s–1980s, as well as the expressed goal of establishing an entirely autonomous political cultural sphere. The interventionists turned instead to small-scale, in-between spaces and ephemeral actions for their work, often illegally infiltrating public squares, corporate websites, libraries, flea markets, housing projects and local political machines in ways not intended to recover a specific meaning or use-value for either art world discourse or private interests. And yet, this emerging interventionist culture also revealed certain definite similarities with the anarcho-entrepreneurial spirit of the neoliberal enterprise, including its highly plastic sense of organizational identity and a romantic distrust of comprehensive administrative structures. Addressing the nature of late twentieth and early twenty-first-century collectivism is key to understanding available forms of political resistance, including its possibilities and its limitations.

The opening essay of Part III, "Counting on Your Collective Silence," examines the process of artistic collectivization that often flows from moments when capitalism is in crisis or, contrarily, when it is delirious with imagined possibilities of endless profitability and prosperity. This text happens to have been written under the second of these circumstances, in 1999, the same year online shopping emerged into the mainstream, sending technology-related stock investing into an "irrational exuberance" as the market appeared incapable of backsliding.[4] Major investors such as George Soros dumped conventional industry stocks to plow their capital into internet start-ups. At one point in 2000 the money manager of his Quantum Fund declared "This is insane. I've never owned a stock that goes from $40 to $250 in a few months."[5] Indeed, the internet itself was viewed not only as capitalism's savior, but also as a libertarian machine for spreading Western democratic ideals. In his highly influential *Code and Other Laws of Cyberspace* from that same year, Harvard Law Professor Lawrence Lessig stated that oppressive nations were about to:

> wake up to find that their telephone lines are tools of free expression, that e-mail carries news of their repression far beyond their borders, that images are no longer the monopoly of state-run television stations but can be transmitted from a simple modem. We have exported to the world, through the architecture of the Internet, a First Amendment *in code* more extreme than our First Amendment *in law*.[6]

And then of course the so-called dot.com bubble imploded, shattering the hallucination of capitalism 2.0 as trillions of (fictitious) dollars disappeared from the global economy. But if "Counting on Your Collective Silence" reflects any aspect of the pre-crash delirium, it does so darkly by questioning the internet's acceleration of a market-based pseudo-collectivism and proposing in response a self-organized activist alternative. The chapter draws on the plot of the 1999 blockbuster movie *The Matrix*, as well as from my own experience co-founding and co-developing two New York City based artists' groups: Political Art Documentation/Distribution (PAD/D, 1980–1988), and REPOhistory (1989–2000). In fact, this essay was completed about a year before REPOhistory also expired, not because of over-capitalization like the stock market, but due in large part to the steeply rising cost of living in NYC, and also the heightened social challenges presented by collective practice about which the "Collective Silence" has much to say. The chapter therefore sets the tone for Part III, the book's concluding section on Resistance, not by celebrating oppositional practices uncritically but by seeking to dig deeply into the complex relationship between self-organized group work and the historical, political and economic realities that play out within the very heart of organized social labor. In short, "Counting on your Collective Silence" reflects upon the possibilities and limits of collectivism after modernism, that is to say, after the end of actually existing socialism as much as Surrealism and other grand Modernist notions of collectivity that had, by the end of the twentieth century, already lost much of their allure for younger artists.[7]

"Collective Silence" also attempts to read communal labor figuratively, as Fredric Jameson might do, by asking what does collectivism represent in the social imaginary of the West following the collapse of actually existing socialism a decade earlier? One answer seemed to be found in popular culture where an image of social cooperation was especially visible in certain science fiction and horror movie narratives. That same year the movie *The Matrix* appeared.[8] With its story pivoting on a ragtag team of multicultural cyberspace guerrillas who are forced into collective action by a mutual desire to awaken from an otherwise veiled state of exploitation and objectification, the movie seemed made to order for my evolving thesis by perfectly illustrating the state of collectivism at the end of the twentieth century.[9] Two other concerns also became paramount as the essay came together. First was a need to tackle the conspicuous absence of informal groups and collectives from the art historical record. Many of my subsequent writings focus on this gap in the official cultural narrative of high art, ultimately leading to the development of the "dark matter" thesis in the late 1990s. However, it was a second and equally pressing concern involving the unstable nature of collective practice itself that "Collective Silence" primarily focuses on, and the explanatory model for this instability has had an equally long-term effect on my thinking. The question that bedeviled me was how to interpret the often intense, interpersonal messiness of group practice, including the challenge of collective decision-making, as well as the appearance of unspoken hierarchies in what is supposed to be a horizontal mode of social organizing? These obstacles to unity included unacknowledged pecking orders reflecting differences in gender, ethnicity, age, education and class, problems that plagued modern social conditions in general and that collective practice was supposed to resolve. The most satisfactory responses led me entirely outside the field of art, or so it seemed.

Drawing on the early writings of Antonio Negri, "Collective Silence" makes use of the Italian philosopher's concept of destructuration, in which working-class self-organization and refusal to work in Italy in the late 1970s simultaneously broke down the disciplinary structures of the factory and made evident the discontinuous and disintegrated nature of working-class experience itself. In such texts as *Marx beyond Marx: Lessons on the Grundrisse* and *Labor of Dionysus: A Critique of State-form* (with Michael Hardt), Negri considered this state of fragmentation and discontinuity to be the direct result of capitalist processes of value extraction through work speed-ups, union busting and automation of production.[10] At the same time, he recognized that this act of destabilization was in turn undermining capital itself, at least in so far as it pushed workers into acts of resistance and even sabotage. But Negri was also criticizing the role of the traditional Communist Party that had long served as a disciplining mechanism in itself, as well as a regulator of working-class resistance and thus was complicit with capital. "The problem of the party today is the present reality of a real contradiction," he writes, adding that it contains "the same contradiction that you find between the personal and the political, between self-valorization and destructuring, between destructuring and destabilization."[11]

Negri's focus on spontaneous acts of direct working-class resistance seemed to resonate with much of my experience working in various self-organized artists' collectives. To underscore this conceivable homology I conducted short interviews about collective experience with other artists. The response involved a mixture of elation and discord perceived to be right at the very core of the collective experience. I scattered excerpts of these observations throughout the essay (later, for the 2011 book *Dark*

Matter, I generated a modest survey of collective practices in an attempt to map their size, longevity, organizational framework and other aspects of this collectivist topography). "Collective Silence" proposes that the contradictions and destructive forces of society at large are not excluded, expelled or resolved within self-organized group formations, but are instead actually amplified whenever individuals consciously seek to work together in a subgroup that is nevertheless surrounded by existing conditions of capitalist exploitation. And yet it is this same heightened tension and concentration of contradictions that forms the source of those exhilarating, short-lived moments of collective enthusiasm when things go well, as well as the extreme distress when they do not. It is in fact this instability that marks the point of departure for the study of collectivism after modernism, as Blake Stimson and I—but also John Roberts, Marc Léger, Brian Holmes, Kim Charnley and others—have endeavored to explore.

Negri's pre-*Empire* theoretical writings were a significant influence on my own ideas and writing. I first read his work sometime in the mid 1980s as a member of the PAD/D Reading Group, where we worked collectively on his unconventional interpretation of Marx's *Grundrisse* (the first English collection of these translated writings was published by Bergin and Garvey in 1984 as *Marx beyond Marx: Lessons from the Grundrisse*). Perhaps it was Negri's direct experience with working-class struggles in 1970s Italy and his attempt to theorize his involvement that spoke to me in the late 1990s in a way that the then popular writings of Ernesto Laclau and Chantal Mouffe did not.[12] Laclau and Mouffe's concept of "agonism" seemed at the time, and still seems today, a means of side-stepping the exploitative inner workings of capital by shifting issues of political resistance away from a struggle over control of one's own time and labor, towards a notion of political conflict manifest at the level of language. While recognizing that Laclau and Mouffe's critique offered a partial corrective to what was an over-emphasis on the determining role of the economic base within all superstructural social formations, their version of agonism did away completely with the primary critique of political economy: that it always reproduces and exacerbates class inequalities. Furthermore, the exact nature of the mechanisms producing their model of antagonistic tension rests, if that is the word, on anti-foundational post-structuralist concepts of difference and discourse theory that, at best, leave Laclau and Mouffe's concept of agonism theoretically fuzzy and at worst politically disarming.

Still, my own background no doubt helped tilt me towards a class-based and ultimately Marxist critique of capital. As the only college graduate in a family of four siblings I paid for classes at the local community college by working as a late-night janitor in a computer hardware factory. Though all employees were gone by the time I arrived at the facility, sometimes after midnight following a full day of studio art classes, I could visualize the supervisors stationed behind oversized interior windows as they watched over rows of wooden workbenches where men and women spent their days soldering electronic circuit boards (a few workstations also contained small craft projects workers produced on breaks, an observation that directly influenced my dark matter thesis many years later). Class stratification, in other words, was deducible from the very layout of the plant I maintained. At the same time, "Collective Silence" also recognizes the evolving nature of class composition, putting to work a comment by the late Gilles Deleuze in which the philosopher mused, "man is no longer man enclosed but man in debt."[13] As much as the late 1990s is characterized by the irrational exuberance of the dot.com stock market, it was also a moment when personal indebtedness rose conspicuously.

Following the late 1970s deregulation of financial industries, "a wave of unscrupulous and excessive practices" was ushered in, as credit card companies engaged in aggressive marketing, lowering minimum payment requirements while raising late fees and other financial penalties. Between 1980 and 1999, credit card debt in the US rose from $111 billion to nearly $600 billion.[14] The very notion of an American middle class, always so central to global capitalist ideology, was beginning to come undone in a process that would only be fully revealed about a decade later during the financial meltdown of 2007–2009. Arriving at the same time as this widespread class decomposition, or as Negri would call it "class destructuration," was the technologically enhanced marketing apparatus of the internet. Consumer behavior could now be tracked in real time, almost like mice in a laboratory maze: their buying habits, lifestyle and interpersonal interactivity gathered into datasets for mining and mapping both the aggregate and individual desire of the population. Primitive by today's standards, late 1990s human marketization technology took advantage of widening internet usage to accelerate the integration of the population into capitalist modes of valorization and consumption. And this was happening not only in places of work, but also at home and even in public spaces, all locations where workers once withdrew from the disciplinary regimes of capitalist production. Simultaneously, this same technology opened up possibilities of connecting forms of communal resistance to the market that had always existed in isolation from one another.

Dark Matter Unconcealed

In reality, fantasy is a specific means of production engaged in a process that is not visible to capital's interest in exploitation: the transformation of the relations between human beings and nature, along with the reappropriation of the dead labor of generations that is sedimented into history.[15]

"Dark Matter: Activist Art and the Counter-public Sphere" (chapter 9) revisits key concerns of my thesis on dark matter first outlined several years earlier, and later developed into book form.[16] Initially presented as a paper written for the conference Marxism and Visual Art Now (MAVAN) held in London in 2002, the text takes to task "radical" art historians for their indifference to oppositional culture and activist art even as they frequently apply their Marxist analysis to the familiar roster of luminaries already valorized by the art world establishment.[17] The chapter also proposes that art has at last merged with life, but that the life it has merged with is appalling. It also touches on the "pre-failed" status of MFA students, the theoretical impact of a withdrawal by this ubiquitous dark matter labor force on the mainstream art world, and the latent reactionary aspects of dark matter as it becomes brighter while acknowledging the importance of pleasurable gift economies that operate within this phenomenon. It seeks to reminds us of the historical, archival narrative from below, while recognizing that it is a fragmented lacuna. But my essay also insists that it is within the archives of this shadowed counter-public sphere of resistant culture that the radical art historian should be at work, and not in the celebrated temples of what O.K. Werckmeister calls Citadel Culture.[18]

The concept of dark matter creativity focuses on three types of cultural producers with differing relationships to the disciplinary regulation of high art, including:

(1) Professionally trained "pre-failed" art students whose academic education most likely emphasized subversive "avant-garde practices" while in reality preparing them to be part of an apparatus of reproduction in which the majority of artists serve the multi-billion dollar industry as museum-goers, magazine subscribers, art supply consumers, part-time art instructors or as poorly paid gallery assistants, art handlers, fabricators and so forth.

(2) Informal, amateur, "non-professional" zinesters, live action fantasy role-play gamers (LARP), "craftavists" knitters, devotees of Goth, Punk, and Do It Yourself (DIY) subcultures, fan filmmakers and cyber-geeks

who are engaged with creative practices focused on pleasure, fantasy and networked communalism, and therefore seemingly in conflict with both the career artist as well as the work ethic of capitalism and its markets.

(3) A smaller number of artists and artist groups, both professional and also informal, who explicitly link their artistic practices to radical social or political transformation and therefore have traditionally been positioned at the outermost margins of the mainstream art world, its history and discourse, and most of all its political economy. *Though this is changing, selectively, as we shall see.*

These three marginal forces resemble what astrophysicists describe as *dark matter* (and also *dark energy*): a gravitational force of unknown make-up that comprises as much as 95% of the known universe. Without the weight of this "missing mass" the visible cosmos would have dispersed into space long ago. Like its astronomical namesake, *creative dark matter* can be said to make up the bulk of the artistic activity that is produced in contemporary societies. However, this type of dark matter has largely been invisible primarily to those who lay claim to the management and interpretation of culture—the critics, art historians, collectors, dealers, museums, curators and arts administrators. It includes makeshift, amateur, informal, unofficial, autonomous, activist, non-institutional, self-organized practices—all work made and circulated in the shadows of the formal art world. Yet, just as the astrophysical universe is dependent on its dark matter, so too is the art world dependent on its dark energy. This is a phenomenon sometimes called the "missing mass problem." The question my thesis asks therefore is this: if celestial dark matter is the principal anchor that slows down cosmic expansion, what role then do redundant artistic producers play in stabilizing the art world?

Three other questions follow from this. First, how does a redundant surplus productivity or even non-productivity benefit, or actually reproduce, the political economy of high culture given that, by definition, what is excess or non-productive is also unnecessary to the normal functioning of a given system? Second, second, how do these three types or "species" of dark matter agency—"failed" artists, activists and amateurs—that initially appear partially or wholly disconnected from one another, form a cohesive conceptual category? The indebted art student who graduates with an MFA and, against all probabilities, continues to play her part in the art system, or the fast-food service employee who spends his weekends engaged in live action role play, or the disgruntled temporary clerk who produces anonymous comic books lampooning his job: how do any of these examples relate to a self-defined radical artist painting banners for a May Day Parade or Black Lives Matter march? And finally, what happens when this dark matter begins to brighten, as it most certainly is doing. Provisional answers to these questions require that we grasp the art world as a total system, one that is nonetheless always in a state of semi-destabilization thanks to internalized class divisions and the asymmetrical distribution of benefits that also serve to unify and reproduce it (see "Introduction I: Welcome to our Art World").

Here my argument parallels Jameson's update of the fundamental Marxist law involving the reserve army of unemployed labor. The original concept proposed that capitalism requires a constant population of redundant, job-seeking laborers who outnumber employed workers and thus, serving as a regulatory threat, keep overall wages low. But this control mechanism is not located within the capitalist mode of production proper and is instead external to it. Jameson argues that at this stage of capitalist subsumption, "the extra-economic or social no longer lies outside capital and economics but has been absorbed into it: so that being unemployed or without economic function is no longer to be expelled from capital but to remain within it."[19] One could conclude that this means that non-productive labor, including art, has been brought within the disciplinary operations of capital *tout court*, suppressing or eliminating what artistic practice represents above all: free self-directed and non-market productivity. Except, conversely, by incorporating the destructured and fragmented actuality of working-class culture and the anti-disciplinary and mimetic free play of art directly into its processes, capitalism can no longer externalize its own negation: that long, attenuated rebellion *from below* with its dangerous, non-utilitarian and resistant surplus archive of uprisings and failures, repetitions and resentment.

Certainly some of this residue is made use of within the pseudo-counterculture and ersatz gift economies found within twenty-first-century hipster anarcho-capitalist marketing. Yet this non-productive productivity simultaneously establishes a negative space directly within the logic of deregulated modern capitalism. Is it therefore also possible that neoliberalism's current financial crisis is as much a result of automation depleting the organic composition of capital as it is the incorporation of useless, redundant labor straight into the aggregate totality of the system, including art? Or does this more or less amount to the same thing, two sides of a single process? In any case, my approach to activist art, as well as so-called dark matter resistance more broadly, is that both are integrated directly to the architecture of the art world as internally excluded agencies, both literally and conceptually.[20] On one level this exile constitutes the chronically under-remunerated productive forces of most professional art workers, and on another level it marks the permanent and necessary demarcation of the art world's perimeter, where non-professional amateurs, as well as self-exiled producers of movement culture and activist art, ply uncharted cultural waters, carry out resistance and occasionally spout into view like Medieval sea monsters, only to submerge from sight again.

Delirium and Resistance

Two years following the great crash when the new normal of austerity and a jobless economic future was being rolled out by neoliberal apologists, these monstrous contradictions rose up again to manifest as spectacular protests and occupations across the public squares of the US, Europe, the Middle East and Latin America. One common element to this global rising was the perceived absence of a better future horizon. It seemed the failed economic policies of the present, or some moderately adjusted version of the same, was all one might expect from now on. This was particularly and understandably dismaying for younger people, including artists and those who made up the so-called creative class, issues that are discussed in Parts 1 and II of the book. Meanwhile, far from Zuccotti Park and just two years after Occupy Wall Street (OWS), thousands took the central Maidan Nezalezhnosti (Independence Square) of Kiev, Ukraine during the winter of 2014 to protest corrupt leadership and demand autonomy from Vladimir Putin's Kremlin. The essay "On the Maidan" (chapter 10) documents the process of installing my collaborative art project entitled *Imaginary Archive* in Kiev in April, just two months after the confrontation now known as the "2014 Ukrainian revolution," but it also seeks to address the complex and conflicted materialization of excluded sensibilities. *Imaginary Archive* is a traveling project containing small pieces by over 90 contributors from numerous countries. It has been exhibited intermittently since 2008. "On the Maidan" compares OWS with the automobile tire barricades of Ukraine's revolution, provoking a further conviction that the surplus archive of dark matter creativity is becoming fully visible, but doing so as a force of reactionary as well as progressive sentiments.

How does the contemporary art world respond to a situation where protests erupt in response to economic upheaval in a world in which everyone is told that they need to adjust and accept austerity, apart from a small group who continue to amass incalculable wealth? Despite claims of radicalism, or ostentatious prohibitions against overt expressions of racism, sexism or anti-LGBTQ sentiments (though seldom classism), the art world system seldom attempts to develop any substantive alternative to its own restricted economy. We might describe this schizoid stance as *prog-servatism*, whereby a roster of socially progressive convictions is tethered to a foundation of managed economic conservatism. The upheaval of centrist social democracy by the tumultuous Brexit and Donald Trump campaigns illustrates this amalgam of the neoliberal status quo with socially progressive posturing, a hybrid ideology and key legacy of the Blair-Clinton era, now thrust aside by the resurgence of the far right. Meanwhile institutional critique, the most highly recognized agonistic offspring of this system, has since devolved from an attempt at critical negation into a project that even one of its best-known proponents, Andrea Fraser, describes as a "victim of its [own] success or failure, swallowed up by the institution it stood against."[21] This does not alter the fact that the art world has sheltered, sometimes heroically, remnants of a once-vibrant bourgeois public sphere that includes the aesthetic-political inheritance of Kantian detached reason and even Marxist theorizing. Except that its primary means of preserving these liberal Enlightenment ideals is compulsory subservience to capitalism, with all of the complications that brings with it (as addressed in the discussion of *bare art* throughout much of this book).

Written in 2015, when the events of 2010, 2011 and 2012 were behind me, "Delirium and Resistance after the Social Turn" (chapter 11) is the final chapter of Part III and the text from which the book takes its title. It seeks to confront the dawning acceptance by the established art world of socially engaged art. The text focuses on events in 2004, the year Nato Thompson curated the watershed exhibition *The Interventionists* for MASS MoCA, but also the year when Critical Art Ensemble founder Steve Kurtz was investigated as a potential bio-terrorist by the US Department of Justice. "Delirium and Resistance" views 2004 as a crucial turning point for socially engaged art, not only because The Interventionists turned a spotlight on these previously submerged practices but also because the energy of the counter-globalization movement was flagging and the war in Iraq and Afghanistan expanding even as images of torture at the Abu Ghraib prison circulated in the mass media.

In November, 2004 George Bush Jr. was re-elected, winning a second presidential term in spite of his administration having waged two illegal and devastating wars in the Middle East, and capitalism was also on a tear as predatory lending exploded and sub-prime mortgage "assets" spiked in supposed value (even though many seeds of the coming downfall were also being sown in 2004). Meanwhile, the commercial art world's markets mushroomed even as state sponsorship for culture dwindled.[22] Against this gloom, tactical media and socially engaged art appeared to offer an antidote. But it is also possible to see the origins of a process of de-radicalization within the ranks of oppositional art that, by 2015, was morphing into tools for "creative cities" planning and urban "placemaking" programs. "Delirium and Resistance" darts sideways rather than strictly forwards, favoring a tactic of conjecture over strict analytical reasoning. It asks how we might re-narrate, or perhaps de-narrate, the history of socially engaged art in order to, at the very least, problematize socially engaged art's cooptation by, and complicity with, the mainstream art world. In a gesture that Jean-Pierre Gorin and Manny Farber would describe as an oblique, crablike movement, "Delirium and Resistance" hacks into the past in order to "prefigure" a different outcome for the present day.[23]

The chapter bases its speculative premise on my own hypothetical art project *Imaginary Archive*, in which an expanding collection of documents describes a series of pasts whose futures never arrived.[24]

Breaking-out

The indiscriminate archive of surplus creativity is rich—actually in truth it is overly rich with content; it is poor in actual resources such as institutional power or capital. Which is why, when artist Andrea Fraser quips "*L'1%, c'est moi*," her (undoubtedly ironic) declaration of identification with privileged elites does not accurately reflect the asymmetrical power relations of the actually existing art world. One need only place this same witticism into the mouth of Guggenheim Museum Director Richard Armstrong to understand my point. Today, the global art *beau monde* stands unashamedly together, off to one side of the undeniably *bare art* world, where they primp and huddle with their partners and patrons, the mega-developers, oligarchs and petro-thugs of the neoliberal new world disorder. This redistribution of the *insensible* (to tweak Jacques Rancière's term) opens up new avenues of appropriation, as high culture is strip-mined for its affective assets. That the Guggenheim and other major museums exploit the vast surplus armies of both migrant, precarious laborers and artists—the former build their art empire but are not welcome inside it, the latter invisibly (though less so all the time) reproduce their art world while never actually being destined to become its content providers, not in any lasting or meaningful way—this is the truly strange weather, as Andrew Ross once put it, for an era of disintegrating habitats, governance and social security.[25]

The speed of finance capital, the rush of data, the demanding agency of living as work and art as life, just how does one describe a world that resembles itself down to the smallest detail with little or no space for metaphor, error or dark matter? Like a simulation that has always already passed the Turing Test, there are no more messages from beyond: only more of the same, everything is now directly in front of us. It's not that we cannot tell the difference, it's that there is no difference. Lacking shadow or depth, the forces of production are repeatedly unconcealed, just as our inability to be shocked by this recurring fact is replayed over and over. With only slight variation this claustrophobic *now* is like Freud's symptom of repetition but without the underlying trauma. Or perhaps more accurately, it is a weird *trauma-less trauma*, a flat automated affect that whatever passes for social collectivity today manufactures as an internalized, subjective accompaniment to Jodi Dean's notion of "politics without politics."[26] We are anxious because we are always at risk, though from what exactly we are not certain, much as the protagonists in Don DeLillo's 1985 novel *White Noise*.[27] It's not that things are hidden from us, instead they are always available in the form of viral factoids, arriving one microsecond, and gone just as fast.

Dark matter may be no longer dark, but contradictions within the sphere of cultural practice have only ratcheted up. As artists and cultural workers

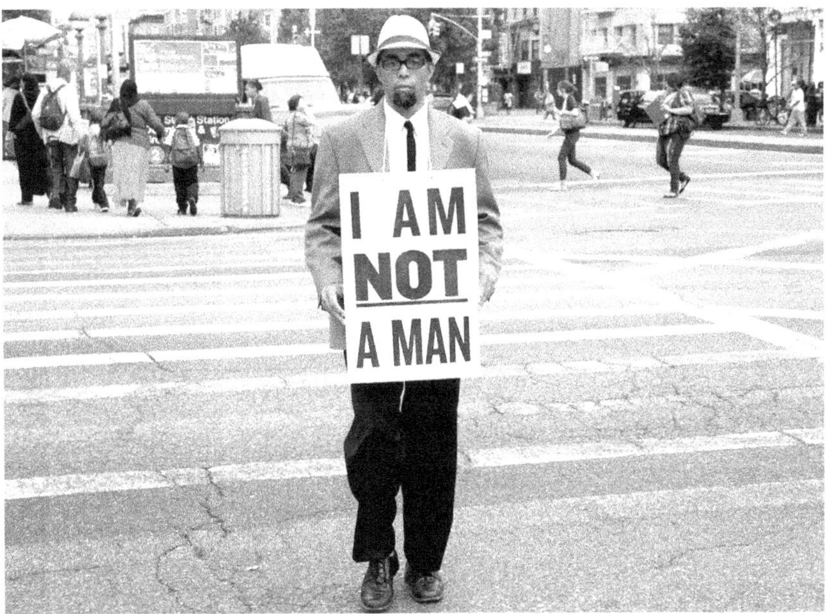

Figure 26 Dread Scott. *I Am Not a Man*, performance, 2009; duration 1 hour. Performance still 22 × 30 inches, pigment print. *I Am Not a Man. I am but I am not. I Am Not a Man* was a performance that was presented on the streets of Harlem, New York (Image Dread Scott)

today we confront a *bare art* world, conspicuously entwined within an equally unconcealed and ongoing capitalist economic and political crisis. Still, now and then, a certain artistic resistance, even *ressentiment*, is also visible, forcing itself onto this overly lit stage set. While social practice art is only one new mechanism for managing both the "oversupply" of artists and their growing discontent, because it mobilizes social production in general, as an abstract thing or medium or agency, the management has good reason to be nervous. And though its predecessor "relational aesthetics" was a prototypical form of this mobilization, not yet ready for prime time and almost entirely confined to a formal level of artistic practice, the boycotts, demonstrations, wage demands and other breaches of conduct committed by a new wave of art activism understand that art's foundation is in social labor. Resentment and resistance fuel one another, the first making the work of the second possible.

Ever seeking to expand and compound itself, Capital, despite claims to the opposite, is stuck in a cycle of unimaginative destruction and mandatory reuse of existing resources. The real crisis, as Hito Steyerl compellingly argues, is that "history seems to have morphed into a loop [and] the future only happens if history doesn't occupy and invade the present."[28] But what if the solution is exactly the opposite? What if the future only happens when history returns to the present, not as a copy of the past or a monument to its wars and delirium, but as a thing that disturbs the status quo whose very strangeness, as opposed to familiarity, liberates us from the eternal return of commodified time, work, culture, life? Perhaps the final question is this: does a prison break have a foreseeable narrative? Or is it always a singular event?

8

Counting on Your Collective Silence: Notes on Activist Art as Collaborative Practice[*]

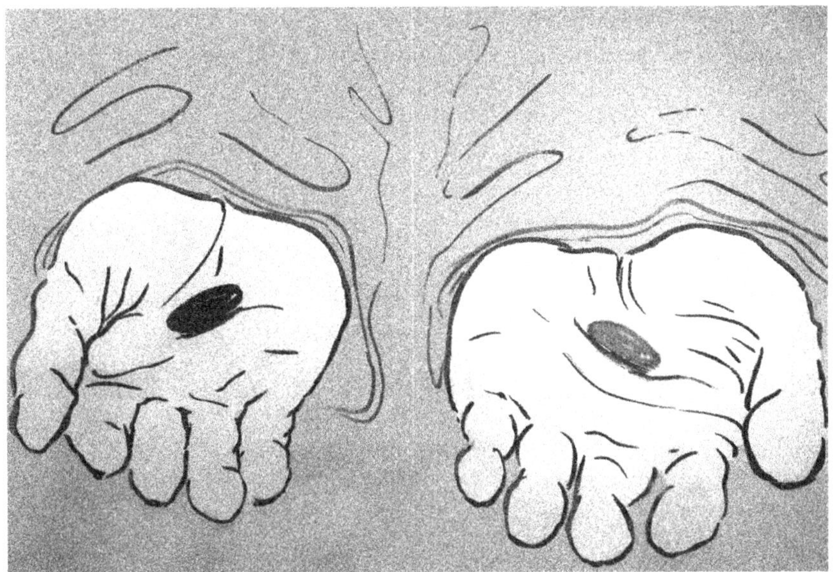

Figure 27   Karl Lorac *Red Pill/Blue Pill*, ink on paper, 18 × 24 inches, 1999 (Image K. Lorac)

Hi Greg,

As I'm thinking about your questions on collective practice etc., I'm disturbed but not surprised to sense that it would be far easier for me to speak about the difficulties of collaborative work than to outline the things, which draw me to it. Here are a few of the positive aspects, however idealized and double-edged, that are important to me: Working as a collective or collaborative means that we can do projects on a scale that one person could only do with great difficulty. Resources, skills, interests, knowledge, and ideas are

*   This chapter was first published in 1999.

167

pooled. This contributes to the overall political and aesthetic complexity, diversity, and effectiveness of the projects. Working on these projects involves developing collaborative practices, which, however problematic, visibly reject a culture of hyper-individualism in favor of other models of "work" and of social (and even "personal") responsibility.

David Thorne, artist and member of the
Resistant Strains art collective, NYC: 1999[1]

Automated Communities?

The Commune [is] the re-absorption of the State power by society as its own living forces, instead of as forces controlling and subduing it, by the popular masses themselves, forming their own force instead of the organized force of their suppression.

Karl Marx[2]

The family, the school, the army, the factory, are no longer the distinct analogical spaces that converge towards an owner—state or private power— but coded figures—deformable and transformable—of a single corporation that now has only stockholders. Even art has left the spaces of enclosure in order to enter into the open circuits of the bank.

Gilles Deleuze[3]

From the swipe of a plastic debit card at the grocery store to regimes of summer recreation, from the surveillance of so-called public spaces to the labels in your undergarments, an administered collectivity hides everywhere in plain sight. Every "I" conceals an involuntary "belonging-ness," every gesture a statistic about the purchasing power, education, and market potential of your desire. A new IBM computer program named "Clever" even detects what its designers call "communities in their nascent stages": these web-based fraternities "spring up spontaneously, even before members are aware of their community's existence."[4]

But if collective formation is so unrelenting it can literally be automated, one might question why non-individualized cultural work—art made cooperatively through collaboration and collective action—requires special attention such as a special issue of *Afterimage*? This raises the question of whether it can be seriously argued today that *the artist* is an autonomous producer who is detachable from politics, history and the market. If we gauge our answer by the unimpeded flow of artists' monographs, by the writing in most art journals, even including that by self-avowed "radical" art historians, the unqualified answer is yes. As the artist's collective Critical Art Ensemble succinctly puts it: "The individual's signature is still the prime collectible, and access to the body associated with the signature is a commodity that is desired more than ever—so much so, that the obsession with the artist's body has made its way into 'progressive' and alternative art networks. Even community art has its stars, its signatures, and its bodies."[5]

While the *auteur* may no longer be thought of as "deep" in the way a Pablo Picasso or Jackson Pollock were once held up as an artistic gold standard, the art industry and its discourse remain dependent on a litany of individual name-brand art producers that circulates like a global aesthetic currency. By contrast, when a group of artists "self-institutionalize" to produce a collaborative or collective the responding art critical narrative, if any, typically falls into one of three story lines: (1) artistic duos like Gilbert and George, Komar and Melamid, or Sophie and Hans Arp, are indiscriminately analyzed using a methodology based on individual art practice to explore their collaboration; (2) collective authorship becomes a backdrop for discussing the evolution of a stellar solo career, for example Kiki Smith as a former member of Collaborative Projects (COLAB), or Joseph Kosuth as a co-founder of Art & Language; (3) the art collective is used to signify an entire historical *mise en scène*, thus the 1930s are the years of organized artistic activism loosely under the umbrella of the Communist Party USA, and the 1980s envisioned as the decade of activist art groups, and so forth. (And no doubt the second decade of the twenty-first-century will one day be described as the rise of networked resistance and collective occupations.)

This chapter will not rectify these critical shortcomings, but it will attempt to open up a set of questions about group art practice, as well as provide specific details regarding collaborative, activist art, much of it drawn from my own experiences, in New York City during the 1980s and 1990s. My text is focused on collective organizations that are both politically engaged and non-hierarchical in structure (at least non-hierarchical in spirit if not always in practice). It is the organizational model I know best, but also it is where the questioning of individuated artistic practice seems to be most contentious. Punctuating my writing the reader will find a series of comments about collective work that I solicited from colleagues. This "symbolic dialogue" is meant to remind both the reader and myself of that larger collective—the intellectual, discursive, practical, material and artistic sphere of present, past and future cultural workers—of which I am at best a ward. My motivation in writing this essay is based in large part on the renewed interest in collective art activism among younger artists and scholars, as well as a conviction that it is not enough to historicize these practices, an endless, even Sisyphean task in itself, but that collective work requires its own analytical approach that does not fall back on modified versions of hagiography, nor slip numbingly into the comforting mystifications of much community-based art.

In her essay "Connective Aesthetics: Art after Individualism" critic Suzi Gablik argues for a new kind of artist who understands that "the boundary between self and Other is fluid rather than fixed: the Other is included within the boundary of selfhood."[6] However, boundaries, both real and imaginary, are historically determined and often harshly material. They are not subject to dissipation by idealized discourse. By contrast, I understand conflict and difference, rather than "merging," to be necessary for the formation of the collective. Furthermore, such incipient abrasiveness cannot but carry over to the routine functioning of the group, thus sparking repercussions, sometimes violent, inside the collective, as well as between the collective and existing institutions and practices. As anyone who has worked in this way will attest, the effort required to sustain collective work rises in direct proportion to the professional and emotional toll extracted on its constituency. Yet it is exactly this state of practical overdetermination—the heterogeneity of membership, the meetings where too much is attempted or rejected, too much brought to the table and left off the table, the fleeting ecstasy of collaborative expenditure, and a space suddenly opened up to the unpredictable effects of class, race, gender, sexual preference, age, divergences in ability, knowledge, and career status—all of this can never be encompassed within the group identity per se but instead forms an excess that is precisely the force making the collective viable.

Perhaps the central concern of this text is therefore to rethink, but also to reconfigure the way collective practice is narrated. Instead of the individual set in opposition to the collective (or the lone artist bestowing his or her talent on a community), my contention is that "collectivity," in one form or another, is virtually an ontological condition of modern life. It precedes divisions of society into the one and the many; the property owner and the commons. Two consequences follow from this supposition. First, it guarantees that no neutral zone can be located from out of which an individual (an *artist* for example) can truly operate alone, as an *individual* in opposition to society. While this does not invalidate the irrepressible desire to escape or radically rewrite what Jean-Jacques Rousseau or Thomas Hobbes considered the social contract or agreement, it does allow us, and this is the second point, to reconfigure the often stated opposition between collective and individual in terms of a topological displacement between two kinds of collective formations: one passive and the other active. Consider Gilles Deleuze in his text "Postscript on the Societies of Control," in which the philosopher describes the new world order as one in which "we no longer find ourselves dealing with the mass/individual pair. Individuals have become '*dividuals*,' and masses, samples, data, markets, or '*banks*.' Man is no longer man enclosed but man in debt."[7]

The Blue Pill

The collective nature of the work can be both exhilarating and exhausting. Working with different people's strengths; balancing individual needs and interests with collective desires and demands; recognizing limits, while opening possibilities, these are challenges perhaps not so different from other administrative positions in mainstream organizations. What is unique, however, to artists is the overriding mythology of genius, and the realities of asymmetrical access to power. This can translate into problems in maintaining a public profile as a collective: making sure the same individuals don't get highlighted again and again in media coverage, allowing different people to speak for the group while maintaining continuity.

There is still the cult of the individual auteur and we as a collective sometimes become kind of invisible.

Lisa Maya Knauer, discussing REPOhistory
at the ten-year mark, NYC, 1999[8]

What I recall most happily are particular periods of working, entering a sort of "flow" state in current jargon together with others, all of us working towards a common goal. This would have to be the "painting parties" held [at ABC No Rio] for various purposes, mostly for Potato Wolf cable TV productions ... There was a general idea of what the set should look like (I don't even recall that there were many if any sketches, just a verbal idea), and then everyone began to make stuff for it. Working was pleasurable, since the mode of working was relatively unusual for me, a writer, and seeing what others had come up with was really exhilarating, especially if the production we were working on was mine. I felt like my ideas were being hyped up and enhanced by others in the group ... All my political actions in the 1970s were based upon my vague and glorified notion of anarchist struggle in Mittel Europa during the last century, of which I knew only some theoretical writings.

Alan W. Moore, NYC, 1999[9]

Reworking the classical Marxian concept of base and superstructure, Fredric Jameson maintains that "the ideological function of mass culture is understood as a process whereby otherwise dangerous and protopolitical impulses are "managed" and defused, rechanneled and offered spurious objects."[10]

Instead of simply masking the true relations of power, as argued by many similar theories, these "spurious objects" satiate a concrete need. That need is abundantly historical, as well as buried from everyday visibility. Borrowing from Walter Benjamin's famed "Theses on the Philosophy of History," Jameson dubs this need the "Political Unconscious." This historical *Other* can no more be wholly repressed than can a passage towards liberation be charted without addressing what "it," this *Other*, wants. In Jameson's terms this means recognizing "such incentives, as well as the impulses to be managed by the mass cultural text, are necessarily Utopian in nature," forming allegorical figures for the ultimate concrete collective life of an achieved Utopian or classless society." If Benjamin argues that the radical historian must "seize hold of a memory as it flashes up at a moment of danger," Jameson would agree and insist that the Utopian impulse is so ubiquitous it is invisibly at work even in the "most degraded of all mass cultural texts, advertising slogans—visions of external life, of the transfigured body, of preternatural sexual gratification—[these] may serve as the model of manipulation on the oldest Utopian longings of humankind."[11]

If Utopian desire, like the background radiation from some radically communal big-bang moment decades, or perhaps centuries past, actually does form a residual political unconscious within mass culture, then so too must some concrete figure of collectivism be present either as image and/or as hidden narrative. And perhaps the most transparent manifestation of collective practice for my purposes is that found in certain science fiction narratives which depict a fantasy in which diverse cells of organized humans actively resist being taken over by hostile invaders (aliens, vampires, zombies and thinking machines in some cases). It is an apocalyptic as well as survivalist narrative that appears in numerous films including John Carpenter's *They Live* (1988), but also such television programs as *Buffy the Vampire Slayer* (1997–2003) or, more recently *The Walking Dead* (2010). This heterotopic figure of underground resistance is perhaps most explicit in the 1980s television series *V* (1983–1985), a mini-series in which human resistance fighters sabotage predacious, reptilian aliens disguised as benevolent "visitors." Reportedly *V* even inspired real-world opposition to white rule in South Africa.[12] Still more useful is the 1999 film *The Matrix*

(1999) and the way it explicitly narrated both desires and anxieties about collectivized human resistance to an alien and alienating enemy.

Set in an apocalyptic near future that looks very much like present-day Chicago, we discover that in fact "the Matrix" is the secret name for a virtual simulation program that almost precisely replicates reality. This simulacrum is fed directly into the cerebellum of the human population who are now grown in liquid-filled vats stacked on top of each other like mile-high versions of Cabrini Green.[13] The Matrix has been digitally fabricated by an artificial intelligence run amuck. This inorganic artisan still needs humans, however, since we are the only source of bioelectrical energy in what appears to be a post-nuclear landscape. Thus the *real world* is in fact little more than an enormous "farm" and the ersatz Chicago is "jacked" into each "human battery" effectively concealing the traumatic "real" that is too awful to directly confront. Happily for us a small band of humans manage to "unplug" themselves from this electronic hegemony, confront the catastrophic landscape of the real world, and in so doing also set about liberating mankind from the machinations of the Matrix.

What interests me about this story most is the way it represents two versions of human collectivization. One is involuntary, and consists of massified bodies digitally dreaming in a cavernous computerized nursery. This is like the bodily awe I sometimes experience attempting to cross Broadway at rush hour or when I try to grasp the magnitude of other people all competing with me for a coffee or subway car or—most disconcertingly perhaps because it is so ephemeral—when using the backed-up telephone system of an airline, bank or other service provider. Opposed to this reflexive collectively are the militarized cells of men and women, white, brown and black, who struggle to release their fellow humans from an invisible bondage. No, this is not the experience I have had as an activist art collaborator, but the way resistance itself is portrayed here is useful.

The Matrix, like *V* and other examples of this sci-fi subgenre, typically represents resistance to mass control as heterogeneous, self-sufficient and culturally diverse. At times the violence of the enemy holding these micro-collectives together barely outweighs their own internal antagonisms, as when for example the Judas-like character in *The Matrix* betrays the group in exchange for returning to the comfort of a simulated reality. But the most important moment for these occupation fantasies is when the horrible nature of the real world is de-concealed. In *The Matrix*, the hero "Neo," played by a nearly inanimate Keanu Reeves, is even offered a choice about this pivotal discovery procedure. When several unplugged humans offer him two pills—one blue and one red—he is asked to choose.

If he swallows the blue pill he remains anesthetized within the Matrix. If, however, he ingests the red pill, then what lies behind the screen is revealed and there is no turning back to the false comfort of the simulated world. As we know, Neo picks the red pill. The now familiar plot of *The Matrix* was developed into two box office busting sequels, but most interesting to me is grafting this figure of revelation, resistance and two competing forms of collectivity directly onto the world of cultural producers. In other words, is it possible to think that when artists choose collective action this is something like taking the red pill? Once one begins to work in a group context, the "blue pill" collectivism that provides an illusion of individuality is displaced by a different collectivity made up of jagged heaps of partial meanings and chunks of resistant histories left over from communal aspirations and failures. It also means that the much vaunted artist-genius narrative is revealed as a fiction. Is it too much of a stretch to suggest that taking the red pill means the mystique of individual artistic practice can never return, at least not with its original luster intact. At some level, I believe artists are always already aware of this choice.

Figuring Collectively

The issue of rupture within community-based artistic collaborations is an important topic because rupture is an inherent part of the process of working with the community ... Communities are not made up of people who are all the same, even if they are the same race. Communities imply a very loose connection of people where cultural, racial and class issues are never a homogeneous mix, and where questions of difference always surface.

From "Some notes on rupture," unpublished text
by artist Tomie Arai, NYC, 1995[14]

The founding or "minting" of any group identity, either corporate or cultural, is always dependent on the material that exceeds this imprint or group signature. However the capitalist, corporate identity aims at purifying this excess, transforming it into a sharply defined brand. This new brand allows the corporation to indefinitely replicate its manufactured identity to consumers with little fear of distraction (which is why image-correcting interventions such as The Yes Men are so difficult to pull off well). For the politicized cultural collective, however, the minting of identity signifies something else: namely, a recognition of the inherently collective texture of the social fabric that surrounds, as well as intersects the group identity at all times. This overdetermination of group identity even affects the day-to-day working procedure of the collective in which too much is attempted, rejected, brought to the table and left off the table and where sudden accelerations of enthusiasm are followed by equally unexpected plunges in spirit. Antonio Negri once described such radical, concentrated excess as a "destructuration," by which I take him to have meant both a demolition of capitalist totality, and the recognition that the nature of today's working class is inherently discontinuous and fragmented. Negri's formulation also implies that such collective arrangements are always therefore at risk of destabilization.[15]

Marx too understood the importance of figuration when discussing political resistance. Writing about the 1871 Paris Commune, he emphasizes the way this historic insurrection was an active reabsorption by the masses of their own alienated powers previously turned against them in the form of the state. Although the Commune lasted only three months, Parisians still managed during this time to declare universal suffrage, to install a communal government, and to decree that all governmental officials be paid only workmen's wages. It is worth contrasting Marx's reappropriation of state control with the "Society of Control" described by Gilles Deleuze. Gone in Deleuze is any single instrument of oppression; this includes the state, the factory or the prison. Today a diffused "universal modulation" forces the individual into a perpetual state of mutation as continuously shifting systems of surveillance, education and work replace any fixed locus of power. Without collapsing these different conceptions of the social body—one analogical the other digital if you like—it is possible to see that each presents us with an economy of forces in which acts of displacement alternate with routines of administration. In both cases resistance depends upon recognizing its very possibility *within* the familiar. Marx describes the predicament this way:

> It is generally the fate of completely new historical creations to be mistaken for the counterpart of older and even defunct forms of social life, to which they may bear a certain likeness. Thus the new Commune, which breaks the modern State power, has been mistaken for a reproduction of the mediaeval Communes, which first preceded, and afterwards became the substratum of, that very State power.[16]

For Marx, the Commune is a displacement in which a unique historical event outwardly replicates an archaic but well-known form: in this case the medieval commune (recall the deceptive role familiarity plays in our pop-culture example *The Matrix*). Deleuze also muses about the possibility of recognizing resistance from within the "society of control." He still manages to ask "can we already grasp the rough outlines of these coming forms, capable of threatening the joys of marketing?"[17] His question, which explicitly adds the problem of pleasure to the one of mere recognition that Marx raises, might be provisionally answered in the form of the politically engaged artists' collective if this is understood, as proposed here, not as a unity of differences, but as the overdetermined arrangement akin to what Toni Negri describes as the "radical, irreducible differentness of the revolutionary movement."[18]

Repetition and Difference

All my angst about collaborative work is hard to separate from the many good times and success that I shared as a member of Blue Funk; Chiefly Brit. A State of Great Terror—a six person 3 male 3 female art group from 1990 to 1995. Authorship was an interesting issue and a given piece was undercut by this transindividual author Blue Funk. The overall result was a strange and liberating experience. We were like some multitracked techno recording that is indistinguishable in a given space. We also rarely used text and all writing was kept to a minimum. For our piece in Sonsbeek 93 in the Netherlands we didn't even have a title. If we followed any model I doubt if we could agree on it—maybe a band that is kept together by the tensions pulling it apart … But the pieces that we made have an interesting ontological shelf life … the archive of Blue Funk is dispersed and the ghost of Blue Funk still lingers on … I think humour was an important element in Blue Funk stemming from the name itself and from our collective friendship, politics and angst.

Brian Hand, Dublin, 1999[19]

Finally, above all else the activist art collective is a de facto critique of the bourgeois public sphere. Not only does the overdetermined nature of such groups upset the alleged separation of public and private space, but the process of self-institutionalization itself inevitably assimilates political functions normally allocated to the bourgeois public sphere. The politicized artists' group not only seizes space, in other words, it also squats organizational structures, transforming these into something both new, and perhaps also quite old. Sometimes the act of self-governing is consciously invoked, at other times simply manifest, but always the politics of the collective are sooner or later thrust into view. For the members of the collective this means deciding among themselves what kind of democratic process they will operate with, as well as establishing rules about membership (should it be open to all who attend meetings, or just active participants?) and voting (do motions pass using a simple majority or through consensus by every member?). Ironically, it is often the process of internal politicization that reveals the lack of historical memory that dominates cultural resistance. Consider the following texts I have excerpted from the minutes of three New York City politically engaged artists collectives: AMCC (Artists Meeting for Cultural Change, 1975–1977), PAD/D (Political Art Documentation and Distribution, 1980–1986, actively), and REPOhistory (1989–2000):

> Our most urgent task right now is to find a more representative method of arriving at true agreement within the group. Not to do this is to doom us to continual tactical maneuvering using these rules—tactics that, as was amply demonstrated last week, lead to destructive polarization and quite palpable disunity ... In this group we are not looking for "victory" of one strand of opinion over another. In fact, this machismo, warlike attitude within the group is entirely contrary to everything that we should be struggling towards. (AMCC document, January 30, 1977)[20]

> I noticed there were certain men or people who could say just about anything and everyone was "attentive." Those who do the most work, those with the most responsibility, those with the most political sophistication and those who have a degree of establishment in the art field have the most "power." We live in a hierarchical world. The fact that some of it translates into PADD is obvious. (Excerpt from an open letter to PAD/D from a former member, October, 1983)[21]

> KL felt that there was a consensus from the last meeting that membership take active tasks ... LK felt that analyzing tasks would help redistribute work. She said that some people have resentment because they do not know where the task openings are.
> KL said that tasks will shift given the projects we are working on. PL thought we should take a look at who's doing what and why.
> HB wanted to understand how this list would relate to project tasks.
> TT thought that the person within a project ... could become the delegate to work in a general REPO working group.
> LK felt that certain people end up doing too much of the work and this person would be doing twice the work ... It is important that more people get involved in this decision. (REPOhistory minutes, January 4, 1993)[22]

LB: what does closed meeting mean anyway? we don't publicize it? what if we just say what it is online, put it out in GG, describe it as retreat, those involved will come.

BR: Closed meeting is having a space to acknowledge some of these things, tensions in the group. Actually, not sure why it needs to be closed.

J: are you creating a safer space, need it to be more trusting? BR: yes.

AB: I wd rather risk a little lack of safety in order to have proposals. Wonder if describe meeting other people wd really want to come anyway.

LB: friendly amendment 20–30 min for proposals.

PW: does closed meeting meaning you can say whatever you want, no minutes, not reported back. or the idea it would be reported back?

LB: yes, no minutes, if talking about what didn't work, don't want that reported out.

BR: can I restate the proposal as use this draft, but describe it not as closed meeting. will dedicate next week to this structure. I guess we could do proposals at end, as long as we keep time.

LB: and friendly amendment re: no recorded minutes. AB: too shady not to advertise it?

LB: too weird for OWS. AB: I get that. (Arts & Labor working group of Occupy Wall Street, minutes from December 6, 2011)[23]

The repetition demonstrated by these documents is all the more remarkable when you consider that the selections span almost 35 years, and that these four groups share various degrees of overlapping membership. Obvious lessons might be drawn from this about the deficiency of not having a history or theory about collective practice, or how the burdens of decision making, divisions of labor, and power sharing are not mitigated simply because people choose to work cooperatively. And because activist art collectives are naturally suspicious of establishment politics, each new group tends to reinvent organizational processes already attempted, sometimes even abandoned by other similar institutions. Therefore what appears to be a blank screen on which to project some new, radical form of self-government might better be understood as a surface so overly etched with traces—of language, history, knowledge and material conditions— that it merely appears empty. These traces cannot be navigated without first recognizing the way in which spatial metaphors are used, consciously or not, by the collective. The problem is similar to that characterized by Jacques Derrida in his essay "The Ends of Man: Reading Us," first published in France in 1969 during the political aftershock of May '68. When the question is what paths lead to radical change the philosopher suggests there remain only two strategies:

> a. To attempt an exit and a deconstruction without changing terrain by repeating what is implicit in the founding concepts and the original problematic by using against the edifice the instruments or stones available in the house, that is equally, in language. Here one risks ceaselessly confirming, consolidating, relifting (*relever*), at an always more certain depth, that which one deconstructs. The continuous process of making explicit, moving toward and opening, risks sinking into the autism of the closure.

> b. To decide to change terrain, in a discontinuous and irruptive fashion, by brutally placing oneself outside, and by affirming an absolute break and difference. Without mentioning all the other forms of *trompe-l'oeil* perspective in which such a displacement can be caught, thereby inhabiting more naively and more strictly than ever the inside one declares one has deserted, the simple practice of language ceaselessly reinstates the new terrain on the oldest ground.[24]

Derrida's solution to this dilemma insists that: "A new writing must weave and interlace these two motifs of deconstruction. Which amounts to saying that one must speak several languages and produce several texts at once."[25] But how can "we" remember and forget, repeat and interrupt, have a history as well as start over again? One possible answer is to map Derrida's musings about ontology onto the very corporeal *plurality* of the activist art collective.

The Red Pill

> *One main factor of this period [early 1980s] was its generosity in trying to include everyone—artist and non artist, good or bad art etc. in exhibitions. This may be why [Lucy R.] Lippard's writing at that time in my eyes was more documentation (in the sense of listing artists and artworks in a matter of fact way) of this growing subculture away from the artmaket, and not criticism directed to judge the quality of a work of art.*
>
> Todd Ayoung, NYC, 1999[26]

Certainly the contingencies Derrida enumerates play themselves out within and around the art collective, including the unwitting consolidation of prevailing power relations—masculinist authority, over-centralization, bureaucracy—and perhaps even more insidiously what he calls a *"trompe-l'oeil"* effect, in which an imagined escape route is but a projection of present limitations. Yet it is the very absence of the collective, in particular the activist art collective, from within the larger cultural discourse (including what goes by the names "left" or Progressive) that seems to indicate a potential for something uncomfortably other and plural. If Derrida's question of "who, we?" were posed to such a group entity the response would come as a shimmer of voices, historical narratives and political positions. Within the "overflowingness" of collective identity, then, are both figures of resistance and something Derrida later termed in *Specters of Marx*

> a certain experience of the promise that one can try to liberate from any dogmatics and even from any metaphysico-religious determination, from any *messianism*. And a promise must be kept, that is, not to remain "spiritual" or "abstract," but to produce effects, new effective forms of action, practice, organization, and so forth.[27]

While Deleuze has asserted that "there is no need to fear or hope, but only to look for new weapons," Derrida still pursues the concept of hope, but in some as yet unrecognized anti-teleological form of the promise, not unlike Jameson's Political Unconscious or Benjamin's moment of historical danger.[28] This "promise," however, *must* be made concrete. And, above all else, what the activist art collective makes tangible, and no doubt what is anathema to the art market and its discourse, is the capacity for self-regulation over one's production and distribution. No doubt this ability is available and suppressed within all artistic practice and within all productive activity, just as regulators, including Societies of Control, always recognize the danger of this promise. Ironically, the activist art collective often displays its own self-control through overproduction and aesthetic incontinence: two operations forbidden by an industry that depends upon the illusion of scarcity and the predictability of goods (the consistency of an artist's style and nowadays even their persona). Perhaps this, more than any imagined threat to some lingering ideology of artistic autonomy, is the danger the collective presents. Let's look a bit more closely at the mechanics of self-control or what Negri calls "self-valorization" before deciding on this question.

First, such artistic self-valorization can be read as a reappropriation directed against the market's own need to rein in an artist's production and stylistic trademark. That restraint is virtually built into an artist's education and reiterated, in one form or another, within the marketplace through dealers, critics and even by other artists. However, within the relative sanctuary of the group identity, this pressure is ameliorated. So much so that being part of a collective often means experimenting with styles and technologies that would otherwise be disruptive to one's career. Second, and even more troubling from the point of view of the culture industry, is the way in which such collectives defiantly establish their own rules about who is and who is not an artist. Such aesthetic self-validation is typically extended, like stolen goods, from the collective to others, including many who feel locked out of traditional venues for reasons of political or cultural content, or simply because of the stinginess of the art market. In the 1980s the artist's collective Group Material went so far as to use the frame of the museum itself to legitimate such munificence. This pilfered aesthetic aura is even transferable from the collective to non-artists, who become ordained as bona fide aesthetic producers. In spite of the "inclusiveness" now dominating the contemporary art world, such cross-disciplinary work remains taboo, except on those occasions when a non-artist is incorporated, readymade fashion, within the work (or even through the body) of a "legitimate artist."

Finally, because all practical issues related to aesthetics today are ultimately settled in the marketplace, we should ask if it is possible to *collect the collective*? Which is to say, under what circumstances would the group signature—it's minting or coinage if you like—be capable of being possessed? Certainly specific objects produced by Group Material, the Guerrilla Girls, Gran Fury and other collectives have, in a limited way, found their way into museums, archives and private collections. But this only raises the question differently: how can one comprehend group authorship as an artist? The answer seems to depend upon the possibility of even conceiving such a thing as a group signature *proper* (as opposed to, say, a collection of signatures or gathering of styles). Such a thing, if it did exist, would openly dispute the fiction of the individual mark: that unique sign which guarantees my absence only by virtue of being infinitely repeatable. It leads us to question the economy of this seemingly unique mark within the art industry and its discourse, and its function within that administered form of collectivity the Society of Control. If we were to answer that artistic value is determined today by a sphincter-like regulation of the individual mark with all that it represents, then, considering what has been said about the excess and instability of group identity—such a thing as a collective signature would by definition be incomprehensible. Not unlike the grotesque truth of *The Matrix*, recognition of this condition demands its price, both personally, and professionally.

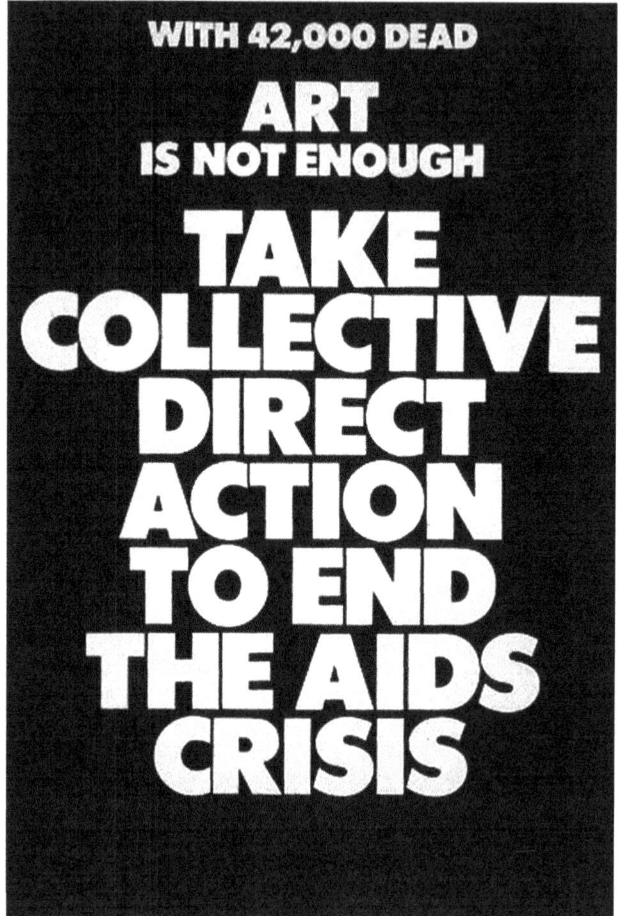

Figure 28   Take Collective Action, a poster by Gran Fury Poster, circa 1986

(Image Gran Fury collective)

Regarding the practice of collective, activist art, this text is neither comprehensive nor conclusive. It is an open question whether the observations here can apply more broadly to other forms of cooperative work. The self-valorizing art collective, with all of its volatility and repetition, may be resistant to what Deleuze calls the Society of Control, if for no other reason than its sheer generosity of material, aesthetic and political production.[29] Overdetermined and discontinuous, the collective assembles the needs, affiliations, differences, sometimes even afflictions of others in a space suddenly open to the possibility of social equality and self-management. Even under the best circumstances, the collective is fueled by these differences as well as destabilized by them. Still, if it was not for the intellectual and sensual pleasure made available, uniquely I believe, through sustained and voluntary collective activity, and undoubtedly linked to this same economy of displacement and reappropriation, no one would ever "ingest the red pill." After all, the art world is counting on your collective silence.

9
Dark Matter: Activist Art and the Counter-Public Sphere

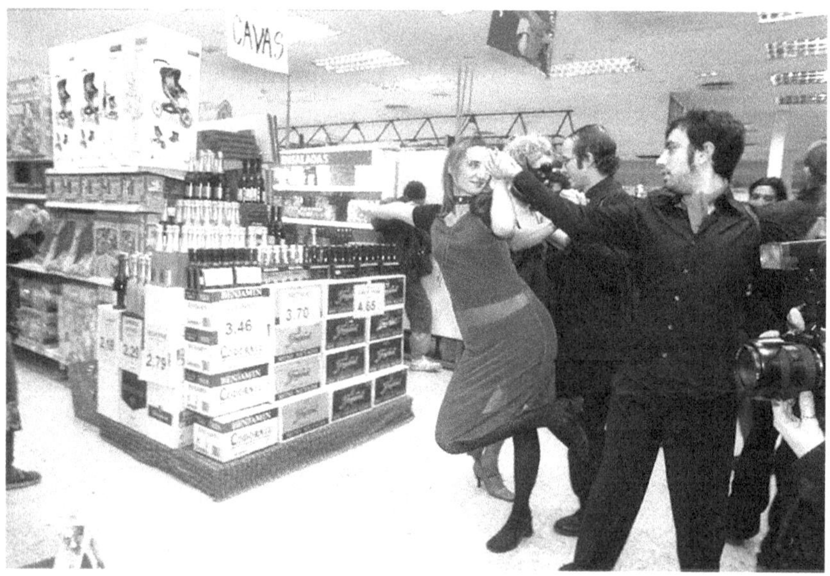

Figure 29 "Yomango Tango" activists flamboyantly "liberate" luxury items from a chain store in Barcelona, Spain using the "Five-Finger Discount" choreographed to live tango music as a protest against austerity following bank failures in Argentina, 2002

(Image Leonidas Martin Saura/Yomango http://beautifultrouble.org/case/yomango/)

The emphasis on the passive element in experience certainly does not claim to be a theory of knowledge … But it is certainly the preliminary condition of any theory of knowledge which is not content with verbalistic and illusory solutions.

Sebastiano Timpanaro, in On Materialism[1]

There is perhaps no current problem of greater importance to astrophysics and cosmology than that of "dark matter."[2]

The MAVAN Conference, and the Battles Lost

What does one make of a conference entitled Marxism and Visual Arts Now (MAVAN), in which examples of contemporary visual art were all but absent and the few speakers who did address recent artistic practices hardly strayed from citing works and practices not already ensconced within the institutional art world? One possible explanation for this conspicuous absence is the understandable resignation that the progressive scholar or artist experiences when confronting a world dominated, almost without exception, by images of a triumphant, global capitalism. This gloom is unintentionally compounded by the MAVAN conference itself, in so far as it concentrates knowledge about the numerous, failed efforts at oppositional artistic practice during the last hundred years. To quote historian O.K. Werckmeister, himself a participant at MAVAN: "After over half a century of progressive abstraction from politics to ideology, from history to utopia, these images are dimming into irrelevancy before our own historical predicament."[3] Such resistant strains of art, if not openly suppressed by state power, either implode from the force of internal contradictions, or do so through a process of institutionalization as they come to resemble the very thing they once opposed. Meanwhile, within the United States today an unfolding spectacle of patriotism and militarism rises amid the subservient and seamless mixture of high fashion and postmodernist irony that assumes the title avant-garde art. This aesthetic of delirium infiltrates galleries and museums, but also public spaces, retail stores, advertising campaigns and even the language of management theory. It is a state of affairs that places a new spin on the classical avant-garde call to transform art into life. Yet if art and life have finally fused, then the life that art has merged with is as corrupt as it is appalling.

At this moment therefore, the battle waged over the symbolic power of artistic practice appears to be finished. Like a scene out of a Russian novel the battlefield is heaped with the remnants of an astonishing array of artistic models, many once aligned with the left and other progressive forces. The defeated in fact fill the museums of twentieth-century art. Among the fallen are those who sought to represent working-class life with compassion and candor, as well as more cerebrally oriented practitioners who endeavored to reveal and subvert the ideological tropes of mass culture.

Here and there are card-carrying modernist nobility and inscrutable formalists whose challenge to the decaying structures of bourgeois society were championed as an immanent critique by T.W. Adorno. Self-segregated in practice, mutual defeat conjoins this mélange of artistic modes and helps explain the missing "Now" witnessed at the MAVAN conference. And while the loss of a strong, pervasive counter-hegemonic visual culture is as deep as the success of the consciousness industry is mountainous, this trope of failure should never become the sole determination of historical and theoretical reflection. Therefore, should you seek still another opportunity to grieve over the prosperity of bourgeois culture, please read no further. All of the lamentations and descriptions of defeat this chapter contains are in the preceding paragraphs. Nor will satisfaction be offered to those who seek another redemptive tract about the critical potential of avant-garde art. Instead, what this chapter attempts is the production, or perhaps the recovery, of space. A space gathered from in between other structures and methods and in which a counter-narrative about the mostly unseen, and sometimes oppositional creative practices already present in the shadows of the culture industry can be articulated. Some will call this activity art and others will refuse that classification, but for my purposes such proper labeling is less the issue than the process of articulating and mapping present coordinates. To that end, this chapter has three, more or less explicit aims. The first of these is as stated: to provide a map of a dimly lit creative realm largely excluded from the economic and discursive structures of the institutionalized art world.[4] Speculating on exactly why this shadow zone has not attracted serious, critical attention, and not even from many radical scholars, is the second goal of the paper. Third, by linking specific aspects of informal creative practice with forms of emerging and residual politicized art, my text calls on progressive scholars and artists to initiate their own critique of what I somewhat mischievously call the artistic "dark matter" of the art world.

Dark Matters

> Who built Thebes of the seven gates?
> In the books you will read the names of kings.
> Did the kings haul up the lumps of rock?
>
> And Babylon, many times demolished,
> Who raised it up so many times? …
>
> Every page a victory.
> Who cooked the feast for the victors?
>
> Every 10 years a great man.
> Who paid the bill?

So many reports.

So many questions
(Bertolt Brecht, "Question from a Worker Who Reads")[5]

I begin with a riddle: what is invisible but has such great mass that its effects are everywhere visible? Consider Brecht's frequently cited poem about a worker who questions the dominant portrayal of history as a string of accomplishments by a few remarkable men. The poet's fictive narrator reveals what Brecht knew from experience: any large-scale project, be it artistic, political or military is decidedly *collaborative* in nature.[6] At the same time, collective experience, as well as the intimation of worker autonomy, poses a potential threat to capitalist management. Collectivism's imprint therefore, on commodities and services, along with its trace of political and symbolic power, are attributes that must be managed through the imposition of clearly discerned, administrative hierarchies, first during production and then through the pseudo-collective imprint of a corporate identity or brand following production. Any additional residue of collectivism is shuttled towards the seemingly autonomous realm of the bourgeois public sphere where it is reconfigured within concepts such as community and nation or, most notably today, as an often dubious form of patriotism.[7] Yet it is precisely the contour of labor's unrepresented collective experience that Brecht's literate worker begins to trace for himself. At the same time, the poem is itself a didactic lesson in so far as Brecht uses it to forge a necessary link between a materialist analysis of ideology and that which is *not* visible. He as much as insists that, before any dialectical or materialist analysis of ideology is initiated, one must first perform a radical reversal of normative, authorial categories. Carrying this methodological inversion over to the realm of the arts, it would seem that any practice claiming to be radical must also take seriously the materiality and structural complexity of unseen creative labor. This includes collective and informal work largely relegated to the shadows of art history, but also non-professional, cultural practices. To do anything less means reducing materialist art history to a mere social history of art that, as Andrew Hemingway asserts, "takes the bourgeois category of art too much for granted, and turns itself into an appendage of that it supposedly seeks to critique."[8] Imagine we were to recast the protagonist of Brecht's poem as a class-conscious, radical art historian? What sort of questions might she ask of the art historical canon and its succession of male geniuses? Was the painting of the *Demoiselles d'Avignon* truly the result of one man's virile talents? Did Pablo Picasso, Matisse or even Bertolt Brecht not draw ideas and material support from an invisible entourage of mistresses, amateur actors and non-Western artists? What percentage of their historic importance owes itself to the skills as well as *the creativity* of artisans who prepared pigments, brushes, engravings or props, sets and stage lighting? Did these other men and women not have talent and ambition of their own? So few great artists: who paid the bills?

Nonetheless, we must go even further than this initial line of questioning because it is not sufficient for a radical scholarship to simply provide conventional art history with a more complete "background" to creative labor and then leave it at that. Instead, a class-conscious and materialist approach to art scholarship and theory must, by necessity, seek to revise radically the very notion of artistic value as it is defined by bourgeois ideology. Besides finding new ways to account for collective artistic authorship it must also theorize the many occasions in which no object is produced or where the artistic practice is a form of creative engagement focused on the process of organization itself. And it needs to theorize concepts of expenditure, including the notion of artistic gift giving as well as the shadowy forms of production and distribution, while simultaneously challenging the emerging rhetoric of artistic administration as evinced by the de-politicized use of the term "cultural capital."[9]

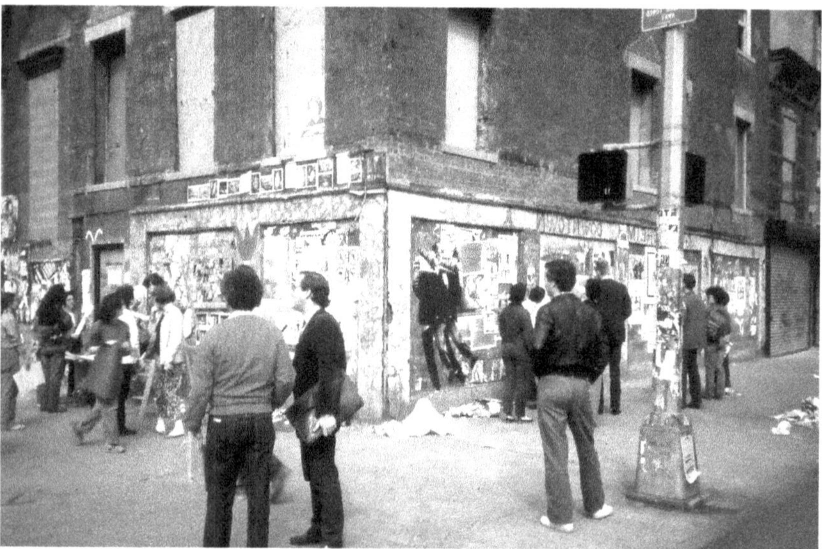

Figure 30 Anti-gentrification street art exhibition by PAD/D opening event at the impromptu gallery "Guggenheim Downtown," temporarily located on the corner of Avenue A and 10th Street in the East Village, NYC, 1984

(Image G. Sholette)

This amounts to a radical re-zoning of art world real estate. This re-mapping also requires the placing of brackets around concepts such as taste or connoisseurship and that means art world property values can be expected to fall hard and fast. Nevertheless, it is the centralized art world itself, with its continuous striving to incorporate prudent examples of the very things that most oppose it, that ironically now opens a door onto a far more radical redistribution of creative value. It is an opening away from high culture and towards the dark matter beyond.

Cosmologists describe *dark matter*, and more recently *dark energy*, as large, invisible entities predicted by the Big Bang theory. So far, dark matter has been perceived only indirectly, by observing the motions of visible astronomical objects such as stars and galaxies. Despite its invisibility and unknown constitution, however, most of the universe, perhaps as much as 96% of it, consists of dark matter. This is a phenomenon sometimes called the "missing mass problem." Like its astronomical cousin, *creative dark matter* also makes up the bulk of the artistic activity produced in our post-industrial society. However, this type of dark matter is invisible primarily to those who lay claim to the management and interpretation of culture—the critics, art historians, collectors, dealers, curators and arts administrators. It includes informal practices such as home-crafts, makeshift memorials, internet art galleries, amateur photography and pornography, Sunday-painters, self-published newsletters and fanzines. Yet, just as the physical universe is dependent on its dark matter and energy, so too is the art world dependent on its shadow creativity. It needs this shadow activity in much the same way certain developing countries secretly depend on their dark or informal economies.[10]

Contemplate for a moment the destabilizing effect on professional artists if hobbyists and amateurs were to stop purchasing art supplies. Consider also the structural "darkness" within which most professionally trained artists actually exist. In the United States alone, several million MFA graduates have been produced since the initiation of the MFA degree in 1944.[11] Assuming even a graduation rate of only 60% (at the time of writing in 2007) the total number of academically trained professional artists holding Master of Fine Arts degrees likely hovers around 24,000 individuals (see chapter 3 this volume for more on this). If trained artists from non-degree programs and those who stopped their education at the BFA level are added to the pool, this number spikes considerably upwards. Yet, given the proportionally few individuals who achieve visibility within the formalized institutions of the art world, are there really any significant structural differences between an earnest amateur and a professional artist made invisible by her "failure" within the art market? Except that perhaps, against all real odds, she still hopes to be discovered? Nonetheless, these shadow-practitioners are essential for the functioning of the institutional and elite art world. For one thing, this dark army makes up the education providers of the next generation of artists. They also work as arts administrators and art fabricators: two increasingly valuable resources given the complexity of producing and managing contemporary, global art. By purchasing journals and books, visiting museums and belonging to professional organizations, these "invisibles" are an essential component of the elite art world whose pyramidal structure looms over them despite the fact that its upper levels remain eternally out of reach.[12] Finally, without an army of allegedly lesser talents to serve as ballast, the privileged treatment of a small number of highly successful artists would be impossible to justify. A class-conscious and materialist analysis begins by turning this equation on its head. New question: what becomes of the economic and ideological foundations of the bourgeois art world if this larger mass of excluded practices were to be given equal consideration as art? This question is now largely in the domain of sociologists and anthropologists. But radical scholars and artists must take that inversion as a starting point and move to the next stage of analysis: the linking of dark matter to those artists who *self-consciously* work outside and/or against the parameters of the mainstream art world for reasons of political and social critique.

These informal, politicized micro-institutions are proliferating today. They create work that infiltrates high schools, flea markets, public squares, corporate websites, city streets, housing projects, and local political machines in ways that do not set out to recover a specific meaning or use-value for art world discourse or private interests. This is due to the fact that many of these activities operate through economies based on pleasure, generosity and the free dispersal of goods and services, rather than the construction of a false scarcity required by the value structure of art world institutions. What can be said of dark matter in general is that, either by choice or circumstance, it displays a degree of autonomy from the critical and economic structures of the art world and moves instead within, or in between, the meshes of the consciousness industry.[13] But this independence is not risk free. Increasingly inexpensive technologies of communication, replication, display and transmission that allow informal and activist artists to network with each other have also made the denizens of this shadowy world ever more conspicuous to the very institutions that once sought to exclude them. In short, dark matter is no longer as *dark* as it once was. Yet, the art world, and global capital, can do little more than immobilize specific, often superficial aspects of this shadow activity by converting it into a fixed consumable or brand. However, even this cultural taxidermy comes at a cost to the elite, contemporary art world because it forces into view the latter's arbitrary value structure. In terms of combat therefore, the double-edged hazards brought on by increasing and decreasing visibility are essential to comprehend.

The Amateurization *of Contemporary Art*

Not only does the amateur status of hobby art dispel the need for costly art lessons, it subverts the intimidation process that takes place when the male domain of "high" art is approached. As it stands, women—and especially women—can make hobby art in a relaxed manner, isolated from the "real" world of commerce and the pressures of professional aestheticism.[14] Evidence that dark matter has affected the world of high art is easy to locate. I will focus on just three examples, starting with the 2002 Whitney Biennial. As curator Larry Rinder explained in the exhibition catalogue the goal of this biennial was to feature those "creative practices" operating "without concern for the art market or art world accolades." Rinder's claims were sardonically commented upon by *New York Times* art reporter Roberta Smith, who suggested that if this exhibition "signals a new openness, [then] the outskirts look very much like the center of town."[15] Among the alleged art world *outsiders* included in the Whitney's high-profile art roundup was Forcefield: a Rhode Island based art group whose installation of hyper-colorful, hand-knit costumes and wigs came with its own reverberating, industrial soundtrack. Yet this ubiquitous, outsider aesthetic Smith alludes to is perhaps more aptly labeled "slack art" by historian Brandon Taylor.[16] Self-consciously amateurish and informal and at the same time the product of a bona-fide MFA degree, this slacker aesthetic was perfectly expressed in a second, very slackly entitled exhibition called K48-3: Teenage Rebel—The Bedroom Show. Organized by Scott Hug for a commercial gallery in the Chelsea district of Manhattan, it boasted work by 50 artists, fashion designers, musicians and graphic designers, all haphazardly displayed on and around an automobile-shaped bed parked on a lime-green shag rug. Snapshots of gun-toting teens, hand-painted sneakers, scrappy pages of doodles, black-light posters, Ken dolls and distressed T-shirts were crammed into every corner of this fictional domestic space. And no less than three of the art writers for the city's major weekly publications deemed Rebel Teen Bedroom essential viewing during the first few weeks of 2003.[17]

My final example of institutionally secure high art influenced by the informality of what I describe as non-professional artistic dark matter is the work of Sarah Lucas, a British artist featured in the controversial *Sensation* show at London's Royal Academy of Art in 1997. Lucas's art consists of objects and installations made from such off-hand materials as stockings and soiled mattresses, a ripe melon, a toilet bowl cast in yellow resin and a cluster of snapshots arranged with that careful indifference to formal, aesthetic schema now typical of slack, or *amateurized* high art.[18] However it is the Lucas piece entitled *Nobby* that most clearly testifies to the sway of dark matter over younger artists. *Nobby* consists of a 1 meter high, plastic "gnome," pushing a wheelbarrow. In all but one respect it is identical to the figures of dwarves that suburban homeowners place on their lawns. The one difference is that both *Nobby* and his wheelbarrow are entirely covered in a "skin" of cigarettes.[19] Because contemporary artistic products are not required to be the work of the presenting artist we must consider the possibility that Lucas purchased this butt-covered dwarf at a flea market, or perhaps on an internet auction site such as ebay. In fact, *Nobby* might just as easily be the work of an anonymous and obsessive smoker or it might be the tedious task of the artist's assistant, or it may be her own handiwork. The answer is irrelevant. However, while this apathy regarding authorship sweeps away several previously valued artistic qualities, including personal expression and the uniqueness of a particular object, it also eliminates from the process of artistic valorization any measurement of the artist's technical capabilities. This raises an obvious question regarding dark matter and, in particular, the practice of amateur artists and "Sunday" painters. Just what is it that prevents this sort of non-professional creative activity from directly entering the value structure of the elite art world? Or, to ask this question in reverse, how is it that the products of art remain "high" or "elite," when cigarette-covered lawn gnomes are scrupulously placed on display by leading, metropolitan art museums? The same question might be posed of artistic authorship. However, in order to answer these questions we first need a working model of the way artistic value is normally produced within the contemporary art world, one that can explain why not just any tobacco-encrusted dwarf gets to enter such an elite domain.

One way to explain why it is that a few artistic producers are rewarded, often quite handsomely, by the art world, while others lose absolutely, is to compare the way value is produced in that arena with value production in competitive sports. The economic anthropologist Stuart Plattner does this by employing a Tournament Model, in which the winning athlete may be a mere fraction of a second faster than one or more of her rivals, yet she is designated the sole winner regardless of the outstanding athletic ability of her competition. According to Plattner, "this model is relevant to the art market because it describes a situation of workers receiving payments that don't seem related to their input of effort."[20] In a close art world competition, however, it is not physical prowess that differentiates the winners from losers, but the quality of *consumption capital* available to the judges. This includes knowing which artist is highly sought after by a prestigious museum or private collector, or what influential critic or curator will soon feature her work in a review or exhibition.[21] Therefore, what stabilizes the borders of the elite art market is *the routine production of relatively minor differences.* These differences may have to do with the context surrounding a particular artwork or the authorship of a given piece, but what is important, and *Nobby* offers concrete evidence of this fact, is that art world valuation has little to do with the formal characteristics of the artwork in itself. Instead, it has everything to do with the way *consumption capital*—accumulated knowledge about art—is produced, circulated and accumulated. This also helps to explain how seemingly identical art products generate artistic value in radically unequal ways.[22] Our re-mapping and ultimate deconstruction of artistic value hinges on this insight.

Look again at the art world and the dark matter it occludes. The lines separating dark and "light" creativity appear almost arbitrary, even from the standpoint of qualities such as talent, vision and other similar mystifying attributes typically assigned to "high art." If indeed the struggle over representational power is reduced to skirmishes and fleeting advancements and retreats, then the reality of this new combat requires a turning away from the realm of the exclusively visual and towards creative practices focused on organizational structures, communicative networks and economies of giving and dissemination. It is an activity that necessarily points to the articulation of what theorists Oskar Negt and Alexander Kluge call the proletarian or counter-public sphere.[23]

The Counter-public Sphere

Federal elections, Olympic ceremonies, the actions of a commando unit, a theatre premiere—all are considered public events. Other events of overwhelming public significance, such as childbearing, factory work, and watching television within one's own four walls, are considered private. The real experiences of human beings, produced in everyday life and work, cut across such divisions ... [T]he weakness characteristic of virtually all forms of the bourgeois public sphere derives from this contradiction: namely, that [it]… excludes substantial life interests and nevertheless claims to represent society as a whole.

Oskar Negt and Alexander Kluge[24]

It is beyond the scope of this chapter to present the full complexity of Negt and Kluge's theories regarding the inherently conflicted constitution of contemporary public spheres, except to say that their polemical displacement of Jürgen Habermas's concept pivots on the actual life experience of workers and others wholly or partially excluded from that idealized realm of citizenship and public opinion. It also seeks to account for the influence that relatively new modes of communication and deception, famously termed the culture industry by Adorno and Horkheimer, continue to have on both worker acquiescence and resistance to capitalist totality. What I will attempt, however, is to introduce two key aspects of their work that are especially relevant to my arguments about dark matter. These include: (1) the subversive potential of working-class fantasy as a counter-productive activity hidden within the capitalist labor process, and (2) Negt and Kluge's insistence that it is politically and theoretically necessary to weave together the fragmented history of resistance to capital into a larger whole or a counter-public sphere. Much like dark matter that is itself often composed of fantastic and libidinous forms of expression, working-class fantasy is never fully absorbed by the antagonistic structures of capitalism. As Negt and Kluge assert: "Throughout history, living labor has, along with the surplus value extracted from it, carried on its own production—within fantasy."[25] The authors further define fantasy as a multi-layered defense mechanism providing, "necessary compensation for the experience of alienated labor process."[26] This does not mean that fantasy, any more than dark matter, represents an inherently progressive force. Instead: "In its unsublated form, as a mere libidinal counterweight to unbearable, alienated relations, fantasy is itself merely an expression of this alienation. Its contents are therefore inverted consciousness. Yet by virtue of its mode of production, fantasy constitutes an unconscious practical critique of alienation."[27]

Working-class fantasy therefore appears to offer a twofold critical function. At its most basic level it is a counter-productive surplus that constitutes a de facto mode of resistance to alienation. This is not merely a metaphysical limit but a material force generated by the "residue of unfulfilled wishes, ideas, of the brain's own laws of movement."[28] However, at the same time, the content of fantasy does occasionally represent specific instances of anti-capitalist or at least anti-authoritarian sentiment. Negt and Kluge approach this repressed content as "promises of meaning and totality—promises that reproduce, in a highly sensitive manner, actual wishes, some of which remain uncensored by the ruling interest."[29]

Examples of workplace fantasies that were turned into action include the convenience store clerk who adjusted his pricing gun to create spontaneous discounts for customers; the model maker who added fantastic machinery to elaborately fabricated coal and nuclear power plant models; the assembly line date pitter who inserted her own messages into the fruit proclaiming such things as, "Hi, I'm your pitter" or simply "stuff it" and "Aaagghhh!!!"; the Heritage Foundation mailroom attendant who shredded fundraising letters meant to raise cash for her employer's conservative agenda; the low-paid, whitecollar stock broker who used his access to a Wall Street phone system to create actual fluctuations in market shares; and the professional muralist who rendered Nazi stormtroopers in the background of a painting made for a Walt Disney hotel and worked images of severed heads into another mural for a restaurant in Las Vegas.[30] However, in so far as these fragmented acts suggest the need for some greater "meaning and totality" yet nevertheless remain unarticulated as such, they are little more than isolated and ultimately impotent moments of a distorted wish fulfilment. Still, both dark matter and working-class fantasy do occasionally resist bourgeois ideology. First, they interrupt its normative structures of production and appropriation. And, second, they present a partial opposition at the level of content even if in an undeveloped form. What must take place before this fragmented experience can be transformed into something more political? According to Negt and Kluge this requires that the "political left must first of all reorganize fantasies in order to make them capable of self-organization."[31]

This brings me to the second aspect of Negt and Kluge's work that directly concerns my argument: the importance of connecting these "unblocked" moments of working-class fantasy with the history, or histories of actual resistance to capital, patriarchy, racism and nationalism. Rather than a smooth, linear narrative, however, this process is one of assembling a montage of "historical fissures—crises, war, capitulation, revolution, counterrevolution," and this is because the proletarian public sphere "has no existence as a ruling public sphere, it has to be reconstructed from such rifts, marginal cases, isolated initiatives."[32] Not unlike the historical re-mapping suggested in Brecht's poem, this reconstruction is built upon acts of interruption, stoppage and skepticism. At the same time, this process also seeks to block capital from appropriating these *other* histories and desires for its own interests. This is an essential point for Negt and Kluge, who believe that with the emergence of the consciousness industry, capital gains the means to reach ever deeper into the shadows of working-class fantasy and with greater sophistication. The same danger of appropriation holds true for dark matter. At the moment these shadows become capable of collectively focused activity, as the margins link up and become visible to themselves, in and for themselves, they simultaneously become discernible to the voracious gaze of capital, with its siren call of "lifestyle" and the joy of consuming.[33] Significantly, activist artists have devised strategies that recognize this dilemma, borrowing dark matter forms such as zines and a do-it-yourself approach to creativity. The final section begins with a description of zine aesthetics before sketching the varied activities of the activist art group known as Las Agencias.

Las Agencias

We need to make ourselves visible without using the mainstream media ...
Riot Grrrl zine[34]

Least available for appropriation by the culture industry is not the slack look of dark matter, but its semi-autonomous and do-it-yourself mode of production and exchange. Zines, for example, are frequently belligerent, self-published newsletters that, as cultural historian Stephen Duncombe argues, do not offer:

> Just a message to be received, but a model of participatory cultural production and organization to be acted upon. The message you get from zines is that you should not just be getting messages, you should be producing them as well. This is not to say that the content of zines— whether anti-capitalist polemics or individual expression—is not important. But what is unique, and uniquely valuable, about the politics of zines and underground culture is their emphasis on the practice of doing it yourself.[35]

Duncombe draws an explicit connection between this reflexivity of the zinester and Walter Benjamin's concept of the author as a producer. Applying Benjamin's analysis to the case of zines, it is exactly their position within the conditions of production of culture that constitutes an essential component of their politics. In an increasingly professionalized culture world, zine producers are decidedly amateur. In producing cheap, multiple-copy objects, they operate against the fetishistic archiving and exhibiting of the high art world and the for-profit spirit of the commercial world. And by their practice of eroding the lines between producer and consumer they challenge the dichotomy between active creator and passive spectator that characterizes our culture and society.[36]

Indeed, with satiric titles such as *Temp Slave, Dishwasher, Welcome to the World of Insurance* and simply *Work*, zines produced by service workers offer an instance of what Negt and Kluge term the "contradictory nature of the public horizon," at least in so far as they represent a sporadic moment of resistance, rather than a means of sustained opposition.[37]

The zine aesthetic and its tactics of recycling and satire bear a certain resemblance to far more self-consciously politicized art-related collectives including: Temporary Services, Las Agencias, Wochen-Klausur, Collectivo Cambalache, the Center for Land Use Interpretation, the Stockyard Institute, Ne Pas Plier, Take Back the Streets, Mejor Vida, RTMark, the Critical Art Ensemble, Ultra Red, the Surveillance Camera Players, the Center for Tactical Magic, Radical Software Group and the Institute for Applied Autonomy. All work within some aspect of public space, and many ascribe their approach as that of tactical media, an activist deployment of new media technology. Yet, the groups mentioned here are difficult to categorize within most definitions of art because their engagement extends well into the public sphere and involves issues of fair housing; the treatment of unemployed people, "guest" workers and prisoners; as well as global politics; biotechnology; and even access to public space itself.[38] Groups such as Temporary Services, Las Agencias, WochenKlausur, Take Back the Street, Ne Pas Plier, the Surveillance Camera Players, the Stockyard Institute and Mejor Vida design participatory projects in which objects and services are made to be given away or used up in public settings or street actions. Other groups, including most notably RTMark use technology to encourage "the intelligent sabotage of mass-produced items."[39] RTMark exists entirely online and its website invites workers, students and other disenfranchised individuals to collaborate with them by purchasing "shares" of RTMark stock. Because the group is a legally registered corporation, it has successfully used limited liability rules to shield its members from personal lawsuits. The list of those who have sought to censor the group because of its "intelligent sabotage" includes major record companies, toy manufacturers and even the World Trade Organization.[40] And, unlike the lone, disaffected rebel worker, RTMark's collective approach raises sabotage to the level of ideological critique, much in the manner proposed by Negt and Kluge.[41]

This same typically humorous reappropriation and do-it-yourself, zine aesthetic is also evident in the work of Las Agencias, an informally structured collective of artists and activists now primarily based in Barcelona but who have collaborated on projects in Madrid, Tarifa, Boston and Milan.[42] Similarly to RTMark, Las Agencias appropriates both the technology and appearance of the consciousness industry, but it also works directly in the streets and barrios to unsettle normative ideological structures and reveal the contradictions and false tranquility of the bourgeois public sphere. Carefully planned group actions have supported local squatters and migratory "guest" workers, while the group has also designed campaigns against gentrification and militarism. But perhaps the work most crucial to my argument is Las Agencias' creative subversion of the riot police during street demonstrations and the group's tactical assault upon *lifestyle* marketing by global corporations. Take for example the group's line of apparel designed for use in demonstrations and street actions. These colorful, "ready to revolt" designs contain hidden pockets that allow the wearer to conceal materials for buffering the blows of police batons or to conceal cameras for documenting abuse by the constabulary. Expanding upon the group's intervention into the couture industry is a more recent project entitled *Yomango*: a word that is slang for shoplifting. Mockingly playing off the retailing strategy of the Mango clothing label that markets itself to young, European professionals, Las Agencias has developed its own "lifestyle" campaign that integrates a range of "anti-consumer" products and services with everyday acts of customer sabotage. Specially adapted clothing and shopping bags are available on the Las Agencias label designed for "disappearing" products out of the retail outlets of global emporiums. Las Agencias also provides workshops on how to defeat security systems through orchestrated teamwork that, on one occasion, to mark the Argentinean riots of December, 2001, took the form of a choreographed dance. For Las Agencias, shoplifting is a type of civil disobedience in which reflexive kleptomania is directed against the homogenizing and instrumentalizing effect of global capital.[43]

For a time, all of Las Agencias' tactics—including counter-couture, anti-war graphics, strategy lessons, street actions and communication systems—came together in the Show Bus: a brightly painted, motor coach equipped with display and networking technologies and topped off by a rooftop platform for public speaking and live performances. With its windows refitted for rear-view projecting of live internet feed, the Show Bus was a combination of mobile organizing space and self-contained agitation apparatus. It also made a conspicuous target for reactionary forces. The Show Bus was demolished and set alight one night by unknown forces, thus forcing the group to reconsider the conspicuousness of this approach.

Nevertheless, the Show Bus was a concrete manifestation of counter-public space in so far as it brought together numerous otherwise fragmented forms of resistance while remaining networked to street culture and yet relatively autonomous with regard to the high art world. And it is important to add a final note about the cunning of Las Agencias in relationship to the art industry. By 2002, the group had gained enough notoriety for a liberal-minded curator to solicit their participation in the Torino Art Biennial. The members met and agreed to bring their *Yomango* campaign into the "white box" of the institutional art museum. But they elected to do so in the form of an "installation" that replicated an actual retail franchise. Within this simulated storefront the audience would be invited to practice shoplifting as well as attend workshops on civil disobedience and activism. Furthermore, all of the shopliftable practice products were themselves to be procured from nearby retail chains prior to the exhibition's opening. The organizers of the biennial, upon hearing about Las Agencias' plans to essentially "squat" their exhibition, acted to evict the group.

However, on other occasions, the group has managed to "leverage" art world funds provided by a museum and use this money to carry out political actions in non-art-related public spaces. Nevertheless, this catty interplay between art activists and art institutions underscores the opportunities as well as potential risks of moving this type of dark matter into greater visibility within the public sphere. And, to the extent that Las Agencias focuses on the process and organization of creative work itself, rather than the production of objects, its "art" is difficult for the art world to appropriate. With group activity divided between theorizing, creating posters, designing clothes, organizing and carrying out actions and giving workshops, as well as networking with other activists and artists, it is simply not possible for the formal institutions of the art world to represent the full extent of Las Agencias' "work." No art objects exist that could summarize group identity and, unlike individuals artists such as Joseph Beuys, the group has so far avoided making fossils and souvenirs of their work for museums and collectors. In addition, because its audience participates in the making of the work and its meaning, it is difficult to imagine what aspect of the group's work would appeal to conventional art collectors. At least to date, the legitimization of collective authorship has been avoided by the culture industry, most likely because it undermines artistic values as defined by collectors, who expect art works to be the product of one individual with one clearly articulated artistic vision. Finally, and most important to my argument, groups such as Las Agencias, Temporary Services and RTMark have adopted forms of creative expenditure and gift giving more typically found within the informal arts that are fundamentally hostile to the functioning of the formal art industry economy. It is my contention that such acts of expenditure without the expectation of a specific return on investment is aimed at building egalitarian social relations rather than optimizing one's position within a market.[44] And it is this adaptation, rather than any formal resemblance to dark matter, that draws these oppositional practices into dark matter's gravitational field and away from the hegemony of the elite art world.

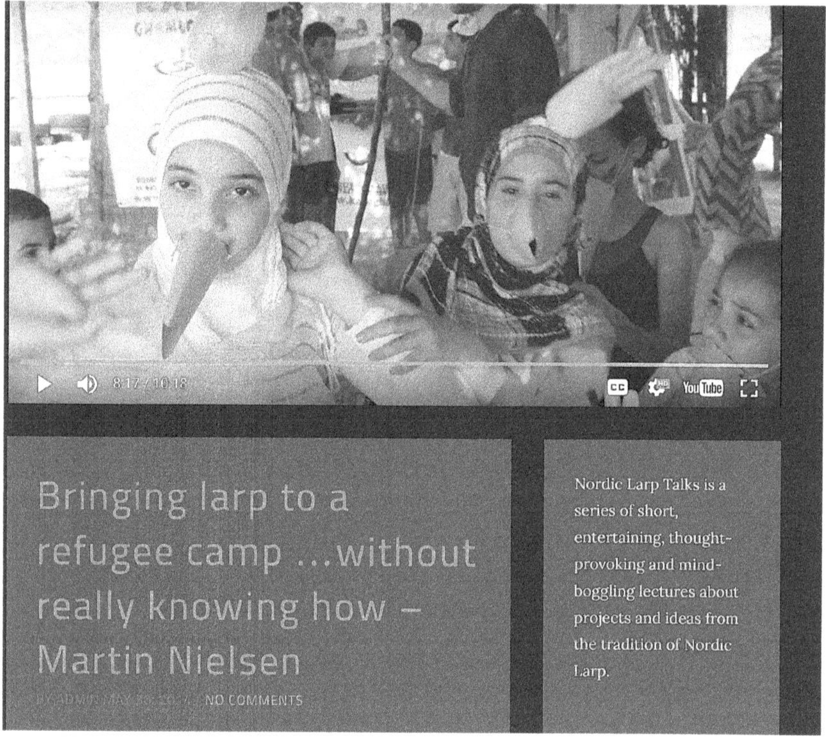

Figure 31 Nordic Live Action Role Play (LARP) Harald Misje, Martin Nielsen and Anita Myhre Andersen with Palestinian children in a refugee camp in Beirut, 2012 (Screen grab from: www.youtube.com/watch?v=9lG5YBkqxFw)

Conclusions

Despite the ideologies of resignation, despite the dense reality of governmental structures in our "control societies," nothing prevents the sophisticated forms of critical knowledge, elaborated in the peculiar temporality of the university, from connecting directly with the new and also complex, highly sophisticated forms of dissent appearing on the streets. This type of crossover is exactly what we have seen in the wide range of movements opposing the agenda of neoliberal globalization.[45]

To paraphrase the cosmologists: there is perhaps no current problem of greater importance to cultural radicals than that of "dark matter." Collectives that operate within the contradictions of the bourgeois public sphere openly and playfully expose its imaginary fault lines dividing private from public, individual from collective, and the light from the dark matter. But while such groups offer important models for cultural resistance, it would be disingenuous of me to suggest that the art collectives and dark activities touched upon in this chapter provide a totally satisfactory solution to the radicalization of creativity now or in the future. Instead, these groups and practices are characterized by their overdetermined and discontinuous nature, by repetitions and instability. Their politics privilege spontaneity. Some favor anarchic forms of direct action over sustained organizational models. What is effective in the short term remains untested on a larger scale. And that is the point we appear to be approaching rapidly. Again, Duncombe neatly summarizes this problem in relation to zine production:

> Tales of sabotage and theft are not just represented in zines, but often by them. Stealing the materials and "borrowing" the technology necessary to produce zines is considered part and parcel of making zines [...] roommates copy zines on midnight shifts at Kinkos and others use postage meters on their jobs. [...] [Yet] with no memories of pre-industrial labor patterns to sustain them, and little in the way of alternative models of labor organization to guide them, these individuals have little hope of taking control of the production process in their workplace, never mind society at large.[46]

Where then are the historians of darkness? What tools will they require to move beyond a mere description of these shadows and dark practices and towards the construction of a counter-public sphere? Clearly, more research is needed on how alternative or counter economic forms link up with collective patterns of engaged art making, as well as how one measures the relative autonomy of critical art practices in relation to the culture industry. One thing is clear however: the construction of a counter-public sphere will necessitate that we move away from the long-standing preoccupation with representation and toward an articulation of the invisible.[47] With this change comes a new horizon filled with possibilities as well as risks. If the domain of representation has up until now belonged to those who have held power over deciding what Jacques Rancière calls the distribution of the sensible, then the politics of invisibility will require an investment in the representation of the excluded and that which is structurally invisible.[48] Still, what steps forth into the light by tactically cutting across zones of representational exclusion may not always be to our liking, as has been seen in recent (2016) votes in the UK and US. The 2014 uprising in Ukraine is an illustration of this paradox to which I now turn.

10
On the Maidan Uprising and *Imaginary Archive, Kiev*[*]

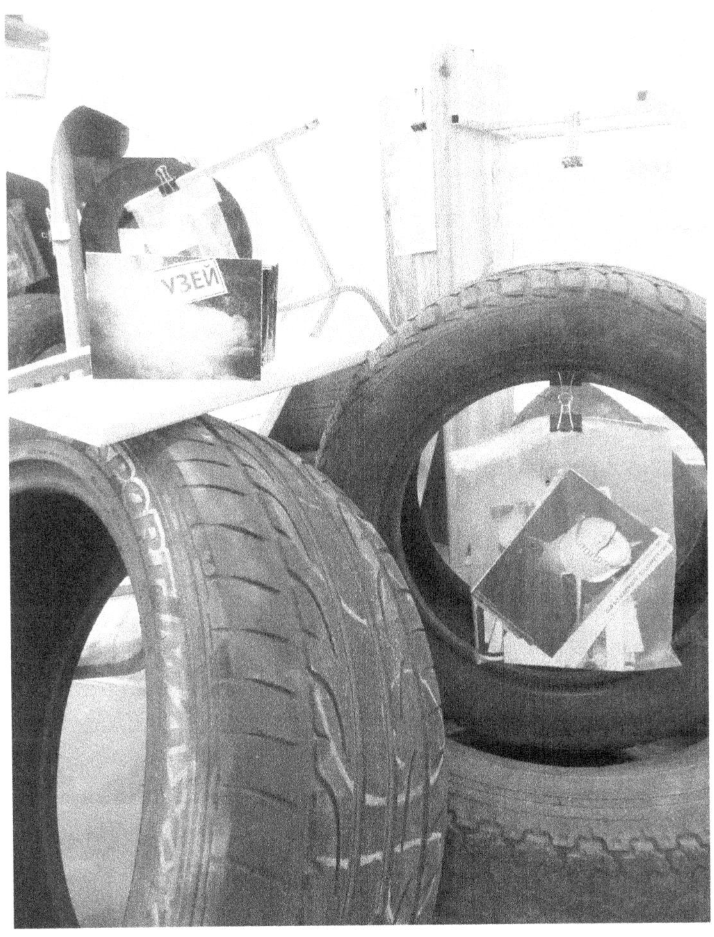

Figure 32   *Imaginary Archive*, Kiev still under construction in the basement of Les Kurbas Center, Greg Sholette with curators Olga Kopenkina and Larissa Babij, Ukraine, April 23, 2014

(Image G. Sholette)

[*] This chapter was first published in 2014.

With a sharp tug the soot-covered tire slides free from a pile stacked over my head. Then another. And another. Soon I have 15 tires loosened. It's April 22, 2014 and, along with local curator Larissa Babij, I am standing on the battle-charred northeast corner of Kiev's Independence Square known locally as the Maidan (square). Only a few months earlier the state's special military units and riot police confronted an assortment of self-organized militias and ordinary citizens here as they attempted, and ultimately succeeded, in ousting their corrupt President Viktor Yanukovych from office. Throughout the battle DIY barricades appeared across all the streets leading to the Maidan. Stacked 3 and 4 meters high, these improvised barriers combined wood shipping pallets with packed ice and assorted objects, from benches to pieces of the dismantled city-sponsored Christmas tree, to automobile tires. The barricades were built to impede the advance of pro-Yanukovych forces, while simultaneously protecting the square's motley crew of demonstrators. Now, after the events of February, these barricades are less functional and more like monuments. Perhaps that is why we were able to cut a deal with the local Maidan "self-defense" to relocate scores of tires to Les Kurbas State Center for Theatre Arts, a nearby cultural space where the Ukrainian edition of *Imaginary Archive* (*IA*) is being hosted.

IA is a traveling installation that I have organized together with curator Olga Kopenkina and artist Matt Greco. For this occasion, curator Larissa Babij makes up the fourth member of our team. *IA* consists of dozens of artist-generated "documents," each of which represents a past whose future never arrived. As it moves from country to country, local artists contribute new fictitious histories, which, despite their fantastical dimension, manage to address concrete political, historical and social struggles. So far *IA* has appeared in New Zealand (2010), Ireland (2011), Austria (2013) and now Ukraine (2014) thanks to support from CEC Artslink and a crowdfunded IndiGoGo campaign.

A principal aim of the project is to release the utopian dimension of history, or, as a reporter from Ukrainian Pravda described *IA*: "At a time when living impressions and personal memory are no longer a reliable instrument for 'digesting' the endless stream of events, the need for an alternative approach to understanding the history, which is unfolding before our eyes, becomes more than relevant."[1]

And so we gather up these readymade materials, rolling them one by one into a waiting cargo van that is quickly filled to capacity. Yet even as we do so small units of camouflaged men huddle about the Maidan on this chilly spring morning. Some chop firewood. Others peel potatoes and tend stoves.

They remain stationed here 24/7, presumably dug-in "just in case." (Or is it because the entire square is now charged with historical significance, or more accurately, with multiple auras of signification?)

Meanwhile, Kiev's residents swarm between these grimy, makeshift obstacles, heading to and from work. At certain points their flow is reduced to single-file. In other words, the barricades still function. Before we pull away, I tuck some folded Hryvnias into a plastic donation box adorned with a small Ukrainian flag. It amounts to only a few US dollars, but in an extraordinarily imploded economy valuable nonetheless. The blue and gold flag is sealed beneath several layers of yellowing packing tape and it dawns on me then that the tape and the box and the tires are all made from the same petrochemical ingredients that sparked the Maidan uprising. It was Yanukovych's Kremlin deal, which had aimed to slash Russian gas import prices in exchange for securing Moscow's vital oil pipelines across Ukraine into Europe, that brought masses of anti-Russian, pro-European Union demonstrators into public squares and spaces starting on November 21. Dubbed Euromaidan (ЄВРОМАЙДАН) via Twitter and then by the press, the crisis peaked on February 22 when Yanukovych fled into exile in Russia, though not before government-loyal forces killed over 100 protesters. Many were shot by unmarked snipers along Institutskaya Street, not far from the National Art Museum. (Notably, those who lost their lives during the Maidan protests were of many nationalities and religions and also from all regions of Ukraine—the first person killed was an Armenian, the second from Belarus.) To *détourne* a Situationist slogan: Beneath the streets, petropolitics: above the streets, blood, tires, asphalt and chaos.

Easy to acquire in large numbers, pneumatic automobile tires have become the "cobblestones" of twenty-first-century uprisings. Made primarily of Styrene-butadiene copolymer, they roll naturally into position and yet are light enough to be stacked into tall, unyielding barriers. But it is thanks to their mostly synthetic carbon composition that their superiority to paving stones becomes evident. At about 140 degrees Celsius (284 Fahrenheit) tires combust, thus amplifying their usefulness as barricades separating protesters from police, or protesters from other protesters as things turned out in Ukraine. For while, at first, the Maidan was a swarm of intermingled Ukrainian bodies: far-right ultra-nationalists, middle-right and middle-middle patriots, and even a small liberal left, made up of feminists, anarchists and anti-Stalinist neo-Marxists, these latter forces never coalesced into a block yet still continued to meet and exert force. In general, precise lines of political stability were difficult to draw. Certainly, from the outset in December there was conflict—often violent—between protesters with varied or opposing political leanings, especially a number of incidents where leftist (sometimes specifically feminist or anarchist) activists were attacked for their political inclination by right activists claiming that there is no place for leftists on the Maidan. Still, there was a unified objective to all this opposition: oust the Yanukovych government. After the government fell, this commingling of positions grew less unified. Insignia and slogans, many of them reflecting strident Christian beliefs and others that reveal archaic historical imagery, all began to crystallize into an array of distinct positions. It was as if a series of micro-nations had sprung up overnight on the Maidan, with each minute grouping generating its own rules, identifiable mottos and imagery, as well as bureaucratic structures.

Imaginary Archive's participants belonged, by and large, to the small, liberal-left intellectual sector. By one artist's estimate it consisted of between 70 and 100 people. Passionate though disorganized, seriously outnumbered, their brief presence on the Maidan was easily and at times brutally suppressed by men wielding clubs. Not surprisingly, many artists turned to the cultural sphere to express their resistance. In the summer and fall of 2012, about a year before the massive Maidan Square protests, many of these artists worked in coordination with staff at the National Art Museum of Ukraine to pressure the Ministry of Culture into hiring a competent director who would prioritize the interests of the museum as a public institution over personal ambitions and political ties. Not unlike Art Workers' Coalition from New York in the late 1960s/early 1970s, or Occupy Museums today, these artists engage in direct action, the wellspring of "institutional critique." The Art Workers' Self-defense Initiative manifesto reads in part: "In a country that declares democracy the preferred mode of interaction, we, as art workers, must impact the formation of new cultural policy principles and how they are put into practice."[2]

But mass political-cultural uprisings today are seldom the sole province of political progressives. The Maidan was no exception. What is striking about the Ukrainian revolution is the degree to which a previously shadowy sphere of ideological interests rapidly cohered, if only momentarily, through acts of self-representation, thanks to a combination of populist activism, networking technology and a significantly weakened central state. And perhaps there is a link between Ukrainian "*zhlob*-art," with its overtly folksy kitsch paintings of unemployed citizens and the Maidan's improvised plywood shields, behind which men bore sticks, rods and makeshift wooden maces. At one point protesters constructed a Molotov-cocktail-launching contraption that resembled a medieval catapult. On another day, *babushka* flashmobs sang quaint Ukrainian folksongs. Illuminated by pyres of flaming tires, this brightening slew of unrestrained fantasies, some at least partially real, though all decidedly heroic, flared rapidly into visibility. As Babij notes:

> Maidan became a platform for certain zhlob-artists to demonstrate their own righteous patriotism and also for accusing other artists (especially those same leftists who were already unwelcome in the square) of not being active enough, especially in day-to-day presence on the square. I bring [this] … up not because I find their work, political positions, or modes of operating in the public sphere sympathetic or thought-provoking; what astounds and disturbs me is their extreme popularity, a kind of channeling of aggressive, populist, patriotic and anti-Other sentiment and their support in the glamour- and scandal-craving wider Ukrainian contemporary art scene. You may recall the photo of some art exhibition that opened just after *IA* with a photo of "Russians" in a cage.[3]

The unleashing of the Maidan's *Imaginary Archive* is just one of many recent examples in which a previously unrepresented cultural mass or "dark matter" has generated its own public presence.[4] Yet even as this

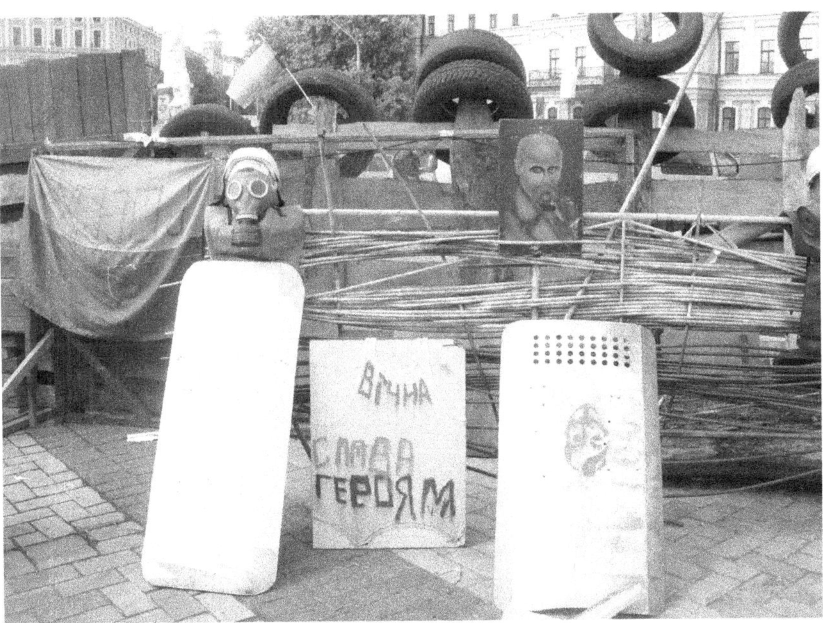

Figure 33   Improvised barricades, shields and other protest equipment in front of St. Michael's Church downtown Kiev, Ukraine, April 2014

(Image G. Sholette)

process of brightening opens up progressive possibilities, it also allows space for reactionary tendencies to gain visibility and coherence. Still, if we sympathize with the "counter-publics" thesis expressed by Kluge and Negt that, "throughout history, living labor has, along with the surplus value extracted from it, carried on its own production—within fantasy," then the often anachronistic and mythopoetic imagery of Euromaidan comes as no surprise.[5] Of course, the political economy of this imaginary production is never neat and orderly. It is instead permeated with hopes as well as resentments. It is also a resource or archive ready to be mined by an ever-expanding culture industry that has moved far beyond the administered Fordist model once proposed by Adorno and Horkheimer. Creativity, collaboration, horizontality: neoliberal capitalism's new business vocabulary applies equally well to the globalized sphere of art as it does to finance. The rapid illumination of this missing cultural mass has become a primary intake-valve for deregulated enterprise culture. Resistance is not futile however, though it can be costly. Not only in terms of one's life or career of course, but also politically, as we now see in Egypt in particular with a return to authoritarian rule after a moment of intense rupture and hope.

IA opened as planned on April 23, 2014. Hours beforehand, however, electrical power was cut to Les Kurbas Center. Using small flashlights and a dose of adrenaline, Olga Kopenkina, Larissa Babij and I completed the installation. Later on, thanks to a portable generator and some gasoline that participating artist Volodymr Kuznetsov biked in from protesters on the Maidan, we installed temporary lighting for our guests. Notably, artist Volodymr Kuznetsov was himself the victim of state censorship when his painted mural *Koliivschina: Judgment Day*, depicting government corruption, was defaced on July 25, 2013 by Natalia Zabolotnaya, director of the Mystetskyi Arsenal art museum, the night before President Viktor Yanukovych was to visit the exhibition.[6] After the opening and the loss of the gas-powered temporary lighting, the exhibition had to be viewed with a flashlight in hand. It now seems that electricity rationing, as well as the privatization of previously public utilities, led to the sudden cutoff, this despite the fact that Kurbas is a state-funded institution. Babij describes the installation itself as resembling or resonating with "the barricades on Maidan" while remaining "consciously artificial."[7] She also pointed out that this congruity of real and synthetic structure echoed the more "formal" barricades constructed in eastern Ukrainian cities as they were being taken over by separatists. Soon after the newly elected mayor of Kiev, Vitaliy Klitschko, called for cleaning crews to dismantle the Maidan barricades. His efforts were met with angry protesters not ready for a return to business as usual. Instead these barricades were tidied up and transformed into genuine monuments to the uprising, and in some places even urban gardens have appeared in Maidan.[8]

Where then does this leave us barricade builders and barricade busters who construct mock-institutional identities to slip between the interstitial spaces of capital? Or what about those who envision the possibilities of progressive dark matter and its imaginary archive? Perhaps by refusing to construct our own absolutist mythologies, and by keeping all notions of identity in play, we produce a kind of alternative *usership*, to deploy a smart, handy term devised by theorist Stephen Wright.[9] In this scenario, art literally attempts to escape its own ontological conditions by seeping out of its autonomous shell to become activity in the everyday world, though while it continues in this vein, it is unrecognized as "art." Not that every artist in *IA* would agree with Wright's objectives, and some in fact are already established figures within the Ukrainian art scene and beyond. In any case, we seem to have arrived at a moment of great possibility and equally great risk. Meanwhile, the socially conscious intellectual never surrenders questioning the substrate of his or her discipline, no matter how squalid its conditions, and never loses hope. "Dark matter" and "imaginary archive" are just two names for this paradox.

11
Delirium and Resistance
After the Social Turn*

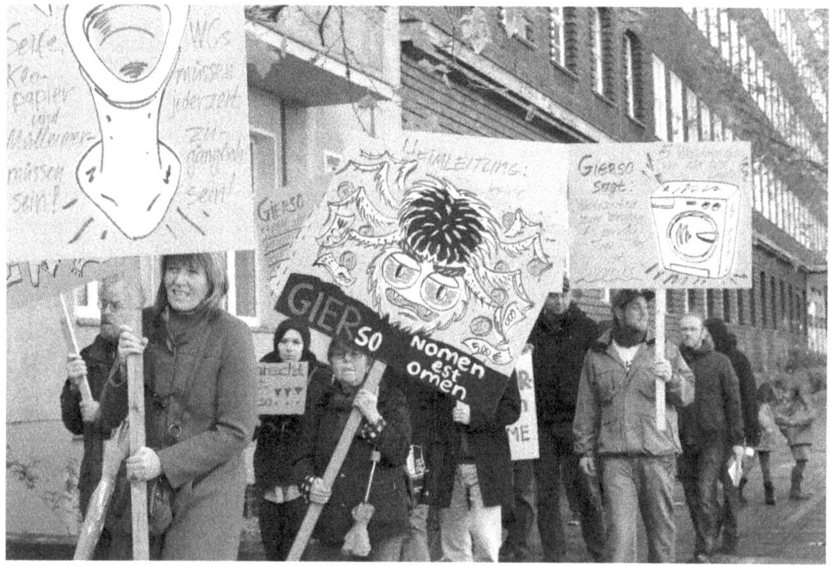

Figure 34 Demonstrators demanding housing rights for immigrants, refugees, students and working people in collaboration with artist Marina Naprushkina and her New Neighborhood Moabit Center, Berlin, Germany, 2014

(Image M. Naprushkina)

To a degree unprecedented in any other social system, capitalism both feeds on and reproduces the moods of populations. Without delirium and confidence, capital could not function.

Mark Fisher, *Capitalist Realism: Is There No Alternative?* (2009)[1]

Art and art-related practices that are oriented toward usership rather than spectatorship are characterized more than anything else by their scale of operations: they operate on the 1:1 scale ... They don't look like anything

---

* This chapter was first published in 2015.

other than what they also are; nor are they something to be looked at and they certainly don't look like art.
Stephen Wright, *Toward a Lexicon of Usership* (2013)[2]

In just a few short years, the emerging field of social practice has gained a considerable following thanks to the way it successfully links an ever-expanding definition of visual art to a broad array of disciplines and procedures, including sustainable design, urban studies, environmental research, performance art and community advocacy, but also such commonplace activities as walking, talking and even cooking.[3] Not just another cultural field or artistic genre, social practice is evolving into a comprehensive sphere of life encompassing over a half dozen academic programs, concentrations, or minors at the graduate and undergraduate levels already dedicated to turning out engaged artists, and still more programs in the pipeline (and, full disclosure, I am part of this pedagogical trend evolving at the City University of New York). Philanthropic foundations, meanwhile, are hurriedly adding community arts related grants to their programming, and major museums are setting aside part of their budgets (primarily from education departments, although that seems about to change) in order to produce ephemeral, participatory projects that have the added benefit, in a cash-strapped financial environment, of being relatively low in cost, of not requiring storage or maintenance, and of generating audience interest in ways that static exhibitions no longer seem to provide.[4] "Art," writes Peter Weibel, "is emerging as a public space in which the individual can claim the promises of constitutional and state democracy. Activism may be the first new art form of the twenty-first century."[5]

And yet all of this ferment is also taking place at a moment when basic human rights are considered a state security risk, when sweeping economic restructuring converts the global majority into a precarious surplus, and when a widespread hostility to the very notion of society has become commonplace rhetoric within mainstream politics. In truth, the public sphere, as both concept and reality, lies in tatters. It is as much a casualty of unchecked economic privatization as it is of anti-government sentiments and failed states. Counter-intuitively, the rise in the number of non-governmental organizations (NGOs) does not reveal a healthy social sphere, but more of a desperate attempt at triage aimed at resolving such complex issues as global labor exploitation, environmental pollution and political misconduct, all of which no longer seem manageable within the framework of democratically elected state governance. The contrast and similarity between socially engaged art collectives and NGOs has been noted by Grant Kester, who cites criticisms by the Dutch architectural collective BAVO regarding "accomodationist" practices that only aim to fix local social problems without questioning the system that gave rise to these problems in the first place.[6] My concerns fall along similar lines, except that here in the United States the situation is less easy to parse. A lack of public funding for art, as well as the absence of an actual left discourse or parties make it difficult to avoid some level of dependency on the institutional art world.

That a relationship exists therefore between the rise of social practice art and the fall of social infrastructures there can be no doubt. And it raises the question, of why art has taken a so-called "social turn," as Claire Bishop proposes, just at this particular historical juncture?[7] I raise this paradox now as engaged art practices appear poised to exit the periphery of the mainstream art world where they have resided for decades, often in the nascent form of "community arts," in order to be embraced today by a degree of institutional legitimacy. The stakes are becoming significantly elevated, not only for artists but also for political activists. This is not a simple matter of good intentions being coopted by evil institutions. We are well beyond that point. The co-dependence of periphery and center, along with the widespread reliance on social networks, and the near-global hegemony of capitalist markets makes fantasies of compartmentalizing social practice from the mainstream as dubious as any blanket vilification of the art world. As Mark Fisher puts it, a delirious confidence permeates our reality under Capitalism 2.0, and I would add that contemporary art is simultaneously its avant-garde and its social realism. I would like to propose a tactical *détournement* of this state of affairs by rerouting capital's deranged affectivity in order to counter its very interests. The goal of my re-examination here is to make trouble for the increasingly normalized theory, history and practice of socially engaged art and its political horizon, or lack thereof, in an attempt to bring about a system-wide reboot. Realistically though, I hope to at least present an outline for future research, discussion and debate regarding the paradoxical ascent of social practice art in a socially bankrupt world.

Capital and art, two seemingly discrete, even antithetical categories, appear to be converging everywhere we look, from the barren sands of Abu Dhabi where Western museums help brand patriarchal monarchies propped up by a surplus of petrodollars and impoverished migrant workers, to online subscriber-driven services like the Mei Moses Fine Art Index, which promotes itself as the "Beautiful Assets Advisor," faithfully keeping track of financial returns on art for the 1% super-rich, much as the Stock Exchange does for other types of investors.[8]

Perhaps it is no coincidence then that both the Mei Moses Index and the future Louvre Abu Dhabi were rolled out in 2007, just as key economic indicators were falling like dominos across the world banking system. It was also the year Apple announced the iPhone, changing the landscape of social networking and setting the stage, some would argue, for a series of "Twitter revolutions," starting in Iran and Moldavia in 2009, and then later across the Arab world.[9] Books such as Naomi Klein's *The Shock Doctrine: The Rise of Disaster Capitalism* (2007) launched a salvo against Milton Friedman-style laissez-faire capitalism, while Antonio Negri and Michael Hardt's re-theorization of imperialism in their bestselling volume *Empire* (2001), followed by *Multitude* (2005), continued to inspire anti-globalization activists in the global justice movement.[10] Still, at this very same moment, a combination of dark derivatives, toxic assets and subprime mortgage tainted hedge funds were beginning to tank as virtually the entire planet was about learn to speak the "grammar of finance."[11] "The financialization of capitalism—the shift in gravity of economic activity from production (and even from much of the growing service sector) to finance—is thus one of the key issues of our time," wrote John Bellamy Foster in a 2007 *Monthly Review* article, adding prophetically "rather than advancing in a fundamental way, capital is trapped in a seemingly endless cycle of stagnation and financial explosion."[12] As the journal containing his essay went to print, the entire global economy began plunging into a massive, prolonged contraction that is still crippling indebted nations and individual workers today.

Astonishingly, one of the few markets to not only weather the crisis, but which also subsequently exploded in aggregate value, even as the rest of the economy remained in deep recession, was that of fine art. On May 9, 2008 Sotheby's sold modern and contemporary paintings worth $362 million, including a record-breaking Francis Bacon triptych. And the sales have not weakened since.[13] It was the same day Fitch Ratings announced they were awarding a subsidiary of Lehman Brothers Holdings Inc. an "A," for a positive financial outlook. Four months later Lehman initiated the largest bankruptcy filing in US history, sending the stock market into a sustained sequence of unprecedented capital losses.[14] Expectations were high that the art market would follow this downward trend, just as it did after the 1987 "Black Monday" crash. And initially the art market did indeed take a hit, with prices for such seemingly stable assets as Impressionist and post-Impressionist painting dropping as much as much as 30% in value by the end of 2008.[15] Then something unexpected took place. Sales of art stabilized and began to rise again, so that by 2013 the global art market grossed €47.42 billion in sales, the second most prosperous year on record since 2007.[16] Since then art sales have continued their dramatic and unprecedented boom, even as the economic crisis continues to plague most of the world's nations. One result of art's cultural potency has been the mutation of works of art themselves, a process in which a relatively fixed capital asset such as a Jackson Pollock painting owned by a well-heeled society elite a few decades ago has today morphed into an investment instrument capable of being bundled together with other assets by clever hedge fund managers. This goes well beyond the merely entrepreneurial marriage between art and commerce exemplified by, say, Jeff Koons who has licensed his metallic, balloon dog brand for use on H&M handbags. This financialization *Zeitgeist* is shifting art all the way down to what might be thought of as its ontological level. Artist and theorist Melanie Gilligan goes so far as to suggest that even the production of artistic work is beginning to resemble a type of finance derivative, which, rather than seeking to generate new forms or new values, instead depends "on the reorganization of something already existing."[17]

Pervasive financialization has also led to the unconcealing of art's political economy. Eyes wide open, the legions of largely invisible artists and cultural workers so fundamental to reproducing what Julian Stallabrass sardonically dubbed Art Incorporated as far back as 2004 are starting to doubt their professional allegiances. We now see in high relief what has always been right in front of us all along: the thousands of invisible, yet professionally trained artist service workers—fabricators, assistants, registrars, shippers, handlers, installers, subscribers, adjunct instructors—who are necessary for reproducing the established hierarchies of the art world. This socialized dark matter is now impossible to unsee, as criticism of the top-heavy distribution of compensation endemic to the field of artistic production intensifies. Some artists are even beginning to organize.

The business-as-usual art world is now facing not one, but two mutinous tendencies. The first involves demands that the art industry be regulated in order to assure a more equitable allocation of resources for all concerned. The other involves escape. Examples of the first tendency include recently formed artists' organizations such as Working Artists and the Greater Economy (WAGE), BFAMFAPhD, ArtLeaks, Gulf Labor Coalition, Debtfair, Arts & Labor (the latter two both offshoots of Occupy Wall Street), and a new Artist's Union being organized in Newcastle, UK. These micro-institutions collectively assert moral and sometimes also legal pressure on the art industry, demanding that it become an all-round better citizen. Redressing economic injustice in the art world, including the average $52,035 of debt owed by art school graduates, has also been the topic of recent conferences, including "Artist as Debtor," the 2015 College Art Association panel entitled "Public Art Dialogue: Student Debt, Real Estate, and the Arts" and "Art Field as Social Factory," sponsored by the Free/Slow University in Warsaw, Poland, in order to address the "division of labor, forms of capital and systems of exploitation in the contemporary cultural production."[18]

The second reaction by artists to the current crisis involves exiting the art world altogether, or at least attempting to put its hierarchical pecking order and cynical winner-takes-all tournament culture at a safe distance.[19] For many artists the primary means of achieving this is withdrawal, or partial withdrawal, which sometimes involves turning to social and political engagement outside of art.[20] In theory, not only is it difficult to monetize acts of, say, artistic gift giving or dialogical conversation, two commonly practiced operations that typify socially engaged art, but also by forming links to non-art professionals in the "real" world one establishes a sense of embodied community quite apart from and affectively far richer than anything possible within the hopelessly compromised relations of the mainstream art world.

In truth, collectively produced art and community-based art have been around for decades. Beginning in the 1970s the British Arts Council began to funnel support to muralists, photographers, theatre troupes and other cultural and media workers operating outside the studio in urban and rural public settings. A similar dissemination of government resources took place in the US under the US Department of Labor's Comprehensive Employment and Training Act (CETA), as well as through National Endowment for the Arts funding. Some of this public support gave rise to artist-run alternative spaces. It also helped establish artists working within labor unions, impoverished inner city neighborhoods, prisons, geriatric facilities and other non-art settings. Exactly what makes current, more celebrated forms of social practice art distinct from these previous incarnations of community art is hard to pinpoint, although several features stand out.

One difference is the move away from producing an artistic "work," such as a mural, exhibition, book, video or some tangible outcome or object, and towards the choreographing of social experience itself as a form of socially engaged art practice. In other words, activities such as collaborative programming, performance, documentation, protest, publishing, shopping, mutual learning, discussion, as well as walking, eating or some other typically ephemeral pursuit is all that social practice sometimes results in. It's not that traditional community-based art generated no social relations, but rather that social practice treats the social itself as a medium and material of expression. Blake Stimson and I began to intuit this shift in 2004. Writing about what we then perceived to be an emerging form of post-war collectivism after modernism:

> This [new collectivism] means neither picturing social form, nor doing battle in the realm of representation but instead engaging with social life as production, engaging with social life itself as the medium of expression. This new collectivism carries with it the spectral power of collectivisms past just as it is realized fully within the hegemonic power of global capitalism.[21]

Second, as theorist Stephen Wright similarly insists in his recent book, *Toward a Lexicon of Usership*, contemporary art is moving beyond the realm of representation altogether and into a one to one correspondence with the world that both we, and it, occupy.[22] Before returning to these provocative claims, let me add a third, less sensational contrast between social practice art and community-based arts. The mainstream critical establishment of the 1960s, 1970s and 1980s treated community-based art either with indifference or derision. It was a level of scorn that community artists returned in spades. Driven by populist ideals as much as contempt for art world glitterati, community artists frequently turned their backs to the established art world, and still do. On those rare occasions when a "serious" critic did "stoop" to address this "unsophisticated" art four issues typically arose.

First, while community artists who were, as often as not, white, middle class and college educated might collaborate with inmates to make "prison art," or choreograph dances with geriatric patients, or train inner city kids to make paintings and sculpture, thereby bringing pleasure and culture to the underserved, they were also, it was argued, undermining art's historically established autonomy from the everyday world. As far as "highbrow" art historians go, this is akin to wearing a large target on your back at a shooting range. Art's allegedly unique state of independence from life has, at least since the time of Schiller and Kant, permitted artists a singular type of freedom from useful labor. It is this purposeless purpose that allows artists to operate in opposition to the banality of the everyday as well as what Theodor W. Adorno and Herbert Marcuse later designated as monopoly capitalism's "totally administered society." That is to say, artistic work retains an ability to withdraw from the everyday world's profaned, degraded routines only by keeping a measured, critical distance from it. By attempting to narrow the gap between art and society, community artists do exactly the opposite. Sin number one.

Second, community arts appear to substitute artist-generated services for genuine public services, thus reforming rather than fundamentally transforming offensive political inequalities that have only grown more extreme over the past 30 years, thanks to the anti-government policies of neoliberal, deregulated capitalism. Following the collapse of the world financial market this "replacement strategy" where artist service-providers take the place of actual social services seems to have accelerated in the US and UK in particular, as governments look for ways to cut public spending. As we well know, artists work cheap. Unionized social workers, educators and therapists do not. In addition, third, community-based art practices run the risk of ensconcing the contemporary artist as some sort of profound, revelatory change agent or, as Grant Kester perceptively wrote, an aesthetic evangelical.[23]

And fourth and finally, who says community is a good thing? Of course this depends on your definition of community but the world is full of tyrannical "communities," where difference, mental, physical, sexual, leads to expulsion or worse. A final sacrilege. Nevertheless, all of these long-standing criticisms of community-based art can just as easily be applied to social practice art today. And yet this new artistic tendency seems to be the unconfirmed major contender for an avant-garde redux. What has changed?

Maybe it was Nicolas Bourriaud's promotion of Relational Aesthetics in the 1990s that began the rehabilitation of community art? Recall that the celebrity curator insisted artist Rirkit Tiravanija's gallery-centered meal sharing established a new, socially participatory paradigm for post-studio artistic practices. It was a claim the art world uncritically devoured for years.[24]

Or perhaps it was the expanding network of artists developing ephemeral actions, research-based public projects and impermanent installations as a response to an ever-shrinking stock of large urban studio spaces? There is still another possibility: the loss of no-strings-attached public funding for art institutions after the 1980s may have ironically brought about a popularization of museum programming by forcing institutions to seek out more interactive, spectacular public events. None of these scenarios disregards the sincerity of artists who seek communal experiences or socially useful applications for their work. Understandably, contemporary artists are seeking a way of remaining relevant in the contemporary art context, while also eyeing an exit from the ironic ineffectuality of the post-modernist paradigm that is still dominant, though fading fast. The question here is what accounts for the positive reception of social practice art today, as opposed to the negative reception of its close kin, community art, only a decade or so ago? One way or the other, it seems that by the early 2000s we find previously widespread art world resistance to socially engaged art practices eroding, though always selectively, so that now, in 2015, the social turn is spinning full-throttle.

It is an inversion of artistic taste so abrupt that it reminds me of the late 1970s when painters still earnestly grappling with Greenbergian "flatness" discovered a decade later that it was an artistic "problem" that had simply vanished as a jubilant, and often juvenile 1980s art scene embraced figurative painting, decorative crafts and even low-brow kitsch, all of which were the bane of most modernist aestheticians. Likewise, drawbacks once dismissively associated with community-based art are just as fugitive today, vanishing in a puff of smoke like the undead at sunrise. Aside from an occasional critic like Ben Davis, who insists that "the genre of 'social practice' art raises questions that it cannot by itself answer," most graduating MFA students today feel obliged to join an art collective and attempt to connect themselves to communities which are not traditionally part of the fine art world.[25] If anything, the focus on socially engaged art by the mainstream art world has actually eclipsed, rather than illuminated the many individuals still active in community arts, turning long-simmering resentments once directed at the art world establishment into charges of appropriation and colonization.[26]

Davis may be right about the blindness of social practice art to its own pre-conceptions. Still, the fact that so many young people today are desperately seeking to redefine the way they live from the point of view of both environmental and social justice adds an impressive robustness to this cultural phenomenon. Art seems to be the one field of recognized, professional activity where a multitude of interests ranging from the aesthetic to the pragmatically everyday coexist, a state of exception that led to artist Chris Kraus's musings on what she calls the ambiguous virtues of art school:

Why would young people enter a studio art program to become teachers and translators, novelists, archivists, and small business owners? Clearly, it's because these activities have become so degraded and negligible within the culture that the only chance for them to appear is within contemporary art's coded yet infinitely malleable discourse.[27]

Socially engaged art practice is becoming such an attractive and paradigmatic model for younger artists that it seems to fulfil Fredric Jameson's proposition that particular historical art forms express a social narrative that paradoxically, "brings into being that very situation to which it is also, at one and the same time, a reaction."[28] At first glance, this seems like the answer to my initial question: why is socially engaged art advancing at a moment when society is bankrupted? Because, with due respect to Jameson, socially engaged art resolves, or seems to resolve, intolerable contradictions in the actual world. But while this explanation may have been applicable to Relational Aesthetics, it seems inadequate just a decade or so later with regard to social practice.

For Jameson, the work of art remains a categorically discrete entity, a novel, building, performance or film framed within a specific historic, cultural and institutional context. It is, in other words, the privileged site where the work of hermeneutic textual interpretation takes place. Works of social practice do not conform to this traditional model. In fact, the success of social practice art has inverted the normative representational framing of art, flipping inside out our spectator-based distance from the world. In a way, this means that everything is outside the frame and nothing remains inside: art has imploded. In Wright's one-to-one thesis, cited in the epigraph to this chapter, the practice of socially engaged art would then simply constitute the remnants of the social itself, emerging into a commodified everyday world as a set of actual social relations or commonplace activities, and not as a deep critical reflection or aesthetic representation of society or its flaws. This is different from a Kaprow/Beuys/Fluxus tactic of inserting anti-art into the everyday. One-to-one art is more subtle: rather than simply close the gap between art and life, it makes art redundant by providing "a function already fulfilled by something else."[29] Neither does Wright's model conform to Shannon Jackson's notion that such heteronomous social activities might be folded into a neat, academic framework via performance studies.[30]

If these emerging practices interact with social life by producing the social itself, then they are neither an experimental trial, nor a performance, nor even a rehearsal for some ideal society. Rather, they are *bare art* as discussed in Part I of this book. They are one-to-one social practices that are virtually redundant within the real world; that is to say, the artists involved carry out activities such as cooking or renovating buildings or operating as business entities, and are consequently also subject to all of the legal, economic and practical consequences as any other real-world activity. Take Pittsburgh-based Conflict Kitchen that specializes in serving food from countries that the United States is in conflict with, including North Korea, Iran and Venezuela. No First Amendment right to free speech typically enjoyed by artists would ever prevent this culinary art project from becoming liable for, say, a food-borne illness, should one be accidentally transmitted to a customer.[31]

By working with human affect and experience as an artistic medium, social practice draws directly upon the state of society that we actually find ourselves in today: fragmented and alienated by decades of privatization, monetization and ultra-deregulation. In the absence of any truly democratic governance, works of socially engaged art seem to be filling an unfulfilled social need by enacting community participation and horizontal collaboration, and by seeking to create micro-collectives and intentional communities. On the surface, it's as if they were making a performative proposition about a truant social sphere they hope will return once the grown-ups notice it's gone missing. If however they are instead incarnating the remains of society, as I am suggesting, then the stakes are radically different, for better and for worse. It is for better when social practice and community-based artists engage with the political, fantastic or even resentful impulses of people, a process that can lead to class awareness or even utopian imaginings much as we saw with Occupy Wall Street. It is for the worse when the social body becomes prime quarry for mainstream cultural institutions and their corporate benefactors who thrive on deep-mining networks of "prosumers" bristling with profitable data. Even the normally optimistic theorist Brian Holmes gloomily warns us that "the myriad forms of contemporary electronic surveillance now constitute a proactive force, the irremediably multiple feedback loops of a cybernetic society, devoted to controlling the future."[32]

One way to grapple with the present paradox of social practice art's predicament is to turn to the archive of past projects and proposals—including those that succeeded and those that failed—in order to reappraise certain moments within the genealogy of socially engaged art that might have unfolded differently. To find vestiges and sparks suggesting unanticipated historical branches that may have sprouted off in directions that would possibly be less vulnerable to the pressures for normalization, institutionalization and administration. One of these significant junctures took place shortly before two world-altering historical occurrences—the global financial crash of 2007/2008 with its devastating economic effects and the widespread surveillance, even criminalization of the electronic commons.

The year 2004–2005 sits at a point where the counter-globalization movement was invisibly beginning to falter, and immediately after unprecedented global peace demonstrations distressingly failed to stop the illegal, US-led invasion of Iraq. It precedes the full disclosure of the emerging national security state complex of today. Nevertheless, these realities had yet to fully sink in as artists, activists and intellectuals remained captivated by the utopian potential of new communications technologies and the "people-power" that seemed to have led to the downfall of the Soviet Union and its Eastern European empire. Coming into focus was a group of tech-savvy, cultural activists whose bold hit-and-run interventions sought to undermine established authority by literally upending public spaces and turning the mainstream media's resources against itself.

Artists Angel Nevarez and Valerie Tevere of the group neuroTransmitter put it this way:

For us this was a moment of heightened media art and activism. Artists were extending the possibilities of new technologies and re-inscribing the use of old media forms. It was a time of innovations in technology and communications media, yet we were interacting in physical space rather than through social media … where we both interacted on the street level as well as in the air.[33]

Decidedly non-ideological in outlook (other than an occasional nod of approval towards the left-libertarian Zapatista Army of National Liberation [EZLN] of Chiapas Mexico), tactical media interventionists dismissed organized politics. Some went so far as to castigate past efforts at achieving progressive political change, describing the utopian aims of the New Left and May '68 as "vaporware"—a derogatory term used for a software product that, while announced with much fanfare, never actually materializes. Geert Lovink and David Garcia argued that tactical media activism sought to hold no ground of its own, instead merely seeking to creatively interrupt the status quo with determined, short-term acts of public sensationalism and cultural sabotage. "Our hybrid forms are always provisional. What counts are the temporary connections you are able to make. Here and now, not some vaporware promised for the future. But what we can do on the spot with the media we have access to."[34]

In truth, tactical media benefitted from a particular historical opening, a quasi-legal loophole that existed before the heavily policed, privatized public sphere emerged full-blown, with its round-the-clock electronic surveillance closing down outlets for resistance, including the kind of

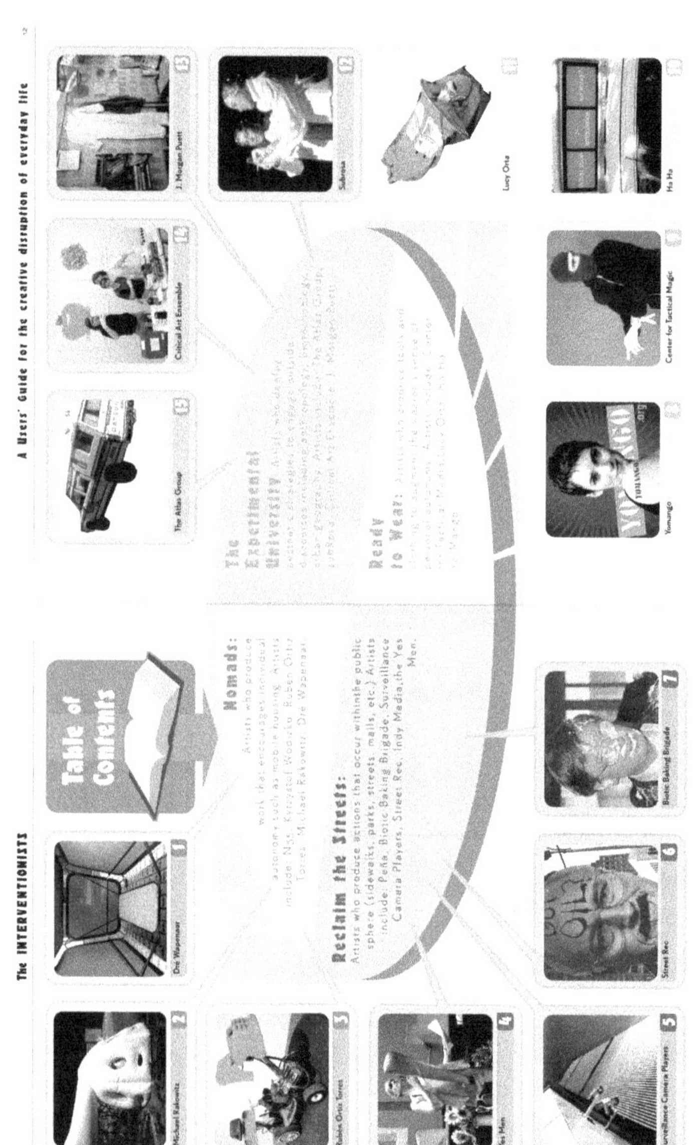

Figure 35   Page spread from the "Users Manual" for The Interventionists exhibition, graphically emphasizing the usefulness of tactical art projects as publicly accessible tools for the "interruption of everyday life." Design by Arjen Noordeman (Image G. Sholette Archive)

analytical gaps exploited by more militantly engaged political artists such as Critical Art Ensemble, which I will discuss below. In other words, the illegal status of distributed denial-of-service (DDoS) attacks clandestinely carried out by hacktivist groups such as Anonymous in recent years were still in a gray zone into the early 2000s. In 1998, Ricardo Dominguez and Electronic Disturbance Theater (EDT) designed a pro-Zapatista virtual sit-in platform aimed at overloading and crashing websites belonging to the Mexican government.[35] But in 2010, University of California Campus Police investigated Dominguez for a tactical media type application he devised that would assist undocumented immigrants crossing the southern US border.[36] This was also before some forms of social practice art began to attract the attention of mainstream cultural institutions.

The second half of this chapter focuses on this tactical media moment as it was presented in the 2004 exhibition The Interventionists: Art in the Social Sphere, organized for the Massachusetts Museum of Contemporary Art (MASS MoCA) by their recently hired curator Nato Thompson. The show was dedicated to artists or artists' collectives who explicitly conceived of art not as an object of contemplation for a passive spectator but as a shareable set of tools for bringing about actual social change. It also reflected a certain optimism that pivoted on the idea of tactics that could be adopted by anyone, not just artists, to improve life conditions. What follows is not intended to serve as a diverting tale of speculative nostalgia. Instead, I hope to put this exhibition forward as one wrinkle in the archive of socially engaged art worthy of re-reading, and possibly rebooting its history. Endeavoring to leverage the euphoric concoction of delirium and confidence Mark Fisher attributes to Capitalism 2.0 for a project of archival redemption, I am reminded of a phrase used by Russian avant-garde theorist Viktor Shklovsky. I proceed therefore with the "optimism of delusion."[37]

After The Interventionists

Conceived of and produced for the Massachusetts Museum of Contemporary Art (MASS MoCA), curator Nato Thompson's 2004 exhibition The Interventionists: Art in the Social Sphere, drew on two precedents: Mary Jane Jacob's 1992–1993 Chicago-based public art project Culture in Action, and the *détournement* or creative "hijacking" of daily life proposed by the Situationist International in the 1960s. It also sought to make a self-conscious break with past attempts to exhibit politically charged contemporary art in a museum setting. Thompson's curatorial statement compares "the sometimes heavy-handed political art of the

1980s" with his selection of interventionist practitioners, who, he insists, had begun to carve out compelling new paths for artistic practice, coupling hardheaded politics with a less heavy, anti-dogmatic visual approach, all the while embracing anarchist Emma Goldman's dictum that revolutions and dancing should never be separated from each other.[38]

This was no gray-on-gray presentation of "message art," intended to dutifully instruct its audience about political realities, any more than some romantic socialist vaporworld. Instead a visitor to MASS MoCA was confronted with a zoo-like menagerie of "magic tricks, faux fashion and jacked-up lawn mowers," packed into the museum's plaintive post-industrial expanse like a sideshow for activists. Rather than didactic lecturing, these projects agitated for social change through ironic critiques, overt lampooning and subtle cooptations of mainstream media and culture cunningly disguised as the real thing. Artist Alex Villar leaps over fences, scales brick facades and squeezes himself into cracks between tenement buildings, temporarily occupying overlooked urban spaces while performing his own Situationist-inspired version of Parkour; the Spanish collective Yomango display fashion accessories for magically making "objects disappear," (i.e. shoplifting with style); and a member of the Danish group N55 rolls a mobile floating unit down a city street, demonstrating the Snail Shell System, a low-cost mobile dwelling useful for transportation and providing "protection from violence during demonstrations."[39] Something subversive pervaded all of these varied works, though exactly what direction this dissidence pointed toward was fuzzy at best.

If the political identity of these interventionist activists was intentionally difficult to pin down, the exhibition certainly proved something else, something that most previous displays of socially engaged art had not attempted: it returned a sense of wonder and surprise to oppositional culture. Subterfuge could be fun. Unfortunately, this aspect of the exhibition's message was easier to take away as a sound bite than its critical intent. Despite being on view for over a year (March, 2004 to May, 2005), The Interventionists received no in-depth reviews, though a one-sentence recommendation for holiday travelers did appear in the *New York Times*, in which the show was cheerfully described as full of "pranksters and fun politically motivated meddlers."[40]

The absence of serious critical response cannot be blamed entirely on the lack of familiarity with Nato Thompson, still an untested curator, or with the exhibition's off-grid location in rural New England. Nor was the carnivalesque enthusiasm that unapologetically permeated The Interventionists a reason for this dismissal. After all, a substantial theoretical discourse already existed for this kind of art, online and in Europe, but its authors, including Gene Ray, Brian Holmes, Rozalinda Borcila, Geert Lovink, Marcelo Exposito, Gerald Raunig, Marc James Léger and Stephen Wright among others, then, as now, have limited impact on cultural discourse in the US. The failure of any critic to develop a substantial political and aesthetic analysis of The Interventionists is unquestionably a lost opportunity, especially when one considers the impoverished state of such criticism even up to today. Still, the exhibition managed to demonstrate two things above all. First, that a thriving group of contemporary artists in 2004 considered social, political and environmental issues paramount to their practice and, second, that their critique could be delivered through the kind of stimulating visual format audiences of contemporary art had come to expect. Even so, there are two overlooked dimensions of The Interventionists more relevant to my argument that is still in need of excavation.

MASS MoCA's sprawling labyrinth of rooms and obsolete industrial apparatus appealed then, as it does today, to vacationers grown tired of Happy Meals and theme parks and searching for that offbeat family experience, but one that promised at least a modicum of educational nourishment. On the occasion of The Interventionists a family outing to the museum delivered something extra, a spectacle of imaginative dissidence whose quintessential onlooker was not the art world elite, but instead these same "holiday travelers," whose demoralized collective unconsciousness theorist Michel de Certeau would call the murmur of the everyday. This was no coincidence. Thompson cut his curatorial teeth co-producing a weekend of guerrilla-style street actions in Chicago under the rubric The Department of Space and Land Reclamation or DSLR. Gleefully bringing together graffiti, agitprop posters, hip-hop, illegal street art and impromptu public actions, DSLR's bottom-up informality simultaneously paid homage to and deconstructed Mary Jane Jacob's landmark 1993 public exhibition Culture in Action, all the while turning a blind eye towards the city's more art savvy neighborhoods. From gigantic balls of trash rolled down Michigan Avenue at lunch hour by men and women dressed up as sanitation workers to anonymous public sculptures attached to traffic signs and absurd performances, including a sofa tagged "Please Loiter" plopped down casually on the sidewalk, DSLR was about as disconnected from the gaze of the art world as one could get in 2001.[41]

No one would argue that MASS MoCA was then or is now disconnected from the contemporary art world, though there is a definite allure generated, even perhaps cultivated, through the museum's measurable distance from the mainstream art world that is quite unlike that of Dia

Beacon's manageable proximity to New York City. This slightly offbeat appeal extends to the type of administered culture found within MASS MoCA, bringing me to my second point. The Interventionists and its venue benefitted from a symbiotic tension that drew on the exhibition's rebellious, Situationist-inspired references, as much as it did from the unusual institutional history of MASS MoCA itself. It was self-made cultural entrepreneur Thomas Krens who conceived of MASS MoCA during the economic upturn of 1984. By sidestepping traditional models of *noblesse oblige*, in which those who "own" high culture generously lend their artistic property to public institutions in order to enlighten the masses, Krens developed a business model that linked a growing interest in contemporary art with the economic resuscitation of North Adams, a former manufacturing town that had fallen into economic decline along with other industrial centers in North America. Strategically located in the bucolic border region where Massachusetts meets Vermont, but also relatively close to New York City with its surplus of sophisticated art consumers and art producers, Krens saw his vision as altogether win-win. Then came the collapse of the savings and loan bubble in 1987. Plans for MASS MoCA were put on hold for over a decade. In 1999, the museum finally opened its doors just one year before the next bubble, the so-called dot.com bubble, also burst sending a pre-Occupy generation of creative workers into states of resentment and near-desperate panic.

At this point Krens had been appointed director of the Solomon R. Guggenheim Foundation in New York City, and soon became the architect of an expanding cultural franchise. Branch museums were established in Berlin, Spain and Las Vegas, with the latest expansion planned for 2017 in Abu Dhabi, United Arab Emirates (UAE), an undertaking that has generated substantial public controversy due to the poor labor conditions of the UAE. Krens was also the first director of a major art museum to hold a Masters of Business Administration (MBA) rather than a degree in art historical scholarship. This last detail becomes more interesting when one considers the nature of Mass MoCA. Lacking a substantial collection of officially sanctioned art objects, the museum plays host to relatively long-term, temporary exhibitions and shorter-term performance events that situate it somewhere between a European Kunsthalle and a Cineplex. Given Krens's background, it is not surprising that the orthodox concept of an art museum has been partially deconstructed at Mass MoCA. Nor is it unusual to find the traditional role of the curator as one who cares for the wellbeing of cultural treasures reinterpreted as that of someone who selects, cultivates and produces projects that combine artistic seriousness with visual pageantry. Notably, Nato Thompson himself was hired by the museum without an advanced degree in art history, but instead with a Master's in Arts Administration from the School of the Art Institute of Chicago. Though what would have proven a professional deficit for a curator at other large cultural institutions likely afforded Thompson certain tactical advantages within the hybridized institutional geography of MASS MoCA. There is also an amusing irony here, when one considers the intersection of these two incongruous, though equally unorthodox, models of cultural programming: MASS MoCA's dedication to "deconstructing" the classical idea of the art museum so as to rebrand it a sensational destination for tourists, and The Interventionists' unapologetic rejection of institutional critique in favor of an eye-popping primer showcasing the subversive possibilities of tactical media as "useful" art.[42]

In the decade following The Interventionists, numerous academic conferences, publications and programs began to engage similar Situationist-inspired themes, as debates about short-term tactics versus strategic sustainability, and artistic instrumentality versus aesthetic value emerged, or rather re-emerged, often recapitulating similar or even identical artistic passions and arguments from key moments in avant-garde art history. Meanwhile, the exuberantly designed exhibition catalog—which I co-edited with Thompson—rapidly went into multiple reprints, most likely keeping pace with a renewed interest in conceiving of art as an instrument for social change. And while the counter-globalization movement began to lose energy after 2004, the World Social Forum, an international policy initiative dedicated to countering neoliberal hegemony, drew thousands of participants to Porto Alegre, Brazil and other locations in the "Global South." In 2004, the forum's host city was Mumbai, India, and those who gathered collectively asserted: "Another world is possible." As if echoing back from a reconverted electronics plant in the winding hills of New England half a world away, The Interventionists seemed to respond yes, and by the way, "another art world is also possible!"[43]

Viewed in this context, The Interventionists coincided with a broader sea change already under way within contemporary art. Not only were many privileged cultural practitioners beginning to raise questions about the social purpose of their professional activities, but the mainstream art world itself was poised to embrace a more performative, participatory, and at times ephemeral artistic experience prefigured by watershed moments such as Okwui Enwezor's Documenta 11 in 2002. Arguably, it is this very shift away from displaying art objects towards generating experimental platforms for discourse and research-based practices that have opened up a legitimizing space for social practice art today. Nevertheless, there was nothing predetermined about the path leading from an exhibition of tactical media troublemakers at MASS MoCA to the white walls of MoMA or the Tate Modern. Furthermore, if we construe Thompson's own tactics as being at least in part a pointed response to Nicolas Bourriaud's incipient concept of Relational Aesthetics, which similarly celebrated everyday social activity but explicitly rejected overt political content or any self-awareness of artistic privilege, then at least one alternative trajectory for social practice art suggests itself. In this scenario art would still engender social interaction, but it would do so without severing such experimentation from a radical critique of either post-Fordism or the deregulated micro-economy of the contemporary art situated within it. But there is another, darker reason The Interventionists might be a significant nodal point for re-thinking the archive of social practice art and its genealogy.

Just prior to the exhibition opening and thanks to sweeping legislation made available by the post-9/11 Patriot Act, a Federal Grand Jury began delivering subpoenas to the friends, colleagues and members of Critical Art Ensemble (CAE) as FBI agents confiscated materials the group planned to use for its MASS MoCA installation *Free Range Grains*. The project involved a DNA sampling apparatus that CAE repurposed so that visitors could "home-test" for genetically mutated fruit and vegetable genes already circulating within the US food supply. Typical of CAE's practice, the goal of *Free Range Grains* was to focus public attention on the intentionally inconspicuous proliferation of government and corporate control over a commons fast disappearing thanks to unfettered privatization. Consider for example, a previous CAE installation in which the artists tried to deploy counter-biological agents against Monsanto's genetically modified Roundup Ready seed stock in an attempt—mostly symbolic—to deprive the agricultural giant of its near-total monopoly over US soy, corn and soybean production.[44] When CAE co-founder Steve Kurtz was falsely accused by the FBI of bio-terrorism in the weeks leading up to the exhibition, the group's MASS MoCA installation materials were seized by the FBI as evidence. Undaunted, curator Nato Thompson and museum director Joe Thompson (no relation) arranged for a facsimile of the project to be placed on display along with a set of informational text panels outlining both the events that had just taken place, as well as the sequestration of CAE's equipment by the government. In fact this incident, and the subsequent public ordeal of Kurtz and his co-defendant Dr. Robert Ferrell, received more press attention from the art world and mainstream media than did the exhibition itself.[45]

CAE's predicament also provided a singular opportunity for socially engaged artists to reconsider what the stakes of their practice were within a broader conception of politics. Sometime around 9 p.m. on May 29, 2004, about 50 people, many of them engaged artists who were attending the opening of The Interventionists, gathered behind the museum's main entrance hall. The objective of the emergency meeting, convened by word of mouth, was to develop a coordinated, collective response in Kurtz's defense. Several of those present had already been issued subpoenas to testify before the Grand Jury or face imprisonment. However, the discussion that ensued quickly divided into two somewhat contrary camps: Kurtz supporters who argued for a pragmatic vindication of the accused based on the right to free speech under the First Amendment, and those hoping to spotlight the investigation's underlying agenda, which, hinged, it was asserted, on George W. Bush's government's efforts to stifle political criticism and criminalize "amateur" scientific research carried out by artists, activists and environmentalists. The late and gifted Beatriz da Costa, who had already been subpoenaed, articulated support for the second, long-range view, pointing out that a collective response to accusations should focus on a broader set of rights. While this was not the minority position within those actively defending Kurtz and Ferrell, and while the artist himself was advised not to speak at this time on advice of his attorney, for practical reasons the discussion that evening ultimately gravitated towards defending the pair based on their constitutional First Amendment right of free speech: to wit, the freedom to critique the privatization and corporatization of science and technology, as well as the ills of biological warfare, using safe representations of these very same methods and techniques as the means of protest.[46] Four years later, after much effort and expense, Kurtz was finally exonerated when a federal judge refused to allow the government's case to go to trial for lack of evidence.

Which brings me to a final point regarding these archival musings. With so many practitioners of tactical media and activist art present for the opening of The Interventionists, an exceptional organizational opportunity was opened up for envisioning a broadly conceived and theoretically nuanced genus of socially engaged art. Ironically, CAE's misfortune might have jump-started a social practice future in which the proven effectiveness of tactical media complemented, rather than eclipsed, a strategic, long-range vision of political transformation. If another art world was possible in the Spring of 2004, ignition failed. Maybe that was inevitable. And yet, it raises the question: did the CAE incident inadvertently scrub clean more militant forms of art, leaving a more manageable strain of socially engaged art behind?[47] Or was the very lack of a broader, strategic political view also to blame? To put this differently, is vaporware really such a bad thing? After all, some version of collectivism operates within even the most battered social terrain. The question is: what does that collective project look like? Stimson puts it this way: "there are only two root forms of collectivist practice—one based in political life and the state and another in economic life and the market—and our time is marked by a historical shift from a greater degree of predominance for the first to an increasingly influential role for the second."[48]

How might our narrative about social practice art collectivism be imagined differently, or perhaps, better yet, how can it be shifted away from the market-based notion of "community as consumer-based demographic" that often surreptitiously dominates it? And yes, we are talking about conscious political resistance, which may ultimately come from any number of unlikely places. It might, for example, involve a process of engagement as disengagement, something akin to Wright's notion of escaping through a trap door.[49] Or perhaps it will emerge as John Roberts proposes, in the form of artistic communization?[50] Recent national demonstrations focusing on police violence against people of color and the unexpected success of the left-wing Syriza party in Greece, Podemos in Spain, or the "Pirate Party" Píratar in Iceland, also suggest possible pathways to politicized collectivism. But resistance could also involve less savory forces, such as the mobilization of a Nietzschean *ressentiment*, something that we can see already visible in Greece's far-right party Golden Dawn, Ukraine's Svobada, France's National Front, Austria's Freedom Party, as well as many who voted for Brexit in the UK and the white supremacist alt-right movement that supported the recent Republican presidential campaign in the United States. It would also be a mistake to overlook the fact that these same political, technological, and economic shifts that gave rise to neoliberal enterprise culture also played midwife to numerous process-oriented, self-organized, collective art organizations as previously robust barriers between artist and audience, artist and curator, and artist and administrator began to blur and blend.

One result is that cultural institutions now resemble components of a "system" that swap and amplify cultural capital, rather than spaces where rare things are collected, guarded and cared for. It's no surprise, therefore, that Thompson's approach to The Interventionists embodied many of these same unresolved contradictions, or that historical contingencies determined which of these threads would prevail and which would be suppressed. Writing about the Museumsquartier in Vienna at about the time as The Interventionists, Brian Holmes observed that, "the welfare states may be shrinking, but certainly not the museum. The latter is rather fragmenting, penetrating ever more deeply and organically into the complex mesh of semiotic production [outside of its walls]."[51] The stage was being set for the current phase of post-Fordist administration and the transformation of cultural institutions into modifiable platforms for staging temporary, project-based installations, spectacles and events. This administrative turn seems to keep pace with a modified neoliberalism in which both risk and regimentation operate side by side, or, as Jan Rehmann summarizes, "neoliberal ideology is continuously permuted by its opposite: its criticism of the state, which is in fact only directed against the welfare state, flows into an undemocratic despotism, its 'freedom' reveals to signify the virtue of submission to pre-given rules."[52] Either way, the question remains: What loopholes of resistance were lost in and around 2004? Which might still remain? And how will we usefully uncover those that might still be present?

In the decade that followed 2004/2005, the massive private appropriation of public capital by self-damaged investment corporations marked a return, already under way since the 1980s, to forms of worker exploitation and precarious inequality typical of capitalism prior to the banking reforms and collective pushback orchestrated by organized labor in the aftermath of the catastrophic 1929 stock market crash. Following the recent financial collapse, an optimistic army of young "knowledge workers," including many artists, probably experienced a shock rivaling that of middle-class homeowners with foreclosed property. These privileged "creatives" had been assured that Capitalism 2.0 needed their non-stop, 24/7 yield of "out-of-the-box" productivity. Well, apparently not. Then came the high-profile prosecutions of Chelsea Manning, the government targeting of WikiLeaks co-founder Julian Assange, and revelations about National Security Administration spying by whistleblower Edward Snowden. Even the realm of non-market, digital democracy was clearly becoming a target of government regulators, to which we can add the increasing move away from fair use worldwide web content, and towards the private corporatization of intellectual property in both physical and http-coded binary form. Nor did the art world provide a refuge for the most challenging forms of tactical media. CAE, for example, stopped experimenting with bio-art after 2007, and the group has found little purchase in the US art world, traveling to Europe for most of its ongoing research projects.

Today, social practice artists are busy planting herb gardens, mending clothes, repairing bicycles, keeping bees and giving out life-coaching advice free of charge. Groups of professional designers are improving the "quality and function of the built environment" in run-down inner city corridors, categorizing what they do with the avant-gardeish rubric "Tactical Urbanism."[53] In the Bronx, working-class tenants are asked to invite a couple of artists into their homes for dinner. In exchange, the artists paint their hosts a still life. Sitting on a sofa, everyone is photographed, with the painting hanging in the background like a commentary on social values that are too often absent from the skeptical art world.[54] In New York City's East Village, a funky storefront installation of assembled found materials highlights the street culture of a gentrifying neighborhood. One artist collaborates with passersby to turn used paper cups into art, as another encourages residents to engage in "critical dialogue" about their precarious future.[55] Artists distribute free beer, hand-picked fruit, glasses of ice tea and home-made waffles to participating members of the public. These gifts are offered up like a sacrifice to some missing deity whose flock has been abandoned.[56] The absent god is of course society itself, defined as a project of collective good, from each according to her ability, to each according to his need. Instead, the community Capitalism 2.0 offers is based on the gospel of mutually shared selfishness, and certainly any attempt at countering such a credo is justified, even participatory waffle sharing, though it must be said here that the road to hell is undoubtedly paved with many good interventions. And now, with the defeat of the politically ineffectual and only moderately oppositional Democrats in the United States, and the rise of a far-right regime with authoritarian and white supremacist tendencies, it is of primary importance to revisit the paradoxes of social practice art as complicit with the global nexus of capital/art/and precarious, surplus labor.

To be sure, the argument put forward here does not deny that artists earnestly struggle to change society, even if the art they produce frequently serves, for better and for worse, as a symbolic resolution to irresolvable social contradictions. And yet what has changed is the phenomenal aggregation of networked social productivity and cultural labor made available today as an artistic medium, and at a time when society is intellectually, culturally and constitutively destitute. Art, along with virtually everything else, has been subsumed by capital, resulting in the socialization of all production. One outcome is that artists are becoming social managers, curators are becoming arts administrators, and academics are becoming tactical urbanistas. Meanwhile, social practice artists collect the bits and pieces of what was once society like a drawer of mismatched socks. Is it any surprise that these social artifacts only seem to feel alive in a space dedicated to collecting and maintaining historical objects (and I am speaking, of course, of the museum)? But in a field that is weakly theorized even in the best of circumstances, art's "social turn" makes the passage of engaged art out of the margins and into some measure of legitimacy all the more compelling as a matter for urgent debate. Because if art has finally merged with life as the early twentieth-century avant-garde once enthusiastically anticipated, it has done so not at a moment of triumphant communal utopia but at a time when life, at least for the 99%, sucks.

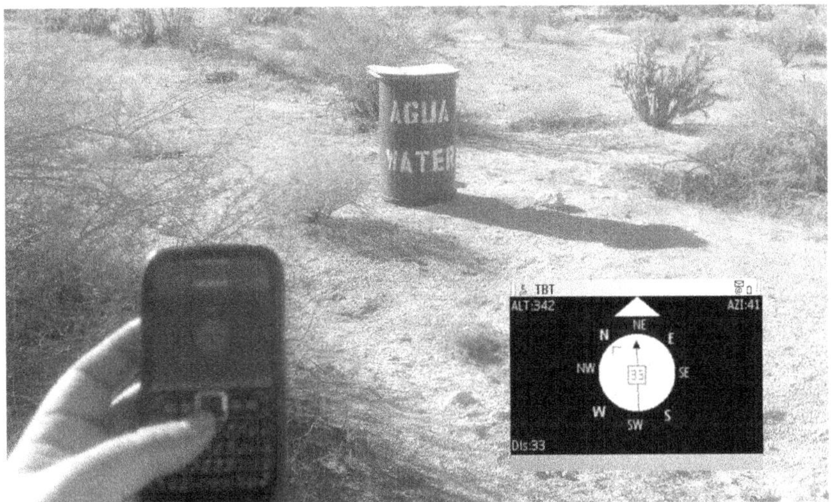

Figure 36 Electronic Disturbance Theater (EDT)/b.a.n.g. lab: Transborder Immigrant Tool, a cell phone hack distributed along the US–Mexico border in 2009 to assist individuals crossing the US–Mexico border using a built-in GPS app to locate water left by volunteer groups and medical help centers

(Image Ricardo Dominguez)

What is called for is imaginative, critical engagement aimed at distancing socially engaged art from both the turbo-charged, contemporary art world, as well as from what Fisher calls "capitalist realism" in the post-Fordist society of control, a world where "'Flexibility', 'nomadism' and 'spontaneity' are the hallmarks of management." As nearly impossible as that struggle seems today, if we do not strive for a broader conception of liberation, then we resign ourselves to nothing less than bad faith, while abandoning hopes of rescuing that *longue durée* of opposition from below that so many before us have endeavored to sustain. Once upon a time, art mobilized its resources to resist becoming kitsch. Now art must avoid becoming a vector for data mining and social asset management, or a means of alleviating unbearable social realities, or a method for withdrawing from politically challenging conflicts whose intensity is clearly on the rise. Nevertheless, delirium and resistance prevail today, forging an indissoluble amalgam of two predictable responses to current circumstances. But it is this same dizzy feverishness that might drive us onwards in the form of a persistent, low-grade fever for social justice. What remains paramount is recognizing the actuality of our plight, including its paradoxes, while asking how we can be more than what the market says we are. The terrain thereafter is a delirious terra incognita. It is waiting to be mapped. We must get there first.

Postscript: December 2016

The neoliberal era in the United States ended with a neofascist bang. The political triumph of Donald Trump shattered the establishments in the Democratic and Republican parties—both wedded to the rule of Big Money and to the reign of meretricious politicians.

Cornel West, commenting on the 2016 US presidential elections[1]

All around us the bodies rose out of the stone, crowded into groups, intertwined, or shattered into fragments, hinting at their shapes with a torso, a propped-up arm, a burst hip, a scabbed shard, always in warlike gestures, dodging, rebounding, attacking, shielding themselves, stretched high or crooked, some of them snuffed out, but with freestanding, forward-pressing foot, a twisted back, the contour of a calf harnessed into a single common motion.

Peter Weiss, describing the Pergamon frieze,
in *The Aesthetics of Resistance*[2]

The delirium and crisis of capitalism—as well as of art—is now the delirium and crisis of liberal democracy. From India and Turkey to the Philippines and the Gulf region, from Hungary to Austria and France, from the US to parts of Central America and the UK, it appears that both developed and developing nations are being equally afflicted with a global contagion of nationalistic and authoritarian sentiment grounded in fear, hatred and, above all, pessimism about any government's or politician's promise to provide a stable and secure future. Neoliberalism's postponement of crisis through consumer credit expansion has run its course. In its place we find a narrative invoking wealthy male leadership, military capacity and warnings of retribution towards one's perceived competitors, be they other militarized states, homeless refugees, migrant workers or even one's own disaffected surplus populace. On the positive side, the rascals previously hiding in the bushes have no more need for camouflage. The stakes have become that much clearer and more urgent.

Meanwhile, art's quarantine from everyday life, already made improbable under the conditions of *bare art*, is clearly no longer viable in light of the gestating political crisis we now face. At this moment, culture cannot serve as a salve for nervous souls, even if the (then) president elect tweeted his disapproval of Broadway actors for using the theater to communicate their doubts about his future administration. Art's peculiar license to speak up, to misbehave, mock and imitate reality, to blur genres and disciplines, this freedom, as long as it lasts, must be deployed to prevent the normalization of the emerging authoritarian paradigm. And if it is blocked, it must then move underground to continue its mission, by retrieving its status as dark matter or what Fred Moten and Stefano Harney call *the undercommons*.[3] Still, as discussed in the essays in this book, socially engaged art is entwined with the rise of a hyper-financialized, totally spectacularized society, the raw condition of *bare art*, which is the negative counterpart of an increasingly politicized, militant art world, is a constant reminder of the fragility of that same social reality. This is the greatest paradox activist artists must come to terms with at the theoretical, political, and artistic levels: how to invent, or how to reinvent, a partisan art praxis now that capitalism has become a dead weight, and its social and political forms begin to implode.

But I suspect we already bear witness to the outlines of this process in groups and actions such as Black Lives Matter, Occupy Wall Street, the Arab uprisings and the Movement of the Squares. Mobilized with the assistance of modern communications technologies, swarms of bodies erupt into public spaces, actively interrupting and deregulating police ordinances segregating those who have access to visibility from those who have little or none. And yet more than one paradox inevitably arises here. Along with the social antagonism networked culture fosters with its panoptic vulnerability to surveillance and self-obsessive tendencies, there is also nothing that prevents assemblies of authoritarian and white supremacist bodies from similarly gathering in an effort to eclipse (or to affirm) their own dark matter obscurity.[4] We have already begun to see this disturbing display in the months leading up to the American election, but also in other nations following the 2008 global financial collapse. Nonetheless, what rigid bodies framed by authoritarian ideology cannot conceal is their fidelity to dogmatic first principles and a fundamentally undemocratic idea of biopolitical sovereignty. In contrast to such fantasies of imperial restoration, movements such as Black Lives Matter or Occupy Wall Street celebrate a critical plurality, and the essential uncertainty of an archive "from below" made concrete through their collective labors of mass protest, no matter how motley, ungainly or informal in appearance.

Two essentially contrasting utopian impulses therefore confront one another, producing in turn contrasting corporeal, visual and narrative public manifestations. One understands history and "whiteness" as a rigid and unchanging guarantee of political dominance. The other recognizes the lacuna of the archive as their inheritance of a struggle "from below," but also a crucial constituent necessary for opening a space for an entirely different social horizon.

Whether or not the coming battlefield where these conflicted notions of history, politics and aesthetics will inevitably soon clash might also give birth to its own generation of chroniclers, depicters, poets and archivists, is an intriguing question. If it does, thanks in part to the totally aestheticized society, they will at long last undoubtedly fulfill the sentiments of Joseph Beuys by proving that "everyone is an artist." In the mean time, what is called for is a grammar of cultural dissent that does not turn innocently away from the chaotic and delirious state of contemporary social realities, or the contradictions of *bare art*, but recognizes this moment, and the confrontation that rises immediately before us, as ultimately historical in nature, and therefore also a time and conflict that will one day be displaced, as all such moments are. To reiterate Derrida's previously cited comment, when it comes to the archive "We will only know tomorrow. Perhaps."[5] However, for now, our obligation is also clear. It calls on us to make certain that any future displacement also reclaims the ghostly presence not only of the current conflict, but also all preceding struggles, no matter how dark or difficult to visualize, no matter how epically everyday in outer appearance.

Notes

Foreword: Is Another Art World Possible?

1. Unsourced quotations in the Foreword are from the text.

Art on the Brink: Bare Art *and the Crisis of Liberal Democracy*

1. Gregory Sholette, *Dark Matter: Art and Politics in the Age of Enterprise Culture*, Pluto Press, 2011.
2. David Harvey, *A Brief History of Neoliberalism*, Oxford University Press, 2005.
3. Sholette, *Dark Matter*, 121–122.
4. Harvey, *A Brief History of Neoliberalism*, 31.
5. Andrew Kliman, *The Failure of Capitalist Production: Underlying Causes of the Great Recession*, Pluto Press, 2012.
6. See Olav Velthuis, *Talking Prices: Symbolic Meanings of Prices in the Market for Contemporary Art*, Princeton University Press, 2005, 5. Velthuis observes the reluctance of art dealers to discuss their pricing strategies.
7. In the immediate aftermath of the British vote to leave the European Union in 2016 the art collector and adviser Stefan Simchowitz was quoted in *Artnet News* to this effect:

   > In the short term, it's bad for all markets, uncertainty creates massive volatility especially in the more mature "blue chip" expensive categories. Art as a store of long-term wealth however is a very good hedge against structural changes in the relative value that currencies have against each other as well as the long-term loss of value that currencies have as central banks print more money to stimulate and stabilize currencies in troubled times. So I think once again, after digesting the short-term BREXIT shock to all markets, art will effectively continue its structural function as an alternative currency that hedges against inflation and currency depreciation. (Rain Embuscado, "The Artworld Responds to Brexit", June 24, 2016, *Artnet News*, https://news.artnet.com/art-world/art-world-re-sponds-brexit-526400).

8. Assemble were awarded the 2015 Turner Prize; Gates was awarded the Artes Mundi 6 Prize, 2015.
9. Yates McKee, *Strike Art! Contemporary Art and the Post-Occupy Condition*, Verso, 2016, 79; Stevphen Shukaitis, *The Composition of Movements to Come: Aesthetics and Cultural Labor after the Avant-garde*, Rowman & Littlefield, 2016.
10. Lucy R. Lippard, "Trojan Horses: Activist Art and Power," in Brian Wallis (ed.) *Art after Modernism: Rethinking Representation*, New Museum of Contemporary Art, 1984, 341–359, 341.
11. Lippard also refers to "art activism" in an essay first published in 1980 (and the author remarks that the passage in question was written in 1977). See: "Hot

Potatoes: Art and Politics in 1980," in Lippard, *Get the Message? A Decade of Art for Social Change*, E.P. Dutton, 1984, 160–172.

12. Important recent examples include: Tom Finkelpearl, *What We Made: Conversations on Art and Social Cooperation*, Duke University Press, 2013; Nato Thompson (ed.) *Living as Form: Socially Engaged Art from 1991–2011*, Creative Time Books and MIT Press, 2012; Claire Bishop, *Artificial Hells: Participatory Art and the Politics of Spectatorship*, Verso, 2012; Sholette, *Dark Matter*; Julia Bryan-Wilson, *Art Workers: Radical Practice in the Vietnam Era*, University of California Press, 2009.

13. McKee, *Strike Art!*.

14. Sholette, *Dark Matter*, 3.

15. See Greg Sholette, "Not Cool Enough to Catalog: Social Movement Culture and its Phantom Archive," in Carol Wells and Ilee Kaplan (eds.) *Peace Press Graphics 1967–1987: Art in the Pursuit of Social Change*, University Art Museum, California State University, LA Center for the Study of Political Graphics, 2011, 91–107, www.gregorysholette.com/wp-content/uploads/2011/11/PEACEPRESS_FINAL_080511-copy.pdf.

16. Lippard, "Trojan Horses," 341.

17. John Walker, *Left Shift: Radical Art in 1970s Britain*, I.B. Tauris, 2002.

18. Sholette, *Dark Matter*, 4.

19. Gerald Raunig, *Art and Revolution: Transversal Activism in the Long Twentieth Century*, Semiotext(e), 2007, 19.

20. Hal Foster, "Against Pluralism," *Recodings: Art, Spectacle, Cultural Politics*, Bay Press, 1985, 13–32.

21. Foster "Against Pluralism," 15.

22. Peter Osborne *Anywhere or Not at All: Philosophy of Contemporary Art*, Verso, 2013, 4.

23. Osborne *Anywhere or Not at All*, chapter 1, "The Fiction of the Contemporary," 15–36, and chapter 4, "Transcategoricality: Post-conceptual Art," 99–116.

24. Sholette, *Dark Matter*, 126.

25. Carol Duncan, "Who Rules the Artworld?," in *The Aesthetics of Power: Essays in Critical Art History*, Cambridge University Press, 1993, 169–188, 180.

26. Andrew Ross, *Nice Work if You Can Get It: Life and Labor in Precarious Times*, New York University Press, 2009.

27. Sholette, *Dark Matter*, 117.

28. See the discussion of Artists Meeting for Cultural Change in this book, page 21 and page 35.

29. Andrew Ross, "The New Geography of Work: Power to the Precarious?" *Theory, Culture & Society* 25(7–8), December 2008, 31–48, 34.

30. Sholette was a student of Hans Haacke, Jean-Pierre Gorin and Benjamin H.D. Buchloh, and a member of Martha Rosler's reading group in the early 1980s. Negri's *Marx beyond Marx* was a key influence; Antonio Negri, *Marx beyond Marx: Lessons from the Grundrisse*, trans. Harry Cleaver, Autonomedia and Pluto Press, 1991. Oskar Negt and Alexander Kluge, *Public Sphere and Experience: Analysis of the Bourgeois and Proletarian Public Sphere*, trans. Peter Labanyi, Jamie Owen Daniel and Assenka Oksiloff, Verso, 2016.

31. Sholette, *Dark Matter*, 4.

32. Joshua Clover, *Riot. Strike. Riot: The New Era of Uprisings*, Verso, 2016, 31.

33. Ibid., 177.

34. Hal Foster, "Postmodernism, a Preface," in Foster (ed.) *The Anti-Aesthetic: Essays on Postmodern Culture*, Bay Press, 1983, ix–xvi.

35. Karl Marx *Capital*, vol. III, chapter 15, "Exposition of the Internal Contradictions of the Law," Lawrence & Wishart, 1977, 242.

36. For some very different approaches to crisis theory see: Paul Mason, *Postcapitalism: A Guide to our Future*, Penguin, 2016; Joshua Clover, *Riot. Strike. Riot*; *Endnotes 3, Gender, Race Class and other Misfortunes*, September 2013, https://endnotes.org.uk/issues/3

37. *Endnotes* 4, "Editorial #4," *Unity in Separation*, October 2015, https://endnotes.org.uk/issues/4

38. John Roberts, *Revolutionary Time and the Avant-garde*, Verso, 2015, 28.

39. Sholette, *Dark Matter*, 22.

40. Ibid., 112.

41. Ibid.

42. See for example: Hito Steyerl. "If You Don't have Bread – Eat Art! Contemporary Art and Derivative Fascisms," *e-flux Journal* 76, October 2016, www.e-flux.com/journal/76/69732/if-you-don-t-have-bread-eat-art-contemporary-art-and-derivative-fascisms/

43. Brian Wallis, "Democracy and Cultural Activism," in Wallis (ed.) *Democracy: A Project by Group Material*, Bay Press and Dia Art Foundation, 1990, 10.

44. Ibid.

45. Wolfgang Streeck, "How Will Capitalism End?," *New Left Review* 87, 2014, 35–64, 38. See also: Wolfgang Streeck, *How will Capitalism End?: Essays on a Failing System* Verso, 2016.

Introduction I: Welcome to Our Art World

1. Marc James Léger, *Brave New Avant-Garde*, Zero Books, 2012, 13.

2. Sholette, "Dark Matter, Activist Art and the Counter-Public Sphere", in M. Beaumont, A. Hemingway, L. Esther and J. Roberts (eds.) *As Radical as Reality Itself: Essays on Marxism and Art for the Twenty-first Century*, Peter Lang, 2007, 429–457.

3. Theodor W. Adorno, *Aesthetic Theory*, Bloomsbury/Berg, 2013, 72.

4. György Lukács, *History and Class Consciousness*, MIT Press, 1972.

5. Arthur C. Danto, "The Artworld", in Carolyn Korsmeyer (ed.) *Aesthetics: The Big Questions*, Blackwell, 1998, 33–43, 40.

6. Carol Duncan, *Civilizing Rituals: Inside the Public Art Museum*, Routledge, 1995.

7. David Joselit, *After Art*, Princeton University Press, 2012, 3.

8. W.J.T. Mitchell, *What do Pictures Want? The Lives and Loves of Images*, University of Chicago Press, 2005, 137.

9. Branden W. Joseph, "Interview with Paolo Virno", *Grey Room* 21, Fall 2005, 35; Fredric Jameson, *Representing Capital: A Reading of Volume One*, Verso, 2011, 17.

10. BFAMFAPhD/Caroline Woolard, "Pedagogies of Payment", *The Enemy* 2(2), 2014, http://theenemyreader.org/pedagogies-of-payment

11. Noah Fischer, "The Dark Arts", *The Enemy* 1(1), 2014, http://theenemyreader.org/the-dark-arts/

12. Lise Soskolne, "What Is Wrong with the Art World and How Would You Fix It?," unpublished WAGE text introducing WAGENCY project, September 24, 2016.

13. Debtfair mission statement by Occupy Museum members Noah Fischer, Kenneth Pietrobono, Tal Beery, Imani Jacqueline Brown and Arthur Polendo, www.noahfischer.org/project/general/214986

14. Gregory Sholette 'Fidelity, Betrayal, Autonomy: In and Beyond the Post Cold-War Art Museum," 2004: http://eipcp.net/transversal/0504/sholette/en

15. See page 34.

16. Stevphen Shukaitis, *The Composition of Movements to Come: Aesthetics and Cultural Labor after the Avant-Garde*, Rowman and Littlefield International, 2015, 8, 29. See also my review of Shukaitis in *Critical Inquiry* 42(4), 2016, 998–1001, http://criticalinquiry.uchicago.edu/that_which_must_not_be_named/.

17. According to Thompson, the union of art and activism defined the anti-globalization movement, but following the terrorist attacks of September 11, 2001 this cultural politics was suppressed only to re-emerge during the period of Occupy Wall Street and the Arab Spring. Nato Thompson, *Seeing Power: Art and Activism in the Twenty-first Century*, Melville House, 2014, 28–30.

18. Ibid., 30.

19. Michel de Certeau, *The Practice of Everyday Life*, University of California Press, 1984, xix.

20. Stephen Wright, who is working with ideas generated by, among others, Yann Moulier Boutang and Henri Lefebvre, argues that "the user's space is lived—not represented." Stephen Wright, *Towards A Lexicon of Usership*, Van Abbemuseum, 2013, 26.

21. Yates McKee, *Strike Art! Contemporary Art and the Post-Occupy Condition*, Verso, 2016, 79.

22. Ibid., 61.

23. Ibid., 61–62.

24. Ibid., 28, 41.

25. Ibid., 27.

26. Ibid., 81.

27. "The Solomon R. Guggenheim Museum has received a major grant from the Edmond de Rothschild Foundation to support Guggenheim Social Practice, a new initiative committed to exploring the ways in which artists can initiate projects that engage community participants," including soliciting a project by Conflict Kitchen co-founder Jon Rubin, we are informed in a press release of May 12, 2016, posted precisely one day and one month after the Guggenheim trustees unilaterally rejected efforts by Gulf Labor Coalition to reform the museum's internationally discredited labor policies in Abu Dhabi. See www.guggenheim.org/press-release/85742 and http://gulflabor.org/

28. McKee, *Strike Art!*, 11.

29. For an extended discussion of social movement art see Greg Sholette, "Merciless Aesthetic: Activist Art as the Return of Institutional Critique. A Response to Boris Groys," *FIELD Journal* 4, Spring 2016, http://field-journal.com/issue-4/merciless-aesthetic-activist-art-as-the-return-of-institutional-critique-a-response-to-boris-groys. In this essay, I discuss the activities of artists, activists and archivists Josh McPhee and the late Dara Greenwald.

30. Olga Kopenkina, "Administered Occupation: Art and Politics at the 7th Berlin Biennale," *Art Journal*, April 18, 2013, http://artjournal.collegeart.org/?p=3457; see also Sebastian Loewe, "When Protest Becomes Art: The Contradictory Transformations of the Occupy Movement at Documenta 13 and Berlin Biennale

7", *FIELD Journal* 1, Spring 2015; and Noah Fischer's response "Agency in a Zoo: The Occupy Movement's Strategic Expansion to Art Institutions," *FIELD Journal*, 2, Fall 2015.

31. Jameson, *Representing Capital*, 6–7.

32. Hito Steyerl, "If You Don't Have Bread, Eat Art! Contemporary Art and Derivative Fascisms," *e-flux Journal* 76, October 2016.

33. These concepts are discussed throughout John Roberts, *Revolutionary Time and the Avant-garde*, Verso, 2015 and Greg Sholette, *Dark Matter: Art and Politics in the Age of Enterprise Culture*, Pluto Press, 2011, respectively.

34. Georges Bataille, "The Notion of Expenditure," *Visions of Excess: Selected Writings 1927–1939*, University of Minnesota Press, 1985.

35. See also Thompson *Seeing Power*, 30; Shukaitis, *The Composition of Movements to Come*, 28 (on Situationist International tactics and the Arab Spring); Thomas Gokey, cited in McKee, *Strike Art!*, 31–32; Gavin Grindon, "Poetry Written in Gasoline: Black Mask and Up Against the Wall Motherfucker", *Art History* 38(1), Fall 2014, 170–209; Gerald Raunig, "The Molecular Strike", 2011, http://eipcp.net/transversal/1011/raunig/en; Brian Holmes, "Art after Capitalism", in Greg Sholette and Oliver Ressler, eds., *It's the Political Economy Stupid*, Pluto Press, 2014, 165–169; and as journalist Michele Elam writes "Occupy art might just be the movement's most politically potent tool," from "How Art Propels Occupy Wall Street," CNN, November 4, 2011, www.cnn.com/2011/11/01/opinion/elam-occupy-art/

36. James C. Scott, *Domination and the Arts of Resistance: Hidden Transcripts*, Yale University Press, 1990.

1   Fidelity, Betrayal, Autonomy:
Within and Beyond the Post-Cold War Art Museum

1. Michel Foucault, "What is an Author?," trans. Donald F. Bouchard and Sherry Simon, in Donald F. Bouchard (ed.) *Language, Counter-memory, Practice*, Cornell University Press, 1977, 124–127.

2. For more on Political Art Documentation/Distribution (PAD/D) see Greg Sholette, "News from Nowhere: Activist Art and After: Report from New York," *Third Text* 45, 1998–1999, 45–62, www.gregorysholette.com/wp-content/uploads/2011/04/13_newsfrom1.pdf.

3. PAD/D newsletter, 1st issue, February 1981.

4. A decade later, Lucy R. Lippard was herself ousted from her post at the *Village Voice*, ostensibly because her political enthusiasm prevented her from writing "objective" art criticism.

5. List compiled from first and second issues of PAD/D newsletter (both published 1981).

6. An example of leveraging is the series of exhibitions entitled Mumia 911 that took place across the United States in the Fall of 1999, which not only called attention to but also provided material support for confronting police brutality and institutionalized racism. Mumia 911 called for an impartial retrial of the outspoken African-American activist Mumia Abu Jamal, who has been on Pennsylvania's death row since 1982, accused of murdering a Philadelphia police officer. International human rights groups have condemned his conviction as legally flawed, even politically motivated by a vindictive police department known for its widespread

racism and corruption. Along with building support for a new trial the Mumia 911 coalition focused public attention on the disproportionate number of non-white people incarcerated and on death row across the United States.

7. The building was finally renovated into the newly named Experimental Station opening in 2006 where, among other occupants over the years, it has housed *The Baffler* magazine, Invisible Institute, Theaster Gates and the Blackstone Bicycle Works, http://experimentalstation.org/aboutus/ (see also "Art after Gentrification," chapter 7 in this volume, page 127).

8. Some of those who worked on the solar technology also developed the start-up company US Robotics that later merged with 3Com with combined assets of $8.5 billion, meanwhile, Peterman's Universal Lab project was assisted by a young, intrepid curator Stephanie Smith, then working at the Smart Museum, as well as former publisher of *The Baffler* Greg Lane and Chicago Resource Center's Ken Dunn also discussed in "Art after Gentrification" (chapter 7 in this volume).

9. Ecologies: Mark Dion, Peter Fend, Dan Peterman was curated by Stephanie Smith and ran from July 6 to August 27, 2000 at the David and Alfred Smart Museum of Art, University of Chicago.

10. Stephanie Smith, *Ecologies: Mark Dion, Peter Fend, Dan* Peterman, University of Chicago Press, 2001, 125.

11. See David Gonzalez, "Lampposts as a Forum for Opinion," *New York Times*, May 12, 1998, B1, Metro edition, and Stuart W. Elliot, "Some Legal History Still Being Overturned," *New York Times*, November 15, 1998, 5.

12. On the structural nature of collectivity see "Counting on Your Collective Silence: Notes on Activist Art as Collaborative Practice" (chapter 8 in this volume, page 167).

13. Michael Hardt and Antonio Negri, *Labor of Dionysus: A Critique of State Form*, University of Minneapolis Press, 1994, 281.

14. For more on this history, see my essay "News from Nowhere."

15. Pier Paolo Pasolini, *Poems*, trans. Norman MacAfee, Noonday Press, 1982, 19.

2   *Let's Do It Again Comrades, Let's Occupy the Museum!*

1. Gilles Deleuze, *Difference and Repetition*, trans. Paul Patton, Columbia University Press, 1995, 1.

2. Jacques Derrida, "Ellipsis," in *Writing and Difference*, University of Chicago Press, 1978, 297.

3. "Invitation to General Assembly at the Museum of Modern Art," January 27, 2012, http://occupywallst.org/article/invitation-general-assembly-museum-modern-art/

4. For more on the Sotheby's strike and art market profits see Carol Vogel, "As Stocks Fall, Art Surges at a $315.8 Million Sale," *New York Times*, November 9, 2011, www.nytimes.com/2011/11/10/arts/sothebys-contemporary-art-sale-totals-316-million.html; see also Marlon Bishop, "Teamsters Art Handlers Picket Sotheby's Following Lockout," WNYC Radio, August 2, 2011, www.wnyc.org/story/150049-art-handlers-picket-sothebys-following-worker-lockout/.

5. Theodor Adorno, "Criticizing Privilege Becomes a Privilege—The World's Course Is as Dialectical as That," in *Negative Dialectics*, trans. E.B. Ashton, Routledge, 1990, 50–53.

3   Bare Art, *Debt, Oversupply, Panic!*
(On the Contradictions of a Twenty-first-century Art Education)

1. Randy Martin, *The Financialization of Daily Life*, Temple University Press, 2002, 17.
2. Libby Kane, "Student Loan Debt in the US has Topped $1.3 Trillion," *Business Insider*, January 13, 2016, www.businessinsider.com/student-loan-debt-state-of-the-union-2016-1.
3. According to US Department of Education data, the percentage of student loans owed to art-focused institutions of higher learning averages around $21,576, see: Ruth Simon and Rob Barry, "A Degree Drawn in Red Ink: Graduates of Arts-focused Schools Are Shown to Rack Up the Most Student Debt," *Wall Street Journal,* February 18, 2013, www.wsj.com/articles/SB10001424127887324432004578306610055834952.
4. For information on the repayment challenge for US artists see Bourree Lam, "M.F.A.s: An Increasingly Popular, Increasingly Bad Financial Decision," *The Atlantic*, December 19, 2014, www.theatlantic.com/business/archive/2014/12/mfas-an-increasingly-popular-increasingly-bad-financial-decision/383706/; and on similar challenges to British artists, despite lower tuition costs, see Susan Jones, "Artists Are Struggling to Make Ends Meet More Than Ever Before," *Guardian*, May 16, 2012, www.theguardian.com/culture-professionals-network/culture-professionals-blog/2012/may/16/artists-finance-statistics-career-problems.
5. Andrew Ross, *Creditocracy And the Case for Debt Refusal*, OR Books, 2014, 125.
6. Michel Kozlowski, Jan Sowa, Kuba Szreder, *The Art Factory*, a report by the Free/Slow University of Warsaw, 2014, 43.
7. The overall number of artists in the US doubled between 1970 and 1990, and then tripled from a mere 737,000 in 1970 to become 6.9% of the professional US labor force by 2005. These figures of course represent all types of artists, but also include some 288,000 painters, sculptors and craft artists, or 11.5% of the total. See the *National Endowment for the Arts Executive Summary of Artists in the Workforce: 1990–2005*, www.arts.gov/sites/default/files/ArtistsInWorkforce_ExecSum.pdf; see also Princeton University's Center for Arts and Cultural Policy Studies, www.princeton.edu/culturalpolicy/quickfacts/artists/lbrfrcartist.html.
8. MA degree stats cited in Bourree Lam, "M.F.A.s: An Increasingly Popular, Increasingly Bad Financial Decision"; and on NYC *creatives* see: *Creative New York*, a Center for an Urban Future report, June 2015, https://nycfuture.org/research/creative-new-york-2015.
9. Artfacts, http://artfacts.australiacouncil.gov.au/overview/.
10. Hill Strategies, *A Statistical Profile of Artists and Cultural Workers in Canada*, 2014, based on 2011 data, www.hillstrategies.com/content/statistical-profile-artists-and-cultural-workers-canada.
11. Nicholas Mirzoeff, *How to See the World: An Introduction to Images, from Self-Portraits to Selfies, Maps to Movies, and More*, Basic Books, 2016, 290. Mirzoeff goes on to speculate that this extraordinary statistic reflects a desire to escape into forms of visual action from the mundane and often precarious service jobs that the global society offers its surplus labor population.
12. "Are There Too Many Artists?" Padwick and Jones Ltd (UK cultural advisors), September 4, 2015, www.padwickjonesarts.co.uk/are-there-too-many-artists/.

13. See Table 2 of Eurostat Statistics on Cultural Employment, http://ec.europa.eu/eurostat/statistics-explained/index.php/Culture_statistics_-_cultural_employment#Focus_on_artists_and_writers.

14. Sharon Zukin, *Loft Living: Culture and Capital in Urban Change*, Johns Hopkins University Press, 1982, Rutgers Reprint edition, 1989, 199.

15. Martha Rosler, "The Artistic Mode of Revolution: From Gentrification to Occupation," *e-flux*, 33, 2012, www.e-flux.com/journal/the-artistic-mode-of-revolution-from-gentrification-to-occupation/.

16. Coco Fusco speaking on a panel entitled Art-Estate, one of the Town Hall Discussions organized by Martha Rosler for her exhibition "If You Can't Afford to Live Here, Mo-o-ove," at Mitchell-Innes & Nash gallery, June 14, 2016.

17. Elizabeth Cabal Curtis, *National Capitalization Project 2010 Summary*, Grantmakers in the Arts, 3, www.tdcorp.org/wp-content/uploads/2014/08/capitalization-project_2010-summary.pdf.

18. Christopher Madden, "Modelling the Economic Impacts of Cultural Policies," *Cultural Policies Australasia* blog, June 17, 2011. Madden suggests regulation of demand as a solution, https://artspolicies.org/2011/06/17/modelling-the-economic-impacts-of-cultural-policies/.

19. From a report by Grantmakers in the Arts, September 2010, www.giarts.org/sites/default/files/capitalization-project_2010-summary.pdf.

20. National Endowment of the Arts Director Rocco Landesman from a 2011 speech on supply and demand reported in *Creative Infrastructure*, https://creativeinfrastructure.org/2011/01/29/supply-demand-and-rocco-landesman/.

21. Diane Ragsdale, then Associate Program Office of the Mellon Foundation, in *Arts Journal*'s blog January 16, 2011, www.artsjournal.com/jumper/2011/01/overstocked-arts-pond-fish-too-big-fish-too-many/.

22. Martin, *Financialization of Daily Life*, 37.

23. Howard Singerman, *Art Subjects: Making Artists in the American University*, University of California Press, 1999, 6.

24. Highlights from the UN Conference on Trade and Development report *Creative Economy: A Feasible Development Option*, http://unctad.org/en/pages/PublicationArchive.aspx?publicationid=946.

25. Chin-Tao Wu, *Privatising Culture: Corporate Art Intervention since the 1980s*, Verso, 2003, 135.

26. Ibid., 284, citing Michael Kimmelman from the *New York Times*, April 19, 1998.

27. From the British Council Creative Economy website, http://creativeconomy.britishcouncil.org/about/.

28. Pierre-Michel Menger, "Artistic Labor Markets and Careers," *Annual Review of Sociology*, 25, 1999, 566; see also H.C. White and C.A. White, *Canvases and Careers: Institutional Change in the French Painting World*, University of Chicago Press, 1993.

29. *The Vermeer Newsletter* online, www.essentialvermeer.com/dutch-painters/dutch_art/ecnmcs_dtchart.html#.V_fjm5MrJhE.

30. Menger, "Artistic Labor Markets and Careers," 566.

31. Ibid., 773.

32. Coco Fusco, Critics Page, *Brooklyn Rail*, December 9, 2015, www.brooklynrail.org/2015/12/criticspage/coco-fusco.

33. Hans Abbing. *Why Are Artists Poor? The Exceptional Economy of the Arts*, Amsterdam University Press, 2002, 197.

34. Abbing's book summary pdf, last page, www.hansabbing.nl/DOCeconomist/ SUMMARY.pdf.

35. Professor Ruth Towse cited in "Are There Too Many Artists?"

36. Dave Beech, *Art and Value: Art's Economic Exceptionalism in Classical, Neoclassical and Marxist Economics*, Haymarket Books, 2016,176.

37. Alexander Forbes, "TEFAF Art Market Report Says 2013 Best Year on Record Since 2007, With Market Outlook Bullish," *artnetnews*, March 12, 2014, http://news. artnet.com/market/tefaf-art-market-report-says-2013-best-year-on-record- since-2007-with-market-outlook-bullish-5358/; and see *Forbes*, "An Overview of Why Microsoft's Worth $42," January 9, 2013, www.forbes.com/sites/greatspeculations/ 2013/01/09/an-overview-why-microsofts-worth-42/#1d48c79b2a34.

38. Robert Frank, "Wealthy Avoiding Stocks, Buying Art," CNBC, February 7, 2014, www.cnbc.com/2014/02/07/wealthy-avoiding-stocks-but-buying-art.html.

39. Katya Kazakina, "Art-flipping Speculators Boost the Young Artist Market," *Bloomberg*, February 13, 2014, www.bloomberg.com/news/articles/2014-02-13/ art-flipping-speculators-boost-the-young-artist-market.

40. Martin, *Financialization of Daily Life*, 17.

41. Anatole Kaletsky, *Capitalism 4.0: The Birth of a New Economy in the Aftermath of Crisis*, Public Affairs Press, 2011.

42. Sophie Quinton, "The Student Debt Crisis at State Community Colleges," PEW Charitable Trusts online, May 10, 2016, www.pewtrusts.org/en/research-and-analysis/blogs/stateline/2016/05/10/the-student-debt-crisis-at-state-community-colleges; and Paul Fain, "Small Loans, Big Problems," *Inside Higher Ed*, September 28, 2015: www.insidehighered.com/news/2015/09/28/four-surprising-findings-debt-and-default-among-community-college-students.

43. Susan M. Dynarski, "The Trouble with Student Loans? Low Earnings, Not High Debt," *Brookings Institution*, January 7, 2016, www.brookings.edu/research/the-trouble-with-student-loans-low-earnings-not-high-debt/.

44. Katy Siegal cited by Mia Fineman in "Looks Brilliant on Paper. But Who, Exactly, Is Going to Make It?," *New York Times*, May 7, 2006: www.nytimes.com/2006/05/07/ arts/design/07fine.html?pagewanted=print Page 4 of 6.

45. Ben Davis, "9.5 Theses on Art and Class," in the book of the same title, Haymarket Books, 2013, 27–37. See also Kim Charnley's review of Davis's book in *Historical Materialism* 23, 2015: 179–196.

46. Jim Edwards, "UK Household Deficit Is at 'Unprecedented' Levels…," *Business Insider*, March 18, 2016, www.businessinsider.com/uk-household-debt-statistics-unprecedented-2016-3?r=UK&IR=T.

47. *Trading Economics* website, www.tradingeconomics.com/united-kingdom/home-ownership-rate.

48. Michael Gerrity, "4.4 Million U.S. Properties Remain in Negative Equity," *World Property Journal*, September 15, 2015, www.worldpropertyjournal.com/ real-estate-news/united-states/irvine/negative-equity-housing-data-2015-frank-nothaft-corelogic-national-home-price-index-hpi-home-foreclosure-data-completed-foreclosures-frank-nothaft-anand-nallathambi-real-estate-news-9358. php.

49. Neil O. Alper and Gregory H. Wassall, "More Than Once in a Blue Moon: Multiple Jobholdings by American Artists," *Research Division Report #40*, NEA, 2000.

50. Charnley review of Davis, *Historical Materialism* 23.

51. Jeroen Boomgaard, "Radical Autonomy: Art in the Era of Process Management," *(In)tolerance*, 10, 2006, 38.

52. Adriano Picinati di Torcello, Senior Manager, Deloitte Luxembourg, "Why Should Art Be Considered as an Asset Class?" Paper presented at the conference Art as an Investment, for the Musée d'Art Moderne, Luxembourg, 2010, 23, www2.deloitte. com/lu/en/pages/art-finance/articles/art-as-investment.html.

53. Beech, *Art and Value*, 20.

54. Marx cited in ibid., 106.

55. Beech, *Art and Value*, 324 (italics added).

56. Esther Leslie, *Hollywood Flatlands: Animation, Critical Theory and the Avant-Garde*, Verso, 2002, 95.

57. Sven Lütticken, "The Coming Exception: Art and the Crisis of Value," *New Left Review*, 99, May/June 2016, 128.

58. Ken Jacobs, Ian Perry and Jenifer MacGillvary, *The High Public Cost of Low Wages*, Research Brief, UC Berkeley Labor Center, April 2015, http://laborcenter.berkeley. edu/the-high-public-cost-of-low-wages/.

59. Roberts, *Revolutionary Time and the Avant-garde*, Verso, 2015, 24; Sholette, *Dark Matter: Art and Politics in the Age of Enterprise Culture*, Pluto Press, 2011, 85.

60. Beech, *Art and Value*, 344.

61. Kerstin Stakemeier and Marina Vishmidt, *Reproducing Autonomy: Work, Money, Crisis and Contemporary Art*, Mute Books, May 2016, 28.

62. Beech, *Art and Value*, 368.

63. Mario Tronti, *Operai e capitale* (*Workers and capital*), Einaudi, 1966, https:// la.utexas.edu/users/hcleaver/TrontiWorkersCapital.html.

64. Andrew Hemingway, *The Mysticism of Money: Precisionist Painting and Machine Age America*, Periscope Press, 2013, 9.

65. Jacques Rancière, *The Politics of Aesthetics*, Continuum Books, 2004, 12–13.

66. Anne-Marie D'Aoust, *Affective Economies, Neoliberalism, and Governmentality*, Routledge, 2015.

67. *Creative New York*, report, 8 and 23.

68. Tom Fleming and A. Erskine, *Supporting Growth in the Arts Economy*, Arts Council England, 2011, 14, http://webarchive.nationalarchives.gov.uk/20160204101926/ www.artscouncil.org.uk/media/uploads/pdf/creative_economy_final210711.pdf.

69. Rachel Bers, Program Director at the Andy Warhol Foundation, cited in Rachel Bers et al., "Convening Common Field," *CAA Art Journal*, 74(3), 2015, 29.

70. Sholette, *Dark Matter*, 134.

71. Luc Boltanski and Eve Chiapello, *The New Spirit of Capitalism*, Verso, 2007. However, not all observers agree. For example, art historian Karen van den Berg stresses that post-Fordism misappropriates the concept of artistic labor production by denying any difference between autonomous art practices and capitalist labor, an argument she explores in Karen van den Berg and Ursula Pasero, *Art Production beyond the Art Market?*, Ram Publications, 2014.

72. David Harvey, *Seventeen Contradictions and the End of Capitalism*, Oxford University Press, 2014, 232.

73. On May 10, 2015 almost the entire Master's of Fine Art class at the prestigious (and expensive) University of Southern California Roski School of Fine Arts staged a walkout of classes, *Art&Eduction*: www.artandeducation.net/school_watch/entire-usc-mfa-1st-year-class-is-dropping-out/.

74. Wright's playfully serious concept is outlined in his paper "Escapology & Then You Disappear," 1 December 2012: http://northeastwestsouth.net/escapology.

75. "Malthus finally discovers, with the help of Sismondi, the beautiful Trinity of capitalistic production: over-production, over-population, over-consumption—three very delicate monsters, indeed." Karl Marx, *Capital* , vol. 1, Penguin Classics reprint edition, 1992, 787.

76. Sholette, citing Simon Sheikh, in *Dark Matter*, 70.

77. Marco Baravalle, "Art, Creativity and Cultural Labor Between Neoliberal Devices and the Drive Towards a Common Use," a paper for m.a.c.lab, University of Venice, Italy, 2014, www.academia.edu/29360147/ART_CREATIVITY_AND_CULTURAL_LABOUR_BETWEEN_NEOLIBERAL_DEVICES_AND_THE_DRIVE_TOWARDS_A_COMMON_USE._THE_CASE_OF_S.A.L.E.-DOCKS_IN_VENICE.

78. See discussions about WAGE, Debtfair, Occupy Museums, Gulf Labor Coalition, and similar groups in the Introduction to Part I: "Welcome to Our Art World," page 19.

Introduction II: Naturalizing the Revanchist City

1. Sharon Zukin, *Naked City: the Death and Life of Authentic Urban Places*, Oxford University Press, 2010, xi.

2. "Aggressive Mimicry," Wikipedia article, https://en.wikipedia.org/wiki/Aggressive_mimicry.

3. Arthur Cotterell, *The Pimlico Dictionary of Classical Mythologies*, Random House, 2000, 83.

4. Christa-Maria Lerm Hayes and Victoria Walters (eds.) *Beuysian Legacies in Ireland and Beyond: Art, Culture and Politics*, Meunster, 2011, 14.

5. A canid is a member of the Canidae, the mammal family that includes dogs, foxes, hyenas, wolves and coyotes. Regarding Beuys's canid, there is no reliable account of either the source of the animal, or its fate after the encounter with the artist, though speculation is that it came from and was returned to a local zoo.

6. Warehousing property amounts to holding useable buildings or spaces vacant in order to rent, lease or sell at a higher value once a neighborhood is fully gentrified. See Picture the Homeless organization: http://picturethehomeless.org/announcing-the-housing-not-warehousing-act/.

7. "Yes, a Police Riot," editorial, *New York Times*, August 26, 1988, www.nytimes.com/1988/08/26/opinion/yes-a-police-riot.html.

8. The defendants spent between six and thirteen years in prison, between the crime in 1989 and their collective exoneration in 2002. On the wolves in blue uniform responsible for the death of Richard Luke see Don Terry, "Angry Protest Assails Police in Man's Death," May 24, 1989, *New York Times*, www.nytimes.com/1989/05/24/nyregion/angry-protest-assails-police-in-man-s-death.html. And on the scandal of the so-called Central Park wilding wolfpack see the Peabody Awarded documentary, *The Central Park Five*, directed by Ken and Sarah Burns, and David Mcmahon, 2013.

9. Artist Dillon de Give was so inspired by the appearance of "Hal" the Central Park coyote that he created a social practice project called *The Coyote Walk Itinerancy*, https://coyotewalks.wordpress.com/.

10. An excellent analysis of the project is found in Julia Rothenberg and Steve Lang, "Repurposing the High Line: Aesthetic Experience and Contradiction in West Chelsea," *City, Culture and Society*, November, 2015.

11. Rosalyn Deutsche, *Evictions: Art and Spatial Politics*. Cambridge, MA: MIT Press, 1996.

12. Neil Smith, *The New Urban Frontier: Gentrification and the Revanchist City*, Routledge, 1996, 227.

13. "Mysteries of the Creative Class" (chapter 5 in this volume, page 112).

14. Richard D. Lloyd, *Neo-Bohemia: Art and Commerce in the Neoliberal City*, Routledge, 2010, 231; Martha Rosler "The Artistic Mode of Revolution," *e-flux*, 33, 2012, www.e-flux.com/journal/the-artistic-mode-of-revolution-from-gentrification-to-occupation/; Zukin, *Naked City*.

15. "Mysteries of the Creative Class" (chapter 5 in this volume).

16. Yates McKee, *Strike Art! Contemporary Art and the Post-Occupy Condition*, Verso, 2016, 87.

17. The Wall Street mascot was first installed illegally by a wealthy Italian artist as push-back against the 1987 stock market crash, and later officially adopted by the city, but one can't help wishing that the *Charging Bull* sculpture had been present a few years earlier when Wadleigh shot his film, the sight of a Wolfen howling on its back would have been delectable.

18. Greg Bankoff, Uwe Lübken and Jordan Sand, eds., *Flammable Cities: Urban Conflagration and the Making of the Modern World*, University of Wisconsin Press, 2011, 352.

19. If anything, the undecidable signification of the Wolfen has only been amplified in 2016 as financial and political crisis eat away at our peace of mind, and a predator becomes President, while the Islamic State and "war on terror" chip away at our sense of stability from without, but also increasingly from within.

20. Albert Finney plays a NYC detective, Diane Venora the criminologist, late tap-dancer and actor Gregory Hines is the coroner, and a young Edward James Olmos appears as a Native American militant, though no tribal affiliation is revealed.

21. Alberto Toscano and Jeff Kinkle, *Cartographies of the Absolute*, Zero Books, 2015, 105.

22. Curiously, there were two other hit "wolfish" films of that era: *The Howling* and *American Werewolf in London* but only *Wolfen*, despite an initial weak box-office showing, transcends the horror genre to address socio-political issues of the day that still appear relevant now.

23. Toscano and Kinkle, *Cartographies*, 135.

24. Ibid., 111.

25. Marc James Léger, "For the De-incapacitation of Community Art Practice," *Journal of Aesthetics and Protest*, 6, 2008, www.joaap.org/6/another/leger.html.

26. Toscano and Kinkle, *Cartographies*, 136.

27. Movoto real estate site: www.movoto.com/blog/top-ten/most-creative-cities/.

28. Rosalyn Deutsche and Cara Gendel Ryan, "The Fine Art of Gentrification", *October*, 31, Winter 1984, 95.

29. Olaf Kaltemeire (ed.) *Selling EthniCity: Urban Cultural Politics in the Americas*, Routledge, 2011, 239.

30. Saskia Sassen, *Expulsions: Brutality and Complexity in the Global Economy*, Belknap Press, 2014; Smith, *New Urban Frontier*.

4   Nature as an Icon of Urban Resistance on NYC's Lower East Side, 1979–1984

1. Alan Moore and Marc Miller, "The ABC's of No Rio and its Times," in Moore and Miller (eds.) *ABC No Rio Dinero: The Story of a Lower East Side Art Gallery*, ABC No Rio, 1985, 1. Available at: http://98bowery.com/return-to-the-bowery/abcnorio-the-book.php.

2. Martha Rosler, "Fragments of a Metropolitan Viewpoint," in Brian Wallis (ed.) *If You Lived Here: The City in Art, Theory and Social Activism*, Bay Press, 1991, 25.

3. Lucy R. Lippard, "Too Close to Home," *The Village Voice*, June 14, 1983, 94–95.

4. A concise analysis of the art world's role in the gentrification of the East Village can be found in two texts from the 1980s. First, a commentary by Craig Owens, "The Problem with Puerilism," first published in *Art in America* in 1984, 135, and reprinted in his volume of collected works: *Beyond Recognition: Representation, Power, and Culture*, University of California Press, 1992, 324–325; see also Rosalyn Deutsche and Cara Gendel Ryan, "The Fine Art of Gentrification", *October*, 31, Winter 1984, 95.

5. Consider the language used in this advertisement from a full page ad in the New *York Times* as quoted by urban geographer Neil Smith: "The Armory [a new condo facility] celebrates the teaming of the Wild Wild West with 10% down payment and twelve months' free maintenance. The trail-blazers have done their work. West 42nd street has been tamed, domesticated, and polished into the most exciting freshest most energetic neighborhoods in New York." Wallis, Rosler, *If You Lived Here: The City in Art, Theory, and Social Activism: A Project by Martha Rosier (Discussions in Contemporary Culture)*, New Press, 1998, 108.

6. Owens, "The Problem with Puerilism."

7. See: Thomas Crow, "Modernism and Mass Culture," in Benjamin Buchloh, Serge Guilbaut and David Solkin (eds.) *Modernism and Modernity*, Press of the Nova Scotia College of Art and Design Culture, 1983, 252–255.

8. Owens, "The Problem with Puerilism."

9. Compare this to Walter Benjamin's description of wall posters in the Arcades of nineteenth-century Paris: "the first drops of a rain of letters that today pours down without let-up day and night on the city and is greeted like the Egyptian plague" or shop signs "recording not so much the habitat as the origin and species of captured animals." From Walter Benjamin's *Passagen-Werk*, quoted by Susan Buck-Morss, *The Dialectics of Seeing: Walter Benjamin and the Arcades Project*, MIT Press, 1989, 66.

10. Steven Hager, *Art after Midnight: The East Village Scene*, St. Martin's Press, 1986, 1.

11. Excerpted from the poem, "Thermidor," in Moore, *ABC No Rio Dinero*, 185.

12. Excerpted from the "'Manifesto or Statement of Intent' Committee for the Real Estate Show, 1980," Moore, *ABC No Rio Dinero*, 56.

13. Ibid., 61.

14. Frank Norris, *The Octopus: A Story of California*, Doubleday, 1901, 48.

15. A useful account of Manhattan's planned urban restructuring from an industrial working-class city to a professional service economy can be found in Robert Fitch, *The Assassination of New York*, Verso, 1993.

16. Moore, *ABC No Rio Dinero*, 57.

17. See: www.abcnorio.org/newbuilding.php.

18. Rupp, quoted from the exhibition catalog of Deborah Wye, *Committed to Print: Social and Political Themes in Recent American Printed Art*, Museum of Modern Art, 1988, 86.
19. Rupp quoted in Moore, *ABC No Rio Dinero*, 78.
20. Rupp quoted in Wye, *Committed to Print*, 86.
21. Details related to these projects derive from materials in the author's own archives, http://www.darkmatterarchives.net/?page_id=72, as well as from the PAD/D Archive at the Museum of Modern Art, New York, https://www.moma.org/research-and-learning/research-resources/library/faq_library_collection?x-iframe=true#padd.
22. Karl Marx and Frederick Engels, *The German Ideology 1845–46*, New York International Publishers, 1979, 62.
23. Ibid.
24. Janet Koenig from PAD/D's journal *Upfront*, 6–7, Summer 1983, 3.
25. Mary Jane Jacob in "Outside the Loop," from the catalog to the exhibition Culture in Action: A Public Art Program of Sculpture Chicago, Bay Press, 1994, 114.

5   *Mysteries of the Creative Class, or, I Have Seen the Enemy and They Is Us (2004)*

1. In 2015 the total number of billionaires had risen to 1,826 according to statistics found on Wikipedia: https://en.wikipedia.org/wiki/Billionaire ; but the 587 number comes from Luisa Kroll, "The Rich Get Richer," February 26, 2004, Forbes online: http://www.forbes.com/2004/02/26/cz_lk_0226mainintrobill04.html.
2. Ironically the bearded "hipster" fashion was only getting under way in 2004, and was mostly confined to the "creative class" neighborhood of Williamsburg Brooklyn at the time.
3. Walter Benjamin, "Theses on the Philosophy of History," in Hannah Arendt (ed.) *Illuminations: Essays and Reflections*, Schocken Books, 1968, 255.

6   *Occupology, Swarmology, Whateverology: The City of (Dis)Order versus the People's Archive*

1. Well, not all of this proto-archive was destroyed, because some museums were already collecting OWS protest signs and other material culture from Zuccotti Park before the police raid, see for example: Cristian Salazar and Randy Herschaft, "Occupy Wall Street: Major Museums and Organizations Collect Materials Produced by Occupy Movement," AP/Huffington Post, December 11, 2011, www.huffingtonpost.com/2011/12/24/occupy-wall-street-museums-organizations_n_1168893.html?ref=new-york&ir=New%20York.
2. Jacques Derrida, *Archive Fever: A Freudian Impression*, trans. Eric Prenowitz, University of Chicago Press, 1995, 36.
3. "One of the most important facts about the current uprising is simply that it has occupied the street and created an existential identification with the homeless. (Though, frankly, my generation, trained in the civil rights movement, would have thought first of sitting inside the buildings and waiting for the police to drag and club us out the door; today, the cops prefer pepper spray and 'pain compliance techniques.') … The genius of Occupy Wall Street, for now, is that it has temporarily

liberated some of the most expensive real estate in the world and turned a privatized square into a magnetic public space and catalyst for protest." Mike Davis, "No More Bubble Gum," *Los Angeles Review of Books*, October 21, 2011. Available at, http://tumblr.lareviewofbooks.org/post/11725867619/no-more-bubble-gum.

4. According to a 2014 report by Coalition for the Homeless, the number of homeless families soared after Mayor Bloomberg took office. See State of the Homeless 2013: http://www.coalitionforthehomeless.org/state-of-the-homeless-2014/. Since that time conditions have continued to worsen in NYC.

5. *Village of the Damned* was based on the novel *The Midwich Cuckoos* by John Wyndham, and was first made into a film in 1960, directed by Wolf Rilla, followed by a 1963 sequel entitled *Children of the Damned* by Anton Leader, and a 1995 remake of the original by John Carpenter.

6. The librarians are quoted in "Destruction of Occupy Wall Street 'People's Library' Draws Ire," *Guardian*, November 23, 2011, www.guardian.co.uk/world/blog/2011/nov/23/occupy-wall-street-peoples-library.

7. For more on my concept of cultural dark matter see Sholette, *Dark Matter: Art and Politics in the Age of Enterprise Culture*, Pluto Press, 2011, as well as chapter 9 in this volume, page 184.

8. "We Are Free People," editorial *Occupied Wall Street Journal*, November 20, 2011, http://occupiedmedia.us/2011/11/we-are-free-people/.

9. "After Conversations with Occupy Wall Street Organizers, Shepard Fairey Releases Revised 'Occupy Hope' Design," November 21, 2011, https://obeygiant.com/occupy-hope-v2/.

10. From two e-mails to the author dated August 6 and August 7, 2011.

11. Jason Adams, "Occupy Time," *Critical Inquiry*, November 16, 2011, http://critinq.wordpress.com/2011/11/16/occupy-time/#more-191.

12. "Occupied Berkeley, 'The Necrosocial,'" November 18, 2009, http://anticapital projects.wordpress.com/2009/11/19/the-necrosocial/.

7 Art after Gentrification

1. *Creative New York*, Center for an Urban Future report, June 2015, https://nycfuture.org/research/creative-new-york-2015, 23.

2. Kerstin Stakemeier and Marina Vishmidt, *Reproducing Autonomy: Work, Money, Crisis and Contemporary Art*, Mute Books, May 2016, 42.

3. A "flash mob" is an assembly of individuals gathered via networking technology to carry out what appears to be a spontaneous short-lived, though typically absurd activity such as dancing or singing in a predetermined public space and just as quickly dispersing again.

4. Google Image search, August 12, 2016.

5. Assemble website: http://assemblestudio.co.uk/?page_id=1030.

6. The 1981 riots are often considered the result of a surge in unemployment amongst Toxteth's largely black community that was already suffering as a result of Margaret Thatcher's monetarist economic policies. Alan Travis, "Thatcher Government Toyed with Evacuating Liverpool after 1981 Riots," *Guardian*, December 29, 2011, www.theguardian.com/uk/2011/dec/30/thatcher-government-liverpool-riots-1981.

7. Eleanor Lee, interviewed by Oliver Wainwright for "The Street that Might Win the Turner Prize: How Assemble are Transforming Toxteth," *Guardian*, May 15, 2015.

8. On the British government's abandonment of the region see Travis, "Thatcher Government Toyed with Evacuating Liverpool after 1981 Riots."

9. According to www.arscapediy.org "Creative Placemaking is an evolving field of practice that intentionally leverages the power of the arts, culture and creativity to serve a community's interest while driving a broader agenda for change, growth and transformation in a way that also builds character and quality of place." See http://www.artscapediy.org/Creative-Placemaking/Approaches-to-Creative-Placemaking.aspx.

10. California's Hollywood Boulevard implemented an Arts Retention Program to "preserve arts and cultural renovations," which amounted to preserving two theaters. This is celebrated by the NEA as a means of "Avoiding Displacement and Gentrification," from Ann Markusen and Anne Gadwa, *Creative Placemaking*, NEA, 2010, 17, https://www.arts.gov/sites/default/files/CreativePlacemaking-Paper.pdf.

11. Josephine B. Slater and Anthony Iles, "No Room to Move: Radical Art and the Regenerate City," *MUTE* Journal, November 24, 2009, www.metamute.org/editorial/articles/no-room-to-move-radical-art-and-regenerate-city.

12. Claire Bishop "The Social Turn: Collaboration and Its Discontents," *Artforum*, February, 2006, 179–185.

13. Keiligh Baker, "A Spruced-up Council Estate …," *Daily Mail*, May 12, 2015: www.dailymail.co.uk/news/article-3078395/Spruced-council-estate-one-year-s- Turner-Prize-hopefuls.html. That said, it is also fair to say that Assemble has built their practice upon models developed by such collectives and individuals as Park Fiction, www.nadir.org/nadir/initiativ/parkfiction/; Rick Lowe's *Project Row Houses*, http://projectrowhouses.org/; Dan Peterman's Experimental Station, http://experimentalstation.org; and the Baltimore Development Cooperative, http://miscprojects.com/tag/baltimore-development- cooperative/.

14. From a Bloomberg Tate Museum short documentary about Assemble at, www.tate.org.uk/whats-on/tramway/exhibition/turner-prize-2015/turner-prize-2015-artists-assemble.

15. Blake Stimson and Gregory Sholette (eds.) *Collectivism after Modernism: Art and Social Imagination after 1945*, University of Minnesota Press, 2006.

16. Gary Younge, "Theaster Gates, the Artist Whose Latest Project is Regenerating Chicago," *Guardian*, October 6, 2014, www.theguardian.com/society/2014/oct/06/theaster-gates-artist-latest-project-is-regenerating-chicago-artes-mundi.

17. White Cube gallery, http://whitecube.com/artists/theaster_gates/information/theaster_gates_cv/.

18. The Rebuild Foundation is at, https://rebuild-foundation.org/. The concept of "intentional community" is discussed in the chapter 11 in this volume, page 210.

19. Without expressly saying so, Gates's *Art Bonds* appear to reference Duchamp's 1919 *Tzanck Check*, a hand-drawn $115 check drawn on the artist's fictitious institution "The Teeth Loan & Trust Company Consolidated of New York."

20. Cited in Andrew M. Goldstein, "Theaster Gates on Using Art (and the Art World) to Remake Chicago's South Side," *Artspace*, September 24, 2015, www.artspace.com/magazine/interviews_features/qa/theaster-gates-interview-53126.

21. Ibid.

22. Enrico, "Theaster Gates: Black Archive/Kunsthaus Bregenz," VernissageTV, April 25, 2016, http://vernissage.tv/2016/04/25/theaster-gates-black-archive-kunsthaus-bregenz/.

23. Bishop, "The Social Turn."

24. Live blog—Walid Raad and Theaster Gates in Conversation, with Mohsen Mostafavi, "On Art and Cities," http://archinect.com/lian/live-blog-walid-raad-and-theaster-gates-in-conversation-with-mohsen-mostafavi-on-art-and-cities.

25. Cited from email to the author from Theaster Gates on November 3, 2016: 6:13 a.m.

26. Laquan McDonald was shot 16 times by a white officer on Chicago's South Side who was subsequently charged with first degree murder. See Invisible Institute's *Citizens Police Data Project,* https://cpdb.co/data/L5Kg6A/citizens-police-data-project; on Peterman and Gates see Rachel Cromidas, "In Grand Crossing, a House Becomes a Home for Art," *New York Times,* April 7, 2011, www.nytimes.com/2011/04/08/us/08cncculture.html?_r=0.

27. The Chicago Creative Reuse Center is at http://resourcecenterchicago.org/.

28. Peterman and Dunn interviewed by A. Laurie Palmer in *Immersive Life Practices,* Daniel Tucker (ed.) *The Chicago Social Practice History Series,* School of the Art Institute of Chicago, 2014, 186.

29. Ibid., 186.

30. Cited in Tim Adams, "Chicago Artist Theaster Gates: 'I'm Hoping Swiss Bankers Will Bail Out My Flooded South Side Bank in the Name of Art,'" *Guardian,* May 3, 2015, www.theguardian.com/artanddesign/2015/may/03/theaster-gates-artist-chicago-dorchester-projects.

31. John Colapinto, "The Real-Estate Artist," *New Yorker Magazine,* January 20, 2014, www.newyorker.com/magazine/2014/01/20/the-real-estate-artist; see also Kim Charnley, "Theaster Gates's Dorchester Projects and the Craft Paradigm," Plymouth College of Art website, http://makingfutures.plymouthart.ac.uk/accepted-abstracts/theaster-gates-s-dorchester-projects-and-the-craft-paradigm/.

32. Ivan Lindsay, "An Unintended Consequence of QE: An Art Market Boom," September 10, 2013, http://stremmelgallery.com/art-word-an-unintended-consequence-of-quantitative-easing-an-art-market-boom/.

33. Julia Rothenberg, cited from an unpublished presentation "Theaster Gates: Chicago's Entrepreneurial Artist," Presented at International Sociological Association meeting in Vienna, Austria, July 12, 2017.

34. Rirkrit Tiravanija's first *pad thai* art work/dinner took place in the Paula Allen Gallery in NYC in 1990 and was celebrated soon after as a form of "relational aesthetics" by critic and curator Nicolas Bourriaud. The cooperative restaurant known as FOOD was founded by Gordon Matta-Clark, Carol Goodden and Tina Girouard in 1971 and closed three years later. It was located on the corner of Prince and Wooster Streets in downtown Manhattan at a time when the New York artists' community was both local and relatively small. FOOD literally helped lay an affective foundation for the city's art world apart from commercial interests. The cooperative was celebrated in 2013 not by a scholarly museum exhibition, or even with a relational aesthetic art project, but by a curated restaurant by Cecilia Alemani installed at the Frieze Art Fair.

35. Conflict Kitchen website: http://conflictkitchen.org/.

36. Trojan horse comments made by Rubin and Weleski during a presentation to ASJWG (Art & Social Justice Working Group) at the Brooklyn home of Paul Ramirez Jonas, February 19, 2015.

37. Pittsburgh was once the anchor of US steel production; today the majority of job occupations there are not working class, but service and administrative related, including office support (16.8%), sales (10.5%), food preparation (8.9%), health

care (7.2%), education (5.7%), business and finance (5.1%), management (4%). By contrast, construction, maintenance, transportation, production, farming and fishing are only 20.5% of total regional employment, according to the US Bureau of Labor Statistics in 2015, www.bls.gov/regions/mid-atlantic/news-release/occupationalemploymentandwages_pittsburgh.htm.

38. See: "New Palestinian Interview Wrappers" online at, http://conflictkitchen.org/2015/04/16/new-palestinian-interview-wrappers/.

39. MIT Comparative Media Studies website, http://cmsw.mit.edu/video-conflict-kitchen-jon-rubin/.

40. Jon Rubin's website, www.jonrubin.net/#/the-waffle-shop-talk-show/.

41. Diana Nelson Jones, "East Liberty Becomes a Vibrant Community," *Pittsburgh Post-Gazette*, June 8, 2009.

42. "The city's housing policies over the past four decades led to 'the forced migration of black people from Pittsburgh to the suburbs,' with the black population declining to 79,789 in 2010 from about 102,000 in 1980, a 22 percent drop," Tom Fontaine, Hill District group: as quoted in "Civic Arena Plan Unfair to Black Residents," *Trib Live*, January 7, 2016, http://triblive.com/news/allegheny/9737974-74/housing-affordable-black.

43. Adrian McCoy, "Waffle Shop to Close in East Liberty in July," *Pittsburgh Post-Gazette*, June 22, 2012, www.post-gazette.com/ae/tv-radio/2012/06/22/Waffle-Shop-to-close-in-East-Liberty-in-July/stories/201206220215.

44. Joe Smydo, "Program Designed to Expand Artwork through Pittsburgh," *Pittsburgh Post-Gazette*, August 13, 2012, www.post-gazette.com/local/neighborhoods/2012/08/13/program-designed-to-expand-artwork-through-pittsburgh/201208130125.

45. Customer reviews from Yelp.com include: "I wouldn't go here for the food alone, but it is a neat little venue with a live talk show, which is something you don't see every day." "Pretty good, actually, but not worth a detour." "The format is irrefutably weird." "Quirky spot. Great for a late night bite." www.yelp.com/biz/waffle-shop-pittsburgh.

46. Artist Jon Rubin's website, www.jonrubin.net/the-waffle-shop-talk-show-1/.

47. Grant Kester, *Conversation Pieces: Community and Communication in Modern Art*, University of California Press, 2004.

48. Both programs emerged from Chicago's satirical comedy troupe *The Second City* whose founder, Paul Sills, in turn employed both the improvisational techniques made famous by Viola Spolin, but also the radical cabaret theater of Bertolt Brecht as reported in Stephen E. Kercher, *Revel with a Cause: Liberal Satire in Postwar America*, University of Chicago Press, 2010, 122.

49. All quotes are from a telephone interview with Mike Rakowitz, conducted March 1, 2015.

50. CK has featured a two-day menu created by local African American and Caribbean chefs celebrating "Juneteenth" (June 19–20), which marks the date in 1865 that Texas finally abolished slavery, thus bringing all states into accordance with President Lincoln's Emancipation Proclamation of 1863.

51. Even MoMA has organized an exhibition entitled Tactical Urbanism, with mixed socioeconomic implications, as reviewer Neil Brenner argues in "Is 'Tactical Urbanism' an Alternative to Neoliberal Urbanism?" http://post.at.moma.org/content_items/587-is-tactical-urbanism-an-alternative-to-neoliberal-urbanism.

52. Marina Vishmidt, "Mimesis of the Hardened and Alienated: Social Practice as Business Model," e-flux, 2013, www.e-flux.com/journal/43/60197/mimesis-of-the-hardened-and-alienated-social-practice-as-business-model/.

53. Cited from an unpublished internet article by Eric Spitznagel on the author's website, www.ericspitznagel.com/unpublished-stories/theaster-gates-inc/.

54. Excerpted from an unpublished memoir by John Preus shared with the author on August 23, 2016, 12:12 p.m.

55. "Conflict Kitchen: Fight for 15", FaceBook page, www.facebook.com/conflict kitchenworkers/?hc_ref=SEARCH.

56. "Edmund" interviewed on "Conflict Kitchen: Fight for 15," ibid.

57. From a telephone interview with Conflict Kitchen employee Clara Gamalski, October 29, 2015.

58. WAGENCY: Artist Certification & Coalition is, according to WAGE, "intended to build economic and political solidarity among artists by uniting them around shared principles of equity"; and on the Guggenheim Bilbao, www.laizquierdadiario.com/Educadores-del-Museo-Guggenheim-de-Bilbao-despedidos-por-hacer-huelga.

59. NYC Art Condo website is at http://artcondo.com.sign-up/.

Introduction III: Critical Praxis/Partisan Art

1. Coa Aly, "No Time for Art", blog, June 15, 2011, 19:47, http://moabdallah.wordpress.com/2011/06/15/no-time-for-art/.

2. Saskia Sassen, *The Global City: New York, London, Tokyo*, Princeton University Press, 2001; Richard D. Lloyd, *Neo-Bohemia: Art and Commerce in the Neoliberal City*, Routledge, 2010; Neil Smith, *The New Urban Frontier: Gentrification and the Revanchist City*, Routledge, 1996.

3. David Garcia and Geert Lovink, "The ABC of Tactical Media," 1997, http://subsol.c3.hu/subsol_2/contributors2/garcia-lovinktext.html.

4. Federal Reserve Board chair Alan Greenspan described the early 1990s technology bubble as "irrational exuberance" at a meeting of the American Enterprise Institute in 1996, immediately pushing the stock market lower, https://en.wikipedia.org/wiki/Irrational_exuberance.

5. Gregory Zuckerman, "Hedged Out: How the Soros Funds Lost Game of Chicken Against Tech Stocks", *Wall Street Journal*, May 22, 2000, www.wsj.com/articles/SB958944419575853588.

6. Lawrence Lessig, *Code and Other Laws of Cyberspace*, Basic Books, 1999, 167.

7. The essay "Collective Silence" also fed directly into the development of the book, Blake Stimson and Gregory Sholette (eds.) *Collectivism after Modernism: Art and Social Imagination after 1945*, University of Minnesota Press, 2006.

8. *The Matrix*, directed by Lana and Lilly Wachowski, Warner Bros.,1999.

9. Slavoj Zizek's Lacanian-inspired exposition of the film, "The Matrix, or, the Two Sides of Perversion," appeared online after my essay was completed. See www.lacan.com/zizek-matrix.htm.

10. Antonio Negri, *Marx beyond Marx*, Bergin & Garvey, 1984; Antonio Negri and Michael Hardt, *Labor of Dionysus*, University of Minnesota Press, 1994.

11. Antonio Negri, "Capitalist Domination and Working Class Sabotage," 1979, Red Notes, https://libcom.org/library/capitalist-domination-working-class-sabotage-negri.

12. Ernesto Laclau and Chantal Mouffe, *Hegemony and Socialist Strategy: Towards a Radical Democratic Politics*, Verso, 1985.

13. Gilles Deleuze, "Post-Script on the Societies of Control," *October*, 59, Winter 1992, 6.

14. Dollars adjusted to 1999 rates in "Borrowing to Make Ends Meet: The Growth of Credit Card Debt in the '90s", a Dēmos policy group publication, 2003, 34, www.demos.org/sites/default/files/publications/borrowing_to_make_ends_meet.pdf.

15. Oskar Negt and Alexander Kluge, *Public Sphere and Experience: Toward an Analysis of the Bourgeois and Proletarian Public Sphere*, University of Minnesota Press, 1993, 80.

16. Greg Sholette, "Heart of Darkness: A Journey into the Dark Matter of the Art World," in John Hall, Blake Stimson and Lisa Tamiris Becker (eds.) *Visual Worlds*, Routledge, 2005, 116–138.

17. An earlier version of this essay was presented as a paper at the Marxism and Visual Art Now (MAVAN) conference held at University College London, April 8–10, 2002. That essay later appeared in the book developed out of that conference: Matthew Beaumont, Andrew Hemingway, Esther Leslie and John Roberts (eds.) *As Radical as Reality Itself: Essays on Marxism and Art for the 21st Century*, Peter Lang, 2007.

18. Otto Karl Werckmeister, *Citadel Culture*, University of Chicago Press, 1991.

19. Fredric Jameson, *Representing Capital: A Reading of Volume One*, Verso, 2014, 71.

20. The ratio of many vibrant, active artists' careers to those few actually rewarded by the system can be directly observed by reviewing decades-old art magazine reviews in which one discovers no obvious difference in the work of the hundreds of artists whose names we do not recognize, and the handful we do know today. New efforts are being made to focus on overlooked practitioners, such as the Queens Museum's retrospective of Mierle Laderman Ukeles influential work, however the surplus archive of dark matter is far larger, as can be witnessed by those many artists whose collective and activist work generated support structures that allowed other careers to thrive. See for instance the remarkable narrative artist Sabra Moore offers in *Openings: A Memoir from the Women's Art Movement, New York City 1970–1992*, New Village Press, 2016.

21. Andrea Fraser, "From the Critique of Institutions to an Institution of Critique," *Artforum*, 44, September 2005, 278–286, www.marginalutility.org/wp-content/uploads/2010/07/Andrea-Fraser_From-the-Critique-of-Institutions-to-an-Institution-of-Critique.pdf.

22. While the National Endowment for the Arts budget in 2004 was a mere $1.5 million in today's dollars, the commercial markets in the US and UK experienced a record jump in prices, with a billion dollars in art sales overall (and with Jeff Koons the most in-demand contemporary artist) and every following year has only been more financially spectacular: see *Art market trends—Tendances du marché de l'art*, http://press.artprice.com/pdf/trends2004.pdf.

23. See Manny Farber, *Negative Space: Manny Farber on the Movies*, Da Capo Press, 2009.

24. *Imaginary Archive*, www.gregorysholetter.com/?page_id=587.

25. Andrew Ross, *Strange Weather: Culture, Science and Technology in the Age of Limits*, Verso, 1991.

26. Jodi Dean, "Politics without Politics," in Paul Bowman, ed., *Reading Rancière: Critical Dissensus*, Bloomsbury, 2011, 79–94.

27. Don DeLillo, *White Noise*, Penguin Books, 1984.

28. Hito Steyerl, "A Tank on a Pedestal: Museums in an Age of Planetary Civil War," *e-flux Journal*, 70, February 2016, www.e-flux.com/journal/70/60543/a-tank-on-a-pedestal-museums-in-an-age-of-planetary-civil-war/.

8   Counting on Your Collective Silence: Notes on Activist Art as Collaborative Practice

1. An excerpt from answers submitted to members of several artists' collectives as research for this essay in 1999. The questions and answers were exchanged via email and consisted of the following inquiries:

   (a) Describe one particular incident—from a crisis to a hilarious situation—that represents some key feature of the process of working with others "beneath" a collective name/project:

   (b) Other than joint authorship what other aspects of collaborative work— aesthetic, political, communal—set it apart from individual cultural production? (again you can use a specific example from your experience):

   (c) Are there any specific historical or theoretical models—pop cultural references, personal incentives—of collaborative/collective work you feel relate to your own experiences?

   (d) Any other thoughts or anecdotes you wish to add?

2. Karl Marx and Friedrich Engels, *Writings on the Paris Commune*, compiled by Hal Draper, Monthly Review Press, 1971, 152.

3. Gilles Deleuze, "Post-Script on the Societies of Control," *October*, 59, Winter 1992, 6.

4. Sara Robinson, "Thousands of Undiscovered Web Communities," *New York Times*, June 10, 1999, D3.

5. Critical Art Ensemble, "Observations on Collective Cultural Action" was originally published in *CAA Art Journal*, Summer 1998, 73–85.

6. Suzi Gablik, "Connective Aesthetics: Art after Individualism," in Suzanne Lacy (ed.) *Mapping the Terrain: New Genre Public Art*, Bay Press, 1995, 84.

7. Deleuze, "Post-Script," 7.

8. Response by Lisa Maya Knaur, former member REPOhistory, to the author's questions (see note 1 of this chapter).

9. Response by Alan W. Moore, former member COLAB, to the author's questions (see note 1).

10. Fredric Jameson, *The Political Unconscious: Narrative as a Socially Symbolic Act*, Cornell University Press, 1981, 287.

11. Ibid., 291.

12. New York City Legal Aid Attorney David Stern in a conversation with the author in the 1990s, and note that this essay was written more than a decade before apocalyptic and survivalist fantasy narratives became fully mainstreamed by the film, television, and popular fiction publishing industries.

13. Demolished in 2011, Chicago's Cabrini-Green public housing project became a notorious national symbol of failed, post-war urban policies aimed at concentrating low-income, and frequently African-American or Latino residents within bunker-like inner-city high-rise structures. A city unto itself with some 3,607 units,

Cabrini-Green was known for violent gang led crime and broken down facilities. See D. Bradford Hunt, *Blueprint for Disaster: The Unraveling of Chicago Public Housing,* University of Chicago Press, 2009.

14. Tomie Arai, artist and former member of New York Chinatown's Basement Workshop in the 1970s sent an unpublished text about collective work as her response to the author's questions (see note 1 in this chapter).

15. Antonio Negri, "Domination and Sabotage," in *Italy: Autonomia Post-Political Politics,* Semiotext(e) Journal, Vol. III, No. 3, 1980, 63.

16. Marx and Engels, *Writings on the Paris Commune,* 75.

17. Deleuze, "Post-Script," 7.

18. Negri, "Domination and Sabotage."

19. Brian Hand, contemporary Irish artist and former member of Blue Funk; a chiefly British state of great terror (see note 1 in this chapter).

20. AMCC document provided by former AMCC member Ann-Marie Rousseau.

21. An open letter to PAD/D dated October 1983, from the author's archive.

22. REPOhistory document dated January 4, 1993, from the author's archive.

23. OWS A&L minutes, www.nycga.net/groups/arts-and-culture/docs/arts-labor-meeting-minutes-12611.

24. Jacques Derrida, "The Ends of Man," in *Margins of Philosophy,* University of Chicago Press, 1982, 135.

25. Ibid.

26. Todd Ayoung, artist and former member of PAD/D and REPOhistory (see note 1 of this chapter).

27. Jacques Derrida, *Specters of Marx: The State of Debt, the Work of Mourning, and the New International,* Routledge, 1994, 89.

28. Walter Benjamin, "Theses on the Philosophy of History," in Hannah Arendt (ed.) *Illuminations: Essays and Reflections,* Schocken Books, 1968, 287.

29. Deleuze, "Post-Script," 4.

9 *Dark Matter: Activist Art and the Counter-public Sphere*

1. Sebastiano Timpanaro, *On Materialism,* trans. by Lawrence Garner, Verso, 1975.

2. http://aether.lbl.gov/www/science/DarkMatter.html.

3. Otto Karl Werckmeister, *Icons of the Left: Benjamin, Eisenstein, Picasso and Kafka after the Fall of Communism,* University of Chicago Press, 1999, 153.

4. By the term "art world" I mean the integrated, transnational economy of auction houses, dealers, collectors, international biennials and trade publications that, together with curators, artists and critics, reproduce the market, as well as the discourse that influences the appreciation and demand for highly valuable artworks.

5. Also translated more suitably as "A Worker Reads History", in *Bertolt Brecht: Selected Poems,* trans. H.R. Hays, Grove Press, 1959, 108.

6. Brecht's practice of collaborating with his wife Helene Weigel and others and sometimes claiming these for his own, merely serves here to underscore my point.

7. For more on the problem of representing positive forms of collectivism in the art world as well as in popular culture see "Counting On Your Collective Silence" (chapter 8 in this volume, page 167).

8. Andrew Hemingway, *Artists on the Left: American Artists and the Communist Movement, 1926–1956,* Yale University Press, 2002, 2.

9. First used by French sociologist Pierre Bourdieu, the term "cultural capital" can now be widely found in the literature of cultural policy think tanks and even economists, albeit stripped of its original, class conscious social critique. See Pierre Bourdieu, *The Field of Cultural Production*, Columbia University Press, 1993.

10. According to the International Labor Organization, 80% of new jobs created between 1990 and 1994 in Latin America were in the informal sector. Furthermore, as many as half of all jobs in Italy are also part of an informal economy that is defined as economic activity taking place outside of government accounting and also goes by the name of the shadow, informal, hidden, black, underground, gray, clandestine, illegal and parallel economy.

11. An estimated 10,000 students entered graduate level art programs within the United States in 1998 alone, see Andrew Hultkrans and Jef Burton's report, "Surf and Turf," *Artforum* Summer, 1998, 106–9.

12. According to the Nationwide Craft & Hobby Consumer Usage and Purchase Study, 2000, 70% of US households reports that at least one member participates in a craft or hobby. Meanwhile, the total sales of hobby supplies was $23 billion in 2000. See Hobby Industry Association, www.hobby.org. And for an enlightening report detailing the massive "cultural capital" of amateur arts in the US see: Alaka Wali, Rebecca Severson and Mario Tongoni, *Informal Arts: Finding Cohesion, Capacity and other Cultural Benefits in Unexpected Places*, Research Report to the Chicago Center for Arts Policy at Columbia College, June, 2002.

13. The digital thievery of mash-ups and the fan cuts are perfect examples of this tendency. Mash-ups are made by pop music fans who illegally copy the vocal track of one pop song and graft it onto the instrumental track of another. The fan cut is similar to the mash-up, but involves a digitally re-edited version of a Hollywood film that is re-cut to please a specific group of fans. An example of the latter is the Phantom Edit, a reconstructed, fan-friendly version of *The Empire Strikes Back*, a George Lucas Star Wars episode. Ignoring issues of copyright infringement, the anonymous editor of this fan cut initially made the Phantom Edit available as a free internet download.

14. Lucy R. Lippard, "Making Something from Nothing (Toward a Definition of Women's 'Hobby Art')", first published in *Heresies* 4, Winter 1978, and cited here from Lippard's book, *Get the Message: A Decade of Art for Social Change*, E.P. Dutton, 1984, 97–105.

15. Roberta Smith, "Bad News for Art However You Define It", *New York Times*, March 31, 2002, 33.

16. Brandon Taylor, *Avant-garde and After: Rethinking Art Now*, H.N. Abrams, 1995, 153.

17. The art writers who endorsed this exhibition included F. Paul Laster in *Time Out New York*, March 1–9, 2003, 59; Kim Levin in the *Village Voice*, January 7, 2003, 60; and, ironically, Roberta Smith, in the *New York Times*, January 31, 2003, 36.

18. In the Tate Modern's "Still Life/Object" room devoted to Lucas's work in April 2002.

19. *Nobby*, 2000, cast plastic garden gnome, cigarettes 70 × 34 × 68.5 cm / 27 1/2 × 13 3/8 × 27 in. Courtesy Sara Coles HQ art gallery, London.

20. Plattner adds that "this model is relevant to the art market because it describes a situation of workers receiving payments that don't seem related to their input of effort." Stuart Plattner, *High Art Down Home: An Economic Ethnography of a Local Art Market*, University of Chicago Press, 1996, 12–13.

21. The significance of such consumption capital is made clear when one considers the odds of an artist without dealer representation ever being chosen for a major art biennial or even getting reviewed in a contemporary art publication.

22. Not surprisingly, the non-art world observer views this phenomenon as entirely arbitrary. Take for example a gestural painting by Yves Klein displayed in a major art museum compared with a well painted, but generic version of abstract expressionism hanging above a sofa in the window of a department store. The viewer with enough accumulated, cultural capital to know which painting is the more valuable will succeed in stabilizing a potentially confusing state of affairs, even if the actual, visual differences between the two paintings are negligible.

23. Oskar Negt and Alexander Kluge, *Public Sphere and Experience: Toward an Analysis of the Bourgeois and Proletarian Public Sphere*, University of Minnesota Press, 1993.

24. Ibid., xliii and xlvi.

25. Ibid., 32.

26. Ibid., 33.

27. Ibid., 33.

28. Ibid., 37. This position regarding the materiality of mental functions is similar to that which Sebastiano Timpanaro raises in his book, *The Freudian Slip: Psychoanalysis and Textual Criticism*, Verso, 2003. See also Timpanaro, *On Materialism*.

29. Negt and Kluge, *Public Sphere and Experience*, 174.

30. These examples are taken from the book, *Sabotage in the American Workplace: Anecdotes of Dissatisfaction, Mischief and Revenge*, edited by Martin Sprouse and illustrated by Tracy Cox, Pressure Drop Press and AK Press, 1992, 5, 86, 21, 92, 137 and 30–31.

31. Negt and Kluge, *Public Sphere and Experience*, 176, and also 296, in which the authors describe the leisure and cultural interests of workers, including hobbies, ideas and fantasies as "linked with one another only in a naturally rooted, random way, at a lower level of production." The introduction of apparent hierarchies between types of resistant actions suggests either a standard of efficacy on one hand, or taste on the other. Yet it is also possible to apply the idea of practice to this problem, that is, practice as the work one does to improve an idea, activity or craft. Curiously, while this drive for self-betterment is found among both professionals and amateurs, the emergence of slack art leaves the amateur artist defending older notions of artistic craft.

32. Ibid., xliii.

33. This new "visibility" also risks attracting the attention of the newly constituted state surveillance institutions in the US. At the same time, the fashion industry already understands the cash potential of dark matter. Worn-out blue jeans and threadbare hooded sweaters with faded screenprinted designs hint at the swap-shop aesthetic of anti-global demonstrators. Ironically, this ersatz "street" aesthetic is produced in volume by sweatshop labor. Indeed, even Nike advertisements for high-end running shoes have mimicked the hand-made style of the fanzine and the street stencil graffiti.

34. From a 1994 issue of the zine *Riot Grrrl*, cited in the book by Stephen Duncombe, *Notes from Underground: Zines and the Politics of Alternative Culture*, Verso, 1997 and 2001, 123.

35. Duncombe, *Notes from Underground*, 129.

36. Ibid., 127.

37. Negt and Kluge, *Public Sphere and Experience*, 171.

38. "Tactical media are what happens when the cheap 'do it yourself media' made possible by the revolution in consumer electronics and the expanded forms of distribution (cable, satellite and internet) are exploited by groups and individuals who feel aggrieved or excluded by the wider culture", Geert Lovink, David Garcia, 2002, http://subsol.c3.hu/subsol_2/contributors2/garcia-lovinktext.html.

39. RTMark website, March 1997, no longer extant. See also https://en.wikipedia.org/wiki/RTMark.

40. The WTO even attempted to prosecute the group over a website the group created parodying the global juridical agency that not only sowed confusion, but spread detailed information about the WTO's neoliberal brand of global profiteering, www.corpwatch.org/article.php?id=2671.

41. For a keen analysis of activist public art using the theories of Negt and Kluge see Philip Glahn's essay, "Public Art: Avant-Garde Practice and the Possibilities of Critical Articulation", *Afterimage* December 2000.

42. More about Las Agencias can be found at: www.sindominio.net/.

43. Information on Yomango can be found at: www.yomango.net.

44. Georges Bataille, "The Notion of Expenditure," in *Visions of Excess: Selected Writings 1927–1939*, University of Minnesota Press, 1985. See also Bruce Barber and Jeff Dayton-Johnson, "Marking the Limit: Re-framing a Micro-economy for the Arts", *Parachute*106, April, May, June 2002, 27 and 39; and Ted Purves, *What We Want Is Free: Generosity and Exchange in Recent Art*, State University of New York Press, 2005, 2nd edn 2014.

45. Brian Holmes, "The Flexible Personality: For a New Cultural Critique," eipcp, 2002, http://eipcp.net/transversal/1106/holmes/en/base_edit.

46. Duncombe, *Notes from Underground*, 81.

47. The act of covering over the copy of Picasso's *Guernica* during Secretary of State Colin Powell's televised call for war against the nation of Iraq at the United Nations on 5 February 2003 suggests that the forces of Empire fully comprehend the nature of this next theatre of cultural battle.

48. Jacques Rancière, *The Politics of Aesthetics: The Distribution of the Sensible*, Continuum, 2004.

10   *On the Maidan Uprising and* Imaginary Archive, *Kiev*

1. "A very timely and out-of-the-ordinary project," Ukrainian Pravda, April 5, 2014, http://life.pravda.com.ua/culture/2014/05/4/166771/view_print/.

2. Manifesto from ICTM Art Workers' Self-defense Initiative at, http://istmkyiv.wordpress.com/manifest/.

3. Email from Larissa Babij to the author June 3, 2014. Other examples of "*zhlob*-art" with commentary can be found at, www.unitedcreativity.org/central_and_easetrn_europe/ukraine/zhlob-ar.html. Similar analysis of Euromaidan's seemingly "regressive" imagery was made by artist Nikita Kadan whose work appears in *Imaginary Archive* during a skype session at New Museum on February 1, 2014, at the height of the struggle, www.newmuseum.org/calendar/view/285/spaceship-skype-session-europe-at-its-best.

4. Gregory Sholette, *Dark Matter: Art and Politics in an Age of Enterprise Culture*, Pluto Press, 2010.

5. Oskar Negt and Alexander Kluge, *Public Sphere and Experience: Analysis of the Bourgeois and Proletarian Public Sphere*, University of Minnesota Press, 1993, 32.

6. For more about this incident see ArtLeaks, https://art-leaks.org/2015/05/19/artist-volodymyr-kuznetsov-has-taken-legal-action-against-the-mystetskii-arsenal-kiev-ukraine/.

7. Babij email, June 3, 2014.

8. By 2016 all that remains of the Maidan uprising is a series of engraved plaques in the square.

9. Stephen Wright, *Towards Lexicon of Usership*, Van Abbesmuseum, 2013.

11   *Delirium and Resistance After the Social Turn*

1. Mark Fisher, *Capitalist Realism: Is There No Alternative?*, Zero Books, 2009, 35.

2. Stephen Wright, *Toward a Lexicon of Usership*, Van Abbesmuseum, 2013.

3. Throughout most of this essay I will use the term "social practice art" to describe the type of cultural production under discussion because this label seems to have gained the widest usage at this point in time. For an interesting hypothesis about the evolution of this terminology see: Larne Abse Gogarty, "Aesthetics and Social Practice," in *Keywords: A (Polemical) Vocabulary of Contemporary Art*, October 3, 2014, http://keywordscontemporary.com/aesthetics-social-practice/.

4. In the past three or four years alone several East Coast institutions of higher education have added some level of social practice or community oriented arts curricula to their offerings. Along with Queens College CUNY this includes NYU, SVA, Pratt, Parsons and Moore College of Art in Philadelphia. Regarding the philanthropic turn towards social practices, in 2014 the Robert Rauschenberg Foundation announced what they describe as a "game changing" $100,000 grant category called Artist as Activist, which is aimed at supporting individuals who address "important global challenges through their creative practice," www.rauschenbergfoundation.org/grants/art-grants/artist-as-activist. There is also the Keith Haring Foundation, which in the same year provided Bard College with $400,000 to support a teaching fellowship in Art and Activism at the school, www.bard.edu/news/releases/pr/fstory.php?id=2516. And just a few years ago, in 2012, an entirely new foundation calling itself A Blade of Grass tells us that it "nurtures socially engaged art," www.abladeofgrass.org/. Meanwhile, the Education Departments at the Museum of Modern Art and Guggenheim Museum sponsor socially engaged art projects with the latter also hosting the think tank/community center known as BMW Guggenheim Lab both inside and outside its museums from 2011 to 2014.

5. From the cover material of Peter Weibel, ed., *Global Activism: Art and Conflict in the 21st Century*, MIT Press, 2015.

6. Grant H. Kester, *The One and the Many: Contemporary Collaborative Art in a Global Context*, Duke University Press, 2011, 223. BAVO's webpage is www.spatialagency.net/database/why/political/bavo.

7. Claire Bishop, *Artificial Hells: Participation Art and the Politics of Spectatorship*, Verso, 2012.

8. Regarding Abu Dhabi's high-priced investment in Western museum branding, see http://gulflabor.org/. On the relationship between art asset funds and ultra-wealth collectors see Andrea Fraser, "There's No Place Like Home / L'1% c'est Moi," a

downloadable pdf is available from *Continent* at www.continentcontinent.cc/index.php/continent/article/view/108.

9. Jared Keller, "Evaluating Iran's Twitter Revolution," *The Atlantic*, June 18, 2010, www.theatlantic.com/technology/archive/2010/06/evaluating-irans-twitter-revolution/58337/.

10. David Graeber, *Direct Action: An Ethnography*, AK Press, 2009.

11. Greg Sholette and Oliver Ressler, "Unspeaking the Grammar of Finance," in Greg Sholette and Oliver Ressler (eds.) *It's the Political Economy, Stupid*, 2013, 8–13.

12. John Bellamy Foster, "The Financialization of Capitalism," *Monthly Review*, March 11, 2007, http://monthlyreview.org/2007/04/01/the-financialization-of-capitalism/.

13. Carol Vogel, "Bacon Triptych Auctioned for Record $86 Million," *New York Times*, May 15, 2008, www.nytimes.com/2008/05/15/arts/design/15auction.html. See also Tierney Sneed, "5 Art Auction Record Breakers That Prove the Industry Is Booming: Art history was made at auctions at Sotheby's and Christie's this week," *US News & World Report*, Nov. 14, 2013, www.usnews.com/news/articles/2013/11/14/christies-142-million-francis-bacon-sale-and-this-weeks-other-art-auction-record-breakers.

14. "Fitch Assigns 'A' to Lehman Brothers Holdings Capital Trust VII," *Business Wire*, May 9, 2007, www.businesswire.com/news/home/20070509006056/en/Fitch-Assigns-Lehman-Brothers-Holdings- Capital-Trust#.VPtOVmTF_1g.

15. Alexandra Peers, "The Fine Art of Surviving the Crash in Auction Prices," *Wall Street Journal*, November 20, 2008, www.wsj.com/articles/SB122713503996042291.

16. Chinese capital, which was not affected by the crash, no doubt played a part in this stability, see: Alexander Forbes, "TEFAF Art Market Report Says 2013 Best Year on Record Since 2007, With Market Outlook Bullish," *artnetnews*, March 12, 2014, http://news.artnet.com/market/tefaf-art-market-report-says-2013-best-year-on-record-since-2007-with-market-outlook-bullish-5358/.

17. Gilligan's examples include Richard Prince's endlessly recycled works, and Seth Price's reworking videos that bear "a striking similarity to financial derivatives in one particularly suggestive way: they derive their value from the value of something else," from Melanie Gilligan, "Derivative Days," in Sholette and Ressler, *It's the Political Economy, Stupid*, 73–81.

18. See "The Artist as Debtor," http://artanddebt.org/; Free/Slow University, www.britishcouncil.pl/en/events/conference-freeslow-university-warsaw, and Erica Ho, "Study: Art School Graduates Rack Up the Most Debt," Feb. 21, 2013, *Time* online, http://newsfeed.time.com/2013/02/21/study-art-school-graduates-rack-up-the-most-debt/.

19. Julian Stallabrass, *Art Incorporated: The Story of Contemporary Art*, Oxford University Press, 2004.

20. For a strong argument to this effect see Tom Finkelpearl, *What We Made: Conversations on Art as Social Cooperation*, Duke University Press, 2013.

21. Blake Stimson and Greg Sholette, "Periodising Collectivism," in *Collectivism after Modernism: Art and Social Imagination after 1945*, University of Minnesota Press, 2006.

22. Wright, *Toward a Lexicon of Usership*.

23. Grant Kester, "Aesthetic Evangelists: The Rhetoric of Empowerment and Conversion in Contemporary Community Art," *Afterimage* 22(6), January 1995, 5–11.

24. The first widely circulated and still most cited critique of Relational Aesthetics did not appear until six years after Bourriaud's book was published, see Claire Bishop, "Antagonism and Relational Aesthetics," *October* 110, Fall 2004, 51–79.

25. See Ben Davis, "A Critique of Social Practice Art: What Does It Mean to be a Political Artist?," *International Socialist Review* 90, July 2013, http://isreview.org/issue/90/critique-social-practice-art.

26. "Is Social Practice Gentrifying Community Arts?" a conversation between Rick Lowe and Nato Thompson at the Creative Time Summit, October 2013, a transcript is available from Bad At Sports at http://badatsports.com/2013/is-social-practice-gentrifying-community-arts/.

27. Chris Kraus, "Ambiguous Virtues of Art School," *Artspace*, March 2, 2015, www.artspace.com/magazine/news_events/chris-kraus-akademie-x.

28. Jameson, *The Political Unconscious: Narrative as a Socially Symbolic Act*, Cornell University Press, 1981, 80–81.

29. Wright, *Towards Lexicon of Usership*, 4.

30. "It is my contention that some socially engaged artworks can be distinguished from others by the degree to which they provoke reflection on the contingent systems that support the management of life. An interest in such acts of support coincides with the project of performance," Shannon Jackson, *Social Works: Performing Art, Supporting Publics*, Routledge, 2011, 29. Wright would likely respond that his idea of usership-driven art is work that is not performed as *art*, but literally and redundantly is action in the "real world," quite unlike performative practices whose content is, first and foremost, art, and then only secondarily perhaps an action, useful or otherwise, in the real world. See Wright, *Towards Lexicon of Usership*, 16.

31. Martin Pengelly, "Pittsburgh Restaurant Receives Death Threats in 'Anti-Israel Messages' furor," *Guardian*, November 9, 2014, www.theguardian.com/world/2014/nov/09/pittsburgh-restaurant-conflict-kitchen-death-threats-israel.

32. Brian Holmes, "Future Map, 2007," http://roundtable.kein.org/node/1332.

33. Quoted from an email to the author, Monday, March 23, 2015 at 10:04 a.m.

34. David Garcia and Geert Lovink, "The ABC of Tactical Media," 1997, http://subsol.c3.hu/subsol_2/contributors2/garcia-lovinktext.html.

35. A discussion of EDT's *floodnet* is found at http://museumarteutil.net/projects/zapatista-tactical-floodnet/.

36. The situation escalated when Dominguez organized a virtual sit-in of the University of California President's website, www.utsandiego.com/news/2010/apr/06/activist-ucsd-professor-facing-unusual-scrutiny/.

37. Viktor Shklovsky, *Energy of Delusion: A Book on Plot*, Dalkey Archive Press, 2007; Fisher, *Capitalist Realism*.

38. Nato Thompson, "Trespassing Toward Relevance," in Nato Thompson and Greg Sholette (eds.) *The Interventionists: Users' Manual for the Creative Disruption of Everyday Life*, MIT Press, 2006, 17.

39. Thompson and Sholette, *The Interventionists*, 60.

40. Choire Sicha, "The Guide," *New York Times*, December 12, 2005. The only lengthier critical responses were by Carlos Basualdo and T.J. Demos in *Artforum*, though these reviews largely recycled existing critical paradigms about site-specific art without successfully engaging in the concept of tactical media in relation to the counter-globalization movement or "the social turn" in art, www.mutualart.com/OpenArticle/-THE-INTERVENTIONISTS–ART-IN-THE-SOCIAL/9FE37A35791E22C3.

41. See Department of Space & Land Reclamation website, www.counter productiveindustries.com/dslr/.

42. Henry Moss, "The Climb to Oatman's Crash Site: Mass MoCA's Discontinued Boiler Plant," *Interventions/Adaptive Reuse* 2, 2011, 6.

43. "Another Art World is Possible," happens to be the title of an essay by theorist Gene Ray from the same year as *The Interventionists* exhibition; in *Third Text* 18(6), 2004, 565–572.

44. Fuzzy Biological Sabotage on CAE website, www.critical-art.net/books/molecular/chapter5.pdf.

45. To read more about the investigation see the Critical Art Ensemble (CAE) Defense Fund, http://critical-art.net/defense/.

46. The CAE Defense Fund, which at the time of The Interventionists opening had already been established by artists Claire Pentecost, Rich Pell, Gregg Bordowitz, Jacques Servin and Igor Vamos of The Yes Men and others, emerged from the emergency meeting with a constituency of supporters ready to go to work raising legal funds and publicizing the senseless injustice of the accusations against Kurtz. While the overall arguments of the Defense Fund's members in their lectures and writings continued to be in favor of amateur scientific research and the right to engage in political disobedience via forms of tactical media, Kurtz's actual legal case pivoted on legal technicalities, while its media publicity focused on the artist's First Amendment guarantee of free speech, a much easier position to spotlight especially within the art world. Ultimately, however, the government's prosecutorial position was defeated by its own flawed legal logic, though not until many thousands of dollars were raised in the artist's defense.

47. This certainly seems to be the position of artist Rubén Ortiz Torres, who was an artist Thompson exhibited in The Interventionists. Torres believes that the occasion of the 2004 show was "supposed to be the moment when the art world (or at least part of it) would recognize the practices that a lot of artists (if not most) do in art schools, and alternative spaces and other circuits outside commercial galleries and museums. However it seemed that the Steve Kurtz incident cancelled or was used to cancel that opportunity." Notably he adds "I see 'social practice' as a very ineffective way to do politics trying to validate them and justify them as art. It seems a way more bureaucratic, moralistic, self righteous and pretentious notion than the more open, anarchist and situationist one of 'Interventionism.'" Cited from an email to me on Monday, October 14, 2013 at 8:45 p.m.

48. Blake Stimson, "The Form of the Informal," *Journal of Contemporary African Art* 34, Spring 2014, 36.

49. "The thing changes not one bit, yet once the trapdoor springs open and the 'dark agents' are on the loose, nothing could be more different." The dark agency is for Wright the allure of the thing that is both a proposition about art, and a completely redundant activity, object, practice of everyday life. Wright, *Towards Lexicon of Usership*, 7.

50. John Roberts, "The Political Economization of Art," in Sholette and Ressler (eds.) *It's the Political Economy, Stupid*, 63–71.

51. Brian Holmes, "A Rising Tide of Contradiction, Museums in the Age of the Expanding Workfare State," Republic Art website, http://republicart.net/disc/institution/holmes03_en.htm.

52. Jan Rehmann, *Theories of Ideology: The Powers of Alienation and Subjection*, Haymarket Books, 2014, 12.

53. Tactical Urbanism/The Street Plans Collaborative, http://issuu.com/streetplans
collaborative.

54. *A Painting for a Family Dinner*, 2012, Alina and Jeff Bliumis. See Tanyanika Samuels,
"Artist Team Offers a Painting in Exchange for Invite to Family Dinner in the
Bronx; Part of Art Exhibition," *NY Daily News*, April 12, 2012, www.nydailynews.
com/new-york/bronx/artist-team-offers-painting-exchange-invite-family-dinner-
bronx-part-art-exhibition-article-1.1059121.

55. No Longer Empty, *Art in Empty Spaces*, June 30, 2011, www.nolongerempty.org/
nc/home/events/events-by-category/event/celebrate-art-in-empty-spaces-with-
community-board/.

56. Examples of gift art are drawn from Ted Purves, *What We Want is Free: Generosity
and Exchange in Recent Art*, State University of New York Press, 2005, 2nd edn
2014.

Postscript

1. Cornel West, "Goodbye, American Neoliberalism. A New Era Is Here," *The Guardian*,
November 17, 2016, https://www.theguardian.com/commentisfree/2016/nov/17/
american-neoliberalism-cornel-west-2016-election.

2. In this opening passage the book's anti-fascist protagonist discovers parallels
between the ancient battle between gods and Titans depicted on the Pergamon
frieze in Berlin, and the partisan struggle he and his comrades are waging against
German National Socialism in the 1930s. Peter Weiss, *The Aesthetics of Resistance*,
vol. 1, trans. Joachim Neugroschel, with a Foreword by Fredric Jameson, Duke
University Press, 2005, 3.

3. "Undercommons" is a term coined by theorists Fred Moten and Stefano Harney to
describe a space of suppressed social antagonism constituted by the black diaspora.
The Undercommons: Fugitive Planning and Black Study, Minor Compositions,
2013.

4. An example of the internet's counter-democratic uses is found in the hacking of
a Gulf Labor Coalition member's email that led to an embargo on her research
travel in the Middle East. See Kristina Borgos, "American Universities in a Gulf
of Hypocrisy," *The New York Times*, Opinion Pages, December 15, 2016, http://
www.nytimes.com/2016/12/15/opinion/american-univisities-nyu-georgetown-in-
a-gulf-of-hypocrisy.html?ref=opinion&_r=0.

5. Jacques Derrida, *Archive Fever: A Freudian Impression*, trans. Eric Prenowitz,
University of Chicago Press, 1995.

Bibliography

Abbing, Hans. *Why Are Artists Poor? The Exceptional Economy of the Arts*. Amsterdam: Amsterdam University Press, 2002.

Adorno, Theodor W. *Negative Dialectics*. London: Bloomsbury, 1981.

——*The Culture Industry: Selected Essays on Mass Culture*. New York: Routledge Classics, 1991.

—— *Aesthetic Theory*. Minneapolis: University of Minnesota, 1998.

Adorno, Theodor W. and Max Horkheimer. *Dialectic of Enlightenment*. London: Continuum, 1994.

Adorno, Theodor W., Ernst Bloch, Walter Benjamin, Bertolt Brecht and Georg Lukács. *Aesthetics and Politics*. London: Verso, 2007.

Agamben, Giorgio. *Homo Sacer: Sovereign Power and Bare Life*. Stanford, CA: Stanford University Press, 1998.

Allen, Felicity. *Education*. Whitechapel: Documents of Contemporary Art. Cambridge, MA: MIT Press, 2011.

Arato, Andrew and Eike Gephardt. *The Essential Frankfurt School Reader*. London: Bloomsbury, 1982.

Ault, Julie (ed.) *Alternative Art New York 1965–1985*. Minneapolis: University of Minnesota, 2002.

—— (ed.) *Show and Tell: A Chronicle of Group Material*. London: Four Corners Books, 2010.

—— (ed.) *Self-Organised*. London and Bergen: Open Editions/Hordaland Art Centre, 2013.

Back, Jon (ed.) *The Cutting Edge of Nordic Larp*. Toptryk Grafisk, Denmark: Knutpunkt, 2014.

Bankoff, Greg, Uwe Lübken and Jordan Sand (eds.) *Flammable Cities: Urban Conflagration and the Making of the Modern World*. Madison: University of Wisconsin Press, 2011.

Barber, Bruce. *Condé and Beveridge: Class Works*. Halifax: Press of the Nova Scotia College of Art and Design, 2008.

Bataille, Georges. *Visions of Excess: Selected Writings 1927–1939*. Minneapolis: University of Minnesota Press, 1985.

Beaumon, Matthew T., J. Roberts, E. Leslie, A. Hemingway (eds.) *As Radical as Reality Itself: Essays on Marxism and Art for the 21st Century*. Oxford: Peter Lang, 2007.

Becker, Howard Saul. *Art Worlds*. Berkeley: University of California Press, 1982.

Beech, Dave. *Art and Value: Art's Economic Exceptionalism in Classical, Neoclassical and Marxist Economics*. Leiden: Brill, 2016.

Benjamin, Walter. *Illuminations: Essays and Reflections*, edited by Hannah Arendt. New York: Schocken Books, 1968.

Bennett, Jane. *Vibrant Matter: A Political Ecology of Things*. Durham, NC: Duke University Press, 2009.

Bishop, Claire. *Artificial Hells: Participatory Art and the Politics of Spectatorship*. London: Verso, 2012.

Boltanski, Luc, Eve Chiapello and Gregory Elliott. *The New Spirit of Capitalism*. London: Verso, 2005.

Boomgaard, Jeroen, Gielen, Pascal, and Paul De Bruyne. *Teaching Art in the Neoliberal Realm: Realism versus Cynicism*. Amsterdam: Valiz, 2012.

Bosteels, Bruno. *The Actuality of Communism*. London: Verso, 2014.

Bourdieu, Pierre. *The Field of Cultural Production: Essays on Art and Literature*. New York: Columbia University Press, 1993.

Bourriaud, Nicolas. *Relational Aesthetics*. Dijon: Les Presses du Réel, 2002.

Brecht, Bertolt. *Selected Poems*, trans. H.R. Hays. New York: Grove Press, 1959.

Bryan-Wilson, Julia. *Cultural Workers: Radical Practice in the Vietnam War Era*. Berkeley: University of California Press, 2009.

Buchloh, Benjamin, Carlos Basualdo and Alison M. Gingeras. *Thomas Hirschhorn*. London: Phaidon, 2004.

Buchloh, Benjamin, Serge Guilbaut and David Solkin (eds.) *Modernism and Modernity*. Halifax: Press of the Nova Scotia College of Art and Design Culture, 1983.

Bürger, Peter. *Theory of the Avant-Garde*. Minneapolis: University of Minnesota Press, 1984.

Cahan, Susan E. *Mounting Frustration: The Art Museum in the Age of Black Power*. Durham, NC: Duke University Press, 2016.

Camille, Michael. *Image on the Edge: The Margins of Medieval Art*. Cambridge, MA: Harvard University Press, 1992.

Cartiere, Cameron and Martin Zebracki. *The Everyday Practice of Public Art: Art, Space, and Social Inclusion*. London: Routledge, 2015.

Chicago Social Practice History Series (books by Mary Jane Jacob, Daniel Tucker, Abigail Satinsky, Stephanie Smith, Rebecca Zorach). School of the Art Institute of Chicago Press, 2015.

Clark, T.J. *Farewell to an Idea: Episodes from a History of Modernism*. New Haven: Yale University Press, 1999.

Cleaver, Harry. *Reading Capital Politically*. Austin: University of Texas Press, 1979.

Crimp, Douglas. *Melancholia and Moralism: Essays on AIDS and Queer Politics*. Cambridge, MA: MIT Press, 2004.

Critical Art Ensemble. *Electronic Disturbance*. New York: Autonomedia, 1994.

Cruz, Teddy, R. Burdett, D. Harvey et al. *Uneven Growth: Tactical Urbanisms for Expanding Megacities*. New York: MoMA, 2014.

Cuoni, Karen. *Entry Points: The Vera List Center Field Guide on Art and Social Justice No. 1*. Durham, NC: Duke University Press, 2015.

Danto, Arthur C. "The Artworld," in Carolyn Korsmeyer (ed.) *Aesthetics: The Big Questions*. Malden, MA: Blackwell, 1998.

Davis, Ben. *9.5 Theses on Art and Class*. Chicago: Haymarket Books, 2013.

de Cauter, Lieven, R. de Roo and Karel Vanhaesebrouck (eds.) *Art and Activism in the Age of Globalization*. Rotterdam: NAi, 2011.

de Certeau, Michel. *The Practice of Everyday Life*, trans. Steen Rendall. Berkeley: University of California Press, 1984.

Dean, Jodi. *Crowds and Party,* London: Verso, 2016.

Debord, Guy. *The Society of the Spectacle*. New York: Zone, 1994.

Deleuze, Gilles. *Difference and Repetition*. New York: Columbia University Press, 1994.

DeLillo, Don. *White Noise*. Harmondsworth: Penguin Books, 1984.

Demos, T.J. *The Migrant Image: The Art and Politics of Documentary during Global Crisis*. Durham, NC: Duke University Press, 2013.

Derrida, Jacques. *Writing and Difference.* Chicago: University of Chicago Press, 1978.

——*Specters of Marx: The State of Debt, the Work of Mourning, and the New International.* London: Routledge, 1994.

Derrida, Jacques. *Archive Fever: A Freudian Impression.* Chicago: University of Chicago Press, 1996.

Deutsche, Rosalyn. *Evictions: Art and Spatial Politics.* Chicago: Graham Foundation, 1996.

Doherty, Claire. *Public Art (now): Out of Time, Out of Place.* London: Art Books, 2015.

Duncan, Carol. *The Aesthetics of Power: Essays in Critical Art History.* Cambridge: Cambridge University Press, 1993.

——*Civilizing Rituals: Inside Public Art Museums.* London: Routledge, 1995.

Duncombe, Stephen. *Notes from Underground: Zines and the Politics of Underground Culture.* Bloomington, IN: Microcosm, 1996.

Esche, Charles and W. Bradley (eds.) *Art and Social Change: A Critical Reader.* London: Tate Publishing/Afterall, 2007.

Evans, Mel. *Artwash: Big Oil and the Arts.* Chicago: University of Chicago Press, 2015.

Federici, Silvia. *Caliban and the Witch.* New York: Autonomedia, 2004.

Felshin, Nina (ed.) *But Is It Art? The Spirit of Art as Activism.* Seattle, WA: Bay Press, 1995.

Finkelpearl, Tom. *What We Made: Conversations on Art and Social Cooperation.* Durham, NC: Duke University Press, 2013.

Fisher, Mark. *Capitalist Realism: Is There No Alternative?* Ropley, Hants: Zero Books, 2009.

Fitch, Robert. *The Assassination of New York.* London: Verso,1993.

Florida, Richard L. *The Rise of the Creative Class: And How It's Transforming Work, Leisure, Community and Everyday Life.* New York: Basic Books, 2002.

Foster, Hal. *The Anti-aesthetic: Essays on Postmodern Culture.* New York: New Press, 2002.

Foster, Hal, Rosalind Krauss, Yve-Alain Bois et al. *Art since 1900: Modernism, Antimodernism, Postmodernism.* London: Thames & Hudson, 2005.

Foucault, Michel. *Language, Counter-memory, Practice,* edited by Donald F. Bouchard. Ithaca, NY: Cornell University Press, 1977.

Gessen, Masha. *Words Will Break Cement: The Passion of Pussy Riot.* New York: Riverhead Books, 2014.

Gielen, Pascal. *The Murmuring of the Artistic Multitude: Global Art, Memory and Post-Fordism.* Amsterdam: Valiz, 2010.

Graeber, David. *Direct Action: An Ethnography.* Edinburgh: AK Press, 2009.

Greenwald, Dara and Josh MacPhee. *Signs of Change: Social Movement Cultures 1960s to Now.* Edinburgh: AK Press & Exit Art, 2010.

Grindon, Gavin and Catherine Flood. *Disobedient Objects.* London: V&A, 2015.

Groys, Boris. *In the Flow.* London: Verso, 2016.

Guerrilla Art Action Group. *GAAG: The Guerrilla Art Action Group.* New York: Printed Matter, 1978.

Guerrilla Girls. *Bitches, Bimbos and Ballbreakers: The Guerrilla Girls' Illustrated Guide to Female Stereotypes.* Harmondsworth: Penguin Books, 2003.

Habermas, Jürgen. *The Theory of Communicative Action,* 3 vols. Boston MA: Beacon Press, 1985.

Haiven, Max. *Cultures of Financialization: Fictitious Capital in Popular Culture and Everyday Life.* London: Palgrave Macmillan, 2014.

Halasz, Judith R. *The Bohemian Ethos: Questioning Work and Making a Scene on the Lower East Side*. London: Routledge, 2014.

Harney, Stefano and Fred Moten. *The Undercommons: Fugitive Planning & Black Study*. New York: Autonomedia, 2013.

Harvey, David. *Seventeen Contradictions and the End of Capitalism*. Oxford: Oxford University Press, 2015.

Helguera, Pablo. *Education for Socially Engaged Art: A Materials and Techniques Handbook*. Bethesda, MD: Jorge Pinto Books, 2011.

Hemingway, Andrew. *The Mysticism of Money: Precisionist Painting and Machine Age America*. Periscope, 2013.

Holmes, Brian. *Unleashing the Collective Phantoms: Essays in Reverse Imagineering*. New York: Autonomedia, 2008.

—— *Escape the Overcode: Activist Art in the Control Society*. Eindhoven: Van Abbemuseum / WHW, 2009.

Horowitz, Noah. *Art of the Deal: Contemporary Art in a Global Financial Market*. Princeton, NJ: Princeton University Press, 2011.

Irish, Sharon. *Suzanne Lacy: Spaces Between*. Minneapolis: University of Minnesota Press, 2010.

Jackson, Shannon. *Social Works: Performing Art, Supporting Publics*. London: Routledge, 2011.

Jacobs, Mary Jane. *Culture in Action: A Public Art Program of Sculpture Chicago*. Seattle, WA: Bay Press, 1995.

Jameson, Fredric. *The Political Unconscious: Narrative as a Socially Symbolic Act*. Ithaca, NY: Cornell University Press, 1981.

—— *Postmodernism, or, The Cultural Logic of Late Capitalism*. Durham, NC: Duke University Press, 1991.

—— *Representing Capital: A Reading of Volume One*. London: Verso, 2011.

Jelinek, Alana. *Art: Activism and Other 'Not-Art'*. London: I.B. Tauris, 2013.

Joselit, David. *After Art*. Princeton, NJ: Princeton University Press, 2012.

Kaletsky, Anatole. *Capitalism 4.0: The Birth of a New Economy in the Aftermath of Crisis*. New York: Public Affairs Press, 2011.

Kaltemeire, Olaf (ed.) *Selling EthniCity: Urban Cultural Politics in the Americas*. London: Routledge, 2011.

Kester, Grant. *Conversation Pieces*. Berkeley: University of California Press, 2004.

—— *The One and the Many: Contemporary Collaborative Art in a Global Context*. Durham, NC: Duke University Press, 2011.

Kliman, Andrew. *The Failure of Capitalist Production: Underlying Causes of the Great Recession*. London: Pluto, 2012.

Kluitenberg, Eric. *Delusive Spaces: Essays on Culture, Media and Technology*. Rotterdam: NAi, 2008.

Kraus, Chris and R. Solnit. *Streetopia*. New York: Brooklyn Press, 2015.

Laclau, Ernesto and Chantal Mouffe. *Hegemony and Socialist Strategy: Towards a Radical Democratic Politics*. London: Verso, 1985.

Lacy, Suzanne (ed.) *Mapping the Terrain: New Genre Public Art*. Seattle, WA: Bay Press, 1995.

Leeson, Loraine. *Art, Communities and Social Change: An Artist's Reflections*. London: Routledge, 2017.

Lefebvre, Henri, Stuart Elden, Elizabeth Lebas and Eleonore Kofman. *Henri Lefebvre: Key Writings*. London: Continuum, 2003.

Léger, Marc James. *Brave New Avant Garde: Essays on Contemporary Art and Politics.* Ropley, Winchester, UK: Zero Books, 2012.

——*The Neoliberal Undead: Essays on Contemporary Art and Politics.* Ropley, Winchester, UK: Zero Books, 2013.

Lerm Hayes, Christa-Maria. *Writing Art and Creating Back: What We Can Do With Art (History)?* Amsterdam: University of Amsterdam Press, 2015.

Lerm Hayes, Christa-Maria and Victoria Walters. *Beuysian Legacies in Ireland and Beyond: Art, Culture and Politics.* Berlin: Lit, 2011.

Leslie, Esther. *Walter Benjamin: Overpowering Conformism.* London: Pluto, 2000.

—— *Hollywood Flatlands: Animation, Critical Theory and the Avant-garde.* London: Verso, 2002.

——*Synthetic Worlds: Nature, Art and the Chemical Industry.* London: Reaktion, 2005.

Lessig, Lawrence. *Code and Other Laws of Cyberspace.* New York: Basic Books, 1999.

Lippard, Lucy. *Six Years: The Dematerialization of the Art Object from 1966 to 1972.* Westport, CT: Praeger, 1973.

—— *Get the Message? A Decade of Art for Social Change.* New York: E.P. Dutton, 1984.

—— *Mixed Blessings.* New York: Pantheon, 1990.

—— *A Different War: Vietnam in Art.* Seattle: Real Comet Press, 1990.

—— *Undermining: A Wilde Ride Through Land Use, Politics, and Art in a Changing West,* New York: New Press, 2014.

Lloyd, Richard D. *Neo-Bohemia: Art and Commerce in the Postindustrial City.* New York: Routledge, 2006.

Lovink, Geert. *Dark Fiber: Tracking Critical Internet Culture.* Cambridge, MA: MIT Press, 2002.

——*Networks without a Cause: A Critique of Social Media.* Cambridge: Polity, 2012.

——*Social Media Abyss: Critical Internet Cultures and the Force of Negation.* Cambridge: Polity, 2016.

Lukács, György. *History and Class Consciousness.* Cambridge, MA: MIT Press, 1972.

Madoff, Steven Henry. *Art School: Propositions for the 21st Century.* Cambridge, MA: MIT Press, 2009.

Malzacher, Florian (ed.) *Truth Is Concrete: A Handbook for Artistic Strategies in Real Politics.* Berlin: Sternberg, 2014.

Marcuse, Herbert. *The Essential Marcuse: Selected Writings of Philosopher and Social Critic Herbert Marcuse,* edited by Andrew Feenberg and William Leiss. Boston, MA: Beacon, 2007.

Martin, Randy. *The Financialization of Daily Life.* Philadelphia, PA: Temple University Press, 2002.

Marx, Karl. *Grundrisse: Foundations of the Critique of Political Economy.* Harmondsworth: Penguin Classics reprint edition, 1973.

——*Capital,* vols. I–III. Harmondsworth: Penguin Classics reprint edition, 1992.

Marx, Karl and Friedrich Engels. *Writings on the Paris Commune,* compiled by Hal Draper. New York: Monthly Review Press, 1971.

—— *The German Ideology 1845–46.* New York: International Publishers, 1979.

Mason, Paul. *Postcapitalism: A Guide to Our Future.* New York: Farrar, Straus and Giroux, 2016.

Mauss, Marcel. *The Gift: Forms and Functions of Exchange in Archaic Societies,* trans. Ian Cunnison, with an introduction by E.E. Evans-Pritchard. New York: Norton,1967.

McKay, George (ed.) *DIY Culture: Party and Protest in Nineties Britain.* London: Verso, 1998.

McKee, Yates. *Strike Art! Contemporary Art and the Post-Occupy Condition.* London: Verso, 2016.

McPhee, Josh and Erik Reuland (eds.) *Realizing the Impossible: Art Against Authority.* Edinburgh: AK Press, 2007.

McRobbie, Angela. *Be Creative: Making a Living in the New Culture Industries.* Cambridge: Polity, 2016.

Menger, Pierre-Michel. *The Economics of Creativity: Art and Achievement under Uncertainty.* Cambridge, MA: Harvard University Press, 2014.

Miles, Malcolm, *Limits to Culture: Urban Regeneration vs. Dissident Art.* London: Pluto Press, 2015.

Mirzoeff, Nicholas. *The Right to Look: A Counterhistory of Visuality.* Durham, NC: Duke University Press, 2011.

—— *How to See the World: An Introduction to Images, from Self-Portraits to Selfies, Maps to Movies, and More.* New York: Basic Books, 2016.

Mitchell, W. J. T., Bernard E. Harcourt and Michael Taussig. *Occupy: Three Inquiries in Disobedience.* Chicago: University of Chicago Press, 2013.

Moore, Alan. *Art Gangs: Protest and Counterculture in New York City.* New York: Autonomedia, 2011.

—— *Occupation Culture: Art and Squatting in the City from Below.* London: Minor Compositions, 2015.

Moore, Alan and Marc Miller. *ABC No Rio Dinero: The Story of a Lower East Side Art Gallery.* New York: No Rio—Self-published, 1985.

Moore, Sabra. *Openings: A Memoir from the Women's Art Movement, New York City 1970–1992.* New York: New Village Press, 2016.

Negri, Antonio. *Marx beyond Marx: Lessons on the Grundrisse.* London: Pluto Press, 1992.

Negri, Antonio and Michael Hardt. *Labor of Dionysus: A Critique of the State-form.* Minneapolis: University of Minnesota Press, 1994.

—— *Empire.* Cambridge, MA: Harvard University Press, 2000.

Negt, Oskar and Alexander Kluge. *Public Sphere and Experience: Toward an Analysis of the Bourgeois and Proletarian Public Sphere.* Minneapolis: University of Minnesota Press, 1993.

Nietzsche, Friedrich. *The Genealogy of Morals.* New York: Dover Books, 2003.

O'Neil, Paul and Mick Wilson. *Curating and the Educational Turn.* London and Amsterdam: Open Editions/De Appel Arts Centre, 2010.

Osborne, Peter. *Anywhere or Not at All: Philosophy of Contemporary Art.* London: Verso, 2013.

Owens, Craig and Scott Bryson, Barbara Kruger, Lynne Tillman, Jane Weinstock (eds.) *Beyond Recognition: Representation, Power, and Culture.* Berkeley: University of California Press, 1992.

Papastergiadis, Nikos. *Cosmopolitanism and Culture.* Cambridge: Polity, 2012.

Plattner, Stuart. *High Art Down Home: An Economic Ethnography of a Local Art Market.* Chicago: University of Chicago Press, 1996.

Pohl, Frances K. *Framing America: A Social History of American Art.* New York: Thames & Hudson, 2002.

Purves, Ted (ed.) *What We Want is Free,* 2nd edn. *Critical Exchanges in Recent Art.* Albany: State University of New York Press, 2014.

Rancière, Jacques. *The Nights of Labor: The Workers' Dream in Nineteenth-century France.* Philadelphia, PA: Temple University Press, 1989.

—— *The Philosopher and His Poor*, edited and with an Introduction by Andrew Parker; trans. John Drury, Corinne Oster and Andrew Parker. Durham, NC: Duke University Press, 2004.

—— *The Politics of Aesthetics: The Distribution of the Sensible*. London: Continuum, 2004.

Raunig, Gerald. *Art and Revolution: Transversal Activism in the Long Twentieth Century*, trans. Aileen Derieg. Los Angeles: Semiotext(e), 2007.

——*Dividuum: Machinic Capitalism and Molecular Revolution*. Los Angeles: Semiotext(e), 2016.

Raunig, Gerald, Gene Ray and Ulf Wuggenig. *Critique of Creativity: Precarity, Subjectivity and Resistance in the 'Creative Industries'*. London: MayFly, 2011.

Ray, Gene (ed.) *Joseph Beuys: Mapping the Legacy*. New York: D.A.P./Ringling Museum of Art, 2001.

Rehmann, Jan. *Theories of Ideology: The Powers of Alienation and Subjection*. Historical Materialism. Leiden: Brill, 2014.

Relyea, Lane. *Your Everyday Art World*. Cambridge, MA: MIT Press, 2013.

Ross, Andrew. *No-collar: The Humane Workplace and Its Hidden Costs*. New York: Basic Books, 2003.

—— *Philosophizing the Everyday: Revolutionary Praxis and the Fate of Cultural Theory*. London: Pluto Press, 2006.

—— *The Intangibilities of Form: Skill and Deskilling in Art after the Readymade*. London: Verso, 2007.

—— *Revolutionary Time and the Avant-garde*. London: Verso, 2015.

Rojek, Chris. *Capitalism and Leisure Theory*. London: Tavistock, 1985.

—— *Ways of Escape: Modern Transformation in Leisure and Travel*. Lanham, MD: Rowman & Littlefield, 1993.

Rosler, Martha and M. Catherine de Zegher. *Martha Rosler: Positions in the Life World*. Birmingham: Ikon Gallery, 1998.

Rosler, Martha and Brian Wallis. *If You Lived Here: The City in Art, Theory and Social Activism*. Seattle, WA: Bay Press, 1991.

Rosler, Martha and Stephen Squibb. *Martha Rosler: Culture Class*. Berlin: Sternberg, 2013.

Ross, Andrew. *Strange Weather: Culture, Science and Technology in the Age of Limits*. London: Verso, 1991.

——*Creditocracy and the Case for Debt Refusal*. New York: OR Books, 2014.

Roth, Gary. *Marxism in a Lost Century: A Biography of Paul Mattick*. Historical Materialism. Leiden: Brill, 2015.

Rothenberg, Julia. *Sociology Looks at the Arts*. London: Routledge, 2014.

Ryan, Susan Elizabeth. *Garments of Paradise: Wearable Discourse in the Digital Age*. Cambridge, MA: MIT Press, 2014.

Sassen, Saskia. *The Global City: New York, London, Tokyo*. Princeton, NJ: Princeton University Press, 2001.

—— *Expulsions: Brutality and Complexity in the Global Economy*. Cambridge, MA: Belknap Press, 2014.

Sauter, Molly. *The Coming Swarm: DDoS Actions, Hacktivism, and Civil Disobedience on the Internet*. London: Bloomsbury Press, 2014.

Scott, James C. *Weapons of the Weak: Everyday Forms of Peasant Resistance*. New Haven: Yale University Press,1985.

Sekula, Allan, Carole Condé and Jan Allen. *Condé and Beveridge: Class Works*. Canada: Nova Scotia College of Art and Design Press, 2009.

Senie, Harriet and Sally Webster. *Critical Issues in Public Art: Content, Context, and Controversy*. Birmingham: Icon Editions, 1992.

Shklovsky, Viktor. *Energy of Delusion: A Book on Plot*. Springfield, IL: Dalkey Archive Press, 2007.

Shklovsky, Viktor and Alexandra Berlina. *Viktor Shklovsky: A Reader*. London: Bloomsbury, 2016.

Sholette, Gregory. *Dark Matter: Art and Politics in the Age of Enterprise Culture*. London: Pluto, 2010.

Sholette, Gregory and Oliver Ressler. *It's the Political Economy, Stupid: The Global Financial Crisis in Art and Theory*. London: Pluto, 2013.

Shukaitis, Stevphen. *The Composition of Movements to Come: Aesthetics and Cultural Labor after the Avant-Garde*. Lanham, MD: Rowman & Littlefield International, 2015.

Simon, Joshua. *Neomaterialism*. Berlin: Sternberg Press, 2013.

Singerman, Howard. *Art Subjects: Making Artists in the American University*. Berkeley: University of California Press, 1999.

Sloterdijk, Peter. *Critique of Cynical Reason*. Minneapolis: University of Minnesota Press, 1987.

Smith, Neil. *The New Urban Frontier: Gentrification and the Revanchist City*. London: Routledge, 1996.

Sprouse, Martin. *Sabotage in the American Workplace: Anecdotes of Dissatisfaction, Mischief and Revenge*, illustrated by Tracy Cox. San Francisco: Pressure Drop Press and Edinburgh: AK Press, 1992.

Stakemeier, Kerstin and Marina Vishmidt. *Reproducing Autonomy: Work, Money, Crisis and Contemporary Art*. New York: Mute Books, 2016.

Stallabrass, Julian. *High Art Lite: British Art in the 1990s*. London: Verso, 1999.

—— *Art Incorporated: The Story of Contemporary Art*. Oxford: Oxford University Press, 2004.

Stimson, Blake. *The Pivot of the World: Photography and Its Nation*. Cambridge, MA: MIT, 2006.

—— *Citizen Warhol*. London: Reaktion Books, 2014.

Stimson, Blake and Gregory Sholette (eds.) *Collectivism after Modernism: The Art of Social Imagination after 1945*. Minneapolis: University of Minnesota Press, 2006.

Taylor, Brandon. *Contemporary Art: Art since 1970*. Upper Saddle River, NJ: Pearson Prentice Hall, 2005.

Temporary Services (collective). *Prisoners' Inventions*. Chicago: WhiteWalls, 2003.

—— *Group Work*. New York: Printed Matter, 2007.

—— *Public Phenomena*. Chicago: Half Letter Press, 2008.

Terranova, Tiziana. *Network Culture: Politics for the Information Age*. London: Pluto Press, 2004.

Thompson, Nato. *Living as Form: Socially Engaged Art from 1991–2011*. Cambridge, MA: MIT Press, 2012.

—— *Seeing Power: Art and Activism in the Twenty-first Century*. New York: Melville House, 2014.

—— *Culture as Weapon: The Art of Influence in Everyday Life*. New York: Melville House, 2017.

Thompson, Nato and Gregory Sholette. *The Interventionists: Users' Manual for the Creative Disruption of Everyday Life*. North Adams, MA: Mass MoCA Publications/ MIT Press, 2004.

Timpanaro, Sebastiano. *On Materialism*, trans. Lawrence Garner. London: Verso, 1975.

Toscano, Alberto and Jeff Kinkle. *Cartographies of the Absolute*. Ropley, Hants: 0 Books, 2015.

Van den Berg, Karen and Ursula Pasero, *Art Production beyond the Art Market?* Santa Monica, CA: Ram Publications, 2014.

Vandeputte, Tom and Tim Ivison (eds.) *Contestations: Learning from Critical Experiments in Education*. London: Bedford Press, 2013.

Vogel, Lise. *Marxism and the Oppression of Women: Toward a Unitary Theory*. New Brunswick, NJ: Rutgers University Press, 1983.

Walker, John A. *Left Shift: Radical Art in 1970s Britain*. London: I.B. Tauris, 2002.

Weibel, Peter. *Global Activism: Art and Conflict in the 21st Century*. Cambridge, MA: MIT University Press, 2015.

Werckmeister, Otto Karl. *Citadel Culture*. Chicago: University of Chicago Press, 1991.

WochenKlausur. *WochenKlausur: Sociopolitical Activism in Art*. Wien: Springer-Verlag, 2001.

Wright, Stephen. *Toward a Lexicon of Usership*. Eindhoven: Van Abbemuseum, 2013.

Wu, Chin-Tao. *Privatising Culture: Corporate Art Intervention since the 1980s*. London: Verso, 2002.

Żmijewski, Artur. *The Applied Social Arts*. Ireland: The Fire Station, 2010.

Zukin, Sharon. *Loft Living: Culture and Capital in Urban Change*. Baltimore, MD: Johns Hopkins University Press, 1982, Rutgers Reprint, 1989.

—— *Naked City: The Death and Life of Authentic Urban Places*. Oxford: Oxford University Press, 2010.

Index